THE AGE OF JIM CROW

A NORTON CASEBOOK IN HISTORY

THE AGE OF JIM CROW

A NORTON CASEBOOK IN HISTORY

Jane Dailey

W. W. NORTON & COMPANY

New York / London

W. W. Norton & Company has been independent since its founding in 1923, when William Warder Norton and Mary D. Herter Norton first published lectures delivered at the People's Institute, the adult education division of New York City's Cooper Union. The Nortons soon expanded their program beyond the Institute, publishing books by celebrated academics from America and abroad. By mid-century, the two major pillars of Norton's publishing program—trade books and college texts—were firmly established. In the 1950s, the Norton family transferred control of the company to its employees, and today—with a staff of four hundred and a comparable number of trade, college, and professional titles published each year—W. W. Norton & Company stands as the largest and oldest publishing house owned wholly by its employees.

Series design by Jo Anne Metsch.
Composition by ElectraGraphics, Inc.
Manufacturing by the Courier Companies—Westford division.
Project editor: Lory A. Frenkel.
Production manager: Christine D'Antonio.

Library of Congress Cataloging-in-Publication Data

Dailey, Jane.
   The age of Jim Crow : a Norton casebook in history / [compiled by] Jane Dailey.
     p. cm. — (Norton casebooks in history series)
   Includes bibliographical references and index.

   ISBN 978-0-393-92758-0 (pbk.)

   1. African Americans—Segregation—Southern States—History—Sources. 2. African Americans—Civil rights—Southern States—History—Sources. 3. African Americans—Legal status, laws, etc.—Southern States—History—Sources. 4. Southern States—Race relations—History—Sources. 5. Racism—Southern States—History—Sources. I. Title.

   E185.61.D23 2008
   975'.04—dc22

                                  2008038536

W. W. Norton & Company, Inc., 500 Fifth Avenue, New York, N.Y. 10110-0017
www.wwnorton.com

W. W. Norton & Company Ltd., Castle House, 75/76 Wells Street, London W1T 3QT

1 2 3 4 5 6 7 8 9 0

CONTENTS

ACKNOWLEDGMENTS

I am grateful for the splendid work of Catherine Jones, who assembled many of the documents in this book and shaped my understanding of the boundaries and meaning of Jim Crow. Many thanks to Charles Eagles, who critiqued an early draft of the introduction, and to David Nirenberg, who commented on multiple drafts. Thanks also to Karl Bakeman, who commissioned this book, and to Kate Feighery and Lory Frenkel, who oversaw its production.

INTRODUCTION

I. Bigger Than a Hamburger

Jim Crow's white southern architects boasted that their creation would last millennia.[1] Yet as a body of law that enforced inequality and discrimination it was outlasted by a long-lived woman. Born in South Carolina when freedmen still sat in public office, Mamie Garvin Fields was in the fourth grade in 1895 when Governor Benjamin Ryan Tillman's followers rewrote the state constitution and disfranchised three-fifths of the state's voters. She was studying to be a teacher in 1900, when a state superintendent of education declared that there was "no opening for the negro in the learned professions" and then wondered whether "the argument often advanced that book-learning carries a negro to the penitentiary [might] have some element of truth." She lived across the street and around the corner from white neighbors in Charleston when South Carolina enacted separate seating on railway coaches in 1898. Her forty-year teaching career was governed by the "separate but equal" principle of school segregation. When she retired from teaching in 1943, Mamie Fields transferred her energy into organizational work with the Young Women's Christian Organization (YWCA), the National Association of Colored Women's Clubs (NACWC), and the South Carolina Federation of Colored Women's Clubs. Elected state president of the Federation in 1948, Fields was part of the successful effort of black South Carolinians to reassert their right to vote. Fifteen years later, her granddaughter recalls, Fields sat down with a group of ladies to decide how they would

---

[1] Glenda Elizabeth Gilmore, *Gender and Jim Crow: Women and the Politics of White Supremacy in North Carolina, 1896–1920* (Chapel Hill, 1996), 225.

show their pride in Harvey Gantt, the first black student to enroll at Clemson University.[2]

Tidy historians bookend eras with dates. This approach works well for moments that have reasonably clear start and end points, such as World War II, or for ages whose beginning or end (if not both) are identifiable, such as the antebellum era. Bounding the creation and dismantling of an entire society is harder. The Age of Jim Crow is most neatly dated from the Supreme Court's decision upholding segregation in *Plessy v. Ferguson* (1896) to passage of the Voting Rights Act of 1965. Yet racial segregation and discrimination did not begin with *Plessy* and did not end entirely with the victories of the civil rights movement. The interwoven legal and economic system, political regimen, and variegated social and cultural world known as Jim Crow was anchored in the antebellum era and continues to structure American society, as revealed in contemporary patterns of wealth distribution, voting, education, and residential geography.

This volume takes an expansive view of the chronology of the Age of Jim Crow and a narrow one of its geography. Though hardly unknown in law and custom elsewhere in the United States, Jim Crow remains most dramatically and enduringly associated with the South. This book is anchored in that region—defined as the eleven states of the former Confederacy[3]—because it was there that Jim Crow flowered most extravagantly and there that the great crusade to uproot it began. Also, although other nonwhite racial minorities have suffered from Jim Crow laws and practices over the years, the original and principal targets of racially discriminatory customs and legislation were African Americans, and they are the central characters here. Jim Crow's roots stretch back to the days of African bondage, and his legacy endures, as the world was reminded in September 2005 when Hurricane Katrina peeled away the outer shell of New Orleans to reveal the segregated inner world of the storm's desperately poor, predominantly African American victims.

[2] Mamie Garvin Fields with Karen Fields, *Lemon Swamp and Other Places: A Carolina Memoir* (New York, 1983), xxii–xxiii; 241.

[3] This definition excludes West Virginia, which did not become a separate state until 1863 and which did not disenfranchise African Americans or initiate many Jim Crow laws.

Jim Crow was originally a dance. To "jump Jim Crow" meant to pass back and forth across a line, and it is useful to keep this idea of motion across boundaries in mind when considering Jim Crow as a social and legal system. Although the origins of the term as applied to black southerners is unknown, it had become an adjective by 1838 and by the 1890s was used commonly to describe the system of law and social rules that structured the South's racially hierarchical society. In the twentieth century, the phrase became a verb: to be Jim Crowed was to be ejected from someplace set aside for whites or forced into an inevitably inferior space designated for blacks.

When under siege in later years, Jim Crow's white southern defenders would refer to it as "our southern way of life." That is an excellent description of Jim Crow viewed at ground level: It was a way of life, a culture, a code of everyday behavior, a mode of experience, a set of mind for whites as well as blacks. Its signs marking services and spaces set aside "for Negroes" and those "for Whites" decorated the common places of the South, and its etiquette informed interactions among the region's people. Like most euphemisms, however, the phrase "our southern way of life" softens and misleads.

First, the phrase's implied timelessness denies the novelty of Jim Crow. Until 1900, the only Jim Crow law common across the South was that segregating rail passengers. This is not to say that there was no segregation before 1900. Through the end of the nineteenth century, however, segregation was more a matter of local custom than of law, and black southern men influenced those laws by exercising their right to vote. The great majority of Jim Crow laws were passed by southern states and municipalities after 1900, in the flush of successful efforts to strip black men of the vote without violating the Fifteenth Amendment and backlit by the glow of the Supreme Court's consent to railway segregation in *Plessy v. Ferguson* (1896). Once started, there was no stopping; there was an internal logic to the codification of Jim Crow that resisted abbreviation, and segregation statutes were applied to nearly every aspect of southern life. Blacks and whites drank from different water pails and dippers by law; they used separate toilets; they walked through separate entrances and exits. The South Carolina Code of 1915 prohibited textile workers of different races from working in the same room or collecting their pay at the same window. Georgia's Separate Park Law meant exactly what it said; Birmingham and Atlanta adopted Mississippi's requirement of separate black and white taxi services. Anxious (one can only speculate) not to offend visitors to the final resting place of their canine friends, the District of Columbia required that animals interred in dog cemeteries be grouped according to the race of their masters.[4]

Second, a narrow focus on the local, everyday social aspects of Jim Crow, encouraged by describing it as a "way of life," obscures the systematic nature of the economic and political discrimination that was the foundation for that way of life. Jim Crow did not draw its strength from segregation and should not be viewed as synonymous with it. Jim Crow's power over African Americans came from exclusion: exclusion from voting booths; from juries; from neighborhoods; from unions and management positions; from higher education; from professions; from hospitals and theaters and hotels. The "southern way of life" of racial hierarchy and segregation was backed up by white economic and political control and secured through the police power of the state. The deep discrimination of the Jim Crow racial order was performed and marked through the practice of segregation, but important though it was, that practice was not its essence. This is why Justice John Marshall Harlan argued that segregated seating was a "badge of servitude" in his dissent to the Supreme Court's decision in *Plessy v. Ferguson* and why the leaders of the sit-in movement in 1960 announced that in their effort to gain access to a lunch counter they were fighting for "something much bigger than a hamburger."[5]

Although there were antebellum antecedents, the specific and systematic racial discrimination that characterized Jim Crow was a product of the post-emancipation era. Anything but timeless, Jim Crow laws and practices represented white victory in a violent forty-year struggle to define and control the postwar southern economy and to deny black men political influence. Contemporaries directly connected the push for Jim Crow at the turn of the century

[4] C. Vann Woodward, *The Strange Career of Jim Crow* (New York, 1974; 1955), 97–102.

[5] *Plessy v. Ferguson*, 163 U.S. 537; at 562; Ella Baker, "Bigger than a Hamburger," *Southern Patriot*, May 1960.

with the increasing economic and political power achieved by African Americans since the war. In an 1899 speech in the House of Representatives, George H. White, the last African American to represent North Carolina in Congress for seventy years, attributed the new Jim Crow laws to black southerners' accomplishments in all realms of life and the assertion of their political equality. "We seem as a race to be going through just now a crucible, a crisis—a peculiar crisis," he mused. "[P]ossibly more than by any one thing it has been brought about by the fact that despite all the oppression which has fallen upon our shoulders we have been rising, steadily rising, and in some instances we hope ere long to be able to measure our achievements with those of all other men and women of the land. This tendency on the part of some of us to rise and assert our manhood along all lines," White concluded, "is, I fear, what has brought about this changed condition."

George White's description of power and achievement in terms of manhood and its repression points to an important truth about Jim Crow that can be difficult to grasp. Formulated in a political universe that reserved the franchise exclusively to men, the limitations and humiliations of Jim Crow were designed to deny a common manhood to whites and blacks and to place the former firmly above the latter. They were, at the same time, designed to constrict the opportunities of all African Americans and to secure a political and economic order that depended on the disenfranchisement and disempowerment of large parts of the southern population as a whole. It is tempting to think of these two aspects of Jim Crow as separate: to consider the first as the product of the South's enduring culture of honor and masculinity and its concern with hierarchy and "place"; and the second as the result of the machinations of a relatively small cohort of elite white southerners to solidify their political and economic dominance. In fact, however, the two were thoroughly interdependent, as practice and as ideology. Black and white southerners drew from a deep well of political thought that imagined masculinity and power—whether economic, political, or physical—in terms of each other. This political world view enabled southern men to translate questions of politics into sexual terms. Northern champions of black equality often ridiculed this view, which they dubbed the "ballot box to bedroom" mentality. "It cannot be possible that any man of common sense can bring himself to believe that marriages between any persons, much less between white and colored people, will take place because a colored man is allowed to drop a little bit of paper into a box," insisted Republican William "Pig Iron" Kelley in 1868. But many men believed exactly that and were susceptible to the toxic arguments of those among them who cast issues of politics and economics in terms of sexual danger. Overcoming this conflation of sexual and political rights was a project of decades, and the greatest challenge opponents of Jim Crow faced.

II. Making Jim Crow: Law, Politics, and Economics, 1865–1900

The slave South did not need Jim Crow laws to discipline its black population. In the antebellum era, racially discriminatory laws were aimed at the nation's *un*enslaved people of color, who clustered in New Orleans and Charleston but resided mainly in the urban North. Numbering never more than a few hundred thousand (as contrasted to four million slaves in 1860), America's free black population was formally free but denied many rights and privileges, including equality in the courts, the right to assemble, and freedom of movement. Racial prejudice, one observer noted in the mid-nineteenth century, "haunts its victim wherever he goes,—in the hospitals where humanity suffers,—in the churches where it kneels to God,—in the prisons where it expiates its offenses,—in the graveyards where it sleeps the last sleep."[6]

After 1865, the largest population of free blacks in America resided south of the Mason-Dixon Line. Emancipation began, rather than ended, a broader political discussion about the meaning of freedom. What was the proper relationship of freedom to equality? Did abolition make everyone equal? When southern state legislatures passed laws known as Black Codes in late 1865, which severely restricted African American movement, freedom of association, and employment, Congress clarified its understanding of abolition. Responding to white persecution of the freed people and the demands of southern blacks for "a republican form of govern-

[6] Leon F. Litwack, *North of Slavery: The Negro in the Free States, 1790–1860* (Chicago, 1961), 97.

ment," Illinois senator Lyman Trumbull drafted the Civil Rights Act of 1866, which defined in legislative terms the essence of the freedom granted by the Thirteenth Amendment (1865). When white southern resistance to black rights continued, Republicans responded with the Fourteenth Amendment (1868), which incorporated the essence of the Civil Rights Act into the Constitution. The Fourteenth Amendment embraced African Americans as citizens, guaranteed "due process of law" and "equal protection of the laws" to every American, and encouraged white southerners to support black suffrage by threatening to reduce the congressional representation of any state that denied the vote to all male citizens aged twenty-one or older.

Although it would, in the long term, become the most powerful constitutional tool for the protection of minority rights in America, in the short term, the Fourteenth Amendment failed spectacularly to guarantee the political participation of black men. In 1868, the Georgia legislature reacted to the election of African American representatives by expelling them, prompting Congress to draft its third and final Reconstruction amendment to the Constitution. The Fifteenth Amendment (1870) prohibited both the federal and the state governments from depriving male citizens on racial grounds of the right to vote. The amendment was silent about the right to hold office and failed to forbid other forms of suffrage restriction, such as literacy tests and educational and property qualifications, causing Henry Adams—Harvard historian and the grandson and great-grandson of two American presidents—to note that the Fifteenth Amendment was "more remarkable for what it does not than for what it does contain." The omissions of the Fifteenth Amendment may be attributed to the desire of Republicans to limit the right to vote in their own regions as well as to protect their party in the South. Enfranchisement of Asians in the West would "kill our party dead as a stone" warned California senator Cornelius Cole, while the repeal of property qualifications on voting in the East would benefit the Democrats far more than the GOP. Yet despite its limitations, the Fifteenth Amendment enshrined in the nation's fundamental law the principle that every man has the right, as its Senate sponsor William Stewart put it, "to protect his own liberty" by participating in the polity.

Freed men and women were quick to embrace their rights. They formalized preexisting marriages, used the courts to establish parental rights over children appropriated as apprentices, joined forces to buy land, and entered the polity as voters, jurors, and officeholders. With one group of whites courting their votes and another determined to nullify them, black southerners organized to protect themselves and promote their interests. Under the watchful eyes of the Union League (which advanced Republican politics and protected black interests at the local level), an occupying army that included black soldiers and a new class of northern-educated African American politicians—what historian Steven Hahn refers to collectively as "the shock troops of political revolution"—the freed people shook the pillars of white domination. During Reconstruction, black men held political office in every state of the former Confederacy. Twenty-two African Americans were elected to Congress between 1870 and 1900, including two U.S. senators, both from Mississippi. More than one hundred won election or appointment to posts with jurisdiction over entire states, and almost eight hundred served in state legislatures. An even greater number held public office at the local level.[7] Probably the last time so large a group of previously dependent people entered the body politic was in the year 211, when the Emperor Caracalla granted full citizenship rights to all freeborn men in the Roman Empire.

In hindsight, it seems odd that the North failed to anticipate southern resistance to Reconstruction, given the revolutionary nature of the constitutional amendments and their enthusiastic embrace by the freedmen. "The presumption [after the war] was that these States would be obedient to the Constitution and the laws," Republican senator James G. Blaine of Maine recalled. "But for this presumption, legislation would be but idle play, and a government of laws would degenerate at once into a government of force. In enacting the Reconstruction laws, Congress proceeded upon the basis of faith in [r]epublican government."[8] This faith turned out to be misplaced. Building on grids of kinship and political patron-

---

[7] Steven Hahn, *A Nation under Our Feet: Black Political Struggles in the Rural South from Slavery to the Great Migration* (Cambridge, MA, 2003), 57, 219, 163.

[8] Blaine quoted in Michael Les Benedict, "Preserving Federalism: Reconstruction and the Waite Court," *Supreme Court Review* 1978: 39–79; 49.

age and fired up by the experience of military defeat, white men across the South reacted to the political mobilization of black men with alacrity and unprecedented violence. Functioning effectively as the paramilitary arm of the Democratic Party, the Ku Klux Klan and other allied organizations were designed to destroy the political infrastructure of black life. Reconstruction was experienced as an organized brawl in many places, as the Democrats captured control of state governments through a combination of intimidation, electoral fraud, and violence, including political assassination.[9]

Faced with resistance to the rule of law in the Reconstruction South but unwilling to employ force to uphold it, the federal government effectively Abandoned the freed people to their own political fate after the 1876 presidential election. Black southerners then had two main options: Abandon the region or make friends with their least objectionable white neighbors. Different groups in different places tried their hands at both. An emigration movement that began in the cotton South took significant numbers of rural blacks west to Kansas, Indiana, and Oklahoma, where land was plentiful and cheap. The Midwest had another distinct advantage over the South: As one settler wrote to a friend in Louisiana, "They do not kill Negroes here for voting."[10]

Other groups of black and white southerners joined forces after the end of Reconstruction. Across the South, but especially in the Upper South, freed blacks and Republican or dissident Democratic whites combined, usually in defense of fiscal policies that would deliver public services for everyone, such as schools and hospitals. These interracial coalition parties did surprisingly well in a political region where partisan divides were expected to parallel the color line and contributed significantly to the volatility of late-nineteenth-century southern politics. The success of each of these parties depended on the ballots of African Americans, who voted in most places throughout the late nineteenth century.

The most important example of this inclination toward interracial third-party politics was the People's Party, or the Populists,

[9] Hahn, *A Nation under Our Feet*, 308.

[10] Davidson et al., *Nation of Nations: A Narrative History of the American Republic*, 5th ed. (Boston, 2005; 1990), 566.

which emerged in the early 1890s in the context of a worldwide depression in agriculture. Representing the "producing classes" of small farmers and wage laborers, the People's Party denounced a nation "brought to the verge of moral, political, and material ruin" by economic inequality and political corruption.[11] Dedicated in principle to the idea that the power of the people should be amplified in government, the Populists were in practice open to the political inclusion of those people most neglected by the national parties: black men.

The Populists insisted that the race problem could not be disconnected from the South's economic system. While the North was experiencing what U.S. history textbooks usually refer to as the Age of Industry, the South's economy remained rooted in the soil, tied to the cash crops of rice, sugar, tobacco, and, especially, cotton. Nonperishable and as easily grown on five acres as on a thousand, cotton seemed a sure bet in a postwar world of uncertainty. But the sure bet held as true for India and Africa as for the American South. By the 1890s, the world market was glutted, and cotton prices plummeted from fifteen to five cents a pound.

Low commodity prices and a ruinous system of credit locked southern farmers into a hopeless cycle of debt. Despite talk of "forty acres and a mule," there was no land redistribution after the Civil War. By the end of the nineteenth century, a minority of southerners owned the vast majority of the region's land. Large landowners did not farm their land themselves: They parceled it out to family farmers, a majority of whom, white as well as black, were landless by the turn of the twentieth century. Sharecroppers worked others' fields for a share of the harvest. Tenants rented land, bargaining that their crop would cover their rent and more. To pay their rent and buy their seed and other necessities, tenants and sharecroppers mortgaged their future crop to merchants and landholders (frequently the same person), who charged exhorbitant rates of interest, shackling farmers with an ever-accruing debt and tying them to the land. As a Louisiana freedman explained, "I was in debt, and the man I rented land from said every year I must rent again to pay the other year, and so I rents and rents and each year

---

[11] Eric Foner, *Give Me Liberty! An American History* (New York, 2005), 639.

I gets deeper and deeper in debt."[12] Moving from the individual to
the structural, other black croppers set their economic analysis to
music:

> De big bee suck de blossom,
> De little bee make de honey,
> De black man makes de cotton and corn,
> And de white man totes de money.[13]

Agricultural depression and the South's exploitative credit system affected black southerners disproportionately because African
Americans had few economic alternatives to farming. Although
black men and women were employed in the tobacco and cigarette
factories of Virginia and North Carolina, on the docks in New Orleans and Baltimore, and in Alabama's coal mines and iron mills,
the highest-paying jobs were always reserved for whites. The newest
and fastest-growing commercial enterprise in the South, cotton textiles, excluded blacks almost entirely and provided a refuge for
white farm families unable to sustain themselves through share-
cropping and tenancy. Although Jim Crow practices of exclusion
supported the creation of a black middle class centered on the
professions (doctors, lawyers, and teachers) and strictly segregated
services such as funeral parlors, most African American businesses
suffered from a lack of credit and the overall poverty of their customers. Until American entry into World War I produced a labor
shortage in the North powerful enough to lower racial barriers to
industrial jobs there, the great majority of southern blacks remained hemmed in by restrictive labor practices at home and the
vagaries of the worldwide commodity market abroad.

While Jim Crow kept black men out of the South's best jobs, the
existence of an army of black labor standing in reserve helped
southern businessmen keep wages low and discouraged organization among white workers. In the 1890s, the Populists became the
first regional political party since the Republicans to point out the
political and economic effects of racial prejudice to their poor
white constituents and to stress their identity of interest with black

---

[12] Davidson et al., *Nation of Nations*, 569.

[13] Leon F. Litwack, *Trouble in Mind: Black Southerners in the Age of Jim Crow* (New York, 1998),
117.

farmers, croppers, and laborers. "You are kept apart that you may
be separately fleeced of your earnings," Georgia Populist Tom
Watson declared to interracial crowds. "This race antagonism perpetuates a monetary system which beggars you both." Watson
promised black men that "if you stand up for your rights and for
your manhood, if you stand shoulder to shoulder with us in this
fight," the People's Party would "wipe out the color line and put
every man on his citizenship irrespective of color."[14]

The Populists' success at convincing poor white and black men
to act in their common political and economic interest galvanized
elite white southerners to use every weapon at their disposal to con-
solidate political power in their own hands and end the threat of
biracial opposition parties. "The Populists and Republicans are our
legitimate political prey," explained one Louisiana newspaper.
"Rob them! You bet!" Political larceny was more easily accomplished some places than others, however. North Carolina had a robust tradition of African American voting and black-white political
cooperation.

Having been eased out of power by an alliance of black Republicans and white Populists in the mid-1890s, North Carolina Democrats turned the election of 1898 into a referendum on white
supremacy. Democratic newspapers complained in bold letters of
"NEGRO DOMINATION" in public life. More ominously, they
also reported a sudden epidemic of black-on-white rapes, which they
connected to black political power. Handbills spread the message in
cartoon form for the illiterate: One showed James H. Young, a black
politician from Raleigh, lurking in a white woman's bedroom.[15]

A few weeks before the election, the editor of the *Wilmington
Record*, North Carolina's only black daily newspaper, responded to
white men's sexual worries. Alexander Manly was the mixed-race
son of Charles Manly, a slave owner and former North Carolina
governor. On the topic of interracial sex, he wrote:

> [O]ur experience among poor white people in the country teaches
> us that women of that race are not any more particular in the mat-

---

[14] Quotes from C. Vann Woodward, *The Strange Career of Jim Crow* (New York, 1974; 1955),
63.

[15] Gilmore, *Gender and Jim Crow*, 83–88.

ter of clandestine meetings with colored men than the white men with colored women. Meetings of this kind go on for some time until the woman's infatuation or the man's boldness brings attention to them, and the man is lynched for rape. Every Negro lynched is called "a Big Burly Black Brute," when, in fact, many of those who have thus been dealt with had white men for their fathers, and were not only not "black and burly," but were sufficiently attractive for white girls of culture and refinement to fall in love with them.[16]

Manly's editorial inflamed North Carolina's white men and allowed the Democrats to cast the election in terms of race and manhood. Instead of focusing on schools, taxes, or the recently inaugurated war with Spain, Charles B. Aycock, the Democratic candidate for governor, ended every speech to white North Carolinians with the same question: "I come to you today on behalf of the goddess of Democracy, the white womanhood of the State, and I appeal to you to come to their relief. Will you come to the rescue? Will you?"[17]

They would. Across the state, white men who had cooperated previously with African Americans abandoned their former allies and voted Democratic. Victory in the state election, however, was not enough. Wilmington, North Carolina's largest city, retained its biracial municipal government, which included three black aldermen, a number of black policemen, two all-black fire companies, and customs collector John Dancy, who represented the federal government at the city's port, its center of trade. In the days following the election, illegal Democratic militia patrolled Wilmington's streets, seized public buildings, and forced the city council to resign. A mob burned Alex Manly's press to the ground; he fled to the North. The armed white men then turned on the black community, killing at least fourteen people and expelling hundreds more, who took what property they could carry and walked away from their former lives at the sharp end of a bayonet.

The federal government might have intervened in North Carolina. It did not, despite pleas from Wilmington's banished black elite and the state's Republican congressmen. The possibility of

[16] Manly, quoted in Adam Fairclough, *Better Day Coming: Blacks and Equality, 1890–2000* (New York, 2001), 9.

[17] Fairclough, *Better Day Coming*, 9.

federal intervention in elections marred by violence remained, however; southern Democrats could not rely forever on political terrorism to destroy their political opponents. Hoping to legitimate their rule rather than operate outside the law through violence and fraud, southern Democrats looked for more legal, and lasting, means to disenfranchise the competition. "There must be devised some legal defensible substitute for the abhorrent and evil methods on which white supremacy lies," one Mississippi newspaper put it unselfconsciously.[18]

The Fifteenth Amendment forbade voter discrimination on the basis of race, color, or previous condition: Outside of these broad guidelines, each state could define its electorate on its own terms. Northerners interested in restricting the suffrage to educated English speakers had already embraced secret (or Australian) ballot laws, which required of the voter either literacy or the aid of someone who could read. Defended by the wealthy and well educated as a progressive reform necessary to discourage fraud and limit black suffrage, adoption of the secret ballot in the South also eliminated a considerable portion of the white electorate, as intended. In Louisiana, the number of black registered voters fell from 130,000 in 1894 to 1,342 a decade later; 80,000 white Louisianans lost the vote during the same period. But illiteracy was not necessarily a permanent condition. More effective in the long term was revision of state constitutions. Beginning in 1890, all eleven states of the former Confederacy rewrote their constitutions in ways calculated to eliminate the votes of black men and potential white political allies.

In addition to representing the determination of the South's Democratic planter elite to reestablish control of politics, the timing of southern disenfranchisement campaigns reflected the resurgence of Republican power in Washington after the election of Benjamin Harrison in 1888 and the potential resuscitation of African American political power in the South. Emboldened by their party's control of the White House and both houses of Congress, black Republicans demanded a greater share of federal patronage and a renewed commitment to black suffrage. In Mississippi, African American Republicans moved to contest three of the

[18] Louisiana quote from Fairclough, *Better Day Coming*, 8; Mississippi quote from Edward L. Ayers, *The Promise of the New South: Life after Reconstruction* (New York, 1992), 147.

state's seven recent congressional elections and nominated the first complete Republican ticket since 1876. In a bid to end black voting power once and for all, Mississippi Democrats called for a constitutional convention to rewrite the state's electoral laws. The new constitution limited black political participation through a combination of complicated registration procedures, a poll tax, a literacy requirement, and what was dubbed an "understanding clause." The purpose of the understanding clause was to guard the interests of illiterate white Democrats, who, while unable to read the state constitution if asked, could presumably provide a "reasonable interpretation" of it. (White Republicans and Populists were unreasonable by definition and could not be expected to interpret the Constitution accurately.) Other southern states followed Mississippi's lead, and in 1898, the U.S. Supreme Court ruled in *Williams v. Mississippi* that poll taxes and literacy tests did not violate the Fifteenth Amendment.

African Americans divided in their response to the white supremacist campaigns of the late nineteenth century. Hoping to distance themselves from the black masses, some educated middle-class black southerners wondered aloud whether suffrage restriction to the literate was such a bad idea after all. The most influential black man in America, Booker T. Washington, a former slave and the founder of the Tuskegee Institute, a vocational school in Alabama, suggested in an 1895 speech at the Cotton States and International Exposition in Atlanta that African Americans leave politics to white men and focus on economic advancement. Suffrage was only one avenue to power, said Washington; labor that resulted in savings amounted to "a little green ballot" that "no one will throw out or refuse to count." Dubbed the "Atlanta Compromise" by more radical African Americans, Washington's position was ridiculed by northern black scholar and activist W. E. B. Du Bois a decade later, who remarked acidly that "the way for a people to gain their reasonable rights is not by voluntarily throwing them away and insisting that they do not want them."

The catastrophic consequences of disenfranchisement for southern blacks cannot be overstated. In the 1880s, more than two-thirds of adult southern males voted. That proportion rose to nearly three-quarters in the 1890s in states that had not yet limited the franchise. By the early 1900s, fewer than one man in three, white or black, voted in the South.[19] If black men could not vote, they could not be elected to office; if they could not be elected to office, they could not shape or administer the laws that governed their community. Sixty-four African Americans sat in Mississippi's state legislature in 1873: None sat there after 1895. At the local level, disenfranchisement meant no black sheriffs, no black justices of the peace, no black members of the school board. As legal historian Michael Klarman points out, because "the preferred method of denying constitutional rights to blacks was to vest discretion in local officials and trust them to preserve white supremacy," the lack of African American representation in public office at the local level was arguably even more devastating than the dearth of black state officials.[20] A conservative mayor beholden to—or afraid of—black voters might squelch a popular movement to segregate streetcars or reduce funding for black schools. That same mayor facing only white voters had little option but to go along or be tagged a "Negro lover." Although many southern whites were disenfranchised alongside their black neighbors and the South as a whole suffered through the creation of an uncompetitive one-party political system, African Americans paid by far the greatest price. Stripped of the vote, black southerners lost what little political leverage they had just when they needed it to fend off the codification of Jim Crow.

III. The Law of Jim Crow, 1896–1954

The legal history of Jim Crow is one of controversial judicial decisions and dramatic reversals. A pile of prize-winning books has been written on the law of race in the twentieth century. Rather than examining the law per se, our focus here will be on its rationale, to see how the same sexual logic that inflamed the 1898 election in Wilmington and fired the politics of Jim Crow elsewhere supported the law that upheld it.

---

[19] Statistic from Fairclough, *Better Day Coming*, 16.

[20] Michael J. Klarman, *From Jim Crow to Civil Rights: The Supreme Court and the Struggle for Racial Equality* (New York, 2004), 32–33.

Although indelibly associated with it, the phrase "separate but equal" appears nowhere in the Supreme Court decision in *Plessy v. Ferguson*, the landmark case that upheld an 1890 Louisiana statute requiring railroads "to provide equal but separate accommodation for the white and colored races." Equal treatment was the concern of the Louisiana legislature, which knew that any legislation along race lines would inevitably be challenged. The Supreme Court, on the other hand, was more concerned with the principal question of whether enforced separation along color lines could be squared with the protections of liberty and equality articulated in the Fourteenth Amendment to the Constitution, which forbade discrimination by race, color, or previous condition of servitude.

Drafted by the 39th Congress under highly partisan, polemical conditions, the Fourteenth Amendment consists almost solely of elliptical phrases that have made it the most scrutinized amendment to the Constitution. There are two sections to the amendment. Of greater interest is the first section, which reads in full: "All persons born or naturalized in the United States, and subject to the jurisdiction thereof, are citizens of the United States and of the State wherein they reside. No State shall make or enforce any law which shall abridge the privileges or immunities of citizens of the United States; nor shall any State deprive any person of life, liberty, or property, without due process of law; nor deny to any person within its jurisdiction the equal protection of the laws."

Such capacious, even vague, language (just what, exactly, were the privileges and immunities of United States citizens? What was the definition of due process? Of equal protection?) invited jurisprudential ingenuity. Against Justice John Marshall Harlan's insistence that "our Constitution is color-blind," his colleagues on the Court found that the Louisiana separate carriage law had nothing to do with the Constitution and especially not with the Fourteenth Amendment, which protected such rights of citizenship as suffrage and jury service, but which, Justice Henry Billings Brown argued, "could not have been intended to abolish distinctions based upon color, or to enforce social, as distinguished from political, equality, or a commingling of the two races upon terms unsatisfactory to either." In a fateful link, Brown gave two examples of legally imposed segregation common across the nation: segregated public schools and racially restrictive marriage laws. Admitting that anti-miscegenation laws "may be said in a technical sense to interfere with the freedom of contract," Brown noted nonetheless that such statutes were universally accepted as a reasonable exercise of the police power of the state "for the preservation of the public peace and good order." Gauged by this standard, the Court concluded, "we cannot say that a law which authorizes or even requires the separation of the two races in public conveyances is unreasonable, or more obnoxious to the [F]ourteenth [A]mendment than the acts of congress requiring separate schools for colored children in the District of Columbia." Legislation, Brown concluded, "is powerless to eradicate racial instincts."[21]

If legislation were powerless to change feelings, it had great power, warned Justice Harlan, to affect behavior. "The present decision, it may well be apprehended," predicted Harlan, "will not only stimulate aggressions, more or less brutal and irritating, upon the admitted rights of colored citizens, but will encourage the belief that it is possible, by means of state enactments, to defeat the beneficent purposes which the people of the United States had in view when they adopted the recent amendments of the constitution." As Harlan anticipated, this violation of the Fourteenth Amendment would lead to still greater violations over time, undoing the emancipatory work of the Civil War generation.

The *Plessy* decision raised more questions than it answered. What were the "political" rights protected by the Fourteenth Amendment? What were the "social" rights beyond the scope of the Constitution? In his dissent, Justice Harlan ridiculed the majority, "who affect to be disturbed at the possibility that the integrity of the white race may be corrupted, or that its supremacy will be imperiled, by contact on public highways with black people." Refusing to be drawn into an argument about schools or marriage, Harlan intoned, "Social equality no more exists between two races when traveling in a passenger coach or a public highway than when members of the same races sit by each other in a street car or in a jury box, or stand or sit with each other in a political assembly, or when they use in common the streets of a city or town, or when

---

[21] *Plessy v. Ferguson*, 544, 545, 550–51.

they are in the same room for the purpose of having their names placed on the registry of voters, or when they approach the ballot box in order to exercise the high privilege of voting." With the exception of sidewalks and streetcars—the latter soon to be segregated, the former a persistent site of racial skirmishes—Harlan's examples of nonsocial equality were drawn exclusively from the all-male world of nineteenth-century politics. Ignoring the reality of life on the rails, in which white women tucked safely into first-class cars could find themselves sharing space with propertied black men and women, Harlan sidestepped what for most other judges was a knock-down argument: That, in the words of the Pennsylvania Supreme Court in another separate car case, integrated rail carriages would promote "promiscuous sitting," which could only lead to "illicit intercourse" and facilitate "intermarriage."[22]

Interracial marriage was regulated in America for over three hundred years. At the time of the *Plessy* decision, twenty-five states considered the marriage of whites with nonwhites a criminal offense. To enforce what were referred to as antimiscegenation laws, authorities had to know who was who, and state legislatures confronted the problem of how to define who was, and who was not, white. Depending on the state and the decade, people who were more than half black, a fourth black, an eighth black, one-sixteenth black, or even one-thirty-second black could not marry anyone defined at law as white. Crossing a state line could change one's legal racial identity and render a marriage and its children illegitimate or vice versa. Aware of the increasing disabilities associated with blackness and mindful of its own antebellum sexual past, the South Carolina constitutional convention of 1895 rejected a proposal to classify as white only those who did not have "any" African heritage. Instead, they decided to play it safe and drew the line at one-eighth: Anyone with one black great-grandparent would be defined as African American and thus ineligible to marry anyone classed as white.

Antimiscegenation statutes and the racial identity laws that supported them were the legal core of Jim Crow, the center from which a multitude of prohibitions and regulations radiated

---

[22] *Plessy v. Ferguson*, 561, 562; *West Chester and Philadelphia R.R. v. Miles*, 55 Pa. 211–12 (1867).

outward. Laws prohibiting interracial marriage provided a firm foundation for other Jim Crow laws and for judicial decisions involving segregation in other realms. In 1904, for example, the state of Kentucky passed a segregated education bill and forced Berea College, founded on the former estate of the abolitionist Cassius M. Clay to "promote the cause of Christ" by educating "all youths of good moral character," to close its doors to black students. When Berea sued, the trial court upheld the statute and opined that "no well-informed person in any section of the country will now deny the position of the Southern people that 'segregation in school, church and society is in the interest of racial integrity, and racial progress.'" The Kentucky Court of Appeals (through which the Berea case passed on its way to the Supreme Court) invoked higher authority and asserted a correspondence of the law of Kentucky with that of God: "The natural law which forbids their intermarriage, and that social amalgamation which leads to a corruption of the races, is as clearly divine as that which imparted to them different natures. . . . From social amalgamation it is but a step to illicit intercourse, and but another to intermarriage."[23] When the Supreme Court upheld the Kentucky statute, the lesson was clear: As the *Harvard Law Review* put it, the right to prohibit miscegenation being established, "to prohibit joint education is not much more of a step."

As Jim Crow's realm expanded in the first two decades of the twentieth century, this slippery-slope rationale for separation was tested by a string of cases. In 1915, the Supreme Court agreed to hear a case that was regarded at the time as the most important test of black rights since *Plessy*. It was called *Buchanan v. Warley*, and it hinged on the twin questions of property rights and racial discrimination.

In the spring of 1914, Louisville, Kentucky, followed the lead of Baltimore and other border-state cities in passing a residential segregation ordinance. This "ordinance to prevent conflict and ill-feeling between the white and colored races" provided that blacks could not occupy a residence on a white-majority block or vice

---

[23] Quoted in Benno C. Schmidt, Jr., "Principle and Prejudice: The Supreme Court and Race in the Progressive Era. Part I: The Heyday of Jim Crow," *Columbia Law Review*, 82, no. 3 (March 1982): 444–524; 447. *Berea College v. Commmonwealth*, 123 Ky. 209, 94 S.W. 623 (1906).

versa. A response to the northward migration of southern blacks and their increasing presence in cities, residential segregation laws were necessary, according to the Kentucky appeals court, "to prevent the mixing of the races in cross breeding." Or, as the attorneys for Louisville put it to the Supreme Court, "It is shown by philosophy, experience and legal decisions, to say nothing of Divine Writ, that . . . the races of the earth shall preserve their racial integrity by living socially by themselves." In addition to aggravating African Americans, such sentiments so alarmed the original custodians of Divine Writ that Louisville officials had to reassure local Jews that they would not be next.

Born in 1909, the same year as the National Association for the Advancement of Colored People (NAACP), residential segregation laws turned out to be an excellent recruitment tool for the new organization. Louisville organized a branch specifically to fight the municipal law, and Baltimore's local branch beat back that city's residential segregation statutes in 1910 and 1911. Argued ably by NAACP president Moorfield Storey, a past president of the American Bar Association and a prominent Boston attorney who based his case squarely on the question of property rights, *Buchanan v. Warley* was only the second case that the NAACP brought before the Supreme Court, and it won.

The decision in *Buchanan* did not end residential discrimination or segregation by race. What was forbidden formally could, the Richmond *News-Leader* reassured its white readers, be maintained "by custom, if not by law." Neighborhood residential covenants, through which individuals circumscribed their own property rights voluntarily by promising not to sell their homes to blacks, Jews, Catholics, and other "undesirables" passed constitutional muster, at least for the moment. Yet, it was nevertheless true, as Norfolk's black *Journal and Guide* pointed out, that "never before in the history of the Supreme Court has that tribunal reached a unanimous decision upon any question upholding the rights of the Negro."

One of the lessons of *Buchanan* was that the miscegenation analogy could be broken, or at least rendered ineffective, by a sufficiently strong counterclaim. Rights of property, in this case, trumped the presumptive power of the state to regulate social relations. Sidestepping the miscegenation question in other arenas would be more difficult. Unlinking sex from schools and moving education from a social to a civil right would be the job of the NAACP. But there was room for optimism. The fact that whites were basing Jim Crow on the miscegenation argument, as opposed to others, was viewed by at least one champion of equality as progress of a sort. In 1913, Moorfield Storey wrote to William Monroe Trotter, Boston's crusading black journalist and head of the National Equal Rights League. "The mills of the Gods grind slowly and patience does its perfect work," the NAACP's legal warrior began. It had been only fifty years since the abolition of slavery, when white men insisted that blacks "are and always must remain hewers of wood and drawers of water because they are incapable of anything else. The cry now," Storey continued, "is that there is danger of racial equality, that colored men will sit at the table with white men and may marry white men's daughters. This is not the fear of an inferior race; it is the fear that a race, though inferior, is proving its right to equality. The very arguments of those who would discriminate against you are admissions of your ability to rise, and of the fact that you have risen and are rising."

Although on record as opposing antimiscegenation laws, challenging them was not a priority for the NAACP. Instead the brilliant team of lawyers that made up the Legal Defense Fund, Inc., (known as "the Inc") set their sights on public education and the right to vote. In a series of victories before the Supreme Court in the 1930s and 1940s, the NAACP chipped away at segregation in higher education. And in what many historians consider an even more consequential decision than that rendered in *Brown v. Board of Education*, in 1944, the Inc succeeded in having racially restrictive primary elections, known as white primaries, declared unconstitutional.

Until 1941, state party primaries were not considered elections in which the right to vote was involved. Political parties defined themselves as private voluntary organizations, with the right to limit their membership. According to this logic, state Democratic parties were no more obliged to open their doors to African Americans than the Masons were to Catholics. This construction of the Democratic Party as a white men's club had significant political consequences across what was, with some short-lived exceptions, the one-party South. In many southern states, the Democratic primary was the only election that mattered. In Texas, for example, every Democratic nominee selected in the primary had won the general election since 1859, with only two exceptions.[24] This method of limiting political participation to whites began to crumble in 1941, when the Supreme Court ruled that the primary and the general election were part of a single electoral process,[25] and it collapsed entirely in 1944 when the Court ruled 8–1 in *Smith v. Allwright* that racially restrictive primaries violated the Fifteenth Amendment.

Smith v. Allwright posed a clear threat to "the southern way of life." As the *New York Times* editorialized approvingly, *Smith* put America "a little closer to a more perfect democracy, in which there will be but one class of citizens."[26] The decision did not, of course, herald the dawn of African American enfranchisement: It would be another twenty years before a majority of black southerners was able to exercise the right to vote without fearing for their lives and livelihoods. But *Smith* did make a difference. In 1946, blacks voted in large numbers in primary elections in Georgia, Florida, and Texas; black voter registration in Georgia exploded from 20,000 in 1940 to 125,000 in 1947.[27] Across the South, returning black veterans from World War II marched straight to city hall and demanded to be registered to vote.[28]

Unapparent in the reaction to *Smith*, the importance of the sexual question became clear once again during the uproar that followed the Supreme Court's decision against segregated public schools in *Brown v. Board of Education* (1954). The *Brown* decision was interpreted by a large and vocal segment of white southerners in explicitly sexual terms. In a typical editorial comment, the Jackson,

---

[24] Hine, *Black Victory: The Rise and Fall of the White Primary in Texas* (Columbia, MO, 2003; 1979), 234–35.

[25] Hine, *Black Victory*, 222. The 1941 case (which originated in Louisiana) is *United States v. Classic* 313 U.S. 299 (1941).

[26] "Primaries Are Not Private," *NYT* April 5, 1944, p. 18. Quoted in Michael Klarman, "The White Primary Rulings: A Case Study in the Consequences of Supreme Court Decisionmaking," *Florida State University Law Review* 29, no. 1 (fall, 2001): 55–109; 64. Richmond's leading papers endorsed the decision. Hine, *Black Victory*, 224.

[27] Hine, *Black Victory*, 238.

[28] John Dittmer, *Local People: The Struggle for Civil Rights in Mississippi* (Urbana, 1994), 1–9; Adam Fairclough, *Race and Democracy: The Civil Rights Struggle in Louisiana, 1915–1972* (Athens, GA, 1995), 111; Steven F. Lawson, *Black Ballots: Voting Rights in the South, 1944–1969* (New York, 1976), 102.

Mississippi, *Daily News* denounced the school decision as "the first step, or an opening wedge, toward mixed marriages, miscegenation, and the mongrelization of the human race." Walter C. Givhan, an Alabama state senator, interpreted the *Brown* decision the same way. "What is the real purpose of this? To open the bedroom doors of our white women to Negro men." Georgia state attorney general Eugene Cook agreed and explained how it would be done. "As I view it," said Cook, "the scope of this decision goes directly to our miscegenation laws. Carried to its ultimate effect it means these laws, too, could be struck down by proper legal attack. Once they are struck down, I foresee an amalgamation stampede."

White southerners used a variety of tactics to prevent this outcome. Southern congressmen declared their unwillingness to abide by the law; their defiance encouraged mobs to prevent the integration of schools and universities across the region. White Citizens' Councils—known across the South as the "uptown Klan"—put a respectable face on social and economic intimidation of civil rights supporters and inundated southern mailboxes with alarmist fliers promising white parents black grandchildren should they not stand together now against school integration. The regular, down and dirty, Klan resurfaced with a vengeance as well. In September 1957, a breakaway group of the North Alabama Klan selected a black man at random to carry a message to Fred Shuttlesworth, Birmingham's charismatic civil rights leader. Tell Shuttlesworth, they said, "to stop sending nigger children and white children to school together or we're gonna do him like we're fixing to do you." Then they castrated J. Edward Aaron and took his scrotum home in a paper cup. In this climate of cultivated white hysteria about black sexuality, eight-year-old African American boys could be made wards of the state for playing a "kissing game" with little white girls and the flirtatious crack of a fourteen-year-old boy could become a death sentence, as it did for Emmett Till in Mississippi in 1955.[29]

---

[29] Glenn T. Eskew, *But for Birmingham: The Local and National Movements in the Civil Rights Struggle* (Chapel Hill, 1997), 114–15; Diane McWhorter, *Carry Me Home: Birmingham, Alabama, the Climactic Battle of the Civil Rights Revolution* (New York, 2001), 124–25. For details on "the kissing case" see Timothy B. Tyson, *Radio Free Dixie: Robert F. Williams and the Roots of Black Power* (Chapel Hill, 1999), 90–125.

The Supreme Court understood the centrality of sex to segregation. The Justices were fully aware of the slippage that occurred between desegregation and interracial sex, and they went to considerable trouble to limit the *Brown* decision's language to segregation in public schools only.[30] They also refused to rule on the constitutionality of antimiscegenation laws. As Justice Felix Frankfurter explained to Circuit Court Judge Learned Hand, "I shall work, within the limits of judicial decency, to put off [a] decision on miscegenation as long as I can. . . . We [have] twice shunted it away and I pray that we may be able to do it again, without being too brazenly evasive." Such evasion was justified, another justice explained to his clerk, as long as "strident opposition is being voiced to less controversial desegregation because it allegedly leads to interracial marriage."

We have dwelt on questions of sex and marriage in this discussion of the law of Jim Crow to highlight the conceptual continuity between the beginning of the Jim Crow legal regime and its end. Arguments about the need to protect white "racial purity" underlay the construction of Jim Crow and blocked efforts to dismantle it. Yet, in addition to preserving the integrity of the white race—as twentieth-century white supremacists would have put it—Jim Crow laws did other work in other realms, to which we will turn now.

IV. Economy and Society, 1896–1954

The architects of the Jim Crow South did not refer to it in those terms. They preferred to call their creation the "New" South, which in their eyes was a South bursting with entrepreneurial energy, abundant natural resources, and cheap labor, primed for northern industrial investment. According to W. H. Harrison, the author of *How to Get Rich in the South*, the region abounded in "tempting inducements to the capitalist for profitable investments." Although often offered as proof of sectional reconciliation, the New South creed, as southern writer W. J. Cash noted in the mid-twentieth century, more resembled "a new charge at Gettysburg." The New South, he continued, "was mainly a South which would

---

[30] See *Naim v. Naim*, 350 U.S. 891 (1955) (per curiam) (motion to recall mandate denied).

be new in this: that it would be so rich and powerful that it might rest serene in its ancient positions, forever impregnable."[31]

And yet there was much that *was* new about the New South. Effectively disenfranchised or not, black men were entitled to vote, which made them potentially powerful should the federal government care to enforce the Fifteenth Amendment. Although still rooted in agriculture, the southern economy did diversify after the Civil War. Some industry developed, such as mining in the Appalachians, steel in Alabama, and textile production in the upcountry, where Georgia, North Carolina, and South Carolina merged. All but textiles were extractive industries, with biracial workforces segregated by task. Needless to say, the skilled jobs and their higher salaries were reserved for whites.

The upcountry cotton mills were almost entirely segregated. Whole families migrated to the mill villages that the textile barons thoughtfully provided. Eyeing the farm wives and their daughters, who could be paid less than white men, mill owners restricted their labor force to whites, neutralizing worries about interracial mixing. By 1900, children under sixteen (the majority of them under thirteen) constituted 30 percent of the cotton mill workforce and southern per capita income stood at 60 percent of the national average.

What was not new about the New South was the position occupied by African Americans on the economic ladder. Bent by the burdens of sharecropping, most black farmers failed to become landowners. Many migrated to the region's fast-growing cities, such as Atlanta, where they found themselves barred from many trades and industries. Most African American city dwellers labored as domestic servants or menial laborers for less than a dollar a day in wages.

Jim Crow's New South boosters justified the racial division of labor in terms designed to appeal to white workers. Here is how William H. Baldwin, director of the Southern Railway, put it:

> Properly directed [the Negro] is the best possible laborer to meet the climactic conditions of the South. He will willingly fill the more menial positions, and do the heavy work, at less wages than the

---

[31] Quotes from James C. Cobb, *Away Down South: A History of Southern Identity* (New York, 2005), 72.

American white man or any foreign race which has yet come to our shores. This will permit the Southern white laborer to perform the more expert labor, and to leave the fields, the mines, and simpler trades for the negro.[32]

Before the Civil War, northern workingmen opposed the expansion of slavery because they did not want their wages eroded through competition with unfree workers who had to be fed and housed but not paid for their labor. Jim Crow promised white workers in the post-emancipation South that they would not have to compete with black workers, who could be paid less than whites: Unless, that is, white workers demanded higher wages, or better living conditions, or banded together politically to outlaw child labor.

What Jim Crow gave white workers with one hand he took away with the other. To encourage the industries that made jobs for white men, southern state legislatures kept taxes low and provided few services. Those they did provide, such as public schools, were underfunded and inadequate as well as segregated and grotesquely unequal. The South led the country in illiteracy and lagged in higher education. Draconian penalties for petty crimes, such as theft, resulted in inflated prison populations in every southern state. Rather than raise taxes to support the prisoners, who were disproportionately black, southern states leased the convicts to local industry. Mines, railroads, and lumber companies leased large numbers of convict laborers and housed them in primitive camps that were hotbeds of disease. The death rates were appallingly high, but there was never a shortage of convicts: As the saying went, "One dies, get another." The availability of involuntary labor helped keep wages for white workers artificially low, which contributed to the overall poverty of the region. The South remained the poorest part of the country throughout the Jim Crow era, many of its rural villages lacking electricity and running water through World War II, its people suffering from nutritional diseases caused by poor diet. Franklin Roosevelt was not exaggerating when he dubbed the South "the nation's number one economic problem" in 1932.

In the mid-1940s, white Georgia author Lillian Smith remarked that "Jim Crow was Mr. Rich White's idea but Mr. Poor White

[32] Quoted in Fairclough, *Better Day Coming*, 51.

made it work."[33] It ought to be clear by now what Mr. Rich White got out of this bargain: A monopoly on political power (which amplified his voice in Washington, D.C., as well as at home), a state legislature that kept his interests always in mind, a segmented labor force that feared and loathed each other. But what did Mr. Poor White get?

It would be fair to answer, "Bad schools, low wages, and pellagra." But poor whites, like all whites, got something more out of Jim Crow: They got privilege. As W. E. B. Du Bois explained in his history of the postwar South, *Black Reconstruction,*

> [T]he white group of laborers, while they received a low wage, were compensated in part by a sort of public and psychological wage. They were given public deference and titles of courtesy because they were white. They were admitted freely with all classes of white people to public functions, public parks, and the best schools.[34]

Jim Crow organized society in a way that made it possible for Mr. Poor White to demand, and receive, deference—if not, perhaps, from many white men, then at least from all African Americans. In this social system the poorest and most degraded white man was considered the superior of the most propertied and refined person of color. It is impossible to set the worth of what some historians have called the "wages of whiteness." But the sentiment "I may not have much, but at least I'm a white man" was a mantra of the Jim Crow era and gained through repetition what it lacked in substance.

Others besides Mr. Poor White made Jim Crow work. A rising urban middle class did its share of the job by passing segregation laws packaged as reform (if black men are banned from white saloons, the chance for racial violence is lessened) and orienting the region's newspapers around an articulate defense of "the southern way of life." White ministers backed up segregation with scripture, arguing that God himself had separated the races; this argument was used to support segregation right through the civil rights movement. And despite growing unease with some aspects of Jim Crow on the part of a small number of southern intellectuals, middle-

---

[33] Lillian Smith, *Killers of the Dream* (New York, 1949), 181.

[34] W. E. B. Du Bois, *Black Reconstruction in America* (New York, 1969; 1935), 700.

class white southerners also turned their heads when confronted with a crucial component of the Jim Crow regime: lynching.

A common form of frontier violence, until the 1880s lynching claimed more white lives than black ones. Beginning in the late 1880s, however, the number of lynchings in the South began to rise; nearly all the victims were African American. Between 1882 and 1946, 4,715 black men, women, and children were killed by white mobs in the American South. Composed of respectable citizens as well as the rabble, defended in the press and frequently in the pulpit, lynch mobs acted without fear of punishment. Local sheriffs colluded with the mob and released black prisoners to it; some joined the mob itself. White grand juries that knew perfectly well who had led the mob refused to indict anyone, insisting instead that lynching victims "died at the hands of persons unknown." Impervious to outside criticism, the white southern establishment considered lynching a regrettable but necessary component of Jim Crow society.

Because it replaced established legal procedures with extralegal violence, lynching is often considered an assault on the authority of the Jim Crow state. But it is perhaps better seen as the purest representation of that state. Rather than undermining the values of the state through their violent extralegal actions, white mobs understood themselves and were understood by others, particularly their victims, as reinforcing those values and the state that upheld them. White men written out of politics through the secret ballot and the poll tax could participate in government through mob action. In the guise of a lynch mob, the disenfranchised became the custodians of the most sacred values of the Jim Crow state.

Although there were broader social and political goals to both segregation and lynching, the rhetorical justification for Jim Crow laws and white mob violence was the protection of white women from the sexual assault of reputedly predatory black men. Despite the pioneering work of Ida B. Wells, who demonstrated that not even a third of black men lynched were *accused* of rape, late-nineteenth-century white southerners convinced themselves that they were surrounded by an African American population increasingly brutalized and criminally inclined. Founded on both sexism and racism, lynching taught every southerner, black or white, male or female, where he stood in the region's social hierarchy. For white women, lynching reaffirmed their dependence on white men; for African American men and women, lynching demonstrated graphically their extreme vulnerability. As Andrew Sledd, a professor of Latin at Emory College in Atlanta, explained in a fiery article in the *Atlantic Monthly* in 1902, the object of such "savagery"—the victim had been burned to death before a large crowd—was to "teach the negro the lesson of abject and eternal servility, [to] burn into his quivering flesh the consciousness that he has not, cannot have, the rights of a free citizen or even of a fellow human creature."[35]

Rooted in sexual fantasies and sometimes in sexual acts, lynchings themselves often had an unmistakably erotic texture. Naked black men were tortured and castrated by white men in full view of white women and children. Newspaper stories about lynchings and the crimes attributed to their victims dwelt lovingly on the details and constituted, in the words of historian Jacquelyn Dowd Hall, a sort of "folk pornography" of the South. W. J. Cash, who occupied the position of regional armchair psychiatrist in the 1940s, admitted that the "Southern rape complex" was irrational, but it was also useful. In a world where white men crossed the sexual color line with impunity, white women became the physical and rhetorical repository of whiteness, the protectors of the race but themselves in need of policing and protection. As segregation became more ingrained, Jim Crow's champions equated any attack on white womanhood with an attack on the region and vice versa. As Cash put it in his epic history *The Mind of the South* (1941), any assault on the Jim Crow South would be felt as an assault on white women, and "the South would inevitably translate its whole battle into terms of her defense." "Protecting" white womanhood was the keystone of an ideology and not just a rhetorical stance.

However, buttressed by the law and sanctioned by society, Jim Crow rested ultimately on force or the threat of force. Lynching was an act of terror, designed to remind black southerners of the boundaries of their lives and the dangerous consequences of crossing them. The fear generated by the possibility of white violence

---

[35] Quoted in Cobb, *Away Down South*, 96–97.

hovered over the everyday world of Jim Crow and reinforced white dominance. As novelist Richard Wright, who grew up in Mississippi, explained in *Black Boy* (1944), "The things that influenced my conduct as a Negro did not have to happen to me directly; I needed but to hear of them to feel their full effects in the deepest layers of my consciousness. Indeed, the white brutality that I had not seen was a more effective control of my behavior than that which I knew."

In addition to the omnipresent threat of violence, the behavior of black boys like Richard Wright was shaped by an intricate code of behavior designed to govern the day-to-day interactions among individual white and black southerners. Like any set of rules, the etiquette of Jim Crow had to be taught. White children could be expected to embrace the dominant role accorded their race. Of his upbringing in small-town North Carolina in the middle of the twentieth century, historian Melton McLaurin recalled,

> [E]arly in life I learned, almost unconsciously, that both races observed the unspoken etiquette of segregation. Blacks who had to enter our house, for whatever reason, came in the back door. Unless employed as domestic servants, blacks conducted business with my father or mother on the back porch, or, on rare occasions, in the kitchen. Blacks never entered our dining or living areas . . . except as domestics. . . . When a black person approached a doorway at the same time as a white adult, the black stepped back and sometimes even held the door open for the white to enter. The message I received from hundreds of such signals was always the same. I was white; I was different; I was superior. It was not a message with which an adolescent boy was apt to quarrel.[36]

The situation was more complicated for black children, who might challenge the message of inferiority but not that of difference. Charles Evers, whose brother Medgar would be among the first civil rights activists murdered for the cause, explained in his autobiography that "Our mothers began telling us about being black from the day we were born. The white folks weren't any better than we were, Momma said, but they sure thought they were. We got it

---

[36] Melton A. McLaurin, *Separate Pasts: Growing Up White in the Segregated South* (Athens, GA, 1987), 13–14.

hammered into us to watch our step, to stay in our place, or to get off the street when a white woman passed."[37]

Many of the rules governing the behavior of black southerners were definite and non-negotiable: Always go to the back door of a white person's house, always doff one's hat in the presence of a white man or woman, wait to be served until white customers have been taken care of, sit only in the "Colored" sections of buses and theaters. But others were more ambiguous; some of Jim Crow's rules could be stretched by creative interpretation and the cooperation of whites, who were themselves expected to conform to racial norms. President Jimmy Carter, who grew up in rural Georgia during the Depression, recalled how African Methodist Episcopal Bishop William Decker Johnson, a propertied man of influence among whites as well as blacks, cheated Jim Crow:

> Bishop Johnson was certainly aware of the racial customs of the day, but he did not consider it appropriate to comply with all of them. It was understood, for instance, that he would not come to our front door when he wished to talk to my father—but neither would he deign to come to the back. After ascertaining through a messenger that we were at home, he would arrive in his chauffeured black Packard or Cadillac, park in our front yard, and sound the horn. My father would go outside to the automobile for a conversation, while Bishop Johnson either stayed in the car or came out so the two men could stand together under the shade of a large magnolia tree.[38]

Jimmy Carter understands this modification of strict Jim Crow racial etiquette as an assertion of dignity and autonomy on the part of Bishop Johnson, which it was. But individual resistance to those constraints in the form of a conversation under a magnolia tree as opposed to a back door still marked Bishop Johnson definitively as a black man and thus reaffirmed rather than challenged the power of Jim Crow to assign racial identity and social position. As Du Bois once commented on the connection between race and place, "A black man is a person who has to ride Jim Crow in Georgia."

[37] Jennifer Ritterhouse, *Growing Up Jim Crow: How Black and White Southern Children Learned Race* (Chapel Hill, 2006), 5.

[38] Jimmy Carter, *An Hour before Daylight: Memories of a Rural Boyhood* (New York, 2001), 23.

Grounded in patriarchy as well as racism, it is fitting that the most successful early assaults on Jim Crow were mounted by organized women. Ignored by whites in the United States, anti-lynching activist Ida B. Wells took her message to Britain in the 1890s and made American mob violence an international cause celèbré. She was supported in the United States by the National Association of Colored Women (NACW), founded in 1896. Unlike the members of contemporaneous white women's clubs, black club women merged gender and race politics, and they took to heart Wells's message, particularly her denial that rape either caused or justified lynching. Molded by years of church work and accustomed to having no formal political power, black women were already organized in voluntary self-help organizations when black men were stripped of the vote at the turn of the twentieth century. The hardening of white supremacy enhanced the importance of these corseted "diplomats to the white community," who lobbied for black interests and worked to improve conditions on a variety of seemingly nonpolitical fronts such as public health and education. Rooted in a growing urban black middle class, club women and other reformers were supported by their local communities and institutions, especially churches. Although overall an economic disaster for southern blacks, Jim Crow did create communities in which African American commerce and institutions flourished, many of which supported the organizations that entered politics through the back door during the era of black disenfranchisement.

Many of black club women's efforts coincided with those of organized white women, some of whom were early proponents of what was called at the time "interracial cooperation." Many fruitful partnerships were forged during the 1920s and 1930s under the auspices of the interracial movement, including the all-male Commission on Interracial Cooperation, the all-female Association of Southern Women for the Prevention of Lynching, and the all-liberal Southern Conference for Human Welfare. Although it made significant contributions toward alleviating the worst excesses of Jim Crow, the interracial cooperation movement was fatally flawed by the belief of all but a handful of its white members that black progress could be achieved within the confines of segregation.

The greatest challenge to southern racial etiquette and in many cases to segregation itself, before the bus boycotts and sit-ins of the mid-century civil rights movement, came during World War II. If not officially under siege by the government, which refused to desegregate the armed forces during the war, the South's social system was challenged more directly, and more systematically, during World War II than it had ever been before. Southern social conventions worked out painstakingly via elaborate municipal laws and local custom came under severe pressure as wartime congestion swelled towns and strained segregated public services. Northern black recruits unfamiliar with the quotidian indignities of Jim Crow clashed on a daily basis with southern white GIs and war workers and chafed against the strictures of segregation. Just how out of touch the black Yanks were with southern social custom may be seen in the acrimonious give and take between black members of the 94th Engineers and local whites in Little Rock, Arkansas. Refused service at a liquor store, a group of black GIs were then confronted by local police who were, as one soldier recalled, "surly and insulting, so the guys turned their car over and burned it." It is hard to say which side was most surprised by this interaction: the police, with their smoldering car, or the 94th Engineers, which pulled out of Camp Robinson the next day and was "rocked, called obscenities, [and] given the full treatment to Gurdon, Arkansas."[39]

The experience of world war—fought, according to the Axis, in the interest of racial and cultural hierarchy and, according to the Allies, to promote democracy and human equality—radically altered the landscape of thinking about domestic segregation in the United States. African American leaders, including those of the NAACP, made an open effort to link Nazi race policies and American segregation. According to sociologist and Howard University professor emeritus Kelly Miller, the chief difference between the United States and Germany in 1935 was that in Germany "Hitler has decreed that proscription against the Jew is a government function while here, especially in the South, every white man arrogates to himself the monitorship over the behavior of colored Americans." Du Bois was characteristically blunter. "The only essential

[39] Mary Penick Motley, ed., *The Invisible Soldier: The Experience of the Black Soldier, World War II* (Detroit, 1975), 42.

difference between a Nazi mob hunting down Jews in Central Europe and an American mob burning black men at the stake in Mississippi is that one is actually encouraged by its national government and the other is merely tolerated," he lectured in *The Crisis*.

Black soldiers considered World War II part of their own struggle against Jim Crow, and they fought for a "Double V"—victory at home and abroad. To this end, African Americans added a fifth freedom, "Freedom from Segregation," to the Four Freedoms already denominated by President Franklin Roosevelt (freedom of speech and religion, freedom from fear and poverty). Chastised by government leaders about putting their own interests ahead of those of the nation, Mary Bethune, the only black woman to hold an administrative position in the federal wartime government, applauded the race militancy of her fellow black citizens. "We have grown tired of turning the other cheek," she declared in June 1942. "Both our cheeks are now so blistered they are too sensitive for further blows."

Early in the war Langston Hughes had insisted that "Pearl Harbor put Jim Crow on the run" and "That Crow can't fight for Democracy, and be the same old Crow he used to be." What would be the extent of his change? What would be Jim Crow's place in postwar America? Aware of the subversive potential of African American service in a citizen army and fearful that events abroad might have altered the racial balance of power at home, white southerners enforced Jim Crow protocols savagely against black soldiers returning from overseas. When ex-Marine Timothy Hood removed the Jim Crow sign from a streetcar in Brichton, Alabama, he was shot five times by the conductor. Chief of police G. B. Fant, who tracked down the wounded serviceman and arrested him, killed Hood later with a single shot to the head.[40] From Tennessee to South Carolina to Texas, returning black veterans encountered what New York congressman and International Labor Defense president Vito Marcantonio termed "a mounting campaign of terror . . . [designed] to re-subjugate the Negro GI returning to civilian life."

[40] "Ex-Marine Slain for Moving Jim Crow Sign," *Chicago Defender*, Feb. 23, 1946, p. 1.

With an eye on the black vote in the North and urged by the National Emergency Committee Against Mob Violence, in 1946, President Harry Truman created an executive committee to investigate the race question in America and recommend policies and procedures to protect the civil rights of all Americans. The Committee's report, *To Secure These Rights*, recommended the "elimination of segregation, based on color, creed, or national origin" from the armed forces, public transportation, housing, health care, and education. Necessary to secure justice at home, the recommendations of the President's Committee on Civil Rights were also designed to deflect foreign criticism of Jim Crow. A signatory to the United Nations Charter (1945), which was dedicated to the goal of achieving human rights and fundamental freedoms "for all without distinction as to race, sex, language, or religion," the United States was vulnerable to charges of hypocrisy. A 1947 State Department report on "Problems of Discrimination and Minority Status in the United States" stated forthrightly that Jim Crow practices were "obviously in conflict with the American creed of democracy and equality of opportunity for all."

African Americans could not have agreed more. In 1946, the National Negro Congress, a left-wing African American organization with Communist ties, petitioned the U. N., "the highest court of mankind," to "end the oppression of the American Negro." The NAACP followed the next year, with a 155-page petition entitled "An Appeal to the World: A Statement on the Denial of Human Rights to Minorities in the Case of Citizens of Negro Descent in the United States of America and an Appeal to the United Nations for Redress." Drafted under the supervision of W. E. B. Du Bois by a group of black academics and lawyers, the Appeal spoke on behalf of fourteen million black citizens of the United States and demanded "elemental Justice against the treatment which the United States has visited upon us for three centuries."

During the late 1940s, a growing number of white Americans, many from the South, joined the NAACP and other organizations dedicated to political and economic change, such as the Southern Regional Council (SRC) and the Southern Conference for Human Welfare. Some, particularly veterans, could no longer stomach the discrepancy between America's professed values of freedom and equality, for which so many had recently given their lives, and the reality of the South's racial hierarchy. Others had commanded African American troops and experienced firsthand the conditions of life on the wrong side of the color line. As Harold Fleming, who would lead the SRC in the 1950s, recalled, "The nearest thing you could be in the army to being black was to be a company officer with black troops, because you lived and operated under the same circumstances they did, and they got crapped all over." Fleming's Army experience did not transform him immediately into a civil rights activist, but it did awaken him to the structural bases of Jim Crow. As he explained years later, "It wasn't that I came to love Negroes; it was that I came to despise the system that did this."

VI. Legacies of Jim Crow

Books about Jim Crow usually have him exit the stage sometime after 1960, when the sit-in movement sparked a massive popular effort to end segregation nationwide. The logic that underlay Jim Crow laws and practices was not addressed until 1967, however, when the Supreme Court struck down state antimiscegenation laws in a case called, appropriately, *Loving v. Virginia*. In a unanimous ruling, Chief Justice Earl Warren declared that marriage was a "vital personal right," a "fundamental freedom," and that to deny it on the basis of racial classifications was "surely to deprive all the State's citizens of liberty without due process of law."[41] A triumph for freedom of marriage and a vindication of the 1954 *Brown* decision, *Loving* nevertheless revealed the pervasive hierarchy of race: From start to finish, Mildred Jeter Loving, whose 1958 marriage to her white neighbor Richard landed them both in jail, denied any African heritage, and insisted vehemently on her legal identity as a Native American.[42]

During the Age of Jim Crow, the color line separated white and non-white in multiple domains—political, economic, social, and

---

[41] *Loving v. Virginia*, 388 U.S. 1 (1967).

[42] Mildred Jeter is identified as Indian on her application for a marriage license. The Lovings are from Caroline County, a triracial community. According to Virginia law at the time, as a Native American, Jeter could marry Loving; as an African American she could not. Jeter fought against her own classification as black even as her lawyers challenged the constitutionality of antimiscegenation laws.

spatial. Today, open barriers have gone: American society is increasingly integrated. But Jim Crow's roots are not so easily eradicated; some of them are very deep indeed, reaching into key national institutions. For example, thanks to segregationist influence in Washington during the New Deal, the United States ended up with what some scholars have dubbed a Jim Crow social welfare state. Southern senators such as South Carolina's Cotton Ed Smith (described once as a "conscientious objector to the twentieth century") resisted any federal legislation that might "put the Negro and the white man on the same basis." Thus the Social Security Act of 1935, still the bedrock of old-age pensions in America, excluded farm laborers and domestic workers, who were also left uncovered by the 1938 Fair Labor Standards Act, which set maximum hours and minimum wages. Workers in these occupations were disproportionately nonwhite, which meant that they were disproportionately left out of the pension system. In the South, between 70 and 80 percent of African Americans were excluded. The NAACP called the Social Security Act "a sieve with holes just big enough for the majority of Negroes to fall through."[43]

Arguably of even greater long-term importance than Social Security was the Selective Service Readjustment Act of 1944. Designed to reintegrate returning soldiers from World War II, the G. I. Bill helped millions to attend college, to buy homes with federally guaranteed low-interest mortgages, to start business ventures with small-business loans, and to find jobs via the United States Employment Service (USES). By advancing the momentum toward suburban living, mass consumption, higher education, and the creation of wealth and economic security, the G. I. Bill vastly expanded the American middle class.

Although race-neutral on their face, both the New Deal social welfare policies and the G.I. Bill were administered locally, which in the South meant according to Jim Crow rules. Some blacks benefited: Mississippi civil rights martyr Medgar Evers attended Alcorn College thanks to his veterans' benefits. But with the options for

---

[43] Ira Katznelson, *When Affirmative Action Was White: An Untold History of Racial Equality in Twentieth Century America* (New York, 2005), 60 (quote), 43 (statistic), 48 (quote).

black veterans limited by the pre-*Brown* world of segregated higher education, the gap in educational attainment between blacks and whites widened, rather than closed, after 1945.

By 1960, as ethnic whites such as Jews and Italians merged with mainstream white culture and joined the surging middle class, African Americans remained on the edge, in marginal class positions. It was largely to address this economic marginality and propel African Americans out of poverty that President Lyndon Johnson launched the social welfare programs he called the "Great Society."[44] But this effort to extend the promise of the New Deal by creating new social welfare policies capable of incorporating African Americans did not result in expansion of state resources available to nonwhites. Rather, it resulted in an erosion of political consensus about the social welfare role of the state and its institutions.[45] In other words, as the proportional participation of African Americans in social welfare programs increased, the political mandate for those programs disintegrated. This is not to say that critics of social welfare or affirmative action programs sought to perpetuate legacies of segregation, and indeed the debate over such programs is seldom explicitly about "the color line." But it is to say, in the words of political scientist Robert Lieberman, that "the color line has not so much faded as shifted, moving away from the surface of American politics—our everyday beliefs and practices—and burrowing deep into the core of American political institutions. . . . Through institutions, our racial past is present even in the silences of our politics."[46]

In 1903, W. E. B. Du Bois declared that "the problem of the twentieth century is the problem of the color line." As the United States crossed the millennial border, important aspects of that problem persisted. African Americans possess ten cents for every dollar of wealth held by whites. Public schools in America are more

---

[44] Katznelson, *When Affirmative Action Was White*, 14.

[45] Robert C. Lieberman, *Shifting the Color Line: Race and the American Welfare State* (Cambridge, MA, 1998), 217.

[46] Lieberman, *Shifting the Color Line*, x, 232.

segregated today than at any time since 1970.[47] The connections between education and economic advancement in the information age grow every day clearer. Cities such as Detroit and Baltimore that were vibrant and partially integrated in the early 1960s have been largely abandoned by whites and middle-class blacks, who have moved their children and their property taxes, to effectively segregated suburbs. Although few people today would openly challenge the voting rights of African Americans, as occurred throughout the age of Jim Crow, periodic congressional attacks on the Voting Rights Act and widespread illegal disfranchisement in recent presidential elections suggest that those rights remain at risk. Even some of the landmark decisions of the Warren Court, most notably *Brown* itself, have been effectively undone in the 2007 decisions of the Roberts Court.[48]

This is not to say that there has been no progress since the *Brown* decision; certainly the second half of the twentieth century saw great movement toward racial equality, and, thanks in good measure to that impulse, toward gender and sexual equality. Yet as those who lived through the onset of the Age of Jim Crow discovered, the steady march of progress can falter and backtrack, leaving vulnerable territory previously considered secure. In a world of constant motion, maintaining the rights of citizens requires diligence and persistence. Many people, including Thomas Jefferson and abolitionist Wendell Phillips, have paraphrased Athenian orator Demosthenes' insistence on the necessity of vigilance to guard liberty. By vigilance, Jefferson and Phillips meant constant awareness of the dangers to liberty, and they believed that Americans should follow Demosthenes' practical advice for freedom's keepers:

> There is one safeguard of the prudent, which is an advantage and security to all, but especially to free states, as against tyrants. What is it? Distrust.
> —Demosthenes: *Philippic 2, sect. 24.*

---

[47] The net worth of a typical white family in 2000 was $81,000 compared to $8,000 for black families. Katznelson, *When Affirmative Action Was White*, 162. On contemporary school resegregation, see Gary Orfield et al., *Schools More Separate: Consequences of a Decade of Resegregation*, report of the Civil Rights Project at Harvard University, July 2001, http://www.civilrightsproject.harvard.edu/research/deseg/separate_schools01.php.

[48] See especially *Parents Involved in Community Schools v. Seattle School District No. 1* (June 2007).

Vigilance, prudence, safeguards, distrust: If these are necessary for the defense of all citizens' rights, all the more so for those whose rights have historically been denied.

THE AGE OF JIM CROW

A NORTON CASEBOOK IN HISTORY

Part I
1865–1908

Reconstruction Amendments' Debates in Congress

Following the conclusion of the Civil War, former Confederates attempted to contain the magnitude of their defeat and the destruction of slavery by passing black codes, laws designed to limit black freedom and protect white supremacy. These laws sought to reestablish strict white control over black labor and restricted the legal rights of the freed people. Overturning President Andrew Johnson's veto, outraged Republicans passed a Civil Rights Act designed to "protect all Persons in the United States in their Civil Rights, and furnish the Means of their Vindication." All those born in the United States, with the exception of Indians untaxed, were declared citizens of the United States, regardless of race and color, and granted the right "to make and enforce contracts, to sue, be parties [to suit], and give evidence, to inherit, purchase, lease, sell, hold, and convey real and personal property, and to full and equal benefit of all laws and proceedings for the security of person and property, as is enjoyed by white citizens." Spirited debate about the definition of rights, and the distinction between "social" and "political" rights, and doubts about the constitutionality of the Civil Rights Act led Congress to incorporate most of its provisions in the Fourteenth Amendment (ratified 1868), albeit in much murkier language.

Lyman Trumbull on the Civil Rights Bill
(January 27, 29, 1866)

Mr. President, I regard the bill to which the attention of the Senate is now called as the most important measure that has been under its consideration since the adoption of the constitutional amendment abolishing slavery. That amendment declared that all persons in the United States should be free. This measure is intended to give effect to that declaration and secure to all persons within the United States practical freedom. There is very little importance in the general declaration of abstract truths and principles unless they can be carried into effect, unless the persons who are to be affected by them have some means of availing themselves of their benefits. Of what avail was the immortal declaration "that all men are created equal; that they are endowed by their Creator with certain inalienable rights; that among these are life, liberty, and the pursuit of happiness," and "that to secure these rights Governments are instituted among men," to the millions of the African race in this country, who were ground down and degraded and subjected to a slavery more intolerable and cruel than the world ever before knew? . . . And of what avail will it now be that the Constitution of the United States has declared that slavery shall not exist, if in the late slaveholding States laws are to be enacted and enforced depriving persons of African descent of privileges which are essential to freemen?

It is the intention of this bill to secure those rights. The laws in the slaveholding states have made a distinction against persons of African descent on account of their color, whether free or slave. . . . When the constitutional amendment was adopted and slavery abolished, all these statutes became null and void, because they were all passed in aid of slavery, for the purpose of maintaining and supporting it. Since the abolition of slavery, the Legislatures which have assembled in the insurrectionary States have passed laws relating to the freedmen, and in nearly all the States they have discriminated against them. They deny them certain rights, subject them to severe penalties, and still impose upon them the very restrictions which were imposed upon them in consequence of the existence of slavery, and before it was abolished. The purpose of the bill under consideration is to destroy all these discriminations, and to carry into effect the constitutional amendment. The first section of the bill . . . declares that all persons of African descent shall be citizens of the United States, and—

That there shall be no discrimination in civil rights or immunities among the inhabitants of any State or Territory of the United States on account of race, color, or previous condition of slavery. . . .

This section is the basis of the whole bill. The other provisions of the bill contain the necessary machinery to give effect to what are declared to be the rights of all persons in the first section. . . .

It is difficult, perhaps, to define accurately what slavery is and what liberty is. Liberty and slavery are opposite terms; one is opposed to the other. We know that in a civil government, in organized society, no such thing can exist as natural or absolute liberty. . . . [E]very man who enters society gives up a part of this natural liberty, which is the liberty of the savage, the liberty which the wild beast has, for the advantages he obtains in the protection which civil government gives him. Civil liberty, or the liberty which a person enjoys in society, is thus defined by Blackstone:

"Civil liberty is no other than natural liberty, so far restrained by human laws and no further, as is necessary and expedient for the general advantage of the public."

That is the liberty to which every citizen is entitled; that is the liberty which was intended to be secured by the Declaration of Independence and the Constitution of the United States originally, and more especially by the amendment which has recently been adopted;[1] and in a note to Blackstone's Commentaries it is stated that—

"In this definition of civil liberty it ought to be understood, or rather expressed, that the restraints introduced by the law should be equal to all, or as much so as the nature of things will admit."

Then, sir, I take it that any statute which is not equal to all, and which deprives any citizen of civil rights which are secured to other citizens, is an unjust encroachment upon his liberty; and is, in fact, a badge of servitude which, by the Constitution, is prohibited. We

---

[1] Thirteenth Amendment.

may, perhaps, arrive at a more correct definition of the term "citizen of the United States" by referring to that clause of the Constitution which I have already quoted,[2] and which declares that "the citizens of each State shall be entitled to all privileges and immunities of citizens in the several States." What rights are secured to the citizens of each State under that provision? Such fundamental rights as belong to every free person. Story, in his Commentaries, in commenting upon this clause of the Constitution of the United States, says:

"The intention of this clause was to confer on citizens, if one may so say, a general citizenship, and to communicate all the privileges and immunities which the citizens of the same State would be entitled to under the like circumstances."

. . . In my judgment, persons of African descent, born in the United States, are as much citizens as white persons who are born in the country. I know that in the slaveholding States a different opinion has obtained. The people of those States have not regarded the colored race as citizens, and on that principle many of their laws making discriminations between the whites and the colored people are based; but it is competent for the Congress to declare, under the Constitution of the United States, who are citizens. If there were any question about it, it would be settled by the passage of a law declaring all persons born in the United States to be citizens thereof.[3] That this bill proposes to do. Then they will be entitled to the rights of citizens. And what are they? The great fundamental rights set forth in this bill: the right to acquire property, the right to go and come at pleasure, the right to enforce rights in the courts, to make contracts, and to inherit and dispose of property. These are the very rights that are set forth in this bill as appertaining to every freeman.

Virginia Commission on Constitutional Government, *The Reconstruction Amendments' Debates* (Richmond, 1967), 121.

---

[2] Privileges and Immunities clause of the Fifth Amendment.

[3] The Fourteenth Amendment declares persons born of African descent citizens: There is debate over whether Congress can declare the freed people citizens through its authority to pass uniform laws of naturalization or whether a constitutional amendment is required to grant citizenship to the freed slaves.

George Julian on White Southern Resistance to Black Suffrage (January 29, 1866)

* * *

. . . Mr. Speaker, I deny that the rebels of the South, who are the rulers of the South, would grant the ballot to the negro if the proposed amendment were now in full force. They would not do it, because their love of domination, their contempt for free labor, and their scorn of an enslaved and downtrodden race are as intense as ever. They hate the negro now, not simply as the ally of the Yankee in foiling their treason, but as the author of all their misfortunes, who, having been villainously misused by them, is of course villainously despised. They hate him with a rancor that feeds unceasingly upon every memory of their humiliation and defeat. They confront him with a hatred so remorseless, withering, consuming, that it crops out to-day in every quarter of the South, in deeds of outrage, violence, and crime, which find no parallel even in the atrocities practiced in that section under the old codes of slavery.

* * *

The leaders of southern opinion openly declare that they would rather die than give the ballot to their former slaves. While it would give their section an increased representation in Congress, that representation would be secured by the votes of negroes, and abolitionists, whose darling purpose would be to Yankeeize and abolitionize the entire South, and put the old slave dynasty hopelessly under their feet. And the old slave dynasty understands this perfectly. They know that negro suffrage, by checking rebel rapacity and restoring order, will reorganize the whole structure of society in their region, and thus doom their prid[e] and sloth to a hopeless conflict with the energy and enterprise of free labor. Do you tell me that men are governed by their own interests, and that the ruling class in the South, finding no other way to serve those interests, will extend suffrage to the negroes? I answer, that long-cherished and traditional prejudices and passions are stronger than interest.

Virginia Commission on Constitutional Government, *The Reconstruction Amendments' Debates* (Richmond, 1967), 57–58.

Mr. Johnson Introduces the Miscegenation Issue (January 30, 1866)

* * *

There is not a State in which these negroes are to be found where slavery existed until recently, and I am not sure that there is not the same legislation in some of the States where slavery has long since been abolished, which does not make it criminal for a black man to marry a white woman, or for a white man to marry a black woman; and they do it not for the purpose of denying any right to the black man or to the white man, but for the purpose of preserving the harmony and peace of society. . . . Do you not repeal all that legislation by this bill? I do not know that you intend to repeal it; but is it not clear that all such legislation will be repealed, and that consequently there may be a contract of marriage entered into as between persons of these different races, a white man with a black woman, or a black man with a white woman? If you are prepared to repeal it, do you think that the repeal will answer any practical purpose? Are you not, on the contrary, rather inclined to believe that, like the fugitive slave law of 1850, if enforced at all, and if these parties are to be protected at all, it must be enforced and the protection must be given by the bayonet? [I.e., miscegenation by force.] Is that not the effect of the law? Still confining myself to the first section, it says that these parties, without distinction of color, "shall have the same right to make and enforce contracts."

Mr. FESSENDEN.   Where is the discrimination against color in the law to which the Senator refers?

Mr. JOHNSON.   There is none; that is what I say; that is the very thing I am finding fault with.

Mr. TRUMBULL.   This bill would not repeal the law to which the Senator refers, if there is no discrimination made by it.

Mr. JOHNSON.   Would it not? We shall see directly. Standing upon this section, it will be admitted that the black man has the same right to enter into a contract of marriage with a white woman as a white man has, that is clear, because marriage is a contract. I was speaking of this without reference to any State legislation.

Mr. FESSENDEN.   He has the same right to make a contract of marriage with a white woman that a white man has with a black woman.

Mr. JOHNSON.   Just wait a moment. My friend from Maine is so quick that he cannot wait for the operation of slower minds. If there were no laws in Maryland on the subject, then the black man could marry a white woman, but there are laws. What is the effect of those laws? The first section of this bill says that there is to be no discrimination. The second section says that "any person who, under color of any law, statute, ordinance, regulation, or custom, shall subject or cause to be subjected any inhabitant of any State or Territory to the deprivation of any right secured or protected by this act, or to different punishment," shall be proceeded against under this bill. Now, there is a State law which says to the black man, "You shall not marry a white woman," and says to the white man, "You may." There is therefore in Maryland one law in relation to this question for the white man, and another law for the black man. The black man marries a white woman and we try to enforce our laws against him. We say to him, "You have done an illegal act, you have offended against the legislation of Maryland by marrying a white woman." He says, "I have done no such thing; I would have done it but for the legislation of Congress; I would have been liable to trial and conviction but for the legislation of Congress; but I set up the legislation of Congress; you may tell me you are prosecuting me under a law of the State of Maryland which makes it a crime in me, but Congress says that that State legislation shall be of no avail; the law of Maryland in reference to the question is at an end." It means that if it means anything. . . . White and black are considered together, put in a mass, and the one is entitled to enter into every contract that the other is entitled to enter into. Of course, therefore, the black man is entitled to enter into the contract of marriage with a white woman.

———————

Congressional Globe, January 30, 1866, p. 505.

Mr. Moulton on Marriage (February 2–3, 1866)

My colleague says that it is a civil right to sit on juries, and that it is a civil right for a black man to marry a white woman. Now, I deny that it is a civil right for anybody to sit on a jury; I deny that it is a civil right for a white man to marry a black woman or for a black man to marry a white women. It is a simple matter of taste, of contract, of arrangement between the parties. No man has a right to marry any particular woman, black or white. It is a matter of mutual taste, contract, and understanding between the parties.

* * *

Mr. THORNTON.   On the point upon which my colleague is now speaking, civil rights, I would ask him if a marriage between a white man and a white woman is a civil right?

Mr. MOULTON.   It is not a civil right.

Mr. THORNTON.   It is not?

Mr. MOULTON.   No, sir, not in my opinion.

Mr. THORNTON.   Then what sort of right is it?

Mr. MOULTON.   Marriage is a contract between individuals competent to contract it.

Mr. THORNTON.   Is it a political or a civil right?

Mr. MOULTON.   It is a social right. I understand that a civil right is a right that a party is entitled to and that he can enforce by operation of the law.

* * *

Mr. COOK.   I would like to ask my colleague [Mr. THORN-TON] whether he thinks that a white man has the right by law now to marry a black woman, and if that is the civil right of the white man? . . . Is it as competent to prevent, by provision of law, a black woman from marrying a white man, as it is to prevent a white man from marrying a black woman?

Mr. THORNTON.   I suppose it is.

Mr. MOULTON.   The remarks that I made in connection with this matter were made for this purpose: I say that the right to marry is not strictly a right at all, because it rests in contract alone between the individuals, and no other person has a right to contract it. It is not a right in any legal or technical sense at all. No one man has any right to marry any woman he pleases. . . . I insist that marriage is not a civil right, as contemplated by the provisions of this bill.

Virginia Commission on Constitutional Government, *The Reconstruction Amendments' Debates* (Richmond, 1967), 632.

Mr. Dawson on the Republicans and Social Equality (January 30–31; February 1, 1866)

It matters not that this Government was made by and for the white race; that the States reserved the right of making their local laws; and that the Union could not otherwise have been formed. It matters not that a million of lives have been sacrificed in the effort to reduce their pernicious theories to practice. Still they falter not in the contest; still they hug to their bosoms the phantom of negro equality; still they claim for one section the right to control the local affairs of others. They hold that the white and black race are equal. This they maintain involves and demands social equality; that negroes should be received on an equality in white families, should be admitted to the same tables at hotels, should be permitted to occupy the same seats in railroad cars and the same pews in churches; that they should be allowed to hold offices, to sit on juries, to vote, to be eligible to seats in the State national Legislatures, and to be judges, or to make and expound laws for the government of white men. Their children are to attend the same schools with white children, and to sit side by side with them. Following close upon this will, of course, be marriages between the races, when, according to these philanthropic theorists, the prejudices of caste will at length have been overcome, and the negro, with the privilege of free miscegenation accorded him, will be in the enjoyment of his true *status*.

To future generations it will be a marvel in the history of our times, that a party whose tenets were such wild ravings and frightful dreams as these should be permitted, in their support, to urge the country into the hugest and most destructive of civil wars, and should, when war was inaugurated, be permitted to shape its policy in furtherance of their peculiar ends. For the full realization of their plans, they are ready to sacrifice not only our priceless system of government, but even our social superiority itself.

* * *

It is impossible that two distinct races should exist harmoniously in the same country, on the same footing of equality by the law. The result must be a disgusting and deteriorating admixture of races, such as is presented in the Spanish States of America by the crossing of the Castilian with the Aztec and the negro. The prejudice of color is one of those facts implanted by Providence for wise purposes. Among others it is doubtless for the purpose of preserving a race homogeneous, which is the source of its true strength and permanent improvement. . . . The Anglo-Saxon, the dominant and most advanced in civilization upon the globe, owes its superiority to its homogeneity or alliance with others of kindred excellence.

We have, then, to insist upon it that this Government was made for the white race. It is our mission to maintain it. Negro suffrage and equality are incompatible with that mission. We must make our own laws and shape our own destiny. Negro suffrage will, in its tendency, force down the Anglo-Saxon to the negro level, and result inevitably in amalgamation and deterioration of our race. The proud spirit of our people will revolt at such certain degradation, while American women, the models of beauty and superiority, will indignantly execrate the men who advise and dictate the policy.

Virginia Commission on Constitutional Government, *The Reconstruction Amendments' Debates* (Richmond, 1967), 541.

Mr. Donnelly on the Black Codes
(February 1, 1866)

Slavery consists in a deprivation of natural rights. A man may be a slave for a term of years as fully as though he were held for life; he may be a slave when deprived of a portion of the wages of his labor as fully as if deprived of all; he may be held down by unjust laws to a degraded and defenseless condition as fully as though his wrists were manacled; he may be oppressed by a convocation of masters called a Legislature as fully as by a single master. In short, he who is not entirely free is necessarily a slave.

What has the South done for the black man since the close of the rebellion?

Let us examine the black codes of the different States adopted since that time.

In South Carolina it is provided that all male negroes between two and twenty, and all females between two and eighteen, shall be bound out to some "master." The adult negro is compelled to enter into contract with a master, and the district judge, not the laborer, is to fix the value of the labor. If he thinks the compensation too small and will not work, he is a vagrant, and can be hired out for a term of service at a rate again to be fixed by the judge. If a hired negro leaves his employer he forfeits his wages for the whole year.

* * *

The black code of Alabama provides that if a negro who has contracted to labor fails to do so he shall be punished with damages; and if he runs away he shall be punished as a vagrant, which probably means that he shall be sold to the highest bidder for a term of years; and that any person who entices him to leave his master, as by the offer of better wages, shall be guilty of a misdemeanor, and may be sent to jail for six months; and further, that these regulations include all persons of negro blood to the third generation, though one parent in each generation shall be pure white; that is, down to the man who has but one eighth negro blood in his veins.

* * *

The black code of Tennessee provides that the vagrant negro may be sold to the highest bidder to pay his jail fees; . . . his children may be bound out against his wish to a master by the county court; if his master fails to pay him he cannot sue him nor testify against him.

* * *

All this means simply the reestablishment of slavery.

* * *

For one, with the help of Almighty God, I shall never consent to such cruel injustice. Having voted to give the negro liberty, I shall vote to give him all things essential to liberty.

If degradation and oppression have, as it is alleged, unfitted him for freedom, surely continued degradation and oppression will not prepare him for it. If he is not to remain a brute you must give him that which will make him a man– opportunity. If he is, as it is claimed, an inferior being and unable to compete with the white man on terms of equality, surely you will not add to the injustice of nature by casting him beneath the feet of the white man. With what face can you reproach him with his degradation at the very moment you are striving to still further degrade him? If he is, as you say, not fit to vote, give him a chance; let him make himself an independent laborer like yourself; let him own his homestead; let the courts of justice be opened to him; and let his intellect, darkened by centuries of neglect, be illuminated by all the glorious lights of education. If after all this he proves himself an unworthy savage and brutal wretch, condemn him, but not till then.

Is the right of suffrage necessary to the negro?

The right to vote is the right of self-protection, through the possession of a share in the Government. Without this a man's rights lie at the mercy of other men who have every selfish incentive to rob and oppress him. This is the great central idea of a republican Government. The absence of this is the source of all despotism. I would ask, what white man would consider himself safe without the right to vote, especially if the Government was exercised exclusively by a hostile race?

* * *

Mr. Speaker, it is as plain to my mind as the sun at noonday, that we must make all the citizens of the country equal before the law; that we must break down all walls of caste; that we must offer equal opportunities to all men.

Virginia Commission on Constitutional Government, *The Reconstruction Amendments' Debates* (Richmond, 1967), 589.

Mr. Thayer on the Rights Included in the Civil Rights Bill (March 2, 1866)

The simple principle of the bill under consideration and its whole essence is contained in its first section. The rest is all matter of detail. The whole life and substance of the bill is in its first section.

* * *

It is an enactment simply declaring that all men born upon the soil of the United States shall enjoy the fundamental rights of citizenship. What rights are these? Why, sir, in order to avoid any misapprehension they are stated in the bill. The same section goes on to define with greater particularity the civil rights and immunities which are to be protected by the bill. They are—

> The right to make and enforce contracts, to sue, be parties and give evidence, to inherit, purchase, lease, sell, hold, and convey real and personal property, and to full and equal benefit of all laws and proceedings for the security of person and property, and to be subject to like punishment, pains, and penalties, and to none other.

Now, sir, I will pay so high a compliment to the intelligence of the gentleman who addressed us yesterday, as to say that I do not think he can believe that this bill extends or alters, or can be construed to extend or alter, the laws regulating suffrage in any of the States.

Virginia Commission on Constitutional Government, *The Reconstruction Amendments' Debates* (Richmond, 1967), 1151.

Dialogue between Mr. Rogers (New Jersey; voted against the Thirteenth Amendment), Mr. Grinnell, and Mr. Cook on the Civil Rights Bill (March 1, 1866)

Mr. ROGERS.   Now, sir, if you pass this bill you will allow the negroes of this country to compete for the high office of President of the United States. Because if they are citizens at all, they come within the meaning and letter of the Constitution of the United States, which allows all natural born citizens to become candidates for the Presidency, and to exercise the duties of that office if elected.

A MEMBER.   Are you afraid of that?

Mr. ROGERS.   I am afraid of degrading this Government. I am afraid of danger to constitutional liberty. I am alarmed at the stupendous strides which this Congress is trying to initiate. And I appeal in behalf of my country . . . that conservative men on the other side should rally to the standard of sovereign and independent States, and blot out this idea which is inculcating itself here, that all the powers of the States must be taken away and the power of the

Czar of Russia or of the Emperor of France must be lodged in the Federal Government.

Sir, where is the civilized country on the face of the earth that gives to the negro the right to hold the highest office within the gift of the sovereign people, or any other office?

Mr. GRINNELL.   Liberia.

[p. 1123–24:]

Mr. COOK.   Mr. Speaker, in listening to the very eloquent remarks of the gentleman from New Jersey, [Mr. ROGERS], I have been astonished to find that in his apprehension this bill is designed to deprive somebody in some State of this Union of some right which he has heretofore enjoyed. I am only sorry that he was not specific enough; that he did not inform us what rights are to be taken away. He has denounced this bill as dangerous to liberty, as calculated in its tendency at least to destroy the liberties of this country. I have examined this bill with some care, and so far as I have been able to understand it, I have found nothing in any provision of it which tends in any way to take from any man, white or black, a single right he enjoys under the Constitution and laws of the United States.

* * *

The gentleman from New Jersey [Mr. ROGERS] commenced his speech by saying that he was in favor of giving civil rights to all men, and that he was a progressive man. He says this bill cannot be passed because it is unconstitutional.[1] The other day when a proposition was made to amend the Constitution in this regard he opposed the amendment to the Constitution.[2] He is for the protection of these men [the freedmen], but against every earthly mode that can be derived for protecting them. . . . Sir, I know of no way by which these men can be protected except it be by the action of Congress, either by passing this bill or by passing a constitutional amendment.

Virginia Commission on Constitutional Government, *The Reconstruction Amendments' Debates* (Richmond, 1967), 1122.

[1] The Civil Rights Bill was ruled unconstitutional by the U.S. Supreme Court in 1883.

[2] The Fourteenth Amendment incorporated the gist of the Civil Rights Bill into the Constitution.

Mr. Rainey on Social Rights
(December 19, 1873)

[Rainey was an African American representative from South Carolina.]

Now, gentlemen, let me say the negro is not asking social equality. We do not ask it of you, we do not ask of the gentleman from Kentucky [Mr. Beck] that the two races should intermarry one with the other. God knows we are perfectly content. I can say for myself that I am contented to be what I am so long as I have my rights; I am contented to marry one of my own complexion, and do not seek intercourse with any other race, because I believe that the race of people I represent, to the extent of the opportunities which they have had, and considering how recently they have escaped from the oppression and wrongs committed upon them, are just as virtuous and hold just as many high characteristics as any class in the country. I think the statistics will prove that there is as much virtue among the negroes as among the whites. Sir, we are not seeking to be put on a footing of social equality. I prefer to choose my own associates, and all my colleagues here and the whole race I belong to prefer to make that choice. We do not ask the passage of any law forcing us upon anybody who does not want to receive us. But we do want a law enacted that we may be recognized like other men in the country. Why is it that colored members of Congress cannot enjoy the same immunities that are accorded to white members? Why cannot we stop at hotels here without meeting objection? Why cannot we go into restaurants without being insulted? We are here enacting laws for the country and casting votes upon important questions; we have been sent here by the suffrages of the people, and why cannot we enjoy the same benefits that are accorded to our white colleagues on this floor?

Virginia Commission on Constitutional Government, *The Reconstruction Amendments' Debates* (Richmond, 1967), 344.

Mr. Ransier on Social Equality
(January 5, 1874)

[Ransier was an African American representative from South Carolina.]

The bugbear of "social equality" is used by the enemies of political and civil equality for the colored man in place of argument. There is not an intelligent white man or black man who does not know that that is the sheerest nonsense; and I would have it distinctly understood that I would most certainly oppose the passage of the pending bill or any similar measure if I believed that its operation would be to force upon me the company of the member from Kentucky [Mr. Beck], for instance, or any one else. These negro-haters would not open school-houses, hotels, places of amusement, common conveyances, or the witness or the jury box to the colored people upon equal terms with themselves, because this contact of the races would, forsooth, "result injuriously to both." Yet they have found agreeable associations with them under other circumstances which at once suggest themselves to us; nor has the result of this contact proved injurious to either race so far as I know, except that the moral responsibility rests upon the more refined and cultivated.

Virginia Commission on Constitutional Government, *The Reconstruction Amendments' Debates* (Richmond, 1967), 382.

Mr. Beck Proposes an Amendment to the Civil Rights Act (January 5–6, 1874)

I desire to offer an amendment to the civil-rights bill, and to have it printed. It is to add to section 1 the following:

> *Provided*, That nothing herein contained shall be so construed as to require hotel-keepers to put whites and blacks into the same rooms, or beds or feed them at the same table, nor to require that whites and blacks shall be put into the same rooms or classes at school, or the same boxes or seats at theaters, or the same berths on steamboats or other vessels, or the same lots in cemeteries.

* * *
[Mr. Durham (KY) responds, p. 406:]

But, sir, when you undertake to legislate as to the civil and social relations of the races, then you will have aroused and embittered the feelings of the Anglo-Saxon race to such an extent that it will be hard to control them. The poorest and humblest white person in my district feels and knows that he or she belongs to a superior race morally and intellectually, and nothing is so revolting to them as social equality with this inferior race. They will treat the freedman kindly, but socially hold aloof from him, as belonging to an inferior race. You may say these are not social relations provided for in this bill; but, sir, if I am compelled to sit side by side with him in the theater, the stage-coach, and the railroad car, to eat with him at the same table at the hotels, and my child to be educated at the same schools with his child—if these are not social relations I do not understand them.

Virginia Commission on Constitutional Government, *The Reconstruction Amendments' Debates* (Richmond, 1967), 405.

Mr. Butler of Massachusetts on Equality (January 7, 1874)

The first objection we meet, but last presented, is that we propose to establish social equality; and the gentleman from Tennessee [Mr. CRUTCHFIELD] offered an amendment that our daughters shall be prohibited by penalty from their right of choice in those who propose marriage to them. If he has got no further than that after hearing the debate of the last few days, then, indeed, I agree with the gentleman from New York, that to some men the debate has been futile and fruitless. If he does not understand that we are not enacting any such proposition, then he could never even appreciate the answer a lady of the North would make to his addresses when she answers "no," which after fathoming his capabilities would assuredly be given.

"Equality!" We do not propose to legislate to establish any equality. I am not one of those who believe that all men were created equal, if equality is to be used in its broadest sense. I believe that "equal" in the Declaration of Independence is a political word, used in a political sense, and means equality of political rights. All men are not equal. Some are born with good constitutions, good health, strength, high mental power; others are not. Now, we cannot by legislation make them equal. God has not made them equal, with equal endowments.

But this is our doctrine: Equality, if I understand it and may be allowed for the moment to speak for the [R]epublican party—and I will embody it in a single phrase, as the true touch-stone of civil liberty—is not that all men are equal, *but that every man has the right to be the equal of every other man if he can*. Let me repeat it. Every man has the inalienable, God-given right to be the equal of every other man if he can.

Virginia Commission on Constitutional Government, *The Reconstruction Amendments' Debates* (Richmond, 1967), 455.

Laws Relating to Freedmen

Problems of legal definition troubled legislators at the state level as well as in Congress. Democrats committed to restoring as much of the antebellum racial regime as possible had first to determine who was black and who was not by establishing legal definitions of race and restricting marriage across the color line. At the same time, southern Republicans, particularly African Americans, sought to incorporate federal definitions of rights into state constitutions and to legislate, as well as they could, race-neutral civility.

Law Forbidding Interracial Marriage, Alabama (1866)

If any white person and any negro, or the descendant of any negro, to the third generation inclusive, though one ancestor of each generation be a white person, intermarry, or live in adultery or fornication with each other, each of them must, on conviction, be imprisoned in the penitentiary, or sentenced to hard labor for the county, for not less than two, nor more than seven years. . . .

Any probate judge, who issues a license for the marriage of any persons who are prohibited by the last preceding section from intermarrying, knowing that they are within the provisions of that section; and any justice of the peace, minister of the gospel, or other person by law authorized to solemnize the rites of matrimony, who performs a marriage ceremony for such persons, knowing that they are within the provisions of said section, must, each, on conviction, be fined not less than one hundred, nor more than one thousand dollars; and may also be imprisoned in the county jail, or sentenced to hard labor for the country, for not less than six months.

Walter L. Fleming, *Documentary History of Reconstruction* (Gloucester, MA, 1960), 274.

Regulations for Freedmen in Louisiana

Senate Ex. Doc. no 2, 39 Cong., 1 Sess., p. 93. It seems to have been a custom for the Louisiana parishes and towns to make such regulations as the following, and, during 1865, they were approved by the military authorities. The legislature of Louisiana passed no laws of importance relating to the blacks, though by custom they were more stringently regulated in Louisiana than in other Southern states. [July, 1865]

Whereas it was formerly made the duty of the police jury to make suitable regulations for the police of slaves within the limits of the parish; and whereas slaves have become emancipated by the action of the ruling powers; and whereas it is necessary for public order, as well as for the comfort and correct deportment of said freedmen, that suitable regulations should be established for their government in their changed condition, the following ordinances are adopted with the approval of the United States military authorities commanding in said parish, viz:

Sec. 1. *Be it ordained by the police jury of the parish of St. Landry*, That no negro shall be allowed to pass within the limits of said parish without special permit in writing from his employer. Whoever shall violate this provision shall pay a fine of two dollars and fifty cents, or in default thereof shall be forced to work four days on the public road, or suffer corporeal punishment as provided hereinafter.

Sec. 2. . . . Every negro who shall be found absent from the residence of his employer after ten o'clock at night, without a written permit from his employer, shall pay a fine of five dollars, or in default thereof, shall be compelled to work five days on the public road, or suffer corporeal punishment as hereinafter provided.

Sec. 3. No negro or freedman shall be permitted to rent or keep a house within the limits of the town under any circumstances, and any one thus offending shall be ejected and compelled to find an employer or leave the town within twenty-four hours. The lessor or furnisher of the house leased or kept as above shall pay a fine of ten dollars for each offense.

Sec. 4. . . . Every negro is required to be in the regular service of some white person, or former owner, who shall be held responsible for the conduct of said negro. But said employer or former owner may permit said negro to hire his own time by special permission in writing, which permission shall not extend over seven days at any one time. Any negro violating the provisions of this section shall be fined five dollars for each offence, or in default of the payment thereof shall be forced to work five days on the public road, or suffer corporeal punishment as hereinafter provided.

Sec. 5. . . . No public meetings or congregations of negroes shall be allowed within said parish after sunset; but such public meetings and congregations may be held between the hours of sunrise and sunset, by the special permission in writing of the captain of patrol, within whose beat such meetings shall take place. This prohibition, however, is not to prevent negroes from attending the usual church services, conducted by white ministers and priests. Every negro violating the provisions of this section shall pay a fine of five dollars, or in default thereof shall be compelled to work five days on the public road, or suffer corporeal punishment as hereinafter provided.

Sec. 6. . . . No negro shall be permitted to preach, exhort, or otherwise declaim to congregations of colored people, without a special permission in writing from the president of the police jury. Any negro violating the provisions of this section shall pay a fine of ten dollars, or in default shall be forced to work ten days on the public road, or suffer corporeal punishment as hereinafter provided.

Sec. 7. . . No negro who is not in the military service shall be allowed to carry fire arms, or any kind of weapons, within the parish, without the special written permission of his employers, approved and indorsed by the nearest and most convenient chief of patrol. Any one violating the provisions of this section shall forfeit his weapons and pay a fine of five dollars, or in default of the payment of said fine, shall be forced to work five days on the public road, or suffer corporeal punishment as hereinafter provided.

Sec. 8. . . No negro shall sell, barter, or exchange any articles of merchandise or traffic within said parish without the special written permission of his employer, specifying the article of sale, barter or traffic. Any one thus offending shall pay a fine of one dollar for each offence, and suffer the forfeiture of said articles, or in default of the payment of said fine shall work one day on the public road, or suffer corporeal punishment as hereinafter provided. . .

Sec. 9. . . Any negro found drunk, within the said parish shall pay a fine of five dollars, or in default thereof work five days on the public road, or suffer corporeal punishment as hereinafter provided.

Sec. 11. . . It shall be the duty of every citizen to act as a police officer for the detection of offences and the apprehension of offenders, who shall be immediately handed over to the proper captain or chief of patrol . . .

Sec. 14. . . The corporeal punishment provided for in the foregoing sections shall consist in confining the body of the offender within a barrel placed over his or her shoulders, in the manner practiced in the army, such confinement not to continue longer than twelve hours, and for such time within the aforesaid limit as shall be fixed by the captain or chief of patrol who inflicts the penalty.

Walter L. Fleming, *Documentary History of Reconstruction* (Gloucester, MA, 1960), 279–81.

North Carolina "Black Code," Definition of "Negro" (1866)

Sec. 1. *Be it enacted by the General Assembly of the State of North Carolina,* . . . That negroes and their issue, even where one ancestor in each succeeding generation to the fourth inclusive is white, shall be deemed persons of color.

Walter L. Fleming, *Documentary History of Reconstruction* (Gloucester, MA, 1960), 290–91.

Correcting the Vocabulary of South Carolina:

Proceedings of Constitutional Convention of South Carolina (1868)

Resolved, That this Convention take such action as it may in its wisdom deem compatible with its powers, and conducive to the public weal, to expunge forever from the vocabulary of South Carolina, the epithets "negro," "nigger," and "Yankee." . . .

Resolved, That the exigencies and approved civilization of the times demand that this Convention, or the Legislative body created by it, enact such laws as will make it a penal offence to use the above epithets in the manner described against an American citizen of this State, and to punish the insult by fine or imprisonment.[1]

Walter L. Fleming, *Documentary History of Reconstruction* (Gloucester, MA, 1960), 450.

Louisiana Constitution (1868)

Art. 2. All persons, without regard to race, color, or previous condition, born or naturalized in the United States, and subject to the jurisdiction thereof, and residents of this State for one year, are citizens of this State. The citizens of this State owe allegiance to the United States; and this allegiance is paramount to that which they

---

[1] The South Carolina constitutional convention was black majority.

owe to the State. They shall enjoy the same civil, political and public rights and privileges, and be subject to the same pains and penalties.

Art. 13. All persons shall enjoy equal rights and privileges upon any conveyance of a public character; and all places of business, or of public resort, or for which a license is required by either State, parish, or municipal authority, shall be deemed places of a public character, and shall be opened to the accommodation and patronage of all persons, without distinction or discrimination on account of race or color.

Walter L. Fleming, *Documentary History of Reconstruction* (Gloucester, MA, 1960), 452.

Proceedings in the Ku Klux Trials at Columbia, South Carolina (November 1871)

In 1866, the Ku Klux Klan emerged in Tennessee and spread rapidly to other southern states. What began as a social club for veterans—including five Confederate generals—developed into a paramilitary organization that terrorized black southerners, northern teachers, and Republican voters and politicians. Although Klansmen claimed to defend their families against violence by lawless freedmen and unscrupulous northerners, their actions revealed a systematic effort to curtail Republican political power and blacks' economic and social autonomy. At the same time, Klansmen policed the domestic behavior of white and black women in an effort to reinforce traditional hierarchies between the sexes. Effectively the paramilitary arm of the Democratic Party, Klansmen's attacks on women at home underscore their perception that private relationships had political implications.

The two interviews here are taken from *Proceedings in the Ku Klux Trials at Columbia, S.C. in the United States Circuit Court, November Term, 1871* (Columbia, 1872). The publication contained the following reporters' note:

The following pages contain a report of the proceedings before the Circuit Court of the United States, at Columbia, S.C., in what are known as the Ku Klux Cases. That portion of the publication which embraces the arguments on the motion to quash the indictment in the case of the United States *vs.* Allen Crosby, *et al.*, and the evidence and arguments in the case of the United States *vs.* Robert Hayes Mitchell, *et al.*, is strictly a *verbatim* report of all that occurred. The evidence in the case of the United States *vs.* John W. Mitchel and Thomas C. Whitesides is also *verbatim*, but the remainder of the report is somewhat condensed. In the latter cause, the arguments are *verbatim*, so far as they relate to questions of general interest, in connection with these Ku Klux prosecutions, and are condensed only in their references to the *alibi* which the defence attempted to prove.

The evidence in the causes tried subsequently is considerably condensed, but no material fact that appeared, and nothing which occurred to indicate the *animus* of witnesses, on either side, has been omitted.

The report of the case of Edward Y. Avery is much more complete than that of John S. Miller, and the statements of those prisoners who pleaded guilty are abstracts only to the extent of the omission of a large number of the questions.

Testimony of Kirkland L. Gunn, Former Member of the Klan

Q. Mr. Gunn, you have stated the general purposes of the order; now will you please state to the jury how those purposes were to be carried into effect?

A. Well, sir; that is known, I think; but the way that I was told that they were going to carry this into effect was by killing off the white Radicals, and by whipping and intimidating the negroes, so as to keep them from voting for any men who held Radical offices.

* * *

A. Pursuant to that mode of intimidating and killing voters, was there anything of the kind done, within your knowledge?

Mr. Stanbery [counsel for the defendant]. We object to that question—object to his saying what he was told. * * * The gentlemen have produced a constitution of the order and given it in evidence, and that has nothing in it about interfering with the suffrage.

There is no such agreement in that paper. Now, I understand the witness to be asked whether he was told by some one that any other body was to intimidate voters. This is not the way to make out the case.

The Court. We think the question may be asked. [To the witness.] State what was done in pursuance of the object of the order. What was done pursuant to the purpose of the order as you have stated it, according to your knowledge?

A.   Their principle was to whip such men as they called Radicals, and men who were ruining the negro population, &c., and they murdered some.

Proceedings in the Ku Klux Trials, 178.

Testimony of Dick Wilson

Q.   Where do you live?

A.   I live in York District, sir.

Q.   On whose place, in York County?

A.   Dr. Lowry's.

Q.   Did you vote at the last election?

A.   Yes, sir.

Q.   Which ticket did you vote?

A.   I voted the Republican ticket.

Q.   Did you vote for Mr. Wallace?

A.   Yes, sir.

Q.   Have you voted there before?

A.   Yes, sir.

Q.   Nobody questioned your right to vote when you did vote?

A.   Not particularly, at the ballot box.

Q.   Now tell us whether the Ku Klux visited you, and where?

A.   Well, they visited me on the 11th April, about two hours before—well, about, 'twixt two and three o'clock in the morning. I had been up till it was light, and laid down and got into a sleep, and I woke up, and these men were in the yard; two of the men came to the house, and the other four went to my son's house.

Q.   What is his name?

A.   Richard. These men came to my house. First words I noticed them saying was, "Open the door." Next word was, "Make up
a light; make up a light." I immediately then jumped up and drew
on my pants, and by that time the door fell in the middle of the
floor. They commenced firing under the door and around the
house. I stood still then. They stopped then for a minute, and asked
me to make up a light again. I jumped to the fire and made up a
light. The next question "Who lives here?" Says I, "Dick Wilson."
"Is this old Dick?" I told them, "Yes, sir." "Where is your son?" "I
don't know, sir, where he is." "You are a dam'd liar, sir; walk out
here; I have a word with you, sir." "Very well, I will come out."
"Come out; come out right now; come out." I walked out. "Go on
down here before me, sir, to the other house." And there was four
men in there; a big light in the house; a good knot of pine on the
fire, and they went searching cupboards and trunks, and looking
everywhere. I could see them as plain as I can see you right now.
Well, they searched the house all over, and they could not find him.
They said, "Look under the floor." Well, they tried to get up the
floor, but the floor was so well nailed they didn't get it up. One of
the men, in the middle of the house, turned around and says,
"What G—d damned rascal you've got there?" Some man says,
"That is old Dick Wilson." "What are you going to do with that
damned old son-of-a-bitch?" "Well, we haint determined on what
we'll do with him." They still searched on, and couldn't find him.

Q.   Couldn't find what?

A.   Couldn't find my son, and they came out. After they came
out, then the question is put me, "Where is your son?" Says I,
"Gentlemen, I don't know." "Your son; don't you call me any gentleman; we are just from hell fire; we haven't been in this country
since Manassas; we come to take Scott and his ring; you damned
niggers are ruining the country, voting for men who are breaking
the treasury; where is your son, I say?" "I don't know, sir, where he
is." "You are a damned liar, sir; and I will make you tell where he
is. Don't you rather the men of this country would rule it, sir, as
these men as is ruling it?" Says I, "I didn't know there was any other
men ruling but the men of this country." "Is Scott a man of this
country, sir?" Says I, "I don't know; I never seen him." "Then, why

is it you don't go to some good old citizen in the country who would tell you how to vote?" Says I, "I went to men who I thought knowed and ought to know." "Who were they?" "Well," I says, "that was Mr. Wallace." "Yes; just as damned a rascal as you are." "I went to Mr. Wallace, and I went to several other gentlemen that I did name out." "Well, what about the League?" I told him that I did belong to the League.

Q. What—the Union league?

A. Yes, sir. "I suppose, then, you are a good old Radical?" Says I, "I don't know whether I have been; I have tried to be." "Yes, and damn you, we'll make a Democrat of you to-night?" That was the next word. Another little one jumped up there, with some horns on his head, and says: "We'll take the damned rascal off and remind him of what we have told him before this; we have told him this long ago, and we want to be obeyed; now we will take satisfaction; walk on here, sir; take the road before me." I walked on. "Drop your breeches, God damn you." I just ran out of them. "Stretch out; we want to make a Democrat out of you tonight." I stretched out full length, just as long as I could get; I would have got a little longer if I could.

Q. Did you drop your pants?

A. Dropped them down—just fell out, full length.

Q. And then what?

A. One went that side and two on this side. Well, they commenced whipping me; I commenced begging them so powerful. "Don't beg, God damn you; if you beg I'll kill you." One of them said, "Stop this whipping right off. One of you gentlemen take that pistol and go to his head, and t'other to his feet, and if he hollows or moves I will blow his brains out." Then they commenced whipping me; they just ruined me; they cut me all to pieces; they did do it, and I wouldn't mind it so much if they had scattered the licks, but they whipped all in one place; that is what they done; they stopped on me then for a while. "Will you vote the Democratic ticket next time?" "Yes, I will vote any way you want me to vote; I don't care how you want me to vote, master, I will vote." Says he, "there now, put it to him; God damn him he has not told us yet where his son is; we have got that much and we will get the balance." They commenced whipping me again. I told them at last I did not know where he was, and I didn't know where he was. After they got done whipping me, they ordered me to get up as quick as I could; I couldn't get up very fast; quick as I got up, I drawed up my pants; couldn't button them nohow. Had them in my hands. "Now let's see how fast you can run." Well, I was going to strain every leader that was in me, because I was hurt so that I could hardly move, but I intended to do my best. The other says, "I have a word or two to speak to him. I will give you ten days—you and your son both—to go and put a card in Grist's* office, and show it; and let it come out in the papers in ten days from now, to show that you are done with the Republican party, Scott, and his damned Ring; and if you don't do it, I will come back for you both again; and if I can't get you at night, I will take you in daylight. Go off in the house, and shut the door." I went off in the house sure enough. I shut the door. I was lying down on the floor. I wasn't able to go to bed. I got worse after I got to the house.

Q.   How bad were you whipped?

A.   I was whipped badly. I had on me a pair of pants too large; and next day I had to tie a string on them so they would meet.

Q.   Your back was all whipped to pieces?

A.   Just all hove up. It was not cut up so, but was bruised.

Q.   What did they whip you with?

A.   With ramrods.

Q.   Take them out of their guns?

A.   Took them out and twisted them up.

Q.   What were they—iron ramrods?

A.   I don't know. There was one felt very much like it. I can't be positive that they was iron ramrods. They had this brass put on them where they rammed the powder and stuff down in the guns. These was there next morning—white oak ramrods.

Q.   Did you find them?

A.   Yes, sir.

Q.   How much did you find of the ramrod?

A.   I found two pieces right at the house, and betwixt my house and the creek I found the other.

---

* Editor of the Yorkville (S.C.) *Enquirer.*

Q. There were three broken?

A. Yes, sir; both of them.

Q. How big were they?

A. About the size of my finger.

Q. Did you go and put a card in the paper as they told you to?

A. No, sir; I did not; I did not do anything.

Q. Did you stay at home nights after that?

A. Yes, sir; I stayed at home; they told me to stay at home, and I done it.

Q. How long before you were able to work after that?

A. I went and knocked about, but I wasn't able to do a piece of work under a week; and to do a good day's work, I wasn't able to do it in two weeks; because I couldn't walk. I couldn't sit down; and when I lay down, I would have to lay right flat down on my stomach.

Q. How many were they there?

A. I didn't see but six.

Q. All have disguises on?

A. Yes, sir.

Cross-Examination by Mr. Stanbery.

Q. Did you know any of them in their disguise?

A. Well, sir, I did.

Q. You did know?

A. I did know.

Q. How could you tell, if they were disguised?

A. I saw the men's hands, shoes, clothing, everything they had on.

Q. Did you know the men?

A. One was Dr. Parker.

Q. Who was the other?

A. Was Mr. John James Miller.

Q. The other?

A. John Lytle.

Q. Who was the other?

A. The other one was Mr. Bill Lowrey.

Q. Who was the other?

A. Now the other man—I believe there were more—but will not swear to that man. I believe they were there.

Q. I only ask who you knew were there?

A. I won't be positive that these men were there; and that was Mr. Bishop Sandifer and Mr. Thomasson; but the other men, I did not say I knew them two men, but these other four, I know them; there were six altogether.

Q. And you told four of the six, notwithstanding they were disguised?

A. I knew four of them out of the six.

Q. How were they disguised?

A. Well, they had a little cloth over the head that came down and fastened back of the head. They had on common coats. This one had on a calico dress, the other one had on a red dress opened down before; the other had on looked like black overcoats, came way down here [indicating below the knee.]

Q. Had they false faces?

A. Well, they first had simply a false face, made to cover over the head, eyes and nose, and all the mouth was out, just a place where they could see, you know.

Q. It was cloth?

A. Yes, sir.

Q. All the head, and the eyes, and the nose, everything, and the face was concealed, but the mouth; but you told four of them because you saw their underclothing?

A. Yes, sir.

Q. You told it from their shoes, and saw their underclothing?

A. I knew their hands, and I knew the men by their conversation. I got a full understanding of their voices.

Q. How far did they live from you?

A. Mr. Miller lived about three mile and a half, or four mile, I say, at the outside.

Q. How far did either of the others live from you?

A. Dr. Parker lived about three miles from me, or a little better.

Q. How far did the other live?

A. Mr. Lytle lived about a mile and a half from me.

Q. How far did the fourth live?

A. Mr. Lowrey lived on the same plantation, about two miles.

Q. Now you told them by their hands, as well as by their underclothing?

A.   Yes, sir.

Q.   How can you be so familiar with their hands?

A.   I know Mr. Lowrey by his hands; I've been working with him; he had been with me the day before.

Q.   What sort of a hand has he?

A.   He has a white hand, but has a finger that stands crooked; and he had sores on his hands, and that is the way I knew him.

Q.   Did each of the other three have fingers of that sort, and sores on their hands?

A.   No, sir.

Q.   How did you know their hands?

A.   I knew the men by their discourse; I knew them by their hands and by their discourse; I didn't say I knew them all by their hands; by their hands I knew two of them.

Q.   You knew one by his hands?

A.   Yes, sir, I went into this thing when they came to my house; they said they had risen from the dead; I wanted to see what sort of men they was; I went a purpose to see who they was; whether they were spirits, or whether they were human; but when I came to find out, they was men like me.

Q.   They told you they would come; back unless you published a card they told you to publish, renouncing Radicalism, and so forth, they would come back and pay you another visit?

A.   Yes, sir.

Q.   Well, did they?

A.   No, sir; they did not.

Q.   They all lived in that neighborhood?

A.   Yes, sir.

Q.   Did you publish the card?

A.   No, sir; I didn't.

Q.   No such card was published, then?

A.   Not by me.

Q.   Was there a grog shop near your house?

A.   There was; three miles from where I lived.

Q.   Do you know this man on trial now?

A.   I don't know him, as I know of.

Q.   Could you tell him by his hand?

A.   I know he is a man; that is all I know about him.

Q. Tell the jury whether you know him?

A. If I had been accustomed to that man, and known what suit of clothing he wore, and known his voice—I knew those other men's voices—I could tell more about them; but just fetch out a stranger—I can't tell anything about it.

Q. But answer my question, whether you recognized this man as one of the men who was at your house?

A. No, sir; I don't recognize him as one of them.

Re-Direct Examination.

Q. Did they use the word Ku Klux? did they call themselves Ku Klux?

A. I don't mind them saying anything about that.

Q. You understood them to be Ku Klux?

Mr. Johnson.   That will not do.

The Court.   Oh! no.

Mr. Corbin.   I think we will stop here, if the Court please.

Mr. Johnson.   Now, we want to know, may it please your Honors, whether they have stopped, not whether they think they have stopped.

The Court.   We will understand that they have stopped.

Proceedings in the Ku Klux Trials, 282–88.

Testimony Taken by the Joint Select Committee to Inquire into the Condition of Affairs in the Late Insurrectionary States (1872)

Washington, D.C., June 15, 1871.

A. WEBSTER SHAFFER sworn and examined.

By the CHAIRMAN:

Question.   Do you live in North Carolina?

Answer.   Yes, sir.

Question.   What part of it?

Answer.   Raleigh.

Question.   Do you hold any official position there?

Answer. I am register in bankruptcy and United States commissioner.

Question. How long have you held that position?

Answer. I have been register in bankruptcy in that district since 1868. I was formerly register in the sixth district; my present district is the fourth.

Question. How long have you been United States commissioner?

Answer. I was appointed United States commissioner while I resided in the sixth district, in 1867—the latter part of that year or the first part of 1868; it was during the December term of 1867 of the United States circuit court; whether it ran into January I do not know. The date of the appointment I do not remember.

Question. In the discharge of your duties as United States commissioner have you had occasion to inquire into the commission of acts of violence and lawlessness in any part of North Carolina?

Answer. I have since the act of May 21, 1870, in my capacity as commissioner.

Question. State, as briefly as you can, the facts that have come under your observation, and the condition of things as affected by those acts of violence, down to the present time.

Answer. The warrants issued from my office have run into Johnson, Chatham, Harnett, and Moore Counties, chiefly against persons who had, during the night-time, disguised, assaulted the persons and houses of chiefly colored people, whipping, shooting, and otherwise mutilating them, in crowds of from eight to twenty and twenty-five—sometimes thirty. I should think the number of cases was about twenty-five. I could tell very readily the exact number of cases I have heard. I do not know that I could tell the number of warrants I have issued which have been carried before other commissioners.

Question. By cases you have heard, you mean heard before you as commissioner?

Answer. Yes, sir; where the marshal returns prisoners before me. I could tell the exact number of cases to-day, if I wanted to do so, by reference to some papers I have here.

Question. State, as briefly as you can, what has been the character of those cases.

Answer. The parties who made oath for the issue of the warrants testified that parties in disguise had come there in the night-time, assaulted their houses and persons, broken down their doors, and in most cases taken the inmates—men, women, and children—and whipped and mutilated them.

* * *

By the CHAIRMAN:

Question. So far as you recollect individual cases that have been before you, proceed in order and give them.

Answer. There are several cases that I never issued warrants upon, for the reason that while the outrages have been terrible, in some respects, there is no testimony upon them. One is the case of Frances Gilmore, a colored woman from Chatham, in the vicinity of Locksville.

Question. When?

Answer. About two months ago.

Question. What was her statement?

Answer. She came to my office and complained that she had been whipped; that disguised persons had visited her house in the night-time, taken her out, and whipped her; laid her on the floor, taken her clothes off, and whipped her with a board; turned her over and whipped her again; then with matches burned the hair from her private parts, and cut her with a knife; and that she had been lying there about three weeks, unable to get to me before. I asked if she could identify any of the parties. She said she could not. I asked if there was anybody there who could do so. She said nobody was there who knew any of them except by suspicion. It is so very difficult to prove anything where they do identify them, that it is very discouraging to undertake to arrest persons purely on suspicion for such an offense as that. I desire to say that she was a colored woman, because I wish to make this case distinct; there were two cases very similar. Right after that there was another case in which another Frances Gilmore was interested.

By MR. POOL:

Question. Was she a white woman?

Answer. Yes, sir.

Question. From what county?

Answer. Chatham County. In this last case the white woman belonged to a party of contractors on the Chatham Railroad. The principal contractor with the road was a man named Howle, from Richmond. These women were about the road; I do not know what they were doing. The Ku-Klux came there in the night-time—some forty or fifty of them, as the testimony showed—and entered the camp of these persons, firing right and left, and hooting and halloing. The contractors, I think, got away. They did not catch them. They had notified them before that they were going to drive them out of the country, as the testimony was given. Howle and some of his friends and laborers got away. They went to the house of this Mrs. Frances Gilmore and found two negroes there sleeping on a pallet.

By MR. VAN TRUMP:

Question.   Men or women?

Answer.   Men. They found one white man, named Gilmore, and four women.

By the CHAIRMAN:

Question.   Did the testimony develop whether these were women of good or bad character?

Answer.   They were of rather bad character—rather worse than the generality of the country people, whose character is not always very good. They entered the house and took one negro out and whipped him. They then undertook to take the other out, and he got through the door, and ran to get away. They shot him. That man was not able to travel when the parties were arrested and brought before me. He is still there, but recovering, I think. The testimony showed that one colored man was very severely whipped, and the women were whipped; also a girl, the only girl there was in the whole crowd; I should judge she was about sixteen to eighteen years of age; they took her clothes off, whipped her very severely, and then lit a match and burned her hair off, and made her cut off herself the part that they did not burn off with the match.

By MR. POOL:

Question.   Was she a white girl?

Answer.   Yes, sir, a white girl.

By the CHAIRMAN:

Question.   Did the testimony disclose whether the men who committed this act gave as a reason for it the presence of those women of bad character?

Answer.   They did not give any testimony as to the cause of it.

Question.   In the examination was there proof of what they had said at the time?

Answer. I do not recollect the testimony as to what was said at the time. The only testimony that went to show the animus of the thing, that seemed to be given for that purpose, was testimony as to the character of those people.

By MR. VAN TRUMP:

Question. Is there any information or public impression down there that there are frequently counterfeit Ku-Klux; that other parties assume masks to correct the morals of the people? What is the state of opinion down there in regard to that?

Answer. If you mean to ask whether it is intended to instruct the people in good morals, I do not know that it is. It is said that it is not political; the conservatives say that it is not political.

Question. Are there many private broils and much trouble among the negro population themselves?

Answer. No, sir.

Question. Not at all?

Answer. No, sir; the colored people of Chatham County are as orderly, quiet, respectful a people as I ever saw in my life anywhere.

Question. Do they never have any quarrels among themselves?

Answer. I do not know that they do. In the towns they do have quarrels, of course; they are a little disorderly; they will steal, and I suppose do worse sometimes.

Question. Do you say that the negroes as a race are free from any disturbances among themselves?

Answer. I am speaking from information that I have. I do not know and have not heard of any disturbance among the negroes of Chatham County, nor Harnett, nor Moore. I have not heard of any broils or disturbances among them, or anything of that nature.

Question. Nothing that might induce any of them to assume masks and punish disorders among themselves?

Answer. No, sir; some of them have been charged with burning barns and other buildings. That is the only thing of the kind I know of. They never attempted to give any testimony of that character before me. They never attempted to show that there were negro Ku-Klux.

Testimony Taken by the Joint Select Committee to Inquire into the Condition of Affairs in the Late Insurrectionary States: North Carolina (Washington, 1871), 31–32, 36–38.

Thomas E. Watson

The Negro Question in the South
(October 1892)

*In 1892, Tom Watson, a Georgia Populist, urged black and white farmers to
shed old political affiliations that paralleled the color line and make common
cause against the economic and political interests he argued held all farmers and
laborers down. Like other white third-party politicians in the postwar South,
Watson was willing for a time to jettison white supremacy in favor of race-
neutral class-based policies. As a member of the Georgia state legislature, Watson supported taxes to fund public education and favored elimination of the
notorious convict lease system; campaigning for reelection to Congress in 1892,
he condemned lynching. In the early years of the twentieth century, Watson retired from public life and published* Watson's Jeffersonian Magazine, *in
which he railed against the exploitative capitalism of New South industrialists
and broadcast his mounting racist, anti-Semitic, and anti-immigrant sentiments.
Sympathetic to black political participation during the Populist years, by the turn
of the century, Watson favored African American disenfranchisement as a remedy to Democratic electoral fraud. As for the Populists, the party was eroded by
factionalism from within and robust opposition from without. By the turn of the
century most white southern Populists, like Tom Watson, returned to a Democratic Party dedicated to white rule.*

The Negro Question in the South has been for nearly thirty years
a source of danger, discord, and bloodshed. It is an ever-present ir-
ritant and menace.

Several millions of slaves were told that they were the prime
cause of the civil war; that their emancipation was the result of the
triumph of the North over the South; that the ballot was placed in
their hands as a weapon of defence against their former masters;
that the war-won political equality of the black man with the white,
must be asserted promptly and aggressively, under the leadership of
adventurers who had swooped down upon the conquered section in
the wake of the Union armies.

No one, who wishes to be fair, can fail to see that, in such a condition of things, strife between the freedman and his former owner

was inevitable. In the clashing of interests and of feelings, bitterness
was born. The black man was kept in a continual fever of suspicion
that we meant to put him back into slavery. In the assertion of his
recently acquired privileges, he was led to believe that the best
proof of his being on the right side of any issue was that his old
master was on the other. When this was the case, he felt easy in his
mind. But if, by any chance, he found that he was voting the same
ticket with his former owner, he at once became reflective and sus-
picious. In the irritable temper of the times, a whispered warning
from a Northern "carpet-bagger," having no justification in rhyme
or reason, outweighed with him a carload of sound argument and
earnest expostulation from the man whom he had known all his
life; who had hunted with him through every swamp and wooded
upland for miles around; who had wrestled and run foot-races with
him in the "Negro quarters" on many a Saturday afternoon; who
had fished with him at every "hole" in the creek; and who had
played a thousand games of "marble" with him under the cool
shade of the giant oaks which, in those days, sheltered a home they
had both loved.

In brief, the end of the war brought changed relations and
changed feelings. Heated antagonisms produced mutual distrust
and dislike—ready, at any accident of unusual provocation on either side, to break out into passionate and bloody conflict.

Quick to take advantage of this deplorable situation, the politicians have based the fortunes of the old parties upon it. Northern
leaders have felt that at the cry of "Southern outrage" they could
not only "fire the Northern heart," but also win a unanimous vote
from the colored people. Southern politicians have felt that at the
cry of "Negro domination" they could drive into solid phalanx
every white man in all the Southern states.

Both the old parties have done this thing until they have constructed as perfect a "slot machine" as the world ever saw. Drop the
old, worn nickel of the "party slogan" into the slot, and the machine does the rest. You might beseech a Southern white tenant to
listen to you upon questions of finance, taxation, and transportation; you might demonstrate with mathematical precision that
herein lay his way out of poverty into comfort; you might have him
"almost persuaded" to the truth, but if the merchant who furnished
his farm supplied (at tremendous usury) or the town politician (who

never spoke to him excepting at election times) came along and cried "Negro rule!" the entire fabric of reason and common sense which you had patiently constructed would fall, and the poor tenant would joyously hug the chains of an actual wretchedness rather than do any experimenting on a question of mere sentiment.

* * *

Now consider: here were two distinct races dwelling together, with political equality established between them by law. They lived in the same section; won their livelihood by the same pursuits; cultivated adjoining fields on the same terms; enjoyed together the bounties of a generous climate; suffered together the rigors of cruelly unjust laws; spoke the same language; bought and sold in the same markets; classified themselves into churches under the same denominational teachings; neither race antagonizing the other in any branch of industry; each absolutely dependent on the other in all the avenues of labor and employment; and yet, instead of being allies, as every dictate of reason and prudence and self-interest and justice said they should be, they were kept apart, in dangerous hostility, that the sordid aims of partisan politics might be served!

So completely has this scheme succeeded that the Southern black man almost instinctively supports any measure the Southern white man condemns, while the latter almost universally antagonizes any proposition suggested by a Northern Republican. We have, then, a solid South as opposed to a solid North; and in the South itself, a solid black vote against the solid white.

That such a condition is most ominous to both sections and both races, is apparent to all.

If we were dealing with a few tribes of red men or a few sporadic Chinese, the question would be easily disposed of. The Anglo-Saxon would probably do just as he pleased, whether right or wrong, and the weaker man would go under.

But the Negroes number 8,000,000. They are interwoven with our business, political, and labor systems. They assimilate with our customs, our religion, our civilization. They meet us at every turn,— in the fields, the shops, the mines. They are a part of our system, and they are here to stay.

Those writers who tediously wade through census reports to prove that the Negro is disappearing, are the most absurd mortals extant. The Negro is not disappearing. A Southern man who looks

about him and who sees how rapidly the colored people increase,
how cheaply they can live, and how readily they learn, has no patience whatever with those statistical lunatics who figure out the final disappearance of the Negro one hundred years hence. The
truth is, that the "black belts" in the South are getting blacker. The
race is mixing less than it ever did. Mulattoes are less common (in
proportion) than during the times of slavery. Miscegenation is further off (thank God) than ever. Neither the blacks nor the whites
have any relish for it. Both have a pride of race which is com-
mendable, and which, properly directed, will lead to the best results
for both. The home of the colored man is chiefly with us in the
South, and there he will remain. It is there he is founding churches,
opening schools, maintaining newspapers, entering the professions,
serving on juries, deciding doubtful elections, drilling as a volunteer
soldier, and piling up a cotton crop which amazes the world.

II

This preliminary statement is made at length that the gravity of the
situation may be seen. Such a problem never confronted any people before.

Never before did two distinct races dwell together under such
conditions.

And the problem is, can these two races, distinct in color, distinct
in social life, and distinct as political powers, dwell together in
peace and prosperity?

Upon a question so difficult and delicate no man should dog-
matize—nor dodge. The issue is here; grows more urgent every
day, and must be met.

It is safe to say that the present status of hostility between the
races can only be sustained at the most imminent risk to both. It is
leading by logical necessity to results which the imagination shrinks
from contemplating. And the horrors of such a future can only be
averted by honest attempts at a solution of the question which will
be just to both races and beneficial to both.

Having given this subject much anxious thought, my opinion is
that the future happiness of the two races will never be assured until the political motives which drive them asunder, into two distinct

and hostile factions, can be removed. There must be a new policy inaugurated, whose purpose is to allay the passions and prejudices of race conflict, and which makes its appeal to the sober sense and honest judgment of the citizen regardless of his color.

To the success of this policy two things are indispensable—a common necessity acting upon both races, and a common benefit assured to both—without injury or humiliation to either.

Then, again, outsiders must let us alone. We must work out our own salvation. In no other way can it be done. Suggestions of Federal interference with our elections postpone the settlement and render our task the more difficult. Like all free people, we love home rule, and resent foreign compulsion of any sort. The Northern leader who really desires to see a better state of things in the South, puts his finger on the hands of the clock and forces them backward every time he intermeddles with the question. This is the literal truth; and the sooner it is well understood, the sooner we can accomplish our purpose.

What is that purpose? To outline a policy which compels the support of a great body of both races, from those motives which imperiously control human action, and which will thus obliterate forever the sharp and unreasoning political divisions of to-day.

The white people of the South will never support the Republican Party. This much is certain. The black people of the South will never support the Democratic Party. This is equally certain.

Hence, at the very beginning, we are met by the necessity of new political alliances. As long as the whites remain solidly Democratic, the blacks will remain solidly Republican.

As long as there was no choice, except as between the Democrats and the Republicans, the situation of the two races was bound to be one of antagonism. The Republican Party represented everything which was hateful to the whites; the Democratic Party, everything which was hateful to the blacks.

Therefore a new party was absolutely necessary. It has come, and it is doing its work with marvellous rapidity.

Why does a Southern Democrat leave his party and come to ours?

Because his industrial condition is pitiably bad; because he struggles against a system of laws which have almost filled him with despair; because he is told that he is without clothing because he produces too much cotton, and without food because corn is too plentiful; because he sees everybody growing rich off the products of labor except the laborer; because the millionnaires who manage the Democratic Party have contemptuously ignored his plea for a redress of grievances and have nothing to say to him beyond the cheerful advice to "work harder and live closer."

Why has this man joined the PEOPLE'S PARTY? Because the same grievances have been presented to the Republicans by the farmer of the West, and the millionnaires who control that party have replied to the petition with the soothing counsel that the Republican farmer of the West should "work more and talk less."

Therefore, if he were confined to a choice between the two old parties, the question would merely be (on these issues) whether the pot were larger than the kettle—the color of both being precisely the same.

* * *

V

The People's Party will settle the race question. First, by enacting the Australian ballot system. Second, by offering to white and black a rallying point which is free from the odium of former discords and strifes. Third, by presenting a platform immensely beneficial to both races and injurious to neither. Fourth, by making it to the *interest* of both races to act together for the success of the platform. Fifth, by making it to the *interest* of the colored man to have the same patriotic zeal for the welfare of the South that the whites possess.

* * *

The white tenant lives adjoining the colored tenant. Their houses are almost equally destitute of comforts. Their living is confined to bare necessities. They are equally burdened with heavy taxes. They pay the same high rent for gullied and impoverished land.

They pay the same enormous prices for farm supplies. Christmas finds them both without any satisfactory return for a year's toil. Dull and heavy and unhappy, they both start the plows again when "New Year's" passes.

Now the People's Party says to these two men, "You are kept apart that you may be separately fleeced of your earnings. You are made to hate each other because upon that hatred is rested the keystone of the arch of financial despotism which enslaves you both. You are deceived and blinded that you may not see how this race antagonism perpetuates a monetary system which beggars both."

This is so obviously true it is no wonder both these unhappy laborers stop to listen. No wonder they begin to realize that no change of law can benefit the white tenant which does not benefit the black one likewise; that no system which now does injustice to one of them can fail to injure both. Their every material interest is identical. The moment this becomes a conviction, mere selfishness, the mere desire to better their conditions, escape onerous taxes, avoid usurious charges, lighten their rents, or change their precarious tenements into smiling, happy homes, will drive these two men together, just as their mutually inflamed prejudices now drive them apart.

Suppose these two men now to have become fully imbued with the idea that their material welfare depends upon the reforms we demand. Then they act together to secure them. Every white reformer finds it to the vital interest of his home, his family, his fortune, to see to it that the vote of the colored reformer is freely cast and fairly counted.

Then what? Every colored voter will be thereafter a subject of industrial education and political teaching.

Concede that in the final event, a colored man will vote where his material interests dictate that he should vote; concede that in the South the accident of color can make no possible difference in the interests of farmers, croppers, and laborers; concede that under full and fair discussion the people can be depended upon to ascertain where their interests lie—and we reach the conclusion that the Southern race question can be solved by the People's Party on the simple proposition that each race will be led by self-interest to support that which benefits it, when so presented that neither is hindered by the bitter party antagonisms of the past.

Let the colored laborer realize that our platform gives him a better guaranty for political independence; for a fair return for his work; a better chance to buy a home and keep it; a better chance to educate his children and see them profitably employed; a better chance to have public life freed from race collisions; a better chance for every citizen to be considered as a *citizen* regardless of color in the making and enforcing of laws,—let all this be fully realized, and the race question at the South will have settled itself through the evolution of a political movement in which both whites and blacks recognize their surest way out of wretchedness into comfort and independence.

* * *

To the emasculated individual who cries "Negro supremacy!" there is little to be said. His cowardice shows him to be a degeneration from the race which has never yet feared any other race. Existing under such conditions as they now do in this country, there is no earthly chance for Negro domination, unless we are ready to admit that the colored man is our superior in will power, courage, and intellect.

Not being prepared to make any such admission in favor of any race the sun ever shone on, I have no words which can portray my contempt for the white man, Anglo-Saxons, who can knock their knees together, and through their chattering teeth and pale lips admit that they are afraid the Negroes will "dominate us."

The question of social equality does not enter into the calculation at all. That is a thing each citizen decides for himself. No statute ever yet drew the latch of the humblest home—or ever will. Each citizen regulates his own visiting list—and always will.

The conclusion, then, seems to me to be this: the crushing burdens which now oppress both races in the South will cause each to make an effort to cast them off. They will see a similarity of cause and a similarity of remedy. They will recognize that each should help the other in the work of repealing bad laws and enacting good ones. They will become political allies, and neither can injure the other without weakening both. It will be to the interest of both that each should have justice. And on these broad lines of mutual interest, mutual forbearance, and mutual support the present will be made the stepping-stone to future peace and prosperity.

The Arena, 6 (October 1892): 540–50. Excerpt here from George Brown Tindall, *A Populist Reader: Selections from the Works of American Populist Leaders* (Gloucester, MA, 1976), 118–28.

Charles Chesnutt

What Is a White Man? (May 30, 1889)

Charles W. Chesnutt was born in Cleveland, Ohio, in 1858 to free African Americans who had emigrated from North Carolina. His life coincided with dramatic changes in the legal and political standing of African Americans. When Charles was eight years old, his family returned to their former home in Fayetteville, North Carolina, where they enjoyed the new opportunities made possible by emancipation and Reconstruction. Educated in a Freedmen's Bureau school, Chesnutt became a teacher himself. Distrustful of the future of interracial democracy in North Carolina, he returned to Ohio in the mid-1880s, where he became a prominent writer. An outspoken critic of racial inequality, Chesnutt explored in his writing the complex workings of race in the South, particularly the blurry edges of the color line on which he himself lived. His own ancestry included mixed-race grandmothers and white grandfathers, making him particularly sensitive to the absurdities of efforts to define and defend whiteness that were crucial to Jim Crow.

The fiat having gone forth from the wise men of the South that the "all-pervading, all-conquering Anglo-Saxon race" must continue forever to exercise exclusive control and direction of the government of this so-called Republic, it becomes important to every citizen who values his birthright to know who are included in this grandiloquent term. It is of course perfectly obvious that the writer or speaker who used this expression—perhaps Mr. Grady of Georgia—did not say what he meant. It is not probable that he meant to exclude from full citizenship the Celts and Teutons and Gauls and Slavs who make up so large a proportion of our population; he hardly meant to exclude the Jews, for even the most ardent fire-eater would hardly venture to advocate the disfranchisement of the thrifty race whose mortgages cover so large a portion of Southern soil. What the eloquent gentleman really meant by this high-sounding phrase was simply the white race; and the substance of the argument of that school of Southern writers to which he belongs, is simply that for the good of the country the Negro should have no voice in directing the government or public policy of the Southern States or of the nation.

But it is evident that where the intermingling of the races has made such progress as it has in this country, the line which separates the races must in many instances have been practically obliterated. And there has arisen in the United States a very large class of the population who are certainly not Negroes in an ethnological sense, and whose children will be no nearer Negroes than themselves. In view, therefore, of the very positive ground taken by the white leaders of the South, where most of these people reside, it becomes in the highest degree important to them to know what race they belong to. It ought to be also a matter of serious concern to the Southern white people; for if their zeal for good government is so great that they contemplate the practical overthrow of the Constitution and laws of the United States to secure it, they ought at least to be sure that no man entitled to it by their own argument, is robbed of a right so precious as that of free citizenship; the "all-pervading, all conquering Anglo-Saxon" ought to set as high a value on American citizenship as the all-conquering Roman placed upon the franchise of his State two thousand years ago. This discussion would of course be of little interest to the genuine Negro, who is entirely outside of the charmed circle, and must content himself with the acquisition of wealth, the pursuit of learning and such other privileges as his "best friends" may find it consistent with the welfare of the nation to allow him; but to every other good citizen the inquiry ought to be a momentous one. What is a white man?

In spite of the virulence and universality of race prejudice in the United States, the human intellect long ago revolted at the manifest absurdity of classifying men fifteen-sixteenths white as black men; and hence there grew up a number of laws in different states of the Union defining the limit which separated the white and colored races, which was, when these laws took their rise and is now to a large extent, the line which separated freedom and opportunity from slavery or hopeless degradation. Some of these laws are of legislative origin; others are judge-made laws, brought out by the exigencies of special cases which came before the courts for determination. Some day they will, perhaps, become mere curiosities of jurisprudence; the "black laws" will be bracketed with the "blue laws," and will be at best but landmarks by which to measure the

progress of the nation. But to-day these laws are in active operation, and they are, therefore, worthy of attention; for every good
citizen ought to know the law, and, if possible, to respect it; and if
not worthy of respect, it should be changed by the authority which
enacted it. Whether any of the laws referred to here have been in
any manner changed by very recent legislation the writer cannot
say, but they are certainly embodied in the latest editions of the revised statutes of the states referred to.

* * *

The states vary slightly in regard to what constitutes a mulatto or
person of color, and as to what proportion of white blood should
be sufficient to remove the disability of color. As a general rule, less
than one-fourth of Negro blood left the individual white—in theory; race questions being, however, regulated very differently in
practice. In Missouri, by the code of 1855, still in operation, so far
as not inconsistent with the Federal Constitution and laws, "any
person other than a Negro, any one of whose grandmothers or
grandfathers is or shall have been a Negro, tho all of his or her pro-
genitors except those descended from the Negro may have been
white persons, shall be deemed a mulatto." Thus the color-line is
drawn at one-fourth of Negro blood, and persons with only one-
eighth are white.

By the Mississippi code of 1880, the color-line is drawn at one-
fourth of Negro blood, all persons having less being theoretically
white.

Under the *code noir* of Louisiana, the descendant of a white and
a quadroon is white, thus drawing the line at one-eighth of Negro
blood. The code of 1876 abolished all distinctions of color; as to
whether they have been re-enacted since the Republican Party
went out of power in that state the writer is not informed.

Jumping to the extreme North, persons are white within the
meaning of the Constitution of Michigan who have less than one-
fourth of Negro blood.

In Ohio the rule, as established by numerous decisions of the
Supreme Court, was that a preponderance of white blood constituted a person a white man in the eye of the law, and entitled him
to the exercise of all the civil rights of a white man. By a retrogres-
sive step the color-line was extended in 1861 in the case of marriage,

which by statute was forbidden between a person of pure white blood and one having a visible admixture of African blood. But by act of legislature, passed in the spring of 1887, all laws establishing or permitting distinctions of color were repealed. In many parts of the state these laws were always ignored, and they would doubtless have been repealed long ago but for the sentiment of the southern counties, separated only by the width of the Ohio River from a former slave-holding state. There was a bill introduced in the legislature during the last session to reenact the "black laws," but it was hopelessly defeated; the member who introduced it evidently mistook his latitude; he ought to be a member of the Georgia legislature.

But the state which, for several reasons, one might expect to have the strictest laws in regard to the relations of the races, has really the loosest. Two extracts from decisions of the Supreme Court of South Carolina will make clear the law of that state in regard to the color line.

> The definition of the term mulatto, as understood in this state, seems to be vague, signifying generally a person of mixed white or European and Negro parentage, in whatever proportions the blood of the two races may be mingled in the individual. But it is not invariably applicable to every admixture of African blood with the European, nor is one having all the features of a white to be ranked with the degraded class designated by the laws of this state as persons of color, because of some remote taint of the Negro race. The line of distinction, however, is not ascertained by any rule of law. . . . Juries would probably be justified in holding a person to be white in whom the admixture of African blood did not exceed the proportion of one-eighth. But it is in all cases a question for the jury, to be determined by them upon the evidence of features and complexion afforded by inspection, the evidence of reputation as to parentage, and the evidence of the rank and station in society occupied by the party. The only rule which can be laid down by the courts is that where there is a distinct and visible admixture of Negro blood, the individual is to be dominated a mulatto or person of color.

In a later case the court held: "The question whether persons are colored or white, where color or feature are doubtful, is for the jury to decide by reputation, by reception into society, and by their exercise of the privileges of the white man, as well as by admixture of blood."

It is an interesting question why such should have been, and should still be, for that matter, the law of South Carolina, and why there should exist in that state a condition of public opinion which would accept such a law. Perhaps it may be attributed to the fact that the colored population of South Carolina always outnumbered the white population, and the eagerness of the latter to recruit their ranks was sufficient to overcome in some measure their prejudice against the Negro blood. It is certainly true that the color-line is, in practice as in law, more loosely drawn in South Carolina than in any other Southern State, and that no inconsiderable element of the population of that state consists of these legal white persons, who were either born in the state, or, attracted thither by this feature of the laws, have come in from surrounding states, and, forsaking home and kindred, have taken their social position as white people. A reasonable degree of reticence in regard to one's antecedents is, however, usual in such cases.

Before the War the color-line, as fixed by law, regulated in theory the civil and political status of persons of color. What that status was, was expressed in the Dred Scott decision. But since the War, or rather since the enfranchisement of the colored people, these laws have been mainly confined—in theory, be it always remembered—to the regulation of the intercourse of the races in schools and in the marriage relation. The extension of the color-line to places of public entertainment and resort, to inns and public highways, is in most states entirely a matter of custom. A colored man can sue in the courts of any Southern State for the violation of his common-law rights, and recover damages of say fifty cents without costs. A colored minister who sued a Baltimore steamboat company a few weeks ago for refusing him first-class accommodation, he having paid first-class fare, did not even meet with that measure of success; the learned judge, a Federal judge by the way, held that the plaintiff's rights had been invaded, and that he had suffered humiliation at the hands of the defendant company, but that "the humiliation was not sufficient to entitle him to damages." And the learned judge dismissed the action without costs to either party.

Having thus ascertained what constitutes a white man, the good citizen may be curious to know what steps have been taken to preserve the purity of the white race. Nature, by some unaccountable oversight having to some extent neglected a matter so important to the future prosperity and progress of mankind. The marriage laws referred to here are in active operation, and cases under them are by no means infrequent. Indeed, instead of being behind the age, the marriage laws in the Southern States are in advance of public opinion; for very rarely will a Southern community stop to figure on the pedigree of the contracting parties to a marriage where one is white and the other is known to have any strain of Negro blood.

In Virginia, under the title "Offenses against Morality," the law provides that "any white person who shall intermarry with a Negro shall be confined in jail not more than one year and fined not exceeding one hundred dollars." In a marginal note on the statute-book, attention is called to the fact that "a similar penalty is not imposed on the Negro"—a stretch of magnanimity to which the laws of other states are strangers. A person who performs the ceremony of marriage in such a case is fined two hundred dollars, one-half of which goes to the informer.

In Maryland, a minister who performs the ceremony of marriage between a Negro and a white person is liable to a fine of one hundred dollars.

In Mississippi, code of 1880, it is provided that "the marriage of a white person to a Negro or mulatto or person who shall have one-fourth or more of Negro blood, shall be unlawful"; and as this prohibition does not seem sufficiently emphatic, it is further declared to be "incestuous and void," and is punished by the same penalty prescribed for marriage within the forbidden degrees of consanguinity.

But it is Georgia, the *alma genetrix* of the chain-gang, which merits the questionable distinction of having the harshest set of color laws. By the law of Georgia the term "person of color" is defined to mean "all such as have an admixture of Negro blood, and the term 'Negro,' includes mulattoes." This definition is perhaps restricted somewhat by another provision, by which "all Negroes, mestizoes, and their descendants, having one-eighth of Negro or mulatto blood in their veins, shall be known in this State as persons of color." A colored minister is permitted to perform the ceremony of marriage between colored persons only, tho white ministers are not forbidden to join persons of color in wedlock. It is further provided that "the marriage relation between white persons and persons of African descent is forever prohibited, and such marriages shall be null and void." This is a very sweeping provision; it will be noticed that the term "persons of color," previously defined, is not employed, the expression "persons of African descent" being used instead. A court which was so inclined would find no difficulty in extending this provision of the law to the remotest strain of African blood. The marriage relation is forever prohibited. Forever is a long time. There is a colored woman in Georgia said to be worth $300,000—an immense fortune in the poverty stricken South. With a few hundred such women in that state, possessing a fair degree of good looks, the color-line would shrivel up like a scroll in the heat of competition for their hands in marriage. The penalty for the violation of the law against intermarriage is the same sought to be imposed by the defunct Glenn Bill for violation of its provisions; i.e., a fine not to exceed one thousand dollars, and imprisonment not to exceed six months, or twelve months in the chain-gang.

Whatever the wisdom or justice of these laws, there is one objection to them which is not given sufficient prominence in the consideration of the subject, even where it is discussed at all; they make mixed blood a *prima-facie* proof of illegitimacy. It is a fact that at present, in the United States, a colored man or woman whose complexion is white or nearly white is presumed, in the absence of any knowledge of his or her antecedents, to be the offspring of a union not sanctified by law. And by a curious but not uncommon process, such persons are not held in the same low estimation as white people in the same position. The sins of their fathers are not visited upon the children, in that regard at least; and their mothers' lapses from virtue are regarded either as misfortunes or as faults excusable under the circumstances. But in spite of all this, illegitimacy is not a desirable distinction, and is likely to become less so as these people of mixed blood advance in wealth and social standing. This presumption of illegitimacy was once, perhaps, true of the majority of such persons; but the times have changed. More than half of the colored people of the United States are of mixed blood; they marry and are given in marriage, and they beget children of complexions similar to their own. Whether or not, therefore, laws which stamp these children as illegitimate, and which by indirection establish a lower standard of morality for a large part of the population than the remaining part is judged by, are wise laws; and whether or not the purity of the white race could not be as well preserved by the exercise of virtue, and the operation of those natural laws which are so often quoted by Southern writers as the justification of all sorts of Southern "policies"—are questions which the good citizen may at least turn over in his mind occasionally, pending the settlement of other complications which have grown out of the presence of the Negro on this continent.

Independent 41 (May 30, 1889): 5–6. Excerpted here from *Charles W. Chesnutt, Essays and Speeches*, ed. Joseph McElrath et al. (Stanford, CA, 1999), 68–73.

Atticus G. Haygood

The Black Shadow in the South (September 1893–February 1894)

A southern progressive who defended secession, Methodist leader Atticus G. Haygood saw a promising future for the South if it pursued new commercial and educational ventures. He advocated expanded access to education for both white and black southerners; he served as the president of Emory College and the agent for the Slater Fund, which provided funds for black schools in the South. In Haygood's opinion, careful, conservative education could solve what many white southerners considered the chief "failure" of Reconstruction: Namely, the assertiveness of the "New Negroes," the generation of African Americans born in freedom (such as Charles Chesnutt). Education could not solve all the South's problems, however, and Haygood defended lynching as a regrettable but acceptable response to black crime. The greatest menace facing the South, in Haygood's estimation, was the new generation of free-born black southerners, which he considered to be dangerously given to criminality, and not the white mobs who shot, hanged, and burned men alive across the region.

I HAVE been asked to explain not the killing, but the torture by burning of two negro men in the United States in the year of grace 1893—one made an end of in Texas, the other in Kentucky. Nowadays, it seems, the killing of negroes is not so extraordinary an occurrence as to need explanation; it has become so common that it no longer surprises. We read of such things as we read of fires that burned a cabin, or a town. Unless the killing occurs in our neighborhood, we do not remember names till the next morning's paper brings us a new story of the contempt shown by an outraged and desperate community for the processes of civil law.

The most alarming fact is that execution by lynching has ceased to surprise us. The area in which mob law asserts itself is a wide and increasing one. In a country unorganized and without government, individuals must punish violations of natural law; there is no other resource. But this is not civilization; it is at best barbarism. In organized society, lynching is a crime against society. It is not a question as to what the victim deserves; it is a question as to what society can afford. In organized society, there is no higher civil or social duty than obedience to law; the lyncher is, of all men, the violator of law. Lynching is a crime against God and man. Lynching breaks the law, defies it, despises it, puts it to open shame. Punishment by government, according to law, represents the judgment of God; punishment by lynching is vengeance. Legal punishment educates men into respect for law; lynching educates them into contempt for law. Lynching does more to put down law than any criminal it takes in hand; lynching kills a man; the lyncher kills the law that protects life; lynching is anarchy. If a government is so weak or bad that it cannot, or will not, enforce the law, the remedy is not lynching; it is revolution. If one private citizen has no moral or civil right to put a man to death, a hundred banded together have not the right. And why not the hundred banded together? Because their object is to overawe and overpower the law. Lynchers are conscious of their lawlessness, and seek protection in masks or numbers. The government that winks at lynching is vicious; the government that does not care is foolish and wicked; the government that cannot put it down is weak.

The burning of a human being for any crime whatsoever, it is thought, is a horror which does not occur, outside the Southern

States of the American Union, in the civilized world. Yet unless assaults by negroes on white women and little white girls come to an end, there will most probably be still further displays of vengeance that will shock the world. While the Texas and Kentucky burnings were going on, men did not think about the world or its opinions. In the white heat of horror and vengeance, they did not so much as remember that there were any people in the world but themselves. For the time, they were beside themselves—absolutely deranged. "Emotional insanity" may dominate a thousand men as certainly and completely as it may dominate one man, driven to the wall and knowing nothing but the emergency that is upon him. And such insanity may be accompanied by the utmost deliberation in seeking its ends. These Texas and Kentucky burnings are monstrous and abnormal things that cannot be approved by any sane and intelligent man. But sane men who are just will consider the provocation. Sane men who are righteous will remember not only the brutish man who dies by the slow torture of fire; they will think also of the ruined woman, worse tortured than he. When they think of the infuriated mob in Paris, Texas, and the negro ruffian tortured most horribly till he was dead, they will think also of a white baby, four years old, first outraged with demoniacal cruelty and then taken by her heels and torn asunder in the mad wantonness of gorilla ferocity. Indeed, the instant comment of a negro man to whom I stated this case was, "He ought to have been burnt." Men, no matter where they live or how high their personal or social development, with human hearts in them, will ask, "What if she had been my baby?"

These horrors—the rapings, the lynchings, the burnings—are not ancient history; they are products of American life in the closing decade of the nineteenth century. These tortures do not belong to that dark time when women were hanged in New England for witchcraft; there is no superstition in Texas or Kentucky about witches, or other supernatural powers—at least among white people. These burnings are not to be accounted for by any theory of superstition, or ignorance, or low human development, but by what we know of the elemental forces that control human nature throughout all time and the world over. Let it be understood that this article does not defend any sort of lynching and that the writer abhors torture with all his soul. The article states only facts and that which they involve. Nor are these statements carelessly made; I have reason to know how serious is the subject herein discussed and to apprehend with clearness of vision the appalling and portentous conditions which make such a discussion even possible.

The Editor of the leading Southern religious paper—estimated by its circulation—the Rev. Dr. E. E. Hoss, of the "Christian Advocate," the chief organ of the Methodist Episcopal Church, South, published from Nashville, Tennessee, said recently in an editorial article that he had reason to believe that "three hundred white women had been raped by negroes within the preceding three months." I believe Dr. Hoss's statement to be under rather than above the facts in the case. Not a few such crimes are never published. And probably some lynchings never get to the newspapers. When Dr. Hoss, at the close of a very vigorous article denouncing all forms of lynch law, added this statement: "But the raping of white women by negroes must cease," every man of both races with a spark of manhood in him, said, "Amen." When it is remembered that the South is a thinly-settled country and that most of these unspeakable outrages upon women occur in out-of-the-way places, just men, putting themselves in the place of the Southern people, will when pronouncing judgment, consider what they would think, feel, and do were the terrible test their own.

On the matters discussed in this article, I have thought much and during many years of opportunity to learn what are the basic facts in Southern social conditions—conditions unmatched in the history of the world; yet lacking a specific request I should probably have remained silent, not caring to discuss for publication a subject both horrible and loathsome, or to offer to the public opinions about facts that make wise men mad.

Some words personal may be allowable in this paper. Any who care to read it may naturally wish to know whether the writer is, in some reasonable degree, a competent witness. He has not lacked opportunity, having been "born and bred" in Middle Georgia, where slavery was at its best, and having been, in later years, familiar with other sections of the Southern country where it was at its worst. He is not a product of *post-bellum* life—which inevitably made the relations between the two races less kindly in their sympathies and friendship—having been a grown man when South Carolina seceded. Opposed to secession, he gave his absolute allegiance to the Confederacy. After Appomattox, recognizing Providence and the invincible facts of history, he soon came to thank Heaven that slavery was done with and that the Union was preserved. Moreover, he has voted always the "regular Democratic ticket." He had no doubt, during the War between the States, of the sacredness of the cause the Confederacy stood for—the rights of the States—nor did he question for a moment the over-ruling Providence that determined the issues of that tremendous revolution. He believed, when it was done, and he believes to this hour, that the unconditional enfranchisement of the negroes was a deadlier crime against republican government and civilization than the extremest Federalist believed secession to be; yet, seeing that the negro was a citizen armed with that thunderbolt of power, the ballot, he laid himself out, through many years of hard service, and with small approval, at the time, from the great body of his own people, to help make of the negro the best citizen possible. His only regret, in looking back at those years of consecration to the negro's cause, is that he could not do more to help his "brother in black" to worthier conceptions of his relations to the government, to society, to the church, and so into better and nobler manhood and womanhood. So much may be pardoned in a Southern man asked to write an article in explanation of the burning of negroes in the South.

Our behavior in the South toward the negro has not been ideally perfect; we might have done better in many things. But I am sure that Southern white people have borne themselves, under trials never known before in history, as well as any people in the world could have borne themselves. In truth, they have done better with and by the negro than any other white people, lacking their training, could have done. It is absolutely certain that, in their ordinary dealings with the negro, the Southern white people are kinder to him and more patient than any other people who come into relations with him. Cruelty of disposition does not explain the torture of the demon men burned to death for assaulting helpless women and tender little girls. The Southern people are not cruel and never were. They are kind-hearted people; good to one another and to all men. They are kind to dumb brutes. Whatever may be true or false about them, they were never cruel-hearted people. They were kind to the negroes when they were slaves; they are kind to them now. That speaker or writer who holds up the worst slave-holder of the old days as the type of all is a slanderer, whether from malice or ignorance; and he who represents a white Southern ruffian of to-day as representative of a whole people in their relation to the negroes is either ignorant, or depraved. Such representations are as devoid of truth and justice as would be the slander of a partisan Southerner who might affirm that a "sweating house" and starving sewing women represent the business of New York City.

I was asked to explain the burning of these negroes, not the killing of them. I give frankly my opinion: the people who burned them were for the time insane. In no other way can the general character of these people and their dealing with these victims of their fierce indignation be accounted for. Take the Paris case. That negro should have been arrested by the sheriff; he should have been duly committed to jail; he should have had a fair trial before a regular court and jury; if convicted, he should have been punished according to law by the officer whose business it is to enforce verdicts and sentences. It was illegal and morally wrong to lynch him by simply hanging or shooting. In organized society, lynching is not only anarchy; it is an anachronism. It is so much of the Dark Ages surviving in modern and civilized life. It was horrible to torture the guilty wretch; the burning was an act of insanity. But had the dismembered form of his victim been the dishonored body of my baby, I might also have gone into an insanity that might have ended never.

There are some collateral considerations that throw some light upon the whole subject before us; I wish to state only recognized facts, not to write in defence of anything wrong in my people. This phrase, "my people," I can but employ so long as the world sits in perpetual judgment upon our behavior, under conditions of which it has little knowledge and no experience. No race, not the most savage, tolerates the rape of women, but it may be said without reflection upon any other people that the Southern people are now and always have been most sensitive concerning the honor of their women—their mothers, wives, sisters, daughters. A single word questioning the purity of Southern women has cost many a man

his life. Hardly any Southern jury will convict him who slays in defence of any woman whose natural protector he is. If a man is shot
dead in the streets for insulting an honorable woman, his slayer will
hardly spend a night in prison. He will generally be released on his
own recognizance; if he need bond, all his neighbors will volunteer
their aid. To these people, rape is a crime so monstrous that they do
not conceive that it can belong to the ordinary categories of crimes.
And it is undoubtedly true that when committed by one of an alien
and recently enslaved race, it has an increment of exasperation not
easy to estimate. The Paris mob would have burned the white
mayor of their city, had he been the guilty man in the monstrous
butchery of that pretty baby; but that their rage was the hotter because the wretch was a negro is most certain. And it would have
been so in Boston: "blood is thicker than water."

The unmistakable increase of this crime—the assaulting of
white women by negro men—enters into the explanation of these
burnings. Legal punishments had been tried, yet the crime increased. Shootings and hangings without law had been tried, yet
the crime increased. It is not to the purpose to remind me that the
increase of crime is, or may be, the natural effect of the unlawful
punishment of crime: I am writing of the influences that led to desperate and mad experiments with fire. Exasperations were cumula-
tive, as in continued doses of digitalis. This particular crime was
practically unknown before Emancipation. Only one case I heard
mentioned from my childhood till after the War. The criminal was
a slave, and he was burned. An ignorant race, that in and through
the ministry of slavery had grown into all that made it better than
naked Africans, were suddenly turned loose, without knowledge of
civil law, into a freedom they did not understand, mistaking most
naturally license for liberty. The recoil was tremendous. It is a wonder that the negro did not do worse. Presently came enfranchisement and complete citizenship without fitness of any sort. Under
the political influences that dominated the negro during the period
of reconstruction—more trying to Southern fortitude than the War
itself—he was taught, in order that others might secure and maintain political control of him, to hate the white people. The manner
of his enfranchisement and the methods employed by self-seeking
demagogues in controlling his vote led him to believe that the gift
of the ballot to him meant two things: first, the peculiar love the

North had for him; second, that it was given to him to keep the old masters and rebels down. The inevitable result was to tend to make the negro lawless in his dealings with his white neighbors.

Added to the evil influences that grew out of corrupt and corrupting reconstruction politics, were unwise methods in the earlier efforts to educate him. Many consecrated, noble-minded, but mistaken missionary-teachers from the North were more impressive, if not more insistent, in teaching the young negro his rights, than in teaching him the responsibilities of citizenship. The result was, he became more anxious to secure his rights than to fit himself for their exercise. All these influences developed in thousands of the younger negroes a spirit of insubordination to the social order. Crimes of violence against the white race were the natural fruitage of the influences that dominated the younger negroes. Under the conditions of Southern life it was inevitable that these crimes should be met by violent punishment without law, and partly for the reason that Southern government was in the hands of strangers and negroes.

* * *

I have called special attention to the influence upon the younger negroes of emancipation and what followed it, for the reason that the older negroes were less affected by the evils of that period. Nearly all crimes of violence by the negroes are committed by those who were children in 1865 or who have been born since that time. Nearly all the negroes in Southern penitentiaries are under thirty-five; if any wish to test these statements, the facts are of record. If men do not wish to take the trouble of looking into records, let them use their eyes. The older negroes, as a class, are the best citizens as well as the best laborers to-day, as all Southern people know.

In these statements is no plea against the education of the enfranchised negro, but an invincible argument for it—which for many years I have made, by pen and tongue, to the best of my ability. The negro must be educated. The conservative influences that secured order under the old *régime* are gone; the uneducated negro is unfitted for the new order. It is absolutely necessary to both races that his education go on. As a rule, rapists and murderers among Southern negroes are not only products of *post-bellum* life; they are uneducated. It is the rarest thing that an educated negro commits these crimes against virtue and life. The great body of the negro population of the country utterly reprobate these crimes. And there is among their leaders a growing sense of the duty of teaching their people that they must come to an end. And it is time for them to think these thoughts. Let their Northern friends and helpers and guides encourage and exhort them to follow these good impressions and impulses. It is vital to the negro race that those they look to for guidance should teach them that rape must cease. At this time let them lay the emphasis of exhortation and warning on this particular crime against the white race. If the negro preachers and negro school-teachers can be awakened to their duty as to this particular matter, they can do more than all others put together. They are everywhere in the South; there are thousands of them; their people look up to them. All primary schools for negro children are taught by negro men and women; all negro pulpits, with exceptions too few to count, are occupied by negro preachers. If these teachers and preachers are brought to understand that upon them, at this time, is the exigent duty of teaching their people that the assaulting of white women must cease; if they use their influence as they can and ought—denouncing rape as much as they do lynching—the crime will be less common in a few weeks; by and by it will be so rare that lynchings will come to an end.

In our extremity we look to wise and just people in the Northern States to help us, to help both races. Without Northern cooperation things will go from bad to worse. At least a million negroes can now read. Let our Northern friends more earnestly (well I know how earnestly many of them have done their duty in all these matters) help them to see that their education puts them under moral obligation to teach, to exhort and to warn their people, and they will begin to do these things. Let our Northern friends impress the negro preachers and teachers with the necessity of teaching, exhorting and warning their people against this particular crime, and they will begin to do these things.

Unless potent influences can be brought to bear upon the negro race that will awaken it to the enormity of assaulting white women, the worst for both races is yet to come and the most dreadful chapters in this sad and fearful history are yet to be written.

The Forum 16 (September 1893–February 1894): 167–75.

Ida B. Wells-Barnett

On Lynchings: Southern Horrors, A Red Record, Mob Rule in New Orleans (1892)

In 1892, a white mob lynched three successful African American businessmen in Memphis, Tennessee, for the crime of running a grocery store that had competed successfully with a local white business. Journalist Ida B. Wells, a friend of the victims, responded to this horror by undertaking a systematic study of lynching to expose the brutality African Americans endured in the Jim Crow South. Wells's statistics on extralegal executions demolished claims that lynchings were attempts to protect the honor of southern women, as attacks on black women regularly went unpunished. She argued further that African American success was the real offense white mobs punished with lynching. Wells continued to publish and speak out against lynching despite threats against her life and the destruction of her property, and brought white southern violence to international attention. Everywhere she went, she encouraged local women to form anti-lynching clubs to promote African American interests and nurture black female leader-ship. A staunch supporter of woman suffrage and one of two black women founders of the NAACP, Wells was for decades a powerful advocate for Afro-America.

Southern Horrors

Chapter I.

The Offense.

Wednesday evening May 24th, 1892, the city of Memphis was fined with excitement. Editorials in the daily papers of that date caused a meeting to be held in the Cotton Exchange Building; a committee was sent for the editors of the "Free Speech" an Afro-American journal published in that city, and the only reason the open threats of lynching that were made were not carried out was because they could not be found. The cause of all this commotion was the following editorial published in the "Free Speech" May 21st, 1892, the Saturday previous.

"Eight Negroes lynched since last issue of the "Free Speech" one at Little Rock, Ark., last Saturday morning where the citizens broke (?) into the penitentiary and got their man; three near Anniston, Ala., one near New Orleans; and three at Clarksville, Ga., the last three for killing a white man, and five on the same old racket—the new alarm about raping white women. The same programme of hanging, then shooting bullets into the lifeless bodies was carried out to the letter.

Nobody in this section of the country believes the old thread bare lie that Negro men rape white women. If Southern white men are not careful, they will over-reach themselves and public sentiment will have a reaction; a conclusion will then be reached which will be very damaging to the moral reputation of their women."

"The Daily Commercial" of Wednesday following, May 25th, contained the following leader:

"Those Negroes who are attempting to make the lynching of individuals of their race a means for arousing the worst passions of their kind are playing with a dangerous sentiment. The Negroes may as well understand that there is no mercy for the negro rapist and little patience with his defenders. A negro organ printed in this city, in a recent issue publishes the following atrocious paragraph: 'Nobody in this section of the country believes the old threadbare lie that negro men rape white women. If Southern white men are not careful they will over-reach themselves, and public sentiment will have a reaction; and a conclusion will be reached which will be very damaging to the moral reputation of their women.'

The fact that a black scoundrel is allowed to live and utter such loathsome and repulsive cal-umnies is a volume of evidence as to the won-derful patience of Southern whites. But we have had enough of it. There are some things that the Southern white man will not tolerate, and the obscene intimations of the foregoing have brought the writer to the very outermost limit of public patience, We hope we have said enough."

* * *

Acting upon this advice, the leading citizens met in the Cotton Exchange Building the same evening, and threats of lynching were freely indulged, not by, the lawless element upon which the deviltry of the South is usually, saddled but by the leading business men, in their leading business centre. Mr Fleming, the business manager and owning a half interest the Free Speech, had to leave town to escape the mob, and was afterwards ordered not to return; letters and telegrams sent me in New York where I was spending my vacation advised me that bodily harm awaited my return. Creditors took possession of the office and sold the outfit, and the "Free Speech" was as if it had never been.

The editorial in question was prompted by the many inhuman and fiendish lynching of Afro-Americans which have recently taken place and was meant as a warning. Eight lynched in one week and five of them charged with rape. The thinking public will not easily believe freedom and education more brutalizing than slavery, and the world knows that the crime of rape was unknown during four years of civil war, when the white women of the South were at the mercy of the race which is all at once charged with being a bestial one.

Since my business has been destroyed and I am au exile from home because of that editorial, the issue has been forced, and as the writer of it I feel that the race and the public generally should have a statement of the facts as they exist. They will serve at the same time as a defense for the Afro Americans Sampsons who suffer themselves to be betrayed by white Delilahs.

The whites of Montgomery, Ala., knew J. C. Duke sounded the keynote of the situation—which they would gladly hide from the world, when he said in his paper, "The Herald," five years ago: Why is it that white women attract negro men now more than in former days? There was a time when such a thing was unheard of. There is a secret to this thing, and we greatly suspect it is the growing appreciation of white Juliets for colored Romeos. "Mr. Duke, like the "Free Speech" proprietors, was forced to leave the city for reflecting on the "honah" of white women and his paper suppressed; but the truth remains that Afro-American men do not always rape (?) white women without their consent.

Mr. Duke, before leaving Montgomery, signed a card disclaiming any intention of slandering Southern white women. The editor of the "Free Speech" has no disclaimer to enter, but asserts instead that there are many white women in the South who would marry colored men if such an act would not place them at once beyond the pale of society and within the clutches of the law. The miscegenation laws of the South only operate against the legitimate union of the races; they leave the white man free to seduce all the colored girls he can, but it is death to the colored man who yields to the force and advances of a similar attraction in white women. White men lynch the offending Afro-American, not because he is a despoiler of virtue, but because he succumbs to the smiles of white women.

* * *

Chapter III

The New Cry.

* * *

To palliate this record (which grows worse as the Afro-American becomes intelligent) and excuse some of the most heinous crimes that ever stained the History of a country, the South is shielding itself behind the plausible screen of defending the honor of its women. This, too, in the face of the fact that only one-third of the 728 victims to mobs have been charged with rape, to say nothing of those of that one-third who were innocent of the charge. A white correspondent of the Baltimore Sun declares that the Afro-American who was lynched in Chestertown, Md., in May for assault on a white girl was innocent; that the deed was done by a white man who had since disappeared. The girl herself maintained that her assailant was a white man. When that poor Afro-American was murdered, the whites excused their refusal of a trial on the ground that they wished to spare the white girl the mortification of having to testify in court.

This cry has had its effect. It has closed the heart, stifled the conscience, warped the judgment and hushed the voice of press and pulpit on the subject of lynch law throughout this "land of liberty." Men who stand high in the esteem of the public for Christian character, for moral and physical courage, for devotion to the principles of equal and exact justice to all, and for great sagacity, stand as cowards who fear to open their mouths before this great outrage. They do not see that by their tacit encouragement, their silent acquiescence, the black shadow of lawlessness in the form of lynch law is spreading its wills over the whole country.

Men who, like Governor Tillman, start the ball of lynch law rolling for a certain crime, are powerless to stop it when drunken or criminal white toughs feel like hanging an Afro-American on any pretext.

Ida B. Wells-Barnett, *On Lynchings: Southern Horrors, A Red Record, Mob Rule in New Orleans* (Salem, NH, 1991), 12–31.

A Red Record

* * *

The Negro has suffered much and is willing to suffer more. He recognizes that the wrongs of two centuries can not be righted in a day, and he tries to bear his burden with patience for to-day and be hopeful for to-morrow. But there comes a time when the veriest worm will turn, and the Negro feels to-day that after all the work he has done, all the sacrifices he has made, and all the suffering he has endured, if he did not, now, defend his name and manhood from this vile accusation, he would be unworthy even of the contempt of mankind, it is to this charge he now feels he must make answer.

If the Southern people in defense of their lawlessness, would tell the truth and admit that colored men and women are lynched for almost any offense, from murder to a misdemeanor, there would not now be the necessity for this defense. But when they intentionally, maliciously and constantly be lie the record and bolster up these falsehoods by the words of legislators, preachers, governors and bishops, then the Negro must give to the world his side of the awful story. A word as to the charge itself. In considering the third reason assigned by the Southern white people for the butchery of blacks, the question must be asked, what the white man means when he charges the black man with rape. Does he mean the crime which the statutes of the civilized states describe as such? Not by any means. With the Southern white man, any misalliance existing between a white woman and a colored man is a sufficient foundation for the charge of rape. The Southern white man says that it is impossible for a voluntary alliance to exist between a white woman and a colored man, and therefore, the fact of an alliance is a proof of force. In numerous instances where colored men have been lynched on the charge of rape, it was positively known at the time of lynching, and indisputably proven after the victim's death, that the relationship sustained between the man and woman was voluntary and clandestine, and that in no court of law could even the charge of assault have been successfully maintained.

* * *

During all the years of slavery, no such charge was ever made, not even during the dark days of the rebellion, when the white man, following the fortunes of war went to do battle for the maintenance of slavery. While the master was away fighting to forge the fetters upon the slave, he left his wife and children with no protectors save the Negroes themselves. And yet during those years of trust and peril, no Negro proved recreant to his trust and no white man returned to a home that had been despoiled.

Likewise during the period of alleged "insurrection," and alarming "race riots," It never occurred to the white man, that his wife and children were in danger of assault. Nor in the Reconstruction era, when the hue and cry was against "Negro Domination," was there ever a thought that the domination would ever contaminate a fireside or strike to death the virtue of womanhood. It must appear strange Indeed, to every thoughtful and candid man, that more than a quarter of a century elapsed before the Negro began to show signs of such infamous degeneration.

In his remarkable apology for lynching, Bishop Haygood, of Georgia, says: "No race, not the most savage, tolerates the rape of woman, but it may be said without reflection upon any other people that the Southern people are now and always have been most sensitive concerning the honor of their women their mothers, wives, sisters and daughters." It is not the purpose of this defense to say one word against the white women of the South. Such need not be said, but it Is their misfortune that the chivalrous white men of that section, in order to escape the deserved execration of the civilized world, should shield themselves by their cowardly and infamously false excuse, and call into question that very honor about which their distinguished priestly apologist claims they are most sensitive. To justify their own barbarism they assume a chivalry which they do not possess. True chivalry respects all womanhood, and no one who reads the record, as it is written in the faces of the minion mulattos in the South, will for a minute conceive that the southern white man had a very chivalrous regard for the honor due the women of his own race or respect for the womanhood which circumstances placed in his power. That chivalry which is "most sensitive concerning the honor of women" can hope for but little respect from the civilized world, when it confines itself entirely to the women who happen to be white. Virtue knows no color line, and the chivalry which depends upon complexion of skill and texture of hair can command no honest respect.

* * *

The Negro may not have known what chivalry was, but he knew enough to preserve inviolate the womanhood of the South which was entrusted to his hands during the war. The finer sensibilities of his soul may have been crushed out by years of slavery, but his heart was full of gratitude to the white women of the North, who blessed his home and inspired his soul in all these years of freedom. Faithful to his trust in both of these instances, he should now have the impartial ear of the civilized world, when he dares to speak for himself as against the infamy wherewith he stands charged.

It is his regret, that, in his own defense, he must disclose to the world that degree of dehumanizing brutality which fixes upon America the blot of a national crime. Whatever faults and failings other nations may have in their dealings with their own subjects or with other people, no other civilized nation stands condemned before the world with a series of crimes so peculiarly national. It becomes a painful duty of the Negro to reproduce a record which shows that a large portion of the American people avow anarchy, condone murder and defy the contempt of civilization.

These pages are written in no spirit of vindictiveness, for all who give the subject consideration must concede that far too serious is the condition of that civilized government in which the spirit of unrestrained outlawry constantly increases in violence, and casts its blight over a continually growing area of territory. We plead not for the colored people alone, but for all victims of the terrible injustice which puts men and women to death without form of law. During the year 1894, there were 132 persons executed in the United States by due form of law, while in the same year, 197 persons were put to death by mobs who gave the victims no opportunity to make a lawful defense.

No comment need be made upon a condition of public sentiment responsible for such alarming results.

—————

Ida B. Wells-Barnett, *On Lynchings: Southern Horrors, A Red Record, Mob Rule in New Orleans* (Salem, NH, 1991), 51–69.

Plessy v. Ferguson, 163 U.S. 537 (1896)

During the 1880s and 1890s, courts and state legislatures steadily eroded the rights black citizens had recently gained through the legal watershed of Reconstruction. In response to an 1890 Louisiana state law requiring "equal but separate" accommodations for black and white passengers in railcars, a group of prosperous New Orleans men of mixed heritage formed the Citizens' Committee to Test the Constitutionality of the Separate Car Law. In an event planned in advance with the cooperation of the railroad company, Homer Plessy, a light-skinned Creole shoemaker, was arrested for sitting in the first-class "white" carriage. Convicted at the district court level by Judge John Howard Ferguson, Plessy's case was heard by the Supreme Court in 1896. Famed Republican jurist Albion Tourgeé argued that the law in question violated both the Thirteenth and the Fourteenth Amendments to the Constitution by establishing, as Plessy had argued before Judge Ferguson, an "insidious distinction and discrimination between citizens of the United States, based on race, which is obnoxious to the fundamental principles of national citizenship." This argument convinced only one justice, John Marshall Harlan, who wrote a stinging dissent to the majority decision in Plessy. *Considered a landmark decision in the history of Jim Crow, one of the most consequential effects of* Plessy *was the Court's embrace of white supremacist reasoning, especially its translation of public rights into social claims. As Justice Henry Billings Brown wrote in the decision, "[The Fourteenth Amendment] could not have been intended to abolish distinctions based on color, or to enforce social, as distinguished from political equality, or a commingling of the two races upon terms unsatisfactory to either."*

May 18, 1896, [163 U.S. 537, 538] This was a petition for writs of prohibition and certiorari originally filed in the supreme court of the state by Plessy, the plaintiff in error, against the Hon. John H.

Ferguson, judge of the criminal district court for the parish of Orleans, and setting forth, in substance, the following facts:

That petitioner was a citizen of the United States and a resident of the state of Louisiana, of mixed descent, in the proportion of seven-eighths Caucasian and one-eighth African blood; that the mixture of colored blood was not discernible in him, and that he was entitled to every recognition, right, privilege, and immunity secured to the citizens of the United States of the white race by its constitution and laws; that on June 7, 1892, he engaged and paid for a first-class passage on the East Louisiana Railway, from New Orleans to Covington, in the same state, and thereupon entered a passenger train, and took possession of a vacant seat in a coach where passengers of the white race were accommodated; that such railroad company was incorporated by the laws of Louisiana as a common carrier, and was not authorized to distinguish between citizens according to their race, but, notwithstanding this, petitioner was required by the conductor, under penalty of ejection from said train and imprisonment, to vacate said coach, and occupy another seat, in a coach assigned by said company for persons not of the white race, and for no other reason than that petitioner was of the colored race; that, upon petitioner's refusal to comply with such order, he was, with the aid of a police officer, forcibly ejected from said coach, and hurried off to, and imprisoned in, the parish jail of [163 U.S. 537, 539] New Orleans, and there held to answer a charge made by such officer to the effect that he was guilty of having criminally violated an act of the general assembly of the state, approved July 10, 1890, in such case made and provided.

* * *

Mr. Justice Harlan dissenting.

A. W. Tourgee and S. F. Phillips, for plaintiff in error.

Alex. Porter Morse, for defendant in error.

Mr. Justice BROWN, after stating the facts in the foregoing language, delivered the opinion of the court.

This case turns upon the constitutionality of an act of the general assembly of the state of Louisiana, passed in 1890, providing for separate railway carriages for the white and colored races. Acts 1890, No. 111, p. 152.

The first section of the statute enacts 'that all railway companies carrying passengers in their coaches in this state, shall provide equal but separate accommodations for the white, and colored races, by providing two or more passenger coaches for each passenger train, or by dividing the passenger coaches by a partition so as to secure separate accommodations: provided, that this section shall not be construed to apply to street railroads. No person or persons shall be permitted to occupy seats in coaches, other than the ones assigned to them, on account of the race they belong to.'

By the second section it was enacted 'that the officers of such passenger trains shall have power and are hereby required [163 U.S. 537, 541] to assign each passenger to the coach or compartment used for the race to which such passenger belongs; any passenger insisting on going into a coach or compartment to which by race he does not belong, shall be liable to a fine of twenty-five dollars, or in lieu thereof to imprisonment for a period of not more than twenty days in the parish prison, and any officer of any railroad insisting on assigning a passenger to a coach or compartment other than the one set aside for the race to which said passenger belongs, shall be liable to a fine of twenty-five dollars, or in lieu thereof to imprisonment for a period of not more than twenty days in the parish prison; and should any passenger refuse to occupy the coach or compartment to which he or she is assigned by the officer of such railway, said officer shall have power to refuse to carry such passenger on his train, and for such refusal neither he nor the railway company which he represents shall be liable for damages in any of the courts of this state.'

The third section provides penalties for the refusal or neglect of the officers, directors, conductors, and employees of railway companies to comply with the act, with a proviso that 'nothing in this act shall be construed as applying to nurses attending children of the other race.' The fourth section is immaterial.

The information filed in the criminal district court charged, in substance, that Plessy, being a passenger between two stations within the state of Louisiana, was assigned by officers of the company to the coach used for the race to which he belonged, but he insisted upon going into a coach used by the race to which he did not belong. Neither in the information nor plea was his particular race or color averred.

The petition for the writ of prohibition averred that petitioner was seven-eights Caucasian and one-eighth African blood; that the mixture of colored blood was not discernible in him; and that he was entitled to every right, privilege, and immunity secured to citizens of the United States of the white race; and that, upon such theory, he took possession of a vacant seat in a coach where passengers of the white race were accommodated, and was ordered by the conductor to vacate [163 U.S. 537, 542] said coach, and take a seat in another, assigned to persons of the colored race, and, having refused to comply with such demand, he was forcibly ejected, with the aid of a police officer, and imprisoned in the parish jail to answer a charge of having violated the above act.

The constitutionality of this act is attacked upon the ground that it conflicts both with the thirteenth amendment of the constitution, abolishing slavery, and the fourteenth amendment, which prohibits certain restrictive legislation on the part of the states.

* * *

A statute which implies merely a legal distinction between the white and colored races—a distinction which is founded in the color of the two races, and which must always exist so long as white men are distinguished from the other race by color—has no tendency to destroy the legal equality of the two races, or re-establish a state of involuntary servitude. Indeed, we do not understand that the thirteenth amendment is strenuously relied upon by the plaintiff in error in this connection.

By the fourteenth amendment, all persons born or naturalized in the United States, and subject to the jurisdiction thereof, are made citizens of the United States and of the state wherein they reside; and the states are forbidden from making or enforcing any law which shall abridge the privileges or immunities of citizens of the United States, or shall deprive any person of life, liberty, or property without due process of law, or deny to any person within their jurisdiction the equal protection of the laws.

* * *

The object of the amendment was undoubtedly to enforce the absolute equality of the two races before the law, but, in the nature of things, it could not have been intended to abolish distinctions

based upon color, or to enforce social, as distinguished from political, equality, or a commingling of the two races upon terms unsatisfactory to either. Laws permitting, and even requiring, their
separation, in places where they are liable to be brought into contact, do not necessarily imply the inferiority of either race to the
other, and have been generally, if not universally, recognized as
within the competency of the state legislatures in the exercise of
their police power. The most common instance of this is connected
with the establishment of separate schools for white and colored
children, which have been held to be a valid exercise of the legislative power even by courts of states where the political rights of the
colored race have been longest and most earnestly enforced.

* * *

Laws forbidding the intermarriage of the two races may be said
in a technical sense to interfere with the freedom of contract, and
yet have been universally recognized as within the police power of
the state. State v. Gibson, 36 Ind. 389.

* * *

In the Civil Rights Cases, 109 U.S. 3, 3 Sup. Ct. 18, it was held
that an act of congress entitling all persons within the jurisdiction
of the United States to the full and equal enjoyment of the accommodations, advantages, facilities, and privileges of inns, public conveyances, on land or water, theaters, and other places of public
amusement, and made applicable to citizens of every race and
color, regardless of any previous condition of servitude, was unconstitutional and void, upon the ground that the fourteenth
amendment was prohibitory upon the states only, and the legislation authorized to be adopted by congress for enforcing it was not
direct legislation on matters respecting which the states were prohibited from making or enforcing certain laws, or doing certain
acts, but was corrective legislation, such as might be necessary or
proper for counter-acting and redressing the effect of such laws or
acts. In delivering the opinion of the court, Mr. Justice Bradley observed that the fourteenth amendment 'does not invest congress
with power to legislate upon subjects that are within the [163 U.S.
537, 547] domain of state legislation, but to provide modes of relief against state legislation or state action of the kind referred to. It
does not authorize congress to create a code of municipal law for

the regulation of private rights, but to provide modes of redress against the operation of state laws, and the action of state officers, executive or judicial, when these are subversive of the fundamental rights specified in the amendment. Positive rights and privileges are undoubtedly secured by the fourteenth amendment; but they are secured by way of prohibition against state laws and state proceedings affecting those rights and privileges, and by power given to congress to legislate for the purpose of carrying such prohibition into effect; and such legislation must necessarily be predicated upon such supposed state laws or state proceedings, and be directed to the correction of their operation and effect.'

* * *

While we think the enforced separation of the races, as applied to the internal commerce of the state, neither abridges the privileges or immunities of the colored man, deprives him of his property without due process of law, nor denies him the equal protection of the laws, within the meaning of the fourteenth amendment, we are not prepared to say that the conductor, in assigning passengers to the coaches according to their race, does not act at his peril, or that the provision of the second section of the act that denies to the passenger compensa-[163 U.S. 537, 549] tion in damages for a refusal to receive him into the coach in which he properly belongs is a valid exercise of the legislative power. Indeed, we understand it to be conceded by the state's attorney that such part of the act as exempts from liability the railway company and its officers is unconstitutional. The power to assign to a particular coach obviously implies the power to determine to which race the passenger belongs, as well as the power to determine who, under the laws of the particular state, is to be deemed a white, and who a colored, person. This question, though indicated in the brief of the plaintiff in error, does not properly arise upon the record in this case, since the only issue made is as to the unconstitutionality of the act, so far as it requires the railway to provide separate accommodations, and the conductor to assign passengers according to their race.

It is claimed by the plaintiff in error that, in a mixed community, the reputation of belonging to the dominant race, in this instance the white race, is 'property,' in the same sense that a right of action or of inheritance is property. Conceding this to be so, for the purposes of this case, we are unable to see how this statute deprives him of, or in any way affects his right to, such property. If he be a white man, and assigned to a colored coach, he may have his action for damages against the company for being deprived of his so-called 'property.' Upon the other hand, if he be a colored man, and be so assigned, he has been deprived of no property, since he is not lawfully entitled to the reputation of being a white man.

In this connection, it is also suggested by the learned counsel for the plaintiff in error that the same argument that will justify the state legislature in requiring railways to provide separate accommodations for the two races will also authorize them to require separate cars to be provided for people whose hair is of a certain color, or who are aliens, or who belong to certain nationalities, or to enact laws requiring colored people to walk upon one side of the street, and white people upon the other, or requiring white men's houses to be painted white, and colored men's black, or their vehicles or business signs to be of different colors, upon the theory that one side [163 U.S. 537, 550] of the street is as good as the other, or that a house or vehicle of one color is as good as one of another color. The reply to all this is that every exercise of the police power must be reasonable, and extend only to such laws as are enacted in good faith for the promotion of the public good, and not for the annoyance or oppression of a particular class.

* * *

So far, then, as a conflict with the fourteenth amendment is concerned, the case reduces itself to the question whether the statute of Louisiana is a reasonable regulation, and with respect to this there must necessarily be a large discretion on the part of the legislature. In determining the question of reasonableness, it is at liberty to act with reference to the established usages, customs, and traditions of the people, and with a view to the promotion of their comfort, and the preservation of the public peace and good order. Gauged by this standard, we cannot say that a law which authorizes or even requires the separation of the two races in public conveyances [163 U.S. 537, 551] is unreasonable, or more obnoxious to the fourteenth amendment than the acts of congress requiring separate schools for colored children in the District of Columbia, the constitutionality of which does not seem to have been questioned, or the corresponding acts of state legislatures.

We consider the underlying fallacy of the plaintiff's argument to consist in the assumption that the enforced separation of the two races stamps the colored race with a badge of inferiority. If this be so, it is not by reason of anything found in the act, but solely because the colored race chooses to put that construction upon it. The argument necessarily assumes that if, as has been more than once the case, and is not unlikely to be so again, the colored race should become the dominant power in the state legislature, and should enact a law in precisely similar terms, it would thereby relegate the white race to an inferior position. We imagine that the white race, at least, would not acquiesce in this assumption. The argument also assumes that social prejudices may be overcome by legislation, and that equal rights cannot be secured to the negro except by an enforced commingling of the two races. We cannot accept this proposition. If the two races are to meet upon terms of social equality, it must be the result of natural affinities, a mutual appreciation of each other's merits, and a voluntary consent of individuals. . . . Legislation is powerless to eradicate racial instincts, or to abolish distinctions based upon physical differences, and the attempt to do so can only result in accentuating the difficulties of the present situation. If the civil and political rights of both races be equal, one cannot be inferior to the other civilly [163 U.S. 537, 552] or politically. If one race be inferior to the other socially, the constitution of the United States cannot put them upon the same plane.

It is true that the question of the proportion of colored blood necessary to constitute a colored person, as distinguished from a white person, is one upon which there is a difference of opinion in the different states; some holding that any visible admixture of black blood stamps the person as belonging to the colored race (State v. Chavers, 5 Jones [N. C.] 1); others, that it depends upon the preponderance of blood (Gray v. State, 4 Ohio, 354; Monroe v. Collins, 17 Ohio St. 665); and still others, that the predominance of white blood must only be in the proportion of three-fourths (People v. Dean, 14 Mich. 406; Jones v. Com., 80 Va. 544). But these are questions to be determined under the laws of each state, and are not properly put in issue in this case. Under the allegations of his petition, it may undoubtedly become a question of importance whether, under the laws of Louisiana, the petitioner belongs to the white or colored race.

The judgment of the court below is therefore affirmed.

Mr. Justice BREWER did not hear the argument or participate in the decision of this case.

Mr. Justice HARLAN dissenting.

By the Louisiana statute the validity of which is here involved, all railway companies (other than street-railroad companies) carry passengers in that state are required to have separate but equal accommodations for white and colored persons, 'by providing two or more passenger coaches for each passenger train, or by dividing the passenger coaches by a partition so as to secure separate accommodations.' Under this statute, no colored person is permitted to occupy a seat in a coach assigned to white persons; nor any white person to occupy a seat in a coach assigned to colored persons. The managers of the railroad are not allowed to exercise any discretion in the premises, but are required to assign each passenger to some coach or compartment set apart for the exclusive use of i[t]s race. If a passenger insists upon going into a coach or compartment not set apart for persons of his race, [163 U.S. 537, 553] he is subject to be fined, or to be imprisoned in the parish jail. Penalties are prescribed for the refusal or neglect of the officers, directors, conductors, and employees of railroad companies to comply with the provisions of the act.

* * *

Thus, the state regulates the use of a public highway by citizens of the United States solely upon the basis of race.

However apparent the injustice of such legislation may be, we have only to consider whether it is consistent with the constitution of the United States.

That a railroad is a public highway, and that the corporation which owns or operates it is in exercise of public functions, is not, at this day, to be disputed. . . . What else does this doctrine mean if not that building a railroad, though it be built by a private corporation, is an act done for a public use?' So, in Township of Pine

Grove v. Talcott, 19 Wall. 666, 676: 'Though the corporation [a railroad company] was private, its work was public, as much so as if it were to be constructed by the state.' So, in Inhabitants of Worcester v. Western R. Corp., 4 Metc. (Mass.) 564: 'The establishment of that great thoroughfare is regarded as a public work, established by public authority, intended for the public use and benefit, the use of which is secured to the whole community, and constitutes, therefore, like a canal, turnpike, or highway, a public easement.' 'It is true that the real and personal property, necessary to the establishment and management of the railroad, is vested in the corporation; but it is in trust for the public.'

In respect of civil rights, common to all citizens, the constitution of the United States does not, I think, permit any public authority to know the race of those entitled to be protected in the enjoyment of such rights. Every true man has pride of race, and under appropriate circumstances, when the rights of others, his equals before the law, are not to be affected, it is his privilege to express such pride and to take such action based upon it as to him seems proper. But I deny that any legislative body or judicial tribunal may have regard to the [163 U.S. 537, 555] race of citizens when the civil rights of those citizens are involved. Indeed, such legislation as that here in question is inconsistent not only with that equality of rights which pertains to citizenship, national and state, but with the personal liberty enjoyed by every one within the United States.

The thirteenth amendment does not permit the withholding or the deprivation of any right necessarily inhering in freedom. It not only struck down the institution of slavery as previously existing in the United States, but it prevents the imposition of any burdens or disabilities that constitute badges of slavery or servitude. It decreed universal civil freedom in this country. This court has so adjudged. But, that amendment having been found inadequate to the protection of the rights of those who had been in slavery, it was followed by the fourteenth amendment, which added greatly to the dignity and glory of American citizenship, and to the security of personal liberty, by declaring that 'all persons born or naturalized in the United States, and subject to the jurisdiction thereof, are citizens of the United States and of the state wherein they reside,' and that 'no state shall make or enforce any law which shall abridge the privileges or immunities of citizens of the United States; nor shall any state deprive any person of life, liberty or property without due process of law, nor deny to any person within its jurisdiction the equal protection of the laws.' These two amendments, if enforced according to their true intent and meaning, will protect all the civil rights that pertain to freedom and citizenship. Finally, and to the end that no citizen should be denied, on account of his race, the privilege of participating in the political control of his country, it was declared by the fifteenth amendment that 'the right of citizens of the United States to vote shall not be denied or abridged by the United States or by any state on account of race, color or previous condition of servitude.'

These notable additions to the fundamental law were welcomed by the friends of liberty throughout the world. They removed the race line from our governmental systems. They had, as this court has said, a common purpose, namely, to secure 'to a race recently emancipated, a race that through [163 U.S. 537, 556] many generations have been held in slavery, all the civil rights that the superior race enjoy.' They declared, in legal effect, this court has further said, 'that the law in the states shall be the same for the black as for the white; that all persons, whether colored or white, shall stand equal before the laws of the states; and in regard to the colored race, for whose protection the amendment was primarily designed, that no discrimination shall be made against them by law because of their color.' We also said: 'The words of the amendment, it is true, are prohibitory, but they contain a necessary implication of a positive immunity or right, most valuable to the colored race,—the right to exemption from unfriendly legislation against them distinctively as colored; exemption from legal discriminations, implying inferiority in civil society, lessening the security of their enjoyment of the rights which others enjoy; and discriminations which are steps towards reducing them to the condition of a subject race' . . . At the present term, referring to the previous adjudications, this court declared that 'underlying all of those decisions is the principle that the constitution of the United States, in its present form, forbids, so far as civil and political rights are concerned, discrimination by the general government or the states against any citizen because of his race. All citizens are equal before the law.' Gibson v. State, 162 U.S. 565, 16 Sup. Ct. 904.

* * *

It was said in argument that the statute of Louisiana does [163 U.S. 537, 557] not discriminate against either race, but prescribes a rule applicable alike to white and colored citizens. But this argument does not meet the difficulty. Every one knows that the statute in question had its origin in the purpose, not so much to exclude white persons from railroad cars occupied by blacks, as to exclude colored people from coaches occupied by or assigned to white persons. Railroad corporations of Louisiana did not make discrimination among whites in the matter of commodation for travelers. The thing to accomplish was, under the guise of giving equal accommodation for whites and blacks, to compel the latter to keep to themselves while traveling in railroad passenger coaches.

* * *

It is one thing for railroad carriers to furnish, or to be required by law to furnish, equal accommodations for all whom they are under a legal duty to carry. It is quite another thing for government to forbid citizens of the white and black races from traveling in the same public conveyance, and to punish officers of railroad companies for permitting persons of the two races to occupy the same passenger coach. If a state can prescribe, as a rule of civil conduct, that whites and blacks shall not travel as passengers in the same railroad coach, why may it not so regulate the use of the streets of its cities and towns as to compel white citizens to keep on one side of a street, and black citizens to keep on the other? Why may it not, upon like grounds, punish whites and blacks who ride together in street cars or in open vehicles on a public road [163 U.S. 537, 558] or street? Why may it not require sheriffs to assign whites to one side of a court room, and blacks to the other? And why may it not also prohibit the commingling of the two races in the galleries of legislative halls or in public assemblages convened for the consideration of the political questions of the day? Further, if this statute of Louisiana is consistent with the personal liberty of citizens, why may not the state require the separation in railroad coaches of native and naturalized citizens of the United States, or of Protestants and Roman Catholics?

* * *

The white race deems itself to be the dominant race in this country. And so it is, in prestige, in achievements, in education, in wealth, and in power. So, I doubt not, it will continue to be for all time, if it remains true to its great heritage, and holds fast to the principles of constitutional liberty. But in view of the constitution, in the eye of the law, there is in this country no superior, dominant, ruling class of citizens. There is no caste here. Our constitution is color-blind, and neither knows nor tolerates classes among citizens. In respect of civil rights, all citizens are equal before the law. The humblest is the peer of the most powerful. The law regards man as man, and takes no account of his surroundings or of his color when his civil rights as guarantied by the supreme law of the land are involved. It is therefore to be regretted that this high tribunal, the final expositor of the fundamental law of the land, has reached the conclusion that it is competent for a state to regulate the enjoyment by citizens of their civil rights solely upon the basis of race.

In my opinion, the judgment this day rendered will, in time, prove to be quite as pernicious as the decision made by this tribunal in the Dred Scott Case.

It was adjudged in that case that the descendants of Africans who were imported into this country, and sold as slaves, were not included nor intended to be included under the word 'citizens' in the constitution, and could not claim any of the rights and privileges which that instrument provided for and secured to citizens of the United States; that, at time of the adoption of the constitution, they were 'considered as a subordinate and inferior class of beings, who had been subjugated by the dominant [163 U.S. 537, 560] race, and, whether emancipated or not, yet remained subject to their authority, and had no rights or privileges but such as those who held the power and the government might choose to grant them.' 17 How. 393, 404. The recent amendments of the constitution, it was supposed, had eradicated these principles from our institutions. But it seems that we have yet, in some of the states, a dominant race,—a superior class of citizens,—which assumes to regulate the enjoyment of civil rights, common to all citizens, upon the basis of race. The present decision, it may well be apprehended, will not only stimulate aggressions, more or less brutal and irritating, upon the admitted rights of colored citizens, but will encourage the belief that it is possible, by means of state enactments, to defeat the beneficent purposes which the people of the United States had in view when they adopted the recent amendments of the constitution, by one of which the blacks of this country were made citizens of the United States and of the states in which they respectively reside, and whose privileges and immunities, as citizens, the states are forbidden to abridge. Sixty millions of whites are in no danger from the presence here of eight millions of blacks. The destinies of the two races, in this country, are indissolubly linked together, and the interests of both require that the common government of all shall not permit the seeds of race hate to be planted under the sanction of law. What can more certainly arouse race hate, what more certainly create and perpetuate a feeling of distrust between these races, than state enactments which, in fact, proceed on the ground that colored citizens are so inferior and degraded that they cannot be allowed to sit in public coaches occupied by white citizens? That, as all will admit, is the real meaning of such legislation as was enacted in Louisiana.

The sure guaranty of the peace and security of each race is the clear, distinct, unconditional recognition by our governments, national and state, of every right that inheres in civil freedom, and of the equality before the law of all citizens of the United States, without regard to race. State enactments regulating the enjoyment of civil rights upon the basis of race, and cunningly devised to defeat legitimate results of the [163 U.S. 537, 561] war, under the pretense of recognizing equality of rights, can have no other result than to render permanent peace impossible, and to keep alive a conflict of races, the continuance of which must do harm to all concerned. This question is not met by the suggestion that social equality cannot exist between the white and black races in this country. That argument, if it can be properly regarded as one, is scarcely worthy of consideration; for social equality no more exists between two races when traveling in a passenger coach or a public highway than when members of the same races sit by each other in a street car or in the jury box, or stand or sit with each other in a political assembly, or when they use in common the streets of a city or town, or when they are in the same room for the purpose of having their names placed on the registry of voters, or when they approach the ballot box in order to exercise the high privilege of voting.

There is a race so different from our own that we do not permit those belonging to it to become citizens of the United States. Persons belonging to it are, with few exceptions, absolutely excluded from our country. I allude to the Chinese race. But, by the statute in question, a Chinaman can ride in the same passenger coach with white citizens of the United States, while citizens of the black race in Louisiana, many of whom, perhaps, risked their lives for the preservation of the Union, who are entitled, by law, to participate in the political control of the state and nation, who are not excluded, by law or by reason of their race, from public stations of any kind, and who have all the legal rights that belong to white citizens, are yet declared to be criminals, liable to imprisonment, if they ride in a public coach occupied by citizens of the white race. It is scarcely just to say that a colored citizen should not object to occupying a public coach assigned to his own race. He does not object, nor, perhaps, would he object to separate coaches for his race if his rights under the law were recognized. But he does object, and he ought never to cease objecting, that citizens of the white and black races can be adjudged criminals because they sit, or claim the right to sit, in the same public coach on a public highway. [163 U.S. 537, 562] The arbitrary separation of citizens, on the basis of race, while they are on a public highway, is a badge of servitude wholly inconsistent with the civil freedom and the equality before the law established by the constitution. It cannot be justified upon any legal grounds.

If evils will result from the commingling of the two races upon public highways established for the benefit of all, they will be infinitely less than those that will surely come from state legislation regulating the enjoyment of civil rights upon the basis of race. We boast of the freedom enjoyed by our people above all other peoples. But it is difficult to reconcile that boast with a state of the law which, practically, puts the brand of servitude and degradation upon a large class of our fellow citizens,—our equals before the law. The thin disguise of 'equal' accommodations for passengers in railroad coaches will not mislead any one, nor atone for the wrong this day done.

* * *

I am of opinion that the state of Louisiana is inconsistent with the personal liberty of citizens, white and black, in that state, and hostile to both the spirit and letter of the constitution of the United States. If laws of like character should be enacted in the several states of the Union, the effect would be in the highest degree mischievous. Slavery, as an institution tolerated by law, would, it is true, have disappeared from our country; but there would remain a power in the states, by sinister legislation, to interfere with the full enjoyment of the blessings of freedom, to regulate civil rights, common to all citizens, upon the basis of race, and to place in a condition of legal inferiority a large body of American citizens, now constituting a part of the political community, called the [163 U.S. 537, 564] 'People of the United States,' for whom, and by whom through representatives, our government is administered. Such a system is inconsistent with the guaranty given by the constitution to each state of a republican form of government, and may be stricken down by congressional action, or by the courts in the discharge of their solemn duty to maintain the supreme law of the land, anything in the constitution or laws of any state to the contrary notwithstanding.

* * *

Congressional Debate on the Treaty of Paris: Benjamin Ryan Tillman and George White (1899)

When Cuban revolutionaries revolted against Spain's colonial control over Cuba in 1895, Americans observed their progress with intense interest. The unexplained explosion of the U.S.S. Maine_'s forward gunpowder magazines and the battleship's subsequent sinking in Havana's harbor in 1898 spurred the United States to intervene in the conflict and declare war on Spain. The Treaty of Paris, which ended the brief war (if not the fighting in the Philippines),_ *granted the United States formal authority over Guam, Puerto Rico, and the Philippine Islands. Although many Americans were enthusiastic about the benefits they expected to flow from these new colonial possessions, a vocal minority opposed the creation of a sprawling American empire on moral and political grounds. Scientific racism informed debate on both sides as Americans again confronted questions about the relationship between citizenship and race, at home as well as abroad.*

Senator Benjamin Tillman of South Carolina

Speech on the Treaty of Paris
(February 7, 1899)

As though coming at the most opportune time possible, you might say, just before the treaty reached the Senate, or about the time it was sent to us, there appeared in one of our magazines a poem by Rudyard Kipling, the greatest poet of England at this time. Mr. President, this poem, unique, and in some places difficult to understand, is to my mind a prophecy. I do not imagine that in the history of human events any poet has ever felt inspired so clearly to portray our danger and our duty. It is called "The White Man's Burden." With the permission of Senators I will read a stanza, and I beg them to listen to it, for it is well worth their attention. This man has lived in the Indies. In fact he is a citizen of the world, and has been all over it, and knows whereof he speaks.

> Take up the White Man's burden—
>   Send forth the best ye breed—
> Go, bind your sons to exile,
>   To serve your captive's need;
> To wait, in heavy harness,
>   On fluttered folk and wild—
> Your new-caught sullen peoples,
>   Half devil and half child.

Mr. President, I will pause here. I intend to read more, but I wish to call attention to a fact which may have escaped the attention of

Senators thus far, that with five exceptions every man in this Chamber who has had to do with the colored race in this country voted against the ratification of the treaty. It was not because we are Democrats, but because we understand and realize what it is to have two races side by side that can not mix or mingle without deterioration and injury to both and the ultimate destruction of the civilization of the higher. We of the South have borne this white man's burden of a colored race in our midst since their emancipation and before.

It was a burden upon our manhood and our ideas of liberty before they were emancipated. It is still a burden, although they have been granted the franchise. It clings to us like the shirt of Nessus, and we are not responsible, because we inherited it, and your fathers as well as ours are responsible for the presence amongst us of that people. Why do we as a people want to incorporate into our citizenship ten millions more of different or of differing races, three or four of them?

* * *

Ah, if we have no other consideration, if no feeling of humanity, no love of our fellows, no regard for others' rights, if nothing but our self-interest shall actuate us in this crisis, let me say to you that if we go madly on in the direction of crushing the Philippines into subjection and submission we will do so at the cost of many, many thousands of the flower of American youth. There are 10,000,000 of these people, some of them fairly well civilized, and running to the other extreme of naked savages, who are reported in our press dispatches as having stood out in the open and fired their bows and arrows, not flinching from the storm of shot and shell thrown into their midst by the American soldiers last Sunday.

The report of the battle claims that we lost only 75 killed and a hundred and odd wounded; but the first skirmish has carried with it what anguish, what desolation, to homes in a dozen States! How many more victims are we to offer up on this altar of Mammon or national greed? When those regiments march back, if they return with decimated ranks, as they are bound to come, if we have to send thousands and tens of thousands of reenforcements there to press onward until we have subdued those ten millions, at whose door will lie these lives—their blood shed for what? An idea. If a man fires upon the American flag, shoot the last man and kill him, no matter how many Americans have to be shot to do it.

The city of Manila is surrounded by swamps and marshes, I am told. A few miles back lie the woods and jungles and mountains. These people are used to the climate. They know how to get about, and if they mean to have their liberties, as they appear to do, at what sacrifice will the American domination be placed over them? Here is another verse of Kipling. I have fallen in love with this man. He tells us what we will reap:

> Take up the White Man's burden,
>   And reap his old reward—
> The blame of those ye better,
>   The hate of those ye guard—
> The cry of hosts ye humor
>   (Ah, slowly!) toward the light—
> "Why brought ye us from bondage,
>   Our loved Egyptian night?"

Those peoples are not suited to our institutions. They are not ready for liberty as we understand it. They do not want it. Why are we bent on forcing upon them a civilization not suited to them and which only means in their view degradation and a loss of self-respect, which is worse than the loss of life itself?

———————

Congressional Record, 55th Congress, 3rd Session, vol. 32, pp. 1531–32.

George White of North Carolina

Speech in the House of Representatives (January 26, 1899)

Mr. Chairman, I supported very cheerfully all measures tending to bring about the recent war for liberating a very much oppressed and outraged people. I supported with equal cheer all appropriations that were necessary for the successful prosecution of that war to a final termination. I thought it was necessary then; I think now that it was a necessity. It has been the province of the people of the

United States at all times to extend a helping hand to the oppressed, to the outraged—I mean, of course, without the borders of the United States.

* * *

Mr. Chairman, it is not so much on account of the recent war with Spain, or the money it took to carry on that war, or the annexation of Cuba, or Porto Rico, or the Philippine Islands that I desire to speak, nor is it so much the pending bill we have before us that I desire to address myself to this House.

But it is another problem, possibly more vexing than the one we have now under consideration. I know that you will pardon me if I do not address myself to the question before us when you recollect that I am the only representative on this floor of 10,000,000 people, from a racial standpoint. They have no one else to speak for them, from a race point of view, except myself. I shall therefore address the remainder of my remarks to another phase of the situation in this country—to another great problem that confronts us, and one which I trust ere long we shall have the manhood to stand up in our places and meet like American citizens, not like sectional cowards. I refer to the race problem. I have sat here in my place and heard discussions pro and con; I have heard my race referred to in terms anything else than dignified and complimentary. I have heard them referred to as savages, as aliens, as brutes, as vile and vicious and worthless, and I have heard but little or nothing said with reference to their better qualities, their better manhood, their developed American citizenship. It is therefore in reply to those seemingly unguarded expressions that I wish to speak.

I have listened to gentlemen here—particularly one of the gentlemen from the State of Mississippi [Mr. WILLIAMS] in his great eloquence about "white supremacy"—just here permit me to say that I have no respect for a "supremacy," white or black, which has been obtained through fraud, intimidation, carnage, and death— "white supremacy" in the great State of Mississippi; about the Anglo-Saxon ruling this country. I did not know that it required any specific reference of this kind for the world to know the fact that the Anglo-Saxon will rule the United States. We constitute as a race less than one-seventh, possibly, of the population. We have been enslaved; we have done your bidding for two hundred and forty years without any compensation; and we did it faithfully. We do not revert to it grumblingly or regretfully, but we refer to it because it seems ungracious in you now, after you have had all this advantage of us, after you have had all this labor of ours, to be unwilling, at this late day, to give us a man's share in the race of life.

That is the only sense in which I refer to it. It is not with a view to digging up the past. It is not with a view of kindling renewed animosity between the races, but only in answer to those who slur at us and remind us of our inferiority. Yes, by force of circumstances, we are your inferiors. Give us two hundred and forty years the start of you, give us your labor for two hundred and forty years without compensation, give us the wealth that the brawny arm of the black man made for you, give us the education that his unpaid labor gave your boys and girls, and we will not be begging, we will not be in a position to be sneered at as aliens or members of an inferior race. Not at all.

We are inferior. We regret it. But if you will only allow us an opportunity we will amend our ways, we will increase our usefulness, we will become more and more intelligent, more and more useful to the nation. It is a chance in the race of life that we crave. We do not expect any special legislation. We do not expect the mythical "40 acres and a mule."

The mule died long ago of old age, and the land grabbers have obtained the 40 acres. We do not expect any of those things. But we have a right to expect a man's chance and opportunity to carve out our own destiny. That is all we ask, and that we demand.

This problem is confronting the nation. We seem as a race to be going through just now a crucible, a crisis—a peculiar crisis. It is not necessary, nor have I the time, to enter into any explanation as to what brought about this crisis. I may say, however, in passing, that possibly more than by any other one thing it has been brought about by the fact that despite all the oppression which has fallen upon our shoulders we have been rising, steadily rising, and in some instances we hope ere long to be able to measure our achievements with those of all other men and women of the land. This tendency on the part of some of us to rise and assert our manhood along all lines is, I fear, what has brought about this changed condition.

Shall the nation stand by listlessly, or shall it uphold the principles that it has established? Shall it recognize, as declared in the organic law, that all men are born free and equal and are endowed
with certain inalienable rights, among which are life, liberty, and
the pursuit of happiness?

* * *

Now, the problem to which I refer not only touches my people,
but in my humble judgment it reaches out and ramifies and affects
every citizen of the American Republic. How long will we sit—I
say "we." I will sit here only two years longer, should I live, and I
am going to try mighty hard to live that long. How long will you sit
in your seats here and see the principles that underlie the foundation of this Government sapped little by little, but nevertheless
surely sapped away? I took the pains this afternoon to run over one
or two of the States that have been harping, through their representatives, most about the colored man on this floor since I have
been in Congress.

I took up Mississippi, because I recall that two gentlemen from
that State especially—I have reference to Congressman ALLEN and
Congressman WILLIAMS—have taken special pains on several occasions to refer to the negro; they referred to him in a slurring way,
referred to him as something to be managed, referred to him as
something to be gotten rid of, referred to him as somebody that
must be—oh, well, Congressman ALLEN told a yarn here one
day—"transferred," I believe he called it. He must be "transferred." Well, now, here is the situation. I could not say much with
reference to him, but here is the situation, taking his district in the
State of Mississippi.

I deal with 1896, because I could not get the figures of last November. I find in the gentleman's district there were only 8,418
votes cast for all the candidates in that district, while the estimated
vote of the district is 28,663. I found in the Second district that the
estimated vote was 34,102. The Congressman said that he got a
plurality of 254 over his opponent, but did not give us the benefit
of how many he got. I presume a few thousand. In the Third district the estimated vote is 36,859, and 4,050 were cast in the Presidential election of 1896. I found in the Fourth district there was an

estimated vote of 42,647. There were votes cast for all the candidates, Democrats, Republicans, Populists, Free-soilers, hottentots,
and everybody else, 11,737.

* * *

I find in the State of South Carolina, adjoining the State that I
hail from, a similar situation of affairs. I suppose I might give these
facts and figures, because the public would like to know these
things, and everyone can not get hold of a Congressional Directory.

In the First district of South Carolina the estimated vote is
34,664; the vote cast, 7,303. In the Second district the estimated
vote is 29,265; the vote cast, 8,634. In the Third district the estimated vote is 30,412 and the votes cast 10,536, or about one-third.

In the Fourth district the estimated vote is 40,000; the vote cast,
12,180. In the Fifth district the estimated vote is 28,350, and the
vote cast is 8,833.

In the Sixth district the estimated vote is 30,770, and we have
this entry, no figures being given at all:

> Elected as a Democrat without opposition, having received the en-
> tire vote cast.

A popular man! In the Seventh district the estimated vote is
35,736, while the vote cast was 9,407. The total vote cast, leaving
out those two districts where the gentlemen did not give the public
the benefit of the votes cast for them—the total vote cast for
Congressmen in that State in that election was 56,953, while the
estimated vote of the State of South Carolina is about 250,000,
about one-fifth of the entire voting population having actually
voted.

Now, I am not going to grumble about the number of votes that
you cast down there in South Carolina, but I want to say to the
Congress of the United States, and through Congress to the people
of the United States, that South Carolina, Louisiana, Mississippi,
and every other State in this Union ought to have the benefit of the
votes that are allowed to be cast in their representation on this floor,
and no more.

It is not fair to the other States of the Union to say that one gentleman shall come here from a district giving 30,000, 40,000,
50,000, or even 60,000 votes, and that a district in Mississippi or a

district in Louisiana or a district in South Carolina, or possibly pretty soon a district in North Carolina, shall come here with a like population with only five or six thousand votes cast, with the others disfranchised and not allowed to vote. If we are unworthy of suffrage, if it is necessary to maintain white supremacy, if it is necessary for the Anglo-Saxon to sway the scepter in those States, then you ought to have the benefit only of those who are allowed to vote, and the poor men, whether they be black or white, who are disfranchised ought not to go into the representation of the district or the State. It is a question that this House must deal with some time, sooner or later.

It may seem a little strange to hear me speak, but nobody else has tackled this question because the boot does not pinch anybody else as it does me and my race. But it will come home to you. You will have to meet it. You have got this problem to settle, and the sooner it is settled the better it will be for all parties concerned. I speak this in all charity. I speak this with no hostility. I am not a pessimist. I take rather the other view. I am optimistic in my views and believe that these problems will adjust themselves one day. I believe that the negro problem in less than fifty years will be a thing of the past.

* * *

Recognize your citizen at home, recognize those at your door, give them the encouragement, give them the rights that they are justly entitled to, and then take hold of the people of Cuba and help establish a stable and fixed government among them; take hold of the Porto Ricans, establish the government there that wisdom predicated, which justice may dictate. Take hold of the Philippine Islands, take hold of the Hawaiian Islands, there let the Christian civilization go out and magnify and make happy those poor, half-civilized people; and then the black man, the white man—yes, all the riff-raff of the earth that are coming to our shores—will rejoice with you in that we have done God's service and done that which will elevate us in the eyes of the world. [Prolonged applause.]

Congressional Record, 55th Congress, 3rd Session, vol. 32, pp. 1124–26.

Paul Lawrence Dunbar

An Ante-Bellum Sermon (1896)

The son of former slaves, Paul Lawrence Dunbar was the first African American poet to gain a national readership. A prolific novelist, essayist, and short-story writer as well as poet, Dunbar was a master of the dialect writing employed by Joel Chandler Harris (in his "Uncle Remus" stories) and others in the late nineteenth century. In the 1920s and 1930s, Dunbar's dialect poetry and his romantic portrait of plantation slave life was criticized by African American writers and activists such as poet and NAACP leader James Weldon Johnson, who considered Dunbar's writings a capitulation to racist stereotypes. This charge cannot be leveled at "An Ante-bellum Sermon," which was composed in 1896 and considered by contemporaries and later readers a protest against the ever-tightening bands of Jim Crow. Himself part of the generation of "New Negroes" who were born in freedom and raised to vote, Dunbar set this poem in the brush arbor Christianity of the slave past. Calling on the deep and lasting connections between African American religion and politics, Dunbar exhorts against fatalism and, in the tradition of Uncle Remus but with an agenda different from that of Joel Chandler Harris, celebrates the wiliness of politically aware slaves.

WE is gathahed hyeah, my brothahs,
    In dis howlin' wildaness,
Fu' to speak some words of comfo't
    To each othah in distress.
An' we chooses fu' ouah subjic'
    Dis—we'll 'splain it by an' by;
"An' de Lawd said, 'Moses, Moses,'
    An' de man said, 'Hyeah am I.'"

Now ole Pher'oh, down in Egypt,
    Was de wuss man evah bo'n,
An' he had de Hebrew chillun
    Down dah wukin' in his co'n;
'Twell de Lawd got tiahed o' his foolin',
    An' sez he: "I'll let him know—

Look hyeah, Moses, go tell Pher'oh
   Fu' to let dem chillun go."

"An' ef he refuse to do it,
   I will make him rue de houah,

Fu' I'll empty down on Egypt
   All de vials of my powah."
Yes, he did—an' Pher'oh's ahmy
   Was n't wuth a ha'f a dime;
Fu' de Lawd will he'p his chillun,
   You kin trust him evah time.

An' yo' enemies may 'sail you
   In de back an' in de front;
But de Lawd is all aroun' you,
   Fu' to ba' de battle's brunt.
Dey kin fo'ge yo' chains an' shackles
   F'om de mountains to de sea;
But de Lawd will sen' some Moses
   Fu' to set his chillun free.

An' de lan' shall hyeah his thundah,
   Lak a blas' f'om Gab'el's ho'n,
Fu' de Lawd of hosts is mighty
   When he girds his ahmor on,
But fu' feah some one mistakes me,
   I will pause right hyeah to say,
Dat I 'm still a-preachin' ancient,
   I ain't talkin' 'bout to-day.

But I tell you, fellah christuns,
   Things 'll happen mighty strange;
Now, de Lawd done dis fu' Isrul,
   An' his ways don't nevah change,
An' de love he showed to Isrul
   Was n't all on Isrul spent;
Now don't run an' tell yo' mastahs
   Dat I 's preachin' discontent.

'Cause I is n't; I 'se a-judgin'
　　Bible people by deir ac's;
I 'se a-givin' you de Scriptuah,
　　I 'se a-handin' you de fac's.
Cose ole Pher'oh b'lieved in slav'ry,
　　But de Lawd he let him see,
Dat de people he put bref in,—
　　Evah mothah's son was free.

An' dahs othahs thinks lak Pher'oh,
　　But dey calls de Scriptuah liar,
Fu' de Bible says "a servant
　　Is a-worthy of his hire."
An' you cain't git roun' nor thoo dat,
　　An' you cain't git ovah it,
Fu' whatevah place you git in,
　　Dis hyeah Bible too 'll fit.

So you see de Lawd's intention,
　　Evah sence de worl' began,
Was dat His almighty freedom
　　Should belong to evah man,
But I think it would be bettah,
　　Ef I 'd pause agin to say,
Dat I 'm talkin' 'bout ouah freedom
　　In a Bibleistic way.

But de Moses is a-comin',
　　An' he 's comin', suah and fas'
We kin hyeah his feet a-trompin',
　　We kin hyeah his trumpit blas'.
But I want to wa'n you people,
　　Don't you git too brigity;
An' don't you git to braggin'
　　'Bout dese things, you wait an' see.

But when Moses wif his powah
　　Comes an' sets us chillun free,
We will praise de gracious Mastah
　　Dat has gin us liberty;

An' we 'll shout ouah halleluyahs,
On dat mighty reck'nin' day,
When we 'se reco'nised ez citiz'—
Huh uh! Chillun, let us pray!

Paul Lawrence Dunbar, *Lyrics of Lowly Life* (New York, 1896). Accessed April 21, 2005 at http://www.libraries.wright.edu/dunbar/lowly2.html.

W. E. B. Du Bois

Of Mr. Booker T. Washington and Others (1906)

In 1903, W. E. B. Du Bois, a professor of sociology at Atlanta University, published The Souls of Black Folk, *a book of essays that earned him acclaim and new prominence as a public intellectual and African American political voice. In "Of Mr. Booker T. Washington and Others," Du Bois attacked the political vision of the most prominent African American of the day. At the height of Jim Crow's assault on black Americans' rights, Washington, a former slave and president of the Tuskegee Institute, advocated acquiescing to the erosion of black social and political rights and focusing on private endeavor and economic improvement. Du Bois and other, largely northern, black leaders objected fiercely to Washington's approach, and they urged African Americans to challenge the injustices they faced in the southern states.*

Easily the most striking thing in the history of the American Negro since 1876 is the ascendancy of Mr. Booker T. Washington. It began at the time when war memories and ideals were rapidly passing; a day of astonishing commercial development was dawning; a sense of doubt and hesitation overtook the freedmen's sons,—then it was that his leading began. Mr. Washington came, with a simple definite programme, at the psychological moment when the nation was a little ashamed of having bestowed so much sentiment on Negroes, and was concentrating its energies on Dollars. His programme of industrial education, conciliation of the South, and submission and silence as to civil and political rights, was not wholly original; the Free Negroes from 1830 up to war-time had striven to build industrial schools, and the American Missionary Association had from the first taught various trades; and Price and others had sought a way of honorable alliance with the best of the Southerners. But Mr. Washington first indissolubly linked these things; he put enthusiasm, unlimited energy, and perfect faith into this programme, and changed it from a by-path into a veritable Way of Life. And the tale of the methods by which he did this is a fascinating study of human life.

It startled the nation to hear a Negro advocating such a programme after many decades of bitter complaint; it startled and won the applause of the South, it interested and won the admiration of the North; and after a confused murmur of protest, it silenced if it did not convert the Negroes themselves.

To gain the sympathy and coöperation of the various elements comprising the white South was Mr. Washington's first task; and this, at the time Tuskegee was founded, seemed, for a black man, well-nigh impossible. And yet ten years later it was done in the word spoken at Atlanta: "In all things purely social we can be as separate as the five fingers, and yet one as the hand in all things essential to mutual progress." This "Atlanta Compromise" is by all odds the most notable thing in Mr. Washington's career. The South interpreted it in different ways: the radicals received it as a complete surrender of the demand for civil and political equality; the conservatives, as a generously conceived working basis for mutual understanding. So both approved it, and to-day its author is certainly the most distinguished Southerner since Jefferson Davis, and the one with the largest personal following.

Next to this achievement comes Mr. Washington's work in gaining place and consideration in the North. Others less shrewd and tactful had formerly essayed to sit on these two stools and had fallen between them; but as Mr. Washington knew the heart of the South from birth and training, so by singular insight he intuitively grasped the spirit of the age which was dominating the North. And so thoroughly did he learn the speech and thought of triumphant commercialism, and the ideals of material prosperity, that the picture of a lone black boy poring over a French grammar amid the weeds and dirt of a neglected home soon seemed to him the acme of absurdities. One wonders what Socrates and St. Francis of Assisi would say to this.

And yet this very singleness of vision and thorough oneness with his age is a mark of the successful man. It is as though Nature must needs make men narrow in order to give them force. So Mr. Washington's cult has gained unquestioning followers, his work has wonderfully prospered, his friends are legion, and his enemies are confounded. To-day he stands as the one recognized spokesman of his ten million fellows, and one of the most notable figures in a nation of seventy millions. One hesitates, therefore, to criticise a life which, beginning with so little, has done so much. And yet the time is come when one may speak in all sincerity and utter courtesy of the mistakes and shortcomings of Mr. Washington's career, as well as of his triumphs, without being thought captious or envious, and without forgetting that it is easier to do ill than well in the world.

The criticism that has hitherto met Mr. Washington has not always been of this broad character. In the South especially has he had to walk warily to avoid the harshest judgments,—and naturally so, for he is dealing with the one subject of deepest sensitiveness to that section. Twice—once when at the Chicago celebration of the Spanish-American War he alluded to the color-prejudice that is "eating away the vitals of the South," and once when he dined with President Roosevelt—has the resulting Southern criticism been violent enough to threaten seriously his popularity. In the North the feeling has several times forced itself into words, that Mr. Washington's counsels of submission overlooked certain elements of true manhood, and that his educational programme was unnecessarily narrow. Usually, however, such criticism has not found open expression, although, too, the spiritual sons of the Abolitionists have not been prepared to acknowledge that the schools founded before Tuskegee, by men of broad ideals and self-sacrificing spirit, were wholly failures or worthy of ridicule. While, then, criticism has not failed to follow Mr. Washington, yet the prevailing public opinion of the land has been but too willing to deliver the solution of a wearisome problem into his hands, and say, "If that is all you and your race ask, take it."

Among his own people, however, Mr. Washington has encountered the strongest and most lasting opposition, amounting at times to bitterness, and even to-day continuing strong and insistent even though largely silenced in outward expression by the public opinion of the nation. Some of this opposition is, of course, mere envy;

the disappointment of displaced demagogues and the spite of narrow minds. But aside from this, there is among educated and thoughtful colored men in all parts of the land a feeling of deep regret, sorrow, and apprehension at the wide currency and ascendancy which some of Mr. Washington's theories have gained. These same men admire his sincerity of purpose, and are willing to forgive much to honest endeavor which is doing something worth the doing. They coöperate with Mr. Washington as far as they conscientiously can; and, indeed, it is no ordinary tribute to this man's tact and power that, steering as he must between so many diverse interests and opinions, he so largely retains the respect of all.

* * *

Mr. Washington represents in Negro thought the old attitude of adjustment and submission; but adjustment at such a peculiar time as to make his programme unique. This is an age of unusual economic development, and Mr. Washington's programme naturally takes an economic cast, becoming a gospel of Work and Money to such an extent as apparently almost completely to overshadow the higher aims of life. Moreover, this is an age when the more advanced races are coming in closer contact with the less developed races, and the race-feeling is therefore intensified; and Mr. Washington's programme practically accepts the alleged inferiority of the Negro races. Again, in our own land, the reaction from the sentiment of war time has given impetus to race-prejudice against Negroes, and Mr. Washington withdraws many of the high demands of Negroes as men and American citizens. In other periods of intensified prejudice all the Negro's tendency to self-assertion has been called forth; at this period a policy of submission is advocated. In the history of nearly all other races and peoples the doctrine preached at such crises has been that manly self-respect is worth more than lands and houses, and that a people who voluntarily surrender such respect, or cease striving for it, are not worth civilizing.

In answer to this, it has been claimed that the Negro can survive only through submission. Mr. Washington distinctly asks that black people give up, at least for the present, three things,—

First, political power,

Second, insistence on civil rights,

Third, higher education of Negro youth,—

and concentrate all their energies on industrial education, the accumulation of wealth, and the conciliation of the South. This policy has been courageously and insistently advocated for over fifteen years, and has been triumphant for perhaps ten years. As a result of this tender of the palm-branch, what has been the return? In these years there have occurred:

1. The disfranchisement of the Negro.

2. The legal creation of a distinct status of civil inferiority for the Negro.

3. The steady withdrawal of aid from institutions for the higher training of the Negro.

These movements are not, to be sure, direct results of Mr. Washington's teachings; but his propaganda has, without a shadow of doubt, helped their speedier accomplishment. The question then comes: Is it possible, and probable, that nine millions of men can make effective progress in economic lines if they are deprived of political rights, made a servile caste, and allowed only the most meagre chance for developing their exceptional men? If history and reason give any distinct answer to these questions, it is an emphatic *No*. And Mr. Washington thus faces the triple paradox of his career:

1. He is striving nobly to make Negro artisans business men and property-owners; but it is utterly impossible, under modern competitive methods, for workingmen and property-owners to defend their rights and exist without the right of suffrage.

2. He insists on thrift and self-respect, but at the same time counsels a silent submission to civic inferiority such as is bound to sap the manhood of any race in the long run.

3. He advocates common-school and industrial training, and depreciates institutions of higher learning; but neither the Negro common-schools, nor Tuskegee itself, could remain open a day were it not for teachers trained in Negro colleges, or trained by their graduates.

This triple paradox in Mr. Washington's position is the object of criticism by two classes of colored Americans. One class is spiritually descended from Toussaint the Savior, through Gabriel, Vesey, and Turner, and they represent the attitude of revolt and revenge; they hate the white South blindly and distrust the white race generally, and so far as they agree on definite action, think that the

Negro's only hope lies in emigration beyond the borders of the United States. And yet, by the irony of fate, nothing has more effectually made this programme seem hopeless than the recent course of the United States toward weaker and darker peoples in the West Indies, Hawaii, and the Philippines,—for where in the world may we go and be safe from lying and brute force?

The other class of Negroes who cannot agree with Mr. Washington has hitherto said little aloud. They deprecate the sight of scattered counsels, of internal disagreement; and especially they dislike making their just criticism of a useful and earnest man an excuse for a general discharge of venom from small-minded opponents. Nevertheless, the questions involved are so fundamental and serious that it is difficult to see how men like the Grimkes, Kelly Miller, J. W. E. Bowen, and other representatives of this group, can much longer be silent. Such men feel in conscience bound to ask of this nation three things:

1. The right to vote.
2. Civic equality.
3. The education of youth according to ability.

They acknowledge Mr. Washington's invaluable service in counselling patience and courtesy in such demands; they do not ask that ignorant black men vote when ignorant whites are debarred, or that any reasonable restrictions in the suffrage should not be applied; they know that the low social level of the mass of the race is responsible for much discrimination against it, but they also know, and the nation knows, that relentless color-prejudice is more often a cause than a result of the Negro's degradation; they seek the abatement of this relic of barbarism, and not its systematic encouragement and pampering by all agencies of social power from the Associated Press to the Church of Christ. They advocate, with Mr. Washington, a broad system of Negro common schools supplemented by thorough industrial training; but they are surprised that a man of Mr. Washington's insight cannot see that no such educational system ever has rested or can rest on any other basis than that of the well-equipped college and university, and they insist that there is a demand for a few such institutions throughout the South to train the best of the Negro youth as teachers, professional men, and leaders.

This group of men honor Mr. Washington for his attitude of conciliation toward the white South; they accept the "Atlanta Compromise" in its broadest interpretation; they recognize, with him, many signs of promise, many men of high purpose and fair judgment, in this section; they know that no easy task has been laid upon a region already tottering under heavy burdens. But, nevertheless, they insist that the way to truth and right lies in straightforward honesty, not in indiscriminate flattery; in praising those of the South who do well and criticising uncompromisingly those who do ill; in taking advantage of the opportunities at hand and urging their fellows to do the same, but at the same time in remembering that only a firm adherence to their higher ideals and aspirations will ever keep those ideals within the realm of possibility. They do not expect that the free right to vote, to enjoy civic rights, and to be educated, will come in a moment; they do not expect to see the bias and prejudices of years disappear at the blast of a trumpet; but they are absolutely certain that the way for a people to gain their reasonable rights is not by voluntarily throwing them away and insisting that they do not want them; that the way for a people to gain respect is not by continually belittling and ridiculing themselves; that, on the contrary, Negroes must insist continually, in season and out of season, that voting is necessary to modern manhood, that color discrimination is barbarism, and that black boys need education as well as white boys.

In failing thus to state plainly and unequivocally the legitimate demands of their people, even at the cost of opposing an honored leader, the thinking classes of American Negroes would shirk a heavy responsibility,—a responsibility to themselves, a responsibility to the struggling masses, a responsibility to the darker races of men whose future depends so largely on this American experiment, but especially a responsibility to this nation,—this common Fatherland. It is wrong to encourage a man or a people in evil-doing; it is wrong to aid and abet a national crime simply because it is unpopular not to do so. The growing spirit of kindliness and reconciliation between the North and South after the frightful differences of a generation ago ought to be a source of deep congratulation to all, and especially to those whose mistreatment caused the war; but if that reconciliation is to be marked by the industrial slavery and civic death of those same black men, with permanent legislation into a position of inferiority, then those black men, if they are really men, are called upon by every consideration of patriotism and loyalty to oppose such a course by all civilized methods, even though such opposition involves disagreement with Mr. Booker T. Washington. We have no right to sit silently by while the inevitable seeds are sown for a harvest of disaster to our children, black and white.

First, it is the duty of black men to judge the South discriminatingly. The present generation of Southerners are not responsible for the past, and they should not be blindly hated or blamed for it. Furthermore, to no class is the indiscriminate endorsement of the recent course of the South toward Negroes more nauseating than to the best thought of the South. The South is not "solid"; it is a land in the ferment of social change, wherein forces of all kinds are fighting for supremacy; and to praise the ill the South is to-day perpetrating is just as wrong as to condemn the good. Discriminating and broad-minded criticism is what the South needs,—needs it for the sake of her own white sons and daughters, and for the insurance of robust, healthy mental and moral development.

To-day even the attitude of the Southern whites toward the blacks is not, as so many assume, in all cases the same; the ignorant Southerner hates the Negro, the workingmen fear his competition, the money-makers wish to use him as a laborer, some of the educated see a menace in his upward development, while others—usually the sons of the masters—wish to help him to rise. National opinion has enabled this last class to maintain the Negro common schools, and to protect the Negro partially in property, life, and limb. Through the pressure of the money-makers, the Negro is in danger of being reduced to semi-slavery, especially in the country districts; the workingmen, and those of the educated who fear the Negro, have united to disfranchise him, and some have urged his deportation; while the passions of the ignorant are easily aroused to lynch and abuse any black man. To praise this intricate whirl of thought and prejudice is nonsense; to inveigh indiscriminately against "the South" is unjust; but to use the same breath in praising Governor Aycock, exposing Senator Morgan, arguing with Mr.

Thomas Nelson Page, and denouncing Senator Ben Tillman, is not only sane, but the imperative duty of thinking black men.

It would be unjust to Mr. Washington not to acknowledge that in several instances he has opposed movements in the South which were unjust to the Negro; he sent memorials to the Louisiana and Alabama constitutional conventions, he has spoken against lynching, and in other ways has openly or silently set his influence against sinister schemes and unfortunate happenings. Notwithstanding this, it is equally true to assert that on the whole the distinct impression left by Mr. Washington's propaganda is, first, that the South is justified in its present attitude toward the Negro because of the Negro's degradation; secondly, that the prime cause of the Negro's failure to rise more quickly is his wrong education in the past; and, thirdly, that his future rise depends primarily on his own efforts. Each of these propositions is a dangerous half-truth. The supplementary truths must never be lost sight of: first, slavery and race-prejudice are potent if not sufficient causes of the Negro's position; second, industrial and common-school training were necessarily slow in planting because they had to await the black teachers trained by higher institutions,—it being extremely doubtful if any essentially different development was possible, and certainly a Tuskegee was unthinkable before 1880; and, third, while it is a great truth to say that the Negro must strive and strive mightily to help himself, it is equally true that unless his striving be not simply seconded, but rather aroused and encouraged, by the initiative of the richer and wiser environing group, he cannot hope for great success.

In his failure to realize and impress this last point, Mr. Washington is especially to be criticised. His doctrine has tended to make the whites, North and South, shift the burden of the Negro problem to the Negro's shoulders and stand aside as critical and rather pessimistic spectators; when in fact the burden belongs to the nation, and the hands of none of us are clean if we bend not our energies to righting these great wrongs.

The South ought to be led, by candid and honest criticism, to assert her better self and do her full duty to the race she has cruelly wronged and is still wronging. The North—her co-partner in guilt—cannot salve her conscience by plastering it with gold. We cannot settle this problem by diplomacy and suaveness, by "policy" alone. If worse come to worst, can the moral fibre of this country survive the slow throttling and murder of nine millions of men?

The black men of America have a duty to perform, a duty stern and delicate,—a forward movement to oppose a part of the work of their greatest leader. So far as Mr. Washington preaches Thrift, Patience, and Industrial Training for the masses, we must hold up his hands and strive with him, rejoicing in his honors and glorying in the strength of this Joshua called of God and of man to lead the headless host. But so far as Mr. Washington apologizes for injustice, North or South, does not rightly value the privilege and duty of voting, belittles the emasculating effects of caste distinctions, and opposes the higher training and ambition of our brighter minds,— so far as he, the South, or the Nation, does this,—we must unceasingly and firmly oppose them. By every civilized and peaceful method we must strive for the rights which the world accords to men, clinging unwaveringly to those great words which the sons of the Fathers would fain forget: "We hold these truths to be self-evident: That all men are created equal; that they are endowed by their Creator with certain unalienable rights; that among these are life, liberty, and the pursuit of happiness."

W. E. B. Du Bois, *The Souls of Black Folk* (New York, 1989), 36–50.

Fannie Barrier Williams

The Club Movement among Colored Women of America (1904)

Denied the vote until 1920, American women were nonetheless important political actors who influenced social and political developments in the nation. The participation of middle-class women in women's clubs and churches enabled them to become effective advocates for social, educational, and domestic reforms; the participation of working women in labor actions helped better conditions in the nation's mills and sweatshops. Almost always denied membership in white women's organizations, black women formed their own clubs, which became influential organizations for the promotion of African American rights and vital training grounds for the leaders who would advance the cause of black civil rights in the twentieth century. In 1906, the National Federation of Afro-American Women merged with National League of Colored Women to form the National Association for Colored Women. The group's original goal was "to furnish evidence of the moral, mental, and material progress made by people of color through the efforts of our women;" its motto "Lifting as We Climb" expressed the commitment of middle-class African American women to address the needs of working mothers and young black women on their own. Its members soon allied with other progressive era women's organizations and added a strong voice to the campaign for woman suffrage and an end to lynching.

Afro-American women of the United States have never had the benefit of a discriminating judgment concerning their worth as women made up of the good and bad of human nature. What they have been made to be and not what they are, seldom enters into the best or worst opinion concerning them.

In studying the status of Afro-American women as revealed in their club organizations, it ought to be borne in mind that such social differentiations as "women's interests; children's interests, and men's interests" that are so finely worked out in the social development of the more favored races are but recent recognitions in the progressive life of the Negro race. Such specializing had no economic value in slavery days, and the degrading habit of regarding the Negro race as an unclassified people has not yet wholly faded into a memory.

The Negro as an "alien" race, as a "problem," as an "industrial factor," as "ex-slaves," as "ignorant" etc . . . are well known and instantly recognized; but colored women as mothers, as home-makers, as the center and source of the social life of the race have received little or no attention. These women been left to grope their way unassisted toward a realization of those domestic virtues, moral impulses and standards of family and social life that are the badges of race respectability. They have had no special teachers to instruct them. No conventions of distinguished women of the more favored race have met to consider their peculiar needs. There has been no fixed public opinion to which they could appeal; no protection against the libelous attacks upon their characters, and no chivalry generous enough to guarantee their safety against man's inhumanity to woman. Certain it is that colored women have been the least known, and the most ill-favored class of women in the country.

Thirty-five years ago they were unsocialized, unclassed and un-recognized as either maids or matrons. There were simply women whose character and personality excited no interest. If within thirty-five years they have become sufficiently important to be stud-ied apart from the general race problem and have come to be rec-ognized as an integral part of the general womanhood of American civilization, that fact is a gratifying evidence of real progress.

In considering the social advancement of these women, it is im-portant to keep in mind the point from which progress began, and the fact that they have been mainly self-taught in all those precious things that make for the social order, purity and character. They have gradually become conscious of the fact that progress includes a great deal more than what is generally meant by the terms cul-ture, education and contact.

The club movement among colored women reaches into the sub-social condition of the entire race. Among white women clubs mean the forward movement of the best women in the interest of the best womanhood. Among colored women the club is an effort of the few competent in behalf of the many incompetent; that is to say that the club is only one of many means for the social uplift of a race. Among white women the club is the onward movement of the already uplifted.

The consciousness of being fully free has not yet come to the great masses of the colored women in this country. The emancipa-tion of the mind and spirit of the race could not be accomplished by legislation. More time, more patience, more suffering and more charity are still needed to complete the work of emancipation.

The training which first enabled colored women to organize and successfully carry on club work was originally obtained in church work. These churches have been and still are the great preparatory schools in which the primary lessons of social order, mutual trust-fulness and united effort have been taught. The churches have been sustained, enlarged and beautified principally through the organized efforts of their women members. The meaning of unity of effort of the common good, the development of social sympathies grew into woman's consciousness through the privileges of church work.

Still another school of preparation for colored women has been their secret societies. "The ritual of these secret societies is not without a certain social value." They demanded a higher order of intelligence than is required for church membership. Care for the sick, provisions for the decent burial of the indigent dead, the care for orphans and the enlarging sense of sisterhood all contributed to the development of the very conditions of heart that qualify women for the more inclusive work of those social reforms that are the aim of women's clubs. The churches and secret societies have helped to make colored women acquainted with the general social condition of the race and the possibilities of social improvement.

With this training the more intelligent women of the race could not fail to follow the example and be inspired by the larger club movement of the white women. The need of social reconstruction became more and more apparent as they studied the results of women's organizations. Better homes, better schools, better protection for girls of scant home training, better sanitary conditions, better opportunities for competent young women to gain employment, and the need of being better known to the American people appealed to the conscience of progressive colored women from many communities.

The clubs and leagues organized among colored women have all been more or less in direct response to these appeals. Seriousness of purpose has thus been the main characteristic of all these organizations. While the National Federation of Woman's Clubs has served as a guide and inspiration to colored women, the club movement among them is something deeper than a mere imitation of white women. It is nothing less than the organized anxiety of women who have become intelligent enough to recognize their own low social condition and strong enough to initiate the forces of reform.

The club movement as a race influence among the colored women of the country may be fittingly said to date from July, 1895, when the first national conference of colored women was held in

Boston, Mass. Prior to this time there were a number of strong clubs in some of the larger cities of the country, but they were not affiliated and the larger idea of effecting the social regeneration of the race was scarcely conceived of.

Among the earlier clubs the Woman's League of Washington, D.C., organized in 1892, and the Woman's Era Club of Boston, organized in January 1893, were and are still the most thorough and influential organizations of the kind in the country.

The kind of work carried on by the Washington League since its organization is best indicated by its standing committees, as follows:

Committee on Education.

Committee on Industries.

Committee on Mending and Sewing.

Committee on Free Class Instruction.

Committee on Day Nursery.

Committee on Building Fund.

These various activities include sewing schools, kindergartens, well-conducted night schools, and mother's meetings. All of which have been developed and made part of the educational and social forces of the colored people of the capital. The league has made itself the recognized champion of every cause in which colored women and children have any special interest in the District of Columbia.

* * *

It will thus be seen that from 1890 to 1895 the character of Afro-American womanhood began to assert itself in definite purposes and efforts in club work. Many of these clubs came into being all unconscious of the influences of the larger club movement among white women. The incentive in most cases was quite simple and direct. How to help and protect some defenseless and tempted young woman, how to aid some poor boy to complete a much-coveted education; how to lengthen the short school term in some impoverished school district; how to instruct and interest deficient mothers in the difficulties of child training are some of the motives of these clubs. These were the first outreachings of sympathy and fellowship felt by women whose lives had been narrowed by the petty concerns of the struggle for existence and removed by human cruelty from all the harmonies of freedom, love and aspirations.

* * *

As already noted some of the more progressive clubs had already conceived the idea of a National organization. The Woman's Era journal of Boston began to agitate the matter in the summer of 1894, and requested the clubs to express themselves through its columns on the question of holding a National convention. Colored women everywhere were quick to see the possible benefits to be derived from a National conference of representative women. It was everywhere believed that such a convention, conducted with decorum, and along the lines of serious purpose might help in a decided manner to change public opinion concerning the character and worth of colored women. This agitation had the effect of committing most of the clubs to the proposal for a call in the summer of 1895. While public-spirited Afro-American women everywhere were thus aroused to this larger vision in plans for race amelioration, there occurred an incident of aggravation that swept away all timidity and doubt as to the necessity of a National conference. Some obscure editor in a Missouri town sought to gain notoriety by publishing a libelous article in which colored women of the country were described as having no sense of virtue and altogether without character. The article in question was in the form of an open letter addressed to Miss Florence Belgarnie of England, who had manifested a kindly interest in behalf of the American Negro as a result of Miss Ida B. Wells' agitation. This letter is too foul for reprint, but the effect of its publication stirred the intelligent colored women of America as nothing else had ever done. The letter, in spite of its wanton meanness, was not without some value in showing to what extent the sensitiveness of colored women had grown. Twenty years prior to this time a similar publication would scarcely have been noticed, beyond the small circles of the few who could read, and were high spirited. In 1893 this open and vulgar attack in the character of a whole race of women was instantly and vehemently resented, in every possible way, by a whole race of women conscious of being slandered. Mass meetings were held in every part of the country to denounce the editor and refute the charges.

The calling of a National Council of colored women was hastened by this coarse assault upon their character. The Woman's

Era Club of Boston took the initiative on concentrating the wide-spread anxiety to do something large and effective, by calling a National conference of representative colored women. The conference was appointed to meet in Berkeley Hall, Boston for a three days' session, July 29, 30, 31, 1895.

In pursuance to this call the 29th day of July, 1895, witnessed in Berkeley Hall the first National convention of colored women ever held in America. About one hundred delegates were present from ten States and representatives of about twenty-five different clubs.

The convention afforded a fine exhibition of capable women. There was nothing amateurish, uncertain or timid in the proceedings. Every subject of peculiar interest to colored women was discussed and acted upon as if by women disciplined in thinking out large and serious problems.

* * *

The importance of this Boston conference to the club movement among colored women can scarcely be overestimated. The bracing effect of its vigorous proceedings and stirring addresses to the public gave a certain inspiration to the women throughout the whole country. The clubs that already existed became stronger and more positive and aggressive in their helpful work.

The national association has steadily grown in power and influence as an organized body, composed of the best moral and social forces of the negro race. It has held three National conventions since its organization, 1895: At Washington, D.C., in 1896; Nashville, Tenn., in 1897 and Chicago, in 1899. At the Chicago convention one hundred and fifty delegates were present, representing clubs from thirty States of the Union. The growing importance of the National organization was evidenced by the generous notices and editorial comments in the press of the country. Fraternal greetings were extended to the Chicago convention from many of the prominent white clubs of the city. It is not too much to say that no National convention of colored people held in the country ever made such a deep impression upon the public and told a more thrilling story of the social progress of the race than the Chicago convention. The interest awakened in colored women, and their peculiar interests, was evidenced in many ways. The National association has made it possible for many bright colored women to enjoy the fellowship and helpfulness of many of the best organizations of American women.

It has certainly helped to emancipate the white women from the fear and uncertainty of contact or association with women of the darker race. In other words the National Association of Colored Women's Clubs is helping to give respect and character to a race of women who had no place in the classification of progressive womanhood in America. The terms good and bad, bright, and dull, plain and beautiful are now as applicable to colored women as to women of other races. There has been created such a thing as public faith in the sustained virtue and social standards of the women who have spoken and acted so well in these representative organizations. The National body has also been felt in giving a new importance and a larger relationship to the purposes and activities of local clubs throughout the country. Colored women everywhere in this club work began to feel themselves included in a wider and better world than their immediate neighborhood. Women who have always lived and breathed the air of ample freedom and whose range of vision has been world-wide, will scarcely know what it means for women whose lives have been confined and dependent to feel the first consciousness of a relationship to the great social forces that include whole nationalities in the sweep of their influences. To feel that you are something better than a slave, or a descendent of an ex-slave, to feel that you are a unit in the womanhood of a great nation and a great civilization, is the beginning of self-respect and the respect of your race. The National Association of Colored Women's Clubs has certainly meant all this and much more to the women of the ransomed race in the United States.

* * *

This chapter on the club movement among colored women would be incomplete without some notice of the leaders of the movement. Nothing that these club women have done or aimed to do is more interesting than themselves. What a variety of accomplishments, talents, successes and ambitions have been brought into view and notice by these hitherto obscure women of a ransomed race! Educated? Yes, besides the thousands educated in the common schools, hundreds of them have been trained in the best colleges and universities in the country, and some of them have spent several years in the noted schools of Europe.

The women thus trained and educated are busily pursuing every kind of avocation not prohibited by American prejudices. As educators, fully twenty thousand of them are at work in the schools, colleges and universities of the country, and some of them teach everything required to be taught from the kindergarten to the university. Among these educators and leaders of Afro-American womanhood are to be found linguists, mathematicians, musicians, artists, authors, newspaper writers, lecturers and reform agitators, with varying degrees of excellence and success. There are women in the professions of law, medicine, dentistry, preaching, trained nursing, managers of successful business enterprises, and women of small independent fortunes made and saved within the past twenty-five years.

There are women plain, beautiful, charming, bright conversationalists, fluent, resourceful in ideas, forceful in execution, and women of all sorts of temperament and idiosyncracies and force and delicacy of character.

All of this of course is simply amazing to people trained in the habit of rating colored women too low and knowing only the menial type. To such people she is a revelation.

The woman thus portrayed is the real new woman in American life. This woman, as if by magic, has succeeded in lifting herself as completely from the stain and meanness of slavery as if a century had elapsed since the day of emancipation. This new woman, with the club behind her and the club service in her heart and mind, has come to the front in an opportune time. She is needed to change the old idea of things implanted in the minds of the white race and there sustained and hardened into a national habit by the debasing influence of slavery estimates. This woman is needed as an educator of public opinion. She is a happy refutation of the idle insinuations and common skepticism as to the womanly worth and promise of the whole race of women. She has come to enrich American life with finer sympathies, and to enlarge the boundary of fraternity and the democracy of love among American women. She has come to join her talents, her virtues, her intelligence, her sacrifices and her love in the work of redeeming the unredeemed from stagnation, from cheapness and from narrowness.

Quite as important as all this she has come to bring new hope and fresh assurances to the hapless young women of her own race. Life is not a failure. All avenues are not closed. Womanly worth of whatever race or complexion is appreciated. Love, sympathy, opportunity and helpfulness are within the reach of those who can deserve them. The world is still yearning for pure hearts, willing hands, and bright minds. This and much more is the message brought by this new woman to the hearts of thousands discouraged and hopeless young colored women.

* * *

The club movement is well purposed. There is in it a strong faith, an enthusiasm born of love and sympathy, and an ever-increasing intelligence in the ways and means of affecting noble results. It is not a fad. It is not an imitation. It is not a passing sentiment. It is not an expedient, or an experiment. It is rather the force of a new intelligence against the old ignorance. The struggle of an enlightened conscience against the whole brood of social miseries born out of the stress and pain of a hated past.

In *A New Negro for a New Century*, ed. J. E. MacBready (Chicago, 1900), 379–405, 414–23.

W. E. B. Du Bois

The Niagara Movement: Declaration of Principles (1906)

Educated at Fisk University, Harvard, and the Humboldt University of Berlin, W. E. B. Du Bois is often remembered for his sharp criticism of Booker T. Washington in The Souls of Black Folk *(1903). In 1905, Du Bois issued a call for "organized, determined and aggressive action on the part of men who believe in Negro freedom and growth." In January 1906, twenty-nine black men, most of them college-educated professionals, gathered on the Canadian side of Niagara Falls. Reflecting their disaffection with Washington's conciliatory response to the increasingly discriminatory and oppressive Jim Crow regime, the Niagara Movement vowed to protest unceasingly until their goal of "the abolition of all caste distinctions based simply on race and color" was realized. Confident of their objective but unsure of how to reach it, plagued by factionalism and underfinanced, the all-black, all-male Niagara Movement collapsed by*

1908. Other supporters of black civil rights learned from its failures, however, including the necessity of organizing in the South and of incorporating white men and public-minded women of both races. The Niagara Movement paved the way for the National Association for the Advancement of Colored People (NAACP), with which it merged in 1909. It also prepared Du Bois to become editor of the Crisis, *the NAACP's official magazine, its "organ of propaganda and defense," as Du Bois put it much later.*

Progress

The members of the conference, known as the Niagara Movement, assembled in annual meeting at Buffalo, July 11th, 12th and 13th, 1905, congratulate the Negro-Americans on certain undoubted evidences of progress in the last decade, particularly the increase of intelligence, the buying of property, the checking of crime, the uplift in home life, the advance in literature and art, and the demonstration of constructive and executive ability in the conduct of great religious, economic and educational institutions.

Suffrage

At the same time, we believe that this class of American citizens should protest emphatically and continually against the curtailment of their political rights. We believe in manhood suffrage; we believe that no man is so good, intelligent or wealthy as to be entrusted wholly with the welfare of his neighbor.

Civil Liberty

We believe also in protest against the curtailment of our civil rights. All American citizens have the right to equal treatment in places of public entertainment according to their behavior and deserts.

Economic Opportunity

We especially complain against the denial of equal opportunities to us in economic life; in the rural districts of the South this amounts to peonage and virtual slavery; all over the South it tends to crush labor and small business enterprises; and everywhere American

prejudice, helped often by iniquitous laws, is making it more difficult for Negro-Americans to earn a decent living.

A three-page leaflet (1905). [This leaflet was issued in an original printing of 750
copies. The actual locale of the meeting was on the Canadian side of Niagara
Falls, not in Buffalo, to avoid discriminatory practices.—ED.]

Education

Common school education should be free to all American children
and compulsory. High school training should be adequately provided for all, and college training should be the monopoly of no
class or race in any section of our common country. We believe
that, in defense of our own institutions, the United States should
aid common school education, particularly in the South, and we especially recommend concerted agitation to this end. We urge an increase in public high school facilities in the South, where the
Negro-Americans are almost wholly without such provisions. We
favor well-equipped trade and technical schools for the training of
artisans, and the need of adequate and liberal endowment for a
few institutions of higher education must be patent to sincere well-
wishers of the race.

Courts

We demand upright judges in courts, juries selected without discrimination on account of color and the same measure of punishment and the same efforts at reformation for black as for white
offenders. We need orphanages and farm schools for dependent
children, juvenile reformatories for delinquents, and the abolition
of the dehumanizing convict-lease system.

Public Opinion

We note with alarm the evident retrogression in this land of sound
public opinion on the subject of manhood rights, republican government and human brotherhood, and we pray God that this nation will not degenerate into a mob of boasters and oppressors, but
rather will return to the faith of the fathers, that all men were created free and equal, with certain unalienable rights.

Health

We plead for health—for an opportunity to live in decent houses and localities, for a chance to rear our children in physical and moral cleanliness.

Employers and Labor Unions

We hold up for public execration the conduct of two opposite classes of men: The practice among employers of importing ignorant Negro-American laborers in emergencies, and then affording them neither protection nor permanent employment; and the practice of labor unions in proscribing and boycotting and oppressing thousands of their fellow-toilers, simply because they are black. These methods have accentuated and will accentuate the war of labor and capital, and they are disgraceful to both sides.

Protest

We refuse to allow the impression to remain that the Negro-American assents to inferiority, is submissive under oppression and apologetic before insults. Through helplessness we may submit, but the voice of protest of ten million Americans must never cease to assail the ears of their fellows, so long as America is unjust.

Color-Line

Any discrimination based simply on race or color is barbarous, we care not how hallowed it be by custom, expediency, or prejudice. Differences made on account of ignorance, immorality, or disease are legitimate methods of fighting evil, and against them we have no word of protest; but discriminations based simply and solely on physical peculiarities, place of birth, color or skin, are relics of that unreasoning human savagery of which the world is and ought to be thoroughly ashamed.

"Jim Crow" Cars

We protest against the "Jim Crow" car, since its effect is and must be to make us pay first-class fare for third-class accommodations, render us open to insults and discomfort and to crucify wantonly our manhood, womanhood and self-respect.

Soldiers

We regret that this nation has never seen fit adequately to reward the black soldiers who, in its five wars, have defended their country with their blood, and yet have been systematically denied the promotions which their abilities deserve. And we regard as unjust, the exclusion of black boys from the military and navy training schools.

War Amendments

We urge upon Congress the enactment of appropriate legislation for securing the proper enforcement of those articles of freedom, the thirteenth, fourteenth and fifteenth amendments of the Constitution of the United States.

Oppression

We repudiate the monstrous doctrine that the oppressor should be the sole authority as to the rights of the oppressed.

The Negro race in America stolen, ravished and degraded, struggling up through difficulties and oppression, needs sympathy and receives criticism; needs help and is given hindrance, needs protection and is given mob-violence, needs justice and is given charity, needs leadership and is given cowardice and apology, needs bread and is given a stone. This nation will never stand justified before God until these things are changed.

The Church

Especially are we surprised and astonished at the recent attitude of the church of Christ—on the increase of a desire to bow to racial prejudice, to narrow the bounds of human brotherhood, and to segregate black men in some outer sanctuary. This is wrong, unchristian and disgraceful to the twentieth century civilization.

Agitation

Of the above grievances we do not hesitate to complain, and to complain loudly and insistently. To ignore, overlook, or apologize for these wrongs is to prove ourselves unworthy of freedom. Persistent manly agitation is the way to liberty, and toward this goal the Niagara Movement has started and asks the co-operation of all men of all races.

Help

At the same time we want to acknowledge with deep thankfulness the help of our fellowmen from the abolitionist down to those who to-day still stand for equal opportunity and who have given and still give of their wealth and of their poverty for our advancement.

Duties

And while we are demanding, and ought to demand, and will continue to demand the rights enumerated above, God forbid that we should ever forget to urge corresponding duties upon our people:
The duty to vote.
The duty to respect the rights of others.
The duty to work.
The duty to obey the laws.
The duty to be clean and orderly.
The duty to send our children to school.
The duty to respect ourselves, even as we respect others.

This statement, complaint and prayer we submit to the American people, and Almighty God.

In *Pamphlets and Leaflets by W. E. B. Du Bois*, ed. Herbert Aptheker (White Plains, NY, 1986), 55–58.

Part II
1909–1945

United States v. *Reynolds*; *United States v. Broughton*, 235 U.S. 133; 35 S. Ct. 86; 1914

Manipulated by unscrupulous landowners into farming arrangements that re-sembled serfdom without that system's customary rights, many southern black croppers and tenant farmers slipped away in the dead of night, leaving irate em-ployers in their wake. Frustrated by their inability to control their laborers, post-war southern landowners took advantage of breach-of-contract statutes in an ef-fort to bind agricultural workers to the land through peonage. A form of involuntary servitude in which a debtor was forced by the state to work for his creditor, peonage found support in an Alabama statute that criminalized share-croppers who breached their contracts. Such arrangements, often established un-der false pretenses and at the expense of illiterate farmers, became the subject of legal challenges. In the case of United States v. Reynolds *(1914), the Supreme Court held that arrangements in which a convicted debtor was bound by an unbreakable contract to work for an aggrieved party to pay off his debts constituted peonage and was therefore in violation of the Thirteenth Amendment. (*United States v. Broughton *was heard with* Reynolds *and dealt with in the same opinion.) Like* Plessy v. Ferguson—*in which the Thirteenth Amend-ment was invoked with less success—this case suggests that the multidimen-sional struggle to ensure the permanent annihilation of slavery required vigilance and the muscle of the courts.*

* * *

Opinion

[*138]

MR. JUSTICE DAY delivered the opinion of the court.

These cases were argued and considered together, and may be disposed of in a single opinion. They come here under the Criminal Appeals Act of March 2, 1907, c. 2564, 34 Stat. 1246, as involving the construction of the statutes of the United States which have for their object the prohibition and punishment of peonage. Case No. 478, *United States v. Reynolds*, was decided upon demurrer and objections to a plea filed to the indictment. The case [*139] against Broughton, No. 479, was decided upon demurrer to the indictment. In both cases the District Court held that no offense was charged. 213 Fed. Red. 345, 352. Both indictments for holding certain persons in a state of peonage were found under Sec. 1990 of the Revised Statutes of the United States, as follows:

"The holding of any person to service or labor under the system known as peonage is abolished and forever prohibited in the Territory of New Mexico, or in any other Territory or State of the United States; and all acts, laws, resolutions, orders, regulations, or usages of the Territory of New Mexico, or of any other Territory or State, which have heretofore established, maintained, or enforced, or by virtue of which any attempt shall hereafter be made to establish, maintain, or enforce, directly or indirectly, the voluntary or involuntary service or labor of any persons as peons, in liquidation of any debt or obligation, or otherwise, are declared null and void," and Sec. 269 of the Criminal Code (Sec. 5526, Rev. Stat.), which provides that—

"Whoever holds, arrests, returns, or causes to be held, arrested or returned, or in any manner aids in the arrest or return of any person to a condition of peonage, shall be fined not more than five thousand dollars, or imprisoned not more than five years, or both."

The facts to be gathered from the indictments and pleas, upon which the court below decided the cases and determined that no offense was charged against the statutes of the United States as above set forth, are substantially these: In No. 478, one Ed Rivers, having

been convicted in a court of Alabama of the offense of petit larceny, was fined $15, and costs $43.75. The defendant Reynolds appeared as surety for Rivers, and a judgment by confession was
entered up against him for the amount of the fine and costs, which
Reynolds afterwards paid to the State. On May 4, 1910, Rivers, the
convict, entered into a written contract with Reynolds to work for
him as a [*140] farm-hand for the term of nine months and
twenty-four days, at the rate of six dollars per month, to pay the
amount of fine and costs. The indictment charges that he entered
into the service of Reynolds, and under threats of arrest and imprisonment if he ceased to perform such work and labor, he worked
until the sixth day of June, when he refused to labor. Thereupon he
was arrested upon a warrant issued at the instance of Reynolds
from the County Court of Alabama, on the charge of violating the
contract of service. He was convicted and fined the sum of one
cent for violating this contract, and additional costs in the amount
of $87.05, for which he again confessed judgment with G. W.
Broughton as surety, and entered into a similar contract with
Broughton to work for him as a farm-hand at the same rate, for a
term of fourteen months and fifteen days.

   In No. 479, the case against Broughton, E. W. Fields, having
been convicted in an Alabama state court, at the July, 1910, term,
of the offense of selling mortgaged property, was fined fifty dollars
and costs, in the additional sum of $69.70. Thereupon Broughton,
as surety for Fields, confessed judgment for the sum of fine and
costs, and afterwards paid the same to the State. On the eighth day
of July, 1910, a contract was entered into, by which Fields agreed
to work for Broughton as a farm and logging hand for the term of
nineteen months and twenty-nine days, at the rate of six dollars per
month, to pay the fine and costs. He entered into the service of
Broughton, and, it was alleged, under threats of arrest and imprisonment if he ceased to labor, he continued so to do until the fourteenth day of September, 1910, when he refused to labor further.
Thereupon Broughton caused the arrest of Fields upon a charge of
violating his contract, and upon a warrant issued upon this charge,
Fields was again arrested.

   The rulings in the court below upon the plea and demurrers,
were that there was no violation of the Federal [*141] statutes,

properly construed, and also held that the conduct of the defendants was justified by the provisions of the Alabama Code, upon which they relied.

* * *

The defendants having justified under this system of law, the question for consideration is, Were the defendants well charged with violating the provisions of the Federal statutes, to which we have referred, notwithstanding they undertook to act under the Alabama laws, particularly under the provisions of Sec. 6846 of the Alabama Code, authorizing sureties to appear and confess judgment and enter into contracts such as those we have described?

The Thirteenth Amendment to the Constitution of the United States provides:

"Section 1. Neither slavery nor involuntary servitude, except as a punishment for crime whereof the party shall have been duly convicted, shall exist within the United States, or any place subject to their jurisdiction.

"Section 2. Congress shall have power to enforce this article by appropriate legislation."

It was under the authority herein conferred, to enforce the provisions of this amendment by appropriate legislation, that Congress passed the section of the Revised Statutes here under consideration. *Clyatt v. United States*, 197 U.S. 207; *Bailey v. Alabama*, 219 U.S. 219.

By these enactments Congress undertook to strike down all laws, regulations and usages in the States and Territories which attempted to maintain and enforce, directly or indirectly, the voluntary or involuntary service or labor of any persons as peons, in the liquidation of any debt or obligation. To determine whether the conduct of the defendants charged in the indictments amounted to holding the persons named in a state of peonage, it is essential to understand what Congress meant in the use of that term prohibiting and punishing those guilty of maintaining it. Extended discussion of this subject is rendered unnecessary in view of the full consideration thereof in the prior adjudications of this [*144] court. *Clyatt v. United States, supra; Bailey v. Alabama, supra.*

Peonage is "a status or condition of compulsory service, based upon the indebtedness of the peon to the master. The basal fact is indebtedness. . . . One fact existed universally; all were indebted to their masters. . . . Upon this is based a condition of compulsory service. Peonage is sometimes classified as voluntary or involuntary, but this implies simply a difference in the mode of origin, but none in the character of the servitude. The one exists where the debtor voluntarily contracts to enter the service of his creditor. The other is forced upon the debtor by some provision of law. But peonage, however created, is compulsory service, involuntary servitude. The peon can release himself therefrom, it is true, by the payment of the debt, but otherwise the service is enforced. A clear distinction exists between peonage and the voluntary performance of labor or rendering of services in payment of a debt. In the latter case, the debtor, though contracting to pay his indebtedness by labor or service, and subject like any other contractor to an action for damages for breach of that contract, can elect at any time to break it, and no law or force compels performance or a continuance of the service." *Clyatt v. United States*, 197 U.S. 207, 215.

Applying this definition to the facts here shown, we must determine whether the convict was in reality working for a debt which he owed the surety, and whether the labor was performed under such coercion as to become a compulsory service for the discharge of a debt. If so, it amounts to peonage, within the prohibition of the Federal statutes. The actual situation is this: The convict instead of being committed to work and labor as the statute provides for the State, when his fines and costs are unpaid, comes into court with a surety, and confesses judgment in the amount of fine and costs, and agrees [*145] with the surety, in consideration of the payment of that fine and costs, to perform service for the surety after he is released because of the confession of judgment. The form of the contract, said to be the usual one entered into in such cases, is given in the record, and reads:

"LABOR CONTRACT.

"The State of Alabama, Monroe County:

"Whereas, at the May term, 1910, of the county court, held in and for said county, I, Ed. Rivers, was convicted in said court of the offense of petit larceny and fined the sum of fifteen dollars, and judgment has been rendered against me for the amount of said fine, and also in the further and additional sum of forty-three and

75/100 dollars, cost in said case, and whereas J. A. Reynolds, together with A. C. Hixon, have confessed judgment with me in said court for said fine and cost. Now, in consideration of the premises, I, the said Ed. Rivers, agree to work and labor for him, the said J. A. Reynolds on his plantation in Monroe County, Alabama, and under his direction as a farm hand to pay fine and cost for the term of 9 months and 24 days, at the rate of $6.00 per month, together with my board, lodging, and clothing during the said time of hire, said time of hire commencing on the 4 day of May, 1910, and ending on the 28 day of Feby., 1911, provided said work is not dangerous in its character.

"Witness our hands this 4 day of May, 1910.

"ED (his x mark) RIVERS.

"J. A. REYNOLDS.

"Witness:

"JOHN M. COXWELL."

It also stands admitted in this record, that the sureties in fact paid the judgment confessed. Looking then to the substance of things, and through the mere form which they have taken, we are to decide the question whether the labor of the convict, thus contracted for, amounted to [*146] involuntary service for the liquidation of a debt to the surety, which character of service it was the intention of the acts of Congress to prevent and punish. When thus at labor, the convict is working under a contract which he has made with his surety. He is to work until the amount which the surety has paid for him—the sum of the fine and costs—is paid. The surety has paid the State and the service is rendered to reimburse him. This is the real substance of the transaction. The terms of that contract are agreed upon by the contracting parties, as the result of their own negotiations. The statute of the State does not prescribe them. It leaves the making of contract to the parties concerned, and this fact is not changed because of the requirement that the judge shall approve of the contract. When the convict goes to work under this agreement, he is under the direction and control of the surety, and is in fact working for him. If he keeps his agreement with the surety, he is discharged from its obligations without any further action by the State. This labor is performed under the constant coercion and threat of another possible arrest and prosecution in case he violates the labor contract which he has made with the surety, and this form of coercion is as potent as it would have been had the law provided for the seizure and compulsory service of the convict. Compulsion of such service by the constant fear of imprisonment under the criminal laws renders the work compulsory, as much so as authority to arrest and hold his person would be if the law authorized that to be done. *Bailey v. Alabama*, 219 U.S. 219, 244; *Ex parte Hollman*, 60 S. E. Rep. 19, 24.

Under this statute, the surety may cause the arrest of the convict for violation of his labor contract. He may be sentenced and punished for this new offense, and undertake to liquidate the penalty by a new contract of a similar nature, and, if again broken, may be again prosecuted, and the convict is thus kept chained to an ever-turning [*147] wheel of servitude to discharge the obligation which he has incurred to his surety, who has entered into an undertaking with the State or paid money in his behalf. The re-arrest of which we have spoken is not because of his failure to pay his fine and costs originally assessed against him by the State. He is arrested at the instance of the surety, and because the law punishes the violation of the contract which the convict has made with him.

Nor is the labor for the surety by any means tantamount to that which the State imposes if no such contract has been entered into, as these cases afford adequate illustration. In the case against Reynolds, Rivers was sentenced to pay $15 fine and $43.75 costs. Under the Alabama Code, he might have been sentenced to hard labor for the county for ten days for the non-payment of the fine, and assuming that he could be sentenced for non-payment of costs under Sec. 7635 of the Alabama Code, he could have worked it out at the rate of seventy-five cents per day, an additional 58 days might have been added, making 68 days as his maximum sentence at hard labor. Under the contract now before us, he was required to labor for nine months and twenty-four days, thus being required to perform a much more onerous service than if he had been sentenced under the statute, and committed to hard labor. Failing to perform the service he may be again rearrested, as he was in fact in this case, and another judgment confessed to pay a fine of one cent and $87.75 costs, for which the convict was bound to work for another surety for the term of fourteen months and seventeen days. In the case against Broughton, Fields was fined $50 and $69.70 costs. Under the law he might have been condemned to hard labor for less than four months. By the contract described, he was required to work for Broughton for a period of nineteen months and twenty-nine days.

* * *

There can be no doubt that the State has authority to impose involuntary servitude as a punishment for crime. This fact is recognized in the Thirteenth Amendment, and such punishment expressly excepted from its terms. Of course, the State may impose fines and penalties which must be worked out for the benefit of the State, and in such manner as the State may legitimately prescribe. See *Clyatt v. United States, supra,* and *Bailey v. Alabama, supra.* But here the State has taken the obligation of another for the fine and costs, imposed upon one convicted for the violation of the laws of the State. It has accepted the obligation of the surety, and, in the present case, it is recited in the record that the money has been in fact paid by the surety. The surety and convict have made a new contract for service, in regard to the terms of which the [*150] State has not been consulted. The convict must work it out to satisfy the surety for whom he has contracted to work. This contract must be kept, under pain of re-arrest, and another similar proceeding for its violation, and perhaps another and another. Thus, under pain of recurring prosecutions, the convict may be kept at labor, to satisfy the demands of his employer.

On our opinion, this system is in violation of rights intended to be secured by the Thirteenth Amendment, as well as in violation of the statutes to which we have referred, which the Congress has enacted for the purpose of making that amendment effective.

It follows that the judgment of the District Court must be reversed.

Judgment accordingly.

W. E. B. Du Bois

Returning Soldiers and Documents of the War (May 1919)

In 1917, the United States abandoned its neutral stance in World War I when it entered the conflict on the side of the Allied powers, pledging to make the world "safe for democracy." W. E. B. Du Bois, a prominent intellectual, activist, and a founder of the National Association of Colored People (NAACP), called on African Americans to support the American war effort but also kept careful watch of the treatment black servicemen received. Over 350,000 black troops served during the war, consigned to segregated units where they regularly endured prejudice and abuse from an all-white officer corps that was disproportionately southern. African Americans experienced the painful inconsistency in a war for democracy that included the exportation of Jim Crow segregation. Following the end of the war, Du Bois used the NAACP magazine Crisis *to publicize the mistreatment African American soldiers had endured and to demand that the United States honor the sacrifices of African American soldiers by making democracy a reality for black citizens at home and abroad.*

Returning Soldiers

We are returning from war! THE CRISIS and tens of thousands of black men were drafted into a great struggle. For bleeding France and what she means and has meant and will mean to us and humanity and against the threat of German race arrogance, we fought gladly and to the last drop of blood; for America and her highest ideals, we fought in far-off hope; for the dominant southern oligarchy entrenched in Washington, we fought in bitter resignation. For the America that represents and gloats in lynching, disfranchisement, caste, brutality and devilish insult—for this, in the hateful upturning and mixing of things, we were forced by vindictive fate to fight, also.

But today we return! We return from the slavery of uniform which the world's madness demanded us to don to the freedom of civil garb. We stand again to look America squarely in the face and call a spade a spade. We sing: This country of ours, despite all its better souls have done and dreamed, is yet a shameful land.

It *lynches*.

And lynching is barbarism of a degree of contemptible nastiness unparalleled in human history. Yet for fifty years we have lynched two Negroes a week, and we have kept this up right through the war.

It *disfranchises* its own citizens.

Disfranchisement is the deliberate theft and robbery of the only protection of poor against rich and black against white. The land that disfranchises its citizens and calls itself a democracy lies and knows it lies.

It encourages *ignorance*.

It has never really tried to educate the Negro. A dominant minority does not want Negroes educated. It wants servants, dogs, whores and monkeys. And when this land allows a reactionary group by its stolen political power to force as many black folk into these categories as it possibly can, it cries in contemptible hypocrisy: "They threaten us with degeneracy; they cannot be educated."

It *steals* from us.

It organizes industry to cheat us. It cheats us out of our land; it cheats us out of our labor. It confiscates our savings. It reduces our wages. It raises our rent. It steals our profit. It taxes us without representation. It keeps us consistently and universally poor, and then feeds us on charity and derides our poverty.

It *insults* us.

It has organized a nation-wide and latterly a world-wide propaganda of deliberate and continuous insult and defamation of black blood wherever found. It decrees that it shall not be possible in travel nor residence, work nor play, education nor instruction for a black man to exist without tacit or open acknowledgment of his inferiority to the dirtiest white dog. And it looks upon any attempt to question or even discuss this dogma as arrogance, unwarranted assumption and treason.

This is the country to which we Soldiers of Democracy return. This is the fatherland for which we fought! But it is *our* fatherland. It was right for us to fight. The faults of *our* country are *our* faults.

Under similar circumstances, we would fight again. But by the God of Heaven, we are cowards and jackasses if now that that war is over, we do not marshal every ounce of our brain and brawn to fight a sterner, longer, more unbending battle against the forces of hell in our own land.

We *return.*

We *return from fighting.*

We *return fighting.*

Make way for Democracy! We saved it in France, and by the Great Jehovah, we will save it in the United States of America, or know the reason why.

The Crisis 18 (May 1919): 13–14.

Documents of the War

The following documents have come into the hands of the Editor [W. E. B. Du Bois]. He has absolute proof of their authenticity. The first document was sent out last August at the request of the American Army by the French Committee which is the official means of communication between the American forces and the French. It represents American and not French opinion and we have been informed that when the French Ministry heard of the distribution of this document among the Prefects and Sous-Prefects of France, they ordered such copies to be collected and burned.

FRENCH MILITARY MISSION

Stationed with the American Army

August 7, 1918.

SECRET INFORMATION CONCERNING

BLACK AMERICAN TROOPS

1. *It is important for French officers who have been called upon to exercise command over black American troops, or to live in close contact with them, to have an exact idea of the position occupied by Negroes in the United States. The information set forth in the following communication ought to be given to these officers and it is to their interest to have these matters known and widely disseminated. It will devolve likewise on the French Military Authorities, through the medium of the Civil Authorities, to give information on this subject to the French population residing in the cantonments occupied by American colored troops.*

2. *The American attitude upon the Negro question may seem a matter for discussion to many French minds. But we French are not in our province if we undertake to discuss what some call "prejudice." American opinion is unanimous on the "color question" and does not admit of any discussion.*

The increasing number of Negroes in the United States (about 15,000,000) would create for the white race in the Republic a menace of degeneracy were it not that an impassable gulf has been made between them.

As this danger does not exist for the French race, the French public has become accustomed to treating the Negro with familiarity and indulgence.

This indulgence and this familiarity are matters of grievous concern to the Americans. They consider them an affront to their national policy. They are afraid that contact with the French will inspire in black Americans aspirations which to them [the whites] appear intolerable. It is of the utmost importance that every effort be made to avoid profoundly estranging American opinion.

Although a citizen of the United States, the black man is regarded by the white American as an inferior being with whom relations of business or service only are possible. The black is constantly being censured for his want of intelligence and discretion, his lack of civic and professional conscience and for his tendency toward undue familiarity.

The vices of the Negro are a constant menace to the American who has to repress them sternly. For instance, the black American troops in France have, by themselves, given rise to as many complaints for attempted rape as all the rest of the army. And yet the [black American] soldiers sent us have been the choicest with respect to physique and morals, for the number disqualified at the time of mobilization was enormous.

CONCLUSION

1. *We must prevent the rise of any pronounced degree of intimacy between French officers and black officers. We may be courteous and amiable with these last, but we cannot deal with them on the same plane as with the white American officers without deeply wounding the latter. We must not eat with them, must not shake hands or seek to talk or meet with them outside of the requirements of military service.*

2. *We must not commend too highly the black American troops, particularly in the presence of [white] Americans. It is all right to recognize their good qualities and their services, but only in moderate terms, strictly in keeping with the truth.*

3. *Make a point of keeping the native cantonment population from "spoiling" the Negroes. [White] Americans become greatly incensed at any public expression of intimacy between white women with black men. They have re-*

cently uttered violent protests against a picture in the "Vie Parisienne" entitled "The Child of the Desert" which shows a [white] woman in a "cabinet particulier" with a Negro. Familiarity on the part of white women with black men is furthermore a source of profound regret to our experienced colonials who see in it an over-weening menace to the prestige of the white race.

* * *

The following letter written by a Negro officer to an American friend illustrates the temper and difficulties of the situation in France.

19 Feb., 1919.

I have been hoping that you would be able to drop in on us here before our departure. We are slated to leave here at 4 A. M. on the 21st supposedly aboard the *Aquitania*. It was my desire to talk with you about the offer to officers and men in the A. E. F. to attend a school in France or England. I made application and was shown the endorsement by the Regt. Commander, that the offer did not apply to transient officers. The knowledge was obtained from a telegram received from Hdq. One of our officers went to the Commanding General of this Camp to obtain a copy of the telegram which could not be or was not produced. Capt. —— —— went in person to the General and requested permission to attend stating that he volunteered for service, left his practise and family at a sacrifice and that he thought the Govt. owed it to him to give him a chance and attend school here. The General took his name and the Organization to which he belongs promising to let him hear from him, but as yet nothing has been done. This Camp is practically a penal institution and prejudice against us is very strong. Some day there is likely to be some grave disturbance here. The conditions are simply awful; mud everywhere, leaky tents and barracks and lack of sufficient and proper toilets. The men are worked quite hard, some at night and others in the day, rain or shine. As a consequence there are quite a number of sick men in our organization. Since our arrival here, the roads have been improved quite a bit (due to the work of the 92nd div.) and you do not have to wade in ankle deep mud. Board walks here to nearly all the tents and barracks. There is so much talk about the rotten conditions that the Camp Officials are making feverish efforts to be ready for the proposed inquiry.

The work of each organization is graded by the Camp Officer in Charge of details and if not satisfactory, the organization may be placed at the bottom of the sailing list or removed temporarily. Commanding Officers of separate units or regiments are practically helpless and if they complain too much against the treatment accorded them, are kept here until the Commanding General sees fit to let them go.

I am beginning to wonder whether it will ever be possible for me to see an American (white) without wishing that he were in his Satanic Majesty's private domain. I must pray long and earnestly that hatred of my fellow man be removed from my heart and that I can truthfully lay claim to being a Christian.

* * *

Addresses Denouncing W. E. B. Du Bois (April 5, 1919)

Following the defeat of Germany in World War I, diplomats and interested observers from around the world met in Paris in 1919 to negotiate a treaty that would redraw global boundaries and politics. Determined to influence international policy regarding the future of Germany's colonial holdings in Africa, W. E. B. Du Bois organized a pan-African Congress to coincide with the Paris Peace Conference. Universal Negro Improvement Association leader Marcus Garvey, a charismatic Jamaican, shared Du Bois's belief that African American contributions to the defeat of Germany should be a prelude to the expansion of democracy around the world. But he rejected Du Bois's vision for the governance of Africa and his articulation of the needs of black people around the world.

ENTHUSIASTIC CONVENTION OF 3,000 AMERICAN, CANADIAN, WEST INDIAN, AFRICAN, SO. & CENTRAL AMERICAN NEGROES DENOUNCED DR. W. E. B. DU BOIS CHARACTERIZED AS REACTIONARY UNDER PAY OF WHITE MEN—RESOLUTION CARRIED UNANIMOUSLY

In our last issue we gave a synopsis of the meeting of the Universal Negro Improvement Association and African Communities

League, held at Mother Zion A.M.E. Church on March 25, for the purpose of denouncing the recent reactionary attitude of Dr. W. E. B. Du Bois with regard to his opposition to the resolutions which appeared in the Negro world of March 1, 1919, and which were presented by Mr. Eliezer Cadet to the Peace Conference and also to determine the most effectual means of protecting the Association's elected delegate. In this issue we are prepared to give, as promised, a full report of the speeches delivered. The meeting was attended by fully 3000 Negroes and several white men representing the Department of Justice. The meeting was opened with the singing of the hymn "From Greenland's Icy Mountains," after which a very inspiring prayer was offered by the Rev. John S. Wilkins, executive secretary of the association. . . .

The chairman before introducing the next speaker took advantage of the opportunity of explaining his psychological view of the efficient members of the Department of Justice, and hoped that the heads of the Department of Justice were doing their duty in crushing autocracy and establishing universal democracy, so that a little may be able to reach the Southern lands. He then introduced the next speaker, Mr. Marcus Garvey, President-General of the Universal Negro Improvement Association and African Communities League.

Mr. Marcus Garvey said: "Mr. Chairman, Ladies and Gentlemen: on behalf of the Universal Negro Improvement Association and [U].N.I.A. and African Communit[i]es' League, this meeting was called. Owing to a cable report sent us on Monday morning [24 March] by our representative, Mr. Eliezer Cadet, now in France, representing the interest of 12,000,000 American, 10,000,000 West Indian Negroes, and 280,000,000 Africans, for which representation he was elected by 7,000 American, African, West Indian, and South and Central American Negroes, at a mass meeting in the Palace Casino on December 1, 1918.

* * *

Men and women, I am indeed glad to see how we are assembled here tonight and to hear the acclamations given to the type of new Negroes, who spoke previous to me. These are men ranging in age from eighteen to thirty-two; men who would have died in this bloody war if it had continued another two years. If the war had continued for two weeks longer I would have had to go to France and Flanders to die for the Belgian. According to the law I would have been compelled to go. I know there are going to be more wars within the next twenty-five years, and Negroes will be called upon. But the Negro is prepared to emancipate himself on the continent of Africa. The time has come for the emancipation of all peoples, whether Russians, Germans, Poles or Jews. Already the Egyptians are fighting for their freedom, and it will not be surprising to hear India also striking the blow for complete emancipation. Egypt is now striking, and I pray Almighty God to be on the side of Egypt. What is good for the white man by way of freedom is also good [*for*] the black man by way of freedom. Why should Europe emancipate herself and keep Africa under the heel of oppression. Africa must be for the Africans, and them exclusively. Dr. Du Bois desires internationalization of Africa for the white man, the capitalistic class of white men. Cannot these hand-picked leaders see that under the League of Nations certain places will be oppressed by mandatories, and unless the entire constitution of the League of Nations be repealed internationalization will be the control of Africa? France, Belgium and Italy have already realized their positions in Africa, because two millions of blacks have gone back to Africa as soldiers. Italy has already lost her individual nationalistic control which she had prior to the outbreak of war. This Government got Dr. Du Bois to go to France so that when he returns and everything is settled they can say, "It i[s] you who asked for these things." Men and women of America, West Indies and Africa. Are you prepared to live in slavery everlasting? "No!" shouted the audience.

* * *

We speak tonight, not in the spirit of cowardice, but as men who died in France in 1914–1918, and since we could have died in France we can now die right here. We remember the words of Patrick Henry one hundred and forty-three years ago in the Virginia Legislature, when he was endeavoring to lay the foundation of independence. "I care not what others may say, but as for me, give me liberty or give me death," and now as a new people representing a new sentiment we will say: "We care not what others may say, but for us give us liberty or give us death." If there are to be white kings, white emperors and white czars, there must also be Negro men representing the same dignitaries. The spirit of the age is freedom; the spirit of the age is liberty; the spirit to sanctify by the blood of the martyr, and I feel quite sure that there are no cowards among you men and women in this church tonight.

Liberty Exploited and Robbed

The object of America, for which George Washington and Patrick Henry fought 140 years ago, are today cast aside and disregarded. Young men and young women, awake! Be ready for the day when Africa shall declare for her independence. And why do I say Africa when you are living in the West Indies and America? Because in these places you will never be safe until you launch your protection internally and externally. The Japanese and Chinese are not lynched in this country because of the fear of retaliation. Behind these men are standing armies and navies to protect them. Such is the case with Frenchmen and Englishmen, but Negroes, representing an undignified and unorganized nation, are lynched, because they know the best that can be done is to hold a mass meeting. It is truly said that we have no original right in America. If the Poles and Hungarians require a national home with national government—and Australia and Canada are white men countries—then it is requisite for 400,000,000 Negroes to have a national home and a national government, and, as I was asked in England and Scotland and Germany what I was doing there, we will also be able to ask somebody, "What are you doing here?"

Objects of the U.N.I.A.

Ladies and gentlemen, I want you to realize that the Universal Negro Improvement Association and African Communities League, the organization which I have the honor to represent, is a worldwide movement that is endeavoring to unite the sentiment of our people. Our objective is to declare Africa a vast Negro empire. We can see no right in Belgium's retention of the Congo. We are going to wait until peace is completely restored, and then will we work Belgium out. And when we ask Belgium, "What are you doing there?" America will have nothing to do with it. Under the League of Nations when Africa revolts America will have to call upon Negroes to fight Negroes, therefore the League of Nations must be defeated by every Negro in America, or it will mean that Africa will have to fight the combined nations of the world.

* * *

This is an age in which we must stand up for our constitutional rights[.] Let your brothers and sisters in the West Indies know that the white man has no privilege, pre-eminence or monopoly over them. I want you to understand clearly that I am not telling you to do anything unconstitutionally.

There are several reasons why we are holding this meeting in the church. We are here because God has always been with the Negro and the Negro with God. We are here because we want the blessing of God. At the crucifixion, white men got hold of Christ, beat him and mocked him but, unlike these, Simon, the Cyrenean, a Negro, took his cross and carried it. Jesus, whom we helped, is now in heaven. If man can be grateful, we know the Divine is much more grateful. When the Divine was in trouble we helped Him, and now that we are in trouble we know that he will help us.

In *The Marcus Garvey and Universal Negro Improvement Association Papers*, vol. 1 (Berkeley, 1983), 394–99.

Marcus Garvey

Speech (September 1921)

Arriving in New York City from London in 1916, Marcus Garvey landed in a city perched on the edge of the Harlem Renaissance and ripe for movement and organization. When the nation exploded with racial and anti-union violence following World War I, the Jamaican-born political activist and printer established a branch of the Universal Negro Improvement Association (UNIA) in Harlem. Through public speaking engagements and his newspaper, the Negro World, *Garvey built UNIA into a pan-African movement that spanned the globe in its effort to unite people of African descent. With colonial boundaries redrawn by the victorious Allied powers after World War I, Garvey argued that black people around the world would not enjoy security and equal opportunity until Africa had been liberated from white control. He preached racial pride and insisted that a better future for the African diaspora lay in black separatism rather than integration and political cooperation with whites. Garvey's assertion that whites would never voluntarily tolerate black equality resonated with many African Americans' experiences of the Jim Crow South, leading them to swell the ranks of UNIA. Garvey's views also brought him into conflict with the NAACP and its most prominent voice, Crisis editor W. E. B. Du Bois.*

Will Stand by Slogan, "Africa for the African at Home and Abroad" (September 7, 1921)

* * *

U.N.I.A. Has Clear-Cut Program

Now understand the Universal Negro Improvement Association. We have a clear-cut program. It is a program of national independence; not staying where you are, to be killed; but national independence, an independence so strong as to enable us to rout others if they attempt to interfere with us. (Applause.) DuBois says he wants to bring about a better harmony, better spirit of unity, among the colored and white people—an impossibility in the present day and under present conditions. Jesus Christ, the Almighty, failed to do that. He came to this world to do that thing and failed. His purpose being to effect the unification of humanity in the worship of God and in the brotherhood of man and the fatherhood of God. That was His mission. He was Jesus Christ, and men refused to accept His ideas, His doctrines, His teachings; and men became to outraged, so offended at the thought of Jesus Christ wanting to unit[e] all mankind into one brotherhood that they killed Him and made Him beat a hasty retreat. And He was God. What God failed to do nearly two thousand years ago is what DuBois, very well meaning though he may be, is trying to do. How impossible! You cannot bring together two people of opposite races if they will remain apart by appealing to their feelings. There is only one way you can bring two such opposing factions to a compromise, and that is by a demonstration of equal strength on the part of both. (Applause.) Man has gone mad, man has gone crazy, and you cannot argue with a man you have to knock down before you can get into his senses, and preachers may preach religion and the philosophers may teach philosophy from now until eternity and you will never be able to change the attitude of the strong toward the weak. But the moment the weak become strong they can compel respect and recognition from those who are strong. That is what the Universal Negro Improvement Association seeks to do. We are not going to waste time here until the white people become sufficiently strong numerically, reaching the 400,000,000 mark, so that they are independent of us economically and can then throw us off as if into a scrap heap; we are not going to do that. We are going to stay here, some of us, for probably another hundred years or so, but we are going to stay here with the protection behind us of the Republic of Africa. (Applause.) So that as African citizens, or a[s] American citizens with African support, we can walk through the South and say: "I am a black man; touch me because I am black if you dare." (This was said with great dramatic effect.) When the Southern white man knows that behind the Negro stands a latest model dreadnought, a latest model cruiser, a latest model submarine, a latest model aeroplane, the latest discovered poisonous gas—ah! he will come to terms. (Applause.) He will come to terms; but not until then, and you cannot build up a separate navy, a separate army, in a country where there is an existing government. So long as you remain here there will be but one government, and that is the government of the United States as controlled by white men, and so long as they are in power there is no need expecting any protection when it comes to a showdown between black and white. But when you have behind you a power that is separate and distinct from the one under which you live, and having that power at your back you can always go behind the might and majesty of that power to protect you. If DuBois thinks white folks are going to go crazy and share their civilization with black folks when black folks have done nothing in their opinion to help them establish their ci[v]ilization, DuBois is crazy and has another thought coming. The white man himself would be crazy. Here it is: I have built up my house on a fine foundation—a marble structure. My house is well adorned and decorated, with the latest furniture and containing everything to make me and my family happy. Do you expect that I am going to pick up a fellow off the street who has no decent home, who has been in the gutter since morning, and take him into my parlor, sit him down, take him to my dining table, introduce him to my wife and beautiful daughter, and after that say to him, "Come inside and sleep next to me?" Imagine a white man doing that!

What I want to portray is this: The white man believes that he has built up this civilization exclusively by himself. His railroads, his steamsh[i]ps, his subways, his elevated railways—all brought into existence through his own energy, and he feels that the black man is impertinent and audacious to want to share equally the comforts of those things with him that he has sacrificed for, and in some cases, died for and which the Negro has never made any effort to help him bring about. That is the white man's attitude, and it is one you cannot blame him for, because I would do it myself. Why, if I bought my suit and paid the tailor for it and saw another man trying to put it on before me, brother, there is going to be some fight. And that is the position now. The cause of this prejudice against black people is because the sober-minded white people believe that the black people have contributed nothing to the civilization they want to enjoy co-equally with them, and that is where the prejudice comes; not so much because you are black, but because we have achieved nothing in comparison to what they have achieved. The white man views the universe—through the Americas, South, Central and North America; through the West Indies, through Africa[—]and he sees no civilization standing to the credit of the black man that he could reciprocate with. If he goes to Africa he sees the naked African and he has to walk his way through the jungles; if he goes to the West Indies he sees the barefooted Negro; if he [go]es to the Southern States he sees the happy-go-lucky coon, and he comes to the conclusion, after all, "why should I accept social equality with a race like this that has done nothing[?]" And that is where the white man gets his argument of inferiority from, and he will adduce that argument until we get out and build (Applause), build our cities, build our nations, build our empires, build our navies, build our armies to protect them, and when he knows you have those things and you can give him a hard battle and whip him he will come to terms, as he has come to terms with Japan. (Applause.) The prejudice of the world is not so much against skin—it is not so much against color—it is against what you have not done. They were prejudiced against the Japanese 70 years ago, and there you have the argument that it was not so much on color; it was on the question of non-achievement. Since the Japanese have achieved what has happened? Our proud and haughty President has is[su]ed an invitation from the White House to nations of equal standing to come and meet in Washington to discuss the question of disarmament. Who are they inviting? We have white France, Anglo-Saxon Britain, white Italy, and among them yellow Japan. And the Universal Negro Improvement Association is working so that when the next President of the United States of America calls a world conference to discuss armament the black African will be invited. (Applause.) The black African will be in the Council Chamber, and any Negro who does not desire that ought to die. (Applause.)

I am tired of having other folks representing me, because they have misrepresented my great-grandfather, and my grandfather and my father, and it is said, "Once bitten always shy." I would be a big fool with all past records to allow them still to represent me. I am going to represent myself. (Applause.) And do you know why? Because civilization has nothing on me. White civilization, yellow civilization have nothing on me. The white statesman has passed through his university; the yellow statesman has passed through his academy, and Marcus Garvey, as a black man, has passed through his. (Applause.) And on the battlefields of domestic politics, of international politics I am prepared to meet them at any time anywhere. (Applause.) The cry of Europe is for Europeans, the cry of Asia is for the Asiatics, and Marcus Garvey raises the cry of "Africa for the Africans, both at home and abroad." (Applause.) I have no apology for this slogan. I live for this slogan and I will die for the realization of this slogan.

Speech given at Liberty Hall, New York, September 7, 1921; excerpted from *The Marcus Garvey and Universal Negro Improvement Association Papers*, vol. ix, ed. Robert A. Hill (Berkeley, 1995), 191–93.

W. E. B. Du Bois

Georgia: Invisible Empire State
(January 21, 1925)

In 1915, a group of Georgians gathered at Stone Mountain to relaunch the Ku Klux Klan. The successful new incarnation of the Klan tapped into white rural Americans' deep sense of dislocation in a rapidly modernizing and increasingly urban America. The Klan's campaigns to "purify" the nation targeted immigrants, Catholics, and Jews, as well as African Americans. Although the modern Klan claimed to be a vestige of the past, it was more truthfully a reflection of the representation of that past in films such as Birth of a Nation *and school textbooks provided and in some cases written by the United Daughters of the Confederacy. Reflecting on Georgia in the 1920s, W. E. B. Du Bois tied Georgia's contemporary racial conflicts to modern economic circumstances, a vestige of, if anything, Henry Grady's New South vision. Grady, a leader in Georgia's Democratic Party in the 1880s, used his position as editor of the* Atlanta Constitution *to promote a booming, industrialized South. As Grady's political enemy Tom Watson had done a generation earlier, Du Bois argued that the prosperity and political power of New South industrialists depended on exploiting racial tensions to prevent black and white working-class Georgians from perceiving their common economic interests.*

Georgia is beautiful. High on the crests of the Great Smoky Mountains some Almighty Hand shook out this wide and silken shawl—shook it and swung it two hundred glistening miles from the Savannah to the Chattahoochee, four hundred miles from the Appalachians to the Southern sea. Red, white, and black is the soil and it rolls by six great rivers and ten wide cities and a thousand towns, thick-throated, straggling, low, busy, and sleepy. It is a land singularly full of lovely things: its vari-colored soil, its mighty oaks and pines, its cotton-fields, its fruit, its hills.

And yet few speak of the beauty of Georgia. Some tourists wait by the palms of Savannah or try the mild winters of Augusta; and there are those who, rushing through the town on its many railroads, glance at Atlanta or attend a convention there. Lovers of the mountains of Tennessee may skirt the mountains of Georgia; but

Georgia connotes to most men national supremacy in cotton and lynching, Southern supremacy in finance and industry, and the Ku Klux Klan.

* * *

When catastrophe came, Georgia was among the first to see a way out. While other States were seeking two impossible and incompatible things, the subjection of the blacks and defiance of the North, Georgia developed a method of her own. With slavery gone the slave baron was bankrupt and two heirs to his power had rushed forward: The poor white from the hills around and above Atlanta and the Northern speculator—"Scalawag" and "Carpet-Bagger" they were dubbed—sought to rebuild the South. In the more purely agricultural regions this involved a mere substitution of owners and black laborers. But the development of Georgia was to be more than agricultural. It was to be manufacturing and mining; transportation, commerce, and finance; and it was to involve both white and colored labor. This was a difficult and delicate task, but there were Georgians who foresaw the way long before the nation realized it. The first prophet of the new day was Henry W. Grady of Atlanta.

* * *

Grady said to Northern capital: Come South and make enormous profits; and to Southern captains of industry: Attract Northern capital by making profit possible. Together these two classes were to unite and exploit the South; and they were to make Georgia not simply an industrial center but what was much more profitable, a center for financing Southern enterprises; and they would furnish industry with labor that could be depended on.

This last point, dependable labor, was the great thing. Here was a vast submerged class, the like or equivalent of which was unknown in the North. Here were a half-million brawny Negro workers and a half-million poor whites. If they could be kept submerged—hard at work in industry and agriculture—they would raise cotton, make cotton cloth, do any number of other valuable things, and build a "prosperous" State. If they joined forces, and went into politics to better their common lot, they would speedily emancipate themselves. How was this to be obviated? How were both sets of laborers to be inspired to work hard and continuously?

The *modus operandi* was worked out slowly but it was done skilfully, and it brought results. These results have been costly, but they have made Georgia a rich land growing daily richer. The new wealth was most unevenly distributed; it piled itself in certain quarters and particularly in Atlanta—birthplace and capital of the new "Invisible Empire."

The method used to accomplish all this was, in addition to much thrift and work, deliberately to encourage race hatred between the mass of white people and the mass of Negroes. This was easy to develop because the two were thrown into economic competition in brick-laying, carpentry, all kinds of mechanical work connected with the new industries. In such work Negroes and whites were personal, face-to-face competitors, bidding for the same jobs, working or willing to work in the same places. The Negroes started with certain advantages. They were the mechanics of the period before the war. The whites came with one tremendous advantage, the power to vote. I remember a campaign in Atlanta. The defeated candidate's fate was sealed by a small circular. It contained a picture of colored carpenters building his house.

* * *

In agriculture poor whites and Negroes were soon brought into another sort of indirect competition. The Negroes worked in the fields, the poor whites in the towns which were the market-places for the fields. Gradually the poor whites became not simply the mechanics but the small storekeepers. They financed the plantations and fleeced the workers. They organized to keep the workers "in their places," to keep them from running away, to keep them from striking, to keep their wages down, to terrorize them with mobs. On the other hand the Negroes worked to own land, to escape from country to city, to cheat the merchants, to cheat the landholders.

Then in larger ways and more indirectly both groups of workers came into competition. They became separated according to different, but supporting and interlocked, industries and occupations. Negroes prepared the road-bed for the railroads; whites ran the trains. Negroes were firemen; whites were engineers. Negroes were porters; whites were mill operatives. Finally there was the Negro servant stretching all the way from the great mansion to the white factory hand's hovel, touching white life at every point.

Soon the subtle rivalry of races in industry began. Soon, to the ordinary Georgia white man, the Negro became a person trying to take away his job, personally degrade him, and shame him in the eyes of his fellows; starve him secretly. To the ordinary Georgia Negro, the average white man was a person trying to take away his job, starve him, degrade him, keep him in ignorance, and return him to slavery. And these two attitudes did not spring from careful reasoning. They were so coiled and hidden with old known and half-known facts that they became matters of instinct and inheritance. You could not argue about them; you could not give or extract information.

It is usual for the stranger in Georgia to think of race prejudices and race hatred as being the great, the central, the unalterable fact and to go off into general considerations as to race differences and the eternal likes and dislikes of mankind. But that line leads one astray. The central thing is not race hatred in Georgia; it is successful industry and commercial investment in race hatred for the purpose of profit.

Skilfully, but with extraordinary ease, the power to strike was gradually taken from both white and black labor. First the white labor vote was used to disfranchise Negroes and the threat of white competition backed by the hovering terror of the white mob made a strike of black workers on any scale absolutely unheard of in Georgia. Continually this disfranchisement went beyond politics into industry and civil life. On the other hand, the power of a mass of cheap black labor to underbid almost any class of white laborers forced white labor to moderate its demands to the minimum and to attempt organization slowly and effectively only in occupations where Negro competition was least, as in the cotton mills.

Then followed the curious and paradoxical semi-disfranchisement of white labor by means of the "white primary." By agreeing to vote on one issue, the Negro, the normal split of the white vote on other questions or the development of a popular movement against capital and privilege is virtually forestalled. Thus in Georgia democratic government and real political life have disappeared. None of the great questions that agitate the nation—international or national, social or economic—can come up for free discussion. Anything that would divide white folk in opinion or action is taboo and only personal feuds survive as the issues of political campaigns. If real issues ever creep in and real difference of opinion appears— "To Your Tents, O Israel"—Do you want your sister to marry a "nigger"?

What induces white labor to place so low a value on its own freedom and true well-being and so high a value on race hatred? The answer involves certain psychological subtleties and yet it is fairly clear. The Southern white laborer gets low wages measured in food, clothes, shelter, and the education of his children. But in one respect he gets high pay and that is in the shape of the subtlest form of human flattery—social superiority over masses of other human beings. Georgia bribes its white labor by giving it public badges of superiority. The Jim Crow legislation was not to brand the Negro as inferior and to separate the races, but rather to flatter white labor to accept public testimony of its superiority instead of higher wages and social legislation. This fiction of superiority invaded public affairs: No Negro schoolhouse must approach in beauty and efficiency a white school; no public competition must admit Negroes as competitors; no municipal improvements must invade the Negro quarters until every white quarter approached perfection or until typhoid threatened the whites; in no city and State affairs could Negroes be recognized as citizens—it was Georgia, Atlanta, the Fourth Ward, and the Negroes.

In return for this empty and dangerous social bribery the white laborer fared badly. Of modern social legislation he got almost nothing; the "age of consent" for girls in Georgia was ten years until 1918, when it was, by great effort and outside pressure, raised to fourteen. Child labor has few effective limitations; children of twelve may work in factories and without birth registration the age is ascertainable with great difficulty. For persons "under twenty-one" the legal workday is still "from sunrise to sunset," and recently Georgia made itself the first State in the Union to reject the proposed federal child-labor amendment. Education is improving, but still the white people of Georgia are one of the most ignorant groups of the Union and the so-called compulsory education law is so full of loopholes as to be unenforceable. And black Georgia? In Atlanta there are twelve thousand Negro children in school and six thousand seats in the schoolrooms! In all legislation tending to limit

profits and curb the exploitation of labor Georgia lingers far behind the nation.

This effort to keep the white group solid led directly to mob law.
Every white man became a recognized official to keep Negroes "in
their places." Negro baiting and even lynching became a form of
amusement which the authorities dared not stop. Blood-lust grew
by what it fed on. These outbreaks undoubtedly affected profits, but
they could not be suppressed, for they kept certain classes of white
labor busy and entertained. Secret government and manipulation
ensued. Secret societies guided the State and administration. The
Ku Klux Klan was quite naturally re-born in Georgia and in
Atlanta.

Georgia is beautiful. Yet on its beauty rests something disturbing
and strange. Physically this is a certain emptiness and monotony, a
slumberous, vague dilapidation, a repetition, an unrestraint. Point
by point one could pick a poignant beauty—one golden river, one
rolling hill, one forest of oaks and pines, one Bull Street. But there
is curious and meaningless repetition until the beauty palls or fails
of understanding. And on this physical strangeness, unsatisfaction,
drops a spiritual gloom. There lies a certain brooding on the land—
there is something furtive, uncanny, at times almost a horror. Some
folk it so grips that they never see the beauty—the hills to them are
haunts of grim and terrible men; the world goes armed with loaded
pistols on the hip; concealed, but ready—always ready. There is a
certain secrecy about this world. Nobody seems wholly frank—neither white nor black; neither child, woman, nor man. Strangers ask
each other pointed searching questions: "What is your name?"
"Where are you going?" "What might be your business?" And they
eye you speculatively. Once satisfied, the response is disconcertingly
quick. They strip their souls naked before you; there is sudden
friendship and lavish hospitality. And yet—yet behind all are the
grim bars and barriers; subjects that must not be touched, opinions
that must not be questioned. Side by side with that warm human
quality called "Southern" stands the grim fact that right here and
beside you, laughing easily with you and shaking your hand cordially, are men who hunt men: who hunt and kill in packs, at odds
of a hundred to one under cover of night. They have lynched five
hundred Negroes in forty years; they have killed unnumbered white

men. There must be living and breathing in Georgia today at least ten thousand men who have taken human life, and ten times that number who have connived at it.

* * *

Nevertheless, there are brave men in Georgia, men and women whose souls are hurt even to death by this merciless and ruthless exploitation of race hatred. But what can they do? It is fairly easy to be a reformer in New York or Boston or Chicago. One can fight there for convictions, and while it costs to oppose power, yet it can be done. It even gains some applause and worth-while friends. But in Atlanta? The students of white Emory College recently invited a student of black Morehouse College to lead a Y.M.C.A. meeting. It was a little thing—almost insignificant. But in Georgia it was almost epochmaking. Ten years ago it would have meant riot. Today it called for rare courage. When the Southern Baptists met in Atlanta recently they did not segregate Negro visitors. Such a thing has seldom if ever happened before in Georgia. It is precisely the comparative insignificance of these little things that shows the huge horror of the bitter fight between Georgia and civilization.

Some little things a liberal public opinion in Georgia may start to do, although the politico-economic alliance stands like a rock wall in the path of real reform. A determined group called "inter-racial" asks for change. Most of them would mean by this the stopping of lynching and mobbing, decent wages, abolition of personal insult based on color. Most of them would not think of demanding the ballot for blacks or the abolition of Jim Crow cars or civil rights in parks, libraries, and theaters or the right of a man to invite his black friend to dinner. Some there are who in their souls would dare all this, but they may not whisper it aloud—it would spoil everything; it would end their crusade. Few of these reformers yet fully envisage the economic nexus, the real enemy encased in enormous profit. They think reform will come by right thinking, by religion, by higher culture, and do not realize that none of these will work its end effectively as long as it pays to exalt and maintain race prejudice.

* * *

[T]here can be no successful economic change in Georgia without the black man's cooperation. First of all the Negroes are property holders. Sixty years after slavery and despite everything

Georgia Negroes own two million acres of land, a space nearly as large as the late kingdom of Montenegro. Their taxable property saved from low wages and systematic cheating has struggled up from twelve million dollars in 1890 to over sixty millions today; and now and then even the remnant of their political power strikes a blow. In 1928 in Savannah a fight within the "white primary" between the corrupt gang and decency gave twelve hundred Negro voters the balance of power. Efforts were made to intimidate the Negroes. Skull and cross-bones signed by the Ku Klux Klan were posted on the doors of eight of the prominent Negro churches with the legend, "This is a white man's fight; keep away." Warning slips were put under the doors of colored citizens. In vain. The colored voters held their own political meetings, financed their own campaign, went into the election, and of their twelve hundred votes it was estimated that less than a hundred went for the gang; the reform mayor was elected.

I am in the hot, crowded, and dirty Jim Crow car, where I belong. A black woman with endless babies is faring forth from Georgia, "North." Two of the babies are sitting on parts of me. I am not comfortable. Then I look out of the window. The hills twist and pass. Slowly the climate changes—cold pines replace the yellow monarchs of the South. There is no cotton. From the door of hewn log cabins faces appear—dead white faces and drawn, thin forms. Here live the remnants of the poor whites.

I look out of the window, and somehow it seems to me that here in the Jim Crow car and there in the mountain cabin lies the future of Georgia—in the intelligence and union of these laborers, white and black, on this soil wet with their blood and tears. They hate and despise each other today. They lynch and murder body and soul. They are separated by the width of a world. And yet—and yet, stranger things have happened under the sun than understanding between those who are born blind.

The Nation 120 (January 21, 1925): 63–67.

Countee Cullen

Incident (1925)

Countee Cullen was one of the most promising poets of the Harlem Renaissance, an outpouring of African American art, music, and literature during the years between World War I and II. Raised by politically active adoptive parents in New York, Cullen graduated phi beta kappa in English and French from New York University in 1925. His 1928 marriage to Yolanda Du Bois, the daughter of W. E. B. Du Bois, was the African American social event of the year. (His divorce from her two years later was accomplished discretely from Paris.) His career in decline by 1934, Cullen took a teaching job at Frederick Douglass High School in New York City. Among his students was James Weldon Johnson, who became a poet and NAACP leader in the 1930s and is remembered for his song "Lift Every Voice and Sing," still referred to as "the Negro national anthem." In this spare poem, written relatively early, Cullen assumes the voice of a young boy to convey the traumatizing, brutalizing effects of Jim Crow sociability on children white and black.

Once riding in old Baltimore,
    Heart-filled, head-filled with glee,
I saw a Baltimorean
    Keep looking straight at me.

Now I was eight and very small,
    And he was no whit bigger,
And so I smiled, but he poked out
    His tongue, and called me, "Nigger."

I saw the whole of Baltimore
    From May until December;
Of all the things that happened there
    That's all that I remember.

From *Color* by Countee Cullen

William Alexander Percy

Fode (1941)

Part autobiography and part narrative history, Mississippi planter and poet William Alexander Percy's Lanterns on the Levee *is an apologetic for a way of life already under fire. A cotton aristocrat of the old school, Percy operated consciously from the position of noblesse oblige, which he applied to his family as well as his employees: At age forty-five, Will Percy adopted and raised his three young second cousins, one of whom grew up to be National Book Award–winning author Walker Percy. Dismissed as racist and paternalistic by liberals and embraced by segregationists,* Lanterns on the Levee *presents the point of view of a thoughtful man of letters considered by local whites in his own time, as Walker Percy put it, "a flaming liberal and a nigger-lover."*

People are divided into Leaners and Leanees: into oaks more or less sturdy and vines quite, quite clinging. I was never a Leaner, yet, although seldom mistaken for one, I find people are constantly feeling impelled to protect me. Invariably they are right and I accept their proffered ministrations gratefully. I cannot drive a car or fix a puncture or sharpen a pencil or swim or skate or give a punch in the jaw to the numerous parties who need punching. My incompetency is almost all-inclusive, but it must have a glow, for it attracts Samaritans from miles around. I have been offered a very fine, quick-working poison for use on my enemies or myself; I have had my rifle carried by a soldier who disliked me, just because I was all in; a bootlegger once asked me to go partners with him because I looked seedy; a top sergeant, icy with contempt, put together my machine-gun when its disjecta membra unassembled would have returned me in disgrace to America; a red-headed friend of mine had to be restrained from flinging a red-headed enemy of mine into the river for some passing insolence; an appreciable percentage of the hard-boiled bastards of the world have patched tires, blown life into sparkplugs, pushed, hauled, lifted, hammered, towed, and sweated for me because they knew that without their aid I should have moldered indefinitely on some wretched, can-strewn landscape. If you mix incompetency with a pinch of the wistful and a heap of good manners, it works pretty well. Men of goodwill are all over the place, millions of them. It is a very nice world—that is, if you remember that while good morals are all-important between the Lord and His creatures, what counts between one creature and another is good manners. A good manner may spring from vanity or a sense of style; it is a sort of pleasant fiction. But good manners spring from well-wishing; they are fundamental as truth and much more useful. No nation or stratum of society has a monopoly on them and, contrary to the accepted estimate, Americans have more than their share.

The righteous are usually in a dither over the deplorable state of race relations in the South. I, on the other hand, am usually in a condition of amazed exultation over the excellent state of race relations in the South. It is incredible that two races, centuries apart in emotional and mental discipline, alien in physical characteristics, doomed by war and the Constitution to a single, not a dual, way of life, and to an impractical and unpracticed theory of equality which deludes and embitters, heckled and misguided by pious fools from the North and impious fools from the South—it is incredible, I insist, that two such dissimilar races should live side by side with so little friction, in such comparative peace and amity. This result is due solely to good manners. The Southern Negro has the most beautiful manners in the world, and the Southern white, learning from him, I suspect, is a close second.

Which reminds me of Ford. (He pronounces his name "Fode" with enormous tenderness, for he is very fond of himself.)

In the South every white man worth calling white or a man is owned by some Negro, whom he thinks he owns, his weakness and solace and incubus. Ford is mine. There is no excuse for talking about him except that I like to. He started off as my caddy, young, stocky, strong, with a surly expression, and a smile like the best brand of sunshine. For no good reason he rose to be my chauffeur; then houseboy; then general factotum; and now, without any contractual relation whatever, my retainer, which means to say I am retained for life by him against all disasters, great or small, for which he pays by being Ford. It was not because of breaking up the first automobile, coming from a dance drunk, or because of breaking up the second automobile, coming from a dance drunk, that our contractual relation was annulled, but for a subtler infamy. I was in the shower, not a position of dignity at best, and Ford strolled in, leaned against the door of the bathroom, in the relaxed pose of the Marble Faun, and observed dreamily: "You ain't nothing but a little old fat man."

A bit of soap was in my eye and under the circumstances it was no use attempting to be haughty anyway, so I only blurted: "You damn fool."

Ford beamed: "Jest look at your stummick."

When one had fancied the slenderness of one's youth had been fairly well retained! Well, taking advantage of the next dereliction, and one occurred every week, we parted; that is to say, I told Ford I was spoiling him and it would be far better for him to battle for himself in this hostile world, and Ford agreed, but asked what he was going to do "seeing as how nobody could find a job nohow." As neither of us could think of the answer, I sent him off to a mechanics' school in Chicago. He returned with a diploma and a thrilling tale of how nearly he had been married against his vehement protest to a young lady for reasons insufficient surely in any enlightened community with an appreciation of romance. With Ford's return the demand for mechanics fell to zero—he always had an uncanny effect on the labor market—so he took to house-painting. His first week he fell off the roof of the tallest barn in the county and instead of breaking his neck, as Giorgione or Raphael would have done, he broke only his ankle and had to be supplied with crutches, medical care, and a living for six weeks. It was then that I left for Samoa.

But I should not complain. Ford has never learned anything from me, but I am indebted to him for an education in more subjects and stranger ones than I took at college, subjects, however, slightly like those the mock-turtle took from the Conger eel. The first lesson might be called "How Not to Faint in Coils." Ford observed:

"You don't understand folks good as I does." I was appalled. "You sees what's good in folks, but you don't see what's bad. Most of the time I'se a good boy, then I goes nigger, just plain nigger. Everybody do that, and when they does, it hurts you." I was pulverized. It may not have taken a wicked person to think that, but it certainly took a wicked one to say it.

That I have any dignity and self-respect is not because of but in spite of Ford. We were returning from a directors' meeting in a neighboring town and he was deeply overcast. At last he became communicative:

"Mr. Oscar Johnston's boy says Mr. Oscar won't ride in no car more'n six months old and he sho ain't goin' to ride in nothin' lessen a Packard."

I received this calmly, it was only one more intimation that my Ford was older than need be and congenitally unworthy. Ford continued:

"He says Mr. Oscar says you ain't got near as much sense as your pa." I agreed, heartily. "He says you ain't never goin' to make no money." I agreed, less heartily. "En if you don't be keerful you goin' to lose your plantation." I agreed silently, but I was nettled, and observed:

"And you sat there like a bump on a log, saying nothing, while I was being run down?"

"Well, I told him you had traveled a lot, a lot more'n Mr. Oscar; you done gone near 'bout everywhere, en he kinder giggled and says: 'Yes, they tells me he's been to Africa,' en I says: 'He is,' en he says: 'You know why he went to Africa?' en I says: ''Cause he wanted to go there,' en he says: 'That's what he tells you, but he went to Africa to 'range to have the niggers sent back into slavery.'"

I exploded: "And you were idiot enough to believe that?"

"I'se heard it lots of times," Ford observed mildly, "but it didn't make no difference to me, you been good to me en I didn't care."

Having fancied I had spent a good portion of my life defending and attempting to help the Negro, this information stunned me and, as Ford prophesied, it hurt. But hiding my wounded vanity as usual in anger, I turned on Ford with:

"You never in your life heard any Negro except that fool boy of Oscar Johnston's say I was trying to put the Negroes back in slavery."

"Lot of 'em," reiterated Ford.

"I don't believe you," I said. "You can't name a single one."

We finished the drive in silence; spiritually we were not en rapport.

The next morning when Ford woke me he was wreathed in smiles, suspiciously pleased with himself. He waited until one eye was open and then announced triumphantly:

"Louisa!" (pronounced with a long i).

"What about Louisa?" I queried sleepily.

"She says you'se goin' to send the niggers back into slavery!"

Louisa was our cook, the mainstay and intimate of the household for fifteen years.

"God damn!" I exploded, and Ford fairly tripped out, charmed with himself.

I dressed thoughtfully and repaired to the kitchen. My intention was to be gentle but desolating. Louisa weighs over three hundred, and despite a physical allure I can only surmise from the stream of nocturnal callers in our back yard, she distinctly suggests in her general contour a hippopotamus. When I entered the kitchen I found her pacing ponderously back and forth through the door that opens on the back gallery. It seemed a strange procedure—Louisa was not given to exercise, at least not of that kind. The following colloquy ensued:

"Louisa, what are you doing?"

"I stuck a nail in my foot."

"Why don't you go to the doctor?"

"I'se gettin' the soreness out."

"You can't walk it out."

"Naw, suh, the nail is *drawing* it out."

"What nail?"

"The nail I stepped on."

"Where is it?"

Louisa pointed to the lintel of the door. A nail hung from it by a piece of string; under it Louisa was pacing. I left her pacing. I didn't mention slavery then or later.

My bitter tutelage didn't conclude here. In late autumn we drove to the plantation on settlement day. Cotton had been picked and ginned, what cash had been earned from the crop was to be distributed. The managers and bookkeeper had been hard at work preparing a statement of each tenant's account for the whole year. As the tenant's name was called he entered the office and was paid off. The Negroes filled the store and overflowed onto the porch, milling and confabulating. As we drove up, one of them asked: "Whose car is dat?" Another answered: "Dat's *us* car." I thought it curious they didn't recognize my car, but dismissed the suspicion and dwelt on the thought of how sweet it was to have the relation between landlord and tenant so close and affectionate that to them my car was their car. Warm inside I passed through the crowd, glowing and bowing, the lord of the manor among his faithful retainers. My mission concluded, I returned to the car, still glowing. As we drove off I said:

"Did you hear what that man said?"

Ford assented, but grumpily.

"It was funny," I continued.

"Funnier than you think," observed Ford sardonically.

I didn't understand and said so.

Ford elucidated: "He meant that's the car *you* has bought with *us* money. They all knew what he meant, but you didn't and they knew you didn't. They wuz laughing to theyselves."

A few days later the managers confirmed this version of the meaning of the phrase and laughed. I laughed too, but not inside.

Yet laughter singularly soft and unmalicious made me Ford's debtor more even than his admonitions and revelations. I still think with gratitude of an afternoon which his peculiarly Negro tact and good manners and laughter made charming. I was in what Ford would call "low cotton." After a hellish day of details and beggars, my nerves raw, I phoned for Ford and the car. On climbing in I asked dejectedly:

"Where shall we drive?"

Ford replied: "Your ruthers is my ruthers" (what you would rather is what I would rather). Certainly the most amiable and appeasing phrase in any language, the language used being not English but deep Southern.

"Let's try the levee," I suggested.

Although nothing further was said and Ford asked no questions, he understood my depression and felt the duty on him to cheer me up. He drove to my favorite spot on the levee and parked where I could watch across the width of waters a great sunset crumbling over Arkansas. As I sat moody and worried, Ford, for the first and only time in his life, began to tell me Negro stories. I wish I could imitate his exact phrases and intonations and pauses, without which they are poor enough stories; but, in spite of the defects of my relaying, anyone can detect their Negro quality, care-free and foolish and innocent—anyone, that is, who has lived among Negroes in the South.

Here are the three I remember in something approximating Ford's diction:

"There wuz a cullud man en he died en went to hevven en the Lawd gevvum all wings, en he flew en he flew" (here Ford hunched his shoulders and gave a superb imitation of a buzzard's flight). "After he flew round there fur 'bout a week he looked down en saw a reel *good*-lookin' lady, a-settin' on a cloud. She wuz *reel* good-lookin'. En he dun the loop-the-loop.

"The Lawd cum en sez: 'Don't you know how to act? There ain't nuthin' but nice people here, en you beehavin' like that. Git out.' But he told the Lawd he jest didn't know en he wuzzent never gonner do nuthin' like that no mo', en please let him stay. So the Lawd got kinder pacified en let him stay. En he flew en he flew. En after he had been flying round fur 'bout a week, he ups en sees that same good-lookin' lady a-settin' on a cloud en he jest couldn't hep it—he dun the loop-the-loop.

"So the Lawd stepped up en he sez: 'You jest don't know how to act, you ain't fitten fur to be with decent folks, you'se a scanlus misbeehavor. Git out.' En he got.

"He felt mighty bad en hung round the gate three or four days tryin' to ease up on St. Peter, but St. Peter 'lowed there wuzn't no way, he jest couldn't let him in en the onliest way he might git in wuz to have a *conference* with the Lawd. Then the man asked if he couldn't 'range fur a conference en they had a lot of back-and-forth. En finally St. Peter eased him in fur a conference." (Ford loved that word, it made him giggle.) "But the Lawd wuz mad, He wuz mad sho-nuff, he wuz hoppin' mad en told him flat-footed to git out en stay out. Then the cullud man sez:

"'Well, jest remember this, Lawd: while I wuz up here in yo' place I wuz the flyin'est fool you had.'"

Since the thirteenth century no one except Ford and his kind has been at ease in heaven, much less confident enough of it to imagine an aeroplane stunt there. And I do hope that good-looking lady saw the loop-the-loop.

The second story is just as inconsequential:

"A fellow cum to a cullud man en promised him a whole wagen-load of watermelons if he would go en set by hisself in a hanted house all night long. Well, the man he liked watermelons en he promised, though he sho didn't like no hanted house, en he sho didn't wanter see no hants. He went in en drug up a cheer en set down en nuthin' happened. After so long a time, in walked a black cat en set down in front of him en jest looked at him. He warn't so skeered because it warn't much more'n a kitten, en they both uvvem jest set there en looked at each uther. Then ernurther cat cum in, a big black 'un, en he set by the little 'un en they jest set there lookin' at him, en ain't sed nothin'. Then ernurther one cum en he wuz big as a dawg en all three uvvem jest set there en looked at him en sed nuthin'. Ernurther one cum, still bigger, en ernurther, en ernurther, en the last one wuz big as a hoss. They all jest set there in a row en sed nuthin' en looked at him. That cullud man he wuz plum skeered en he had ter say sumpin so he 'lowed all nice en p'lite:

"'Whut us gwiner do?'

"En the big 'un sed: 'Us ain't gwiner do nuthin', till Martin comes.'

"The cullud man says reel nice en p'lite: 'Jest tell Martin I couldn't wait,' en he busted out the winder en tore down the big road fast as he could en faster, en he ain't never taken no more in-terest in watermelons since."

"But, Ford," I asked, "who was Martin?"

"I dunno," said Ford and chuckled, "but I reckon he wuz big as er elly-fant."

I reckon so too, and twice as real, so far as I am concerned.

And now the last:

"A cullud man cum to the white folks' house in the country en sed to the man:

"'Boss, I'se hongry; gimme sumpin t'eat.'

"The man sed: 'All right, go round to the back do' en tell the cook to feed you.'

"The cullud man sed: 'Boss, I'se neer 'bout starved, I ain't et fur a whole week.'

"The man sed: 'All right, all right, go round to the kitchen.'

"The cullud man sed: 'Boss, if you gimme sumpin t'eat I'll split up all that stove wood you got in yo' back yard.'

"The man sed: 'All right, all right, go en git that grub like I tole yer.'

"So he went. After 'bout three hours the man went to his back yard en saw the cullud man, who wuz jest settin'. So he sed:

"'Has you et?'

"En he sed: 'Yassir.'

"En he sed: 'Has you chopped up that wood-pile?'

"En he sed: 'Boss man, if you jest let me res' round till dinner time, after dinner I'll go en chop out that patch of cotton fur you.'

"So the man sed: 'All right, but don't you fool me no more.'

"After the cullud man had et him a big dinner he started out to the cotton patch en he met him a cooter [a mud-turtle] en the cooter sed to him:

"'Nigger, you talks too much.'

"The nigger goes tearin' back to the big house en when he gits there the man cums out en sez:

"'Nigger, has you chopped out that cotton?'

"En the nigger sez:

"'Lawd, boss, I wuz on my way, fo' God I wuz, en I met a cooter en he started talkin' to me en I lit out from there en here I is.'

"The boss man was plenty riled and he sez:

"'Nigger, take me to that cooter en if he don't start talkin', I'se goin' to cut your thoat frum year to year."

"So they bof uvvem started fur the cotton patch en there in the middle of the big road set that cooter. En he never opened his mouth, he ain't sed nuthin'. So the man hopped on the nigger en whupped him sumpin' scand'lous en left fur the big house mighty sore at niggers en cooters. Well, the cullud man wuz neer 'bout through breshing hisself off en jest fo' moseying on off when the cooter poked his head out en looks at him en sez:

"'Nigger, I tole you you talks too much.'"

Can it be wondered at, now that Ford is sojourning in the North beyond the infamous housing conditions of the South, comfortable

and healthy in his own little room with four young Negro room-
mates, a single window to keep out the cold and a gas burner for
cooking and heat—can it be wondered, if now when the phone
rings and the operator's voice says: "Detroit, calling collect," that I
accept the charge, although I know who it is and why he is calling?
It is Ford and he is drunk and he is incoherently solicitous for me
and mine and for his mother and wants to come home and needs
five dollars. I reply I am glad to hear his voice, which is true, and
hope he is well, and advise him to be a good boy and stick to his
job, and a letter will follow or shall I wire? Of course, he has no job,
except with the W.P.A., to which he has attached himself by fictions
and frauds with which all good Southern darkies with itching feet
are familiar. I hope the government supports him as long and as
loyally as I did, because if it doesn't, I must. I must because Ford is
my fate, my Old Man of the Sea, who tells me of Martin and ad-
monishing cooters and angels that do the loop-the-loop, my only tie
with Pan and the Satyrs and all earth creatures who smile sunshine
and ask no questions and understand.

I wish my parting with him could have been happier or that I
could forget it. He had abandoned his truck in a traffic jam and for-
feited his job, one that I had procured for him with much difficulty
and some misrepresentation. Then he had got looping drunk and
last, against all precedent and propriety, he had come to see me; it
was late at night when he arrived, stumbling and weeping. He
threw himself across the couch and sobbed without speaking. I
could not get him up or out, and he wouldn't explain his grief. At
last he quieted down and, his face smeared with tears, managed to
gasp:

"You cain't do no good, Mr. Will. It don't make no difference
how hard I tries or how good I bees, I ain't never gonner be nuthin'
but jest Fode."

I wish I had never heard him say that. There are some truths
that facing does not help. Something had brought home to Ford the
tragedy of himself and of his race in an alien world. Had he been
in South Africa or Morocco or Harlem or Detroit, his pitiful cry
would have been equally true, equally hopeless and unanswerable.
What can we do, any of us, how can we help? Let the man who has

the answer cry it from the house-tops in a hundred languages. But there will be no crier in the night, and it is night for all the Fords of the world and for us who love them.

In *Lanterns on the Levee* (Baton Rouge, 1941), 285–97.

Katherine Du Pre Lumpkin

The Making of a Southerner (1946)

Southern autobiographers are as a group recognizable by their attention to the history of their region as well as their relatives and by the central role accorded questions of race and slavery. Like William Alexander Percy, who published his memoir Lanterns on the Levee *in 1941, Katherine Du Pre Lumpkin turned a critical eye on local custom and mores, including those of her family. Unlike Percy, who defended white privilege and condoned only incremental social change, Lumpkin was open to systemic change, particularly in the post–World War II context. Trained as a sociologist at Columbia University, Lumpkin realized that the South's ingrained racial culture could not simply be renounced; it had to be actively unlearned. Much of* The Making of a Southerner *concerns Lumpkin's process of unlearning her upbringing in the years before World War II.*

* * *

One summer morning I had gone aimlessly out into the yard before breakfast. In the kitchen breakfast-preparation had been stirring as I passed. Of a sudden in the house there was bedlam— sounds to make my heart pound and my hair prickle at the roots. Calls and screams were interspersed with blow upon blow. Soon enough I knew someone was getting a fearful beating, and I knew full well it was not one of us: when we children were punished, it might be corporal, but it was an occasion of some dignity for all parties concerned. Carefully keeping my distance, I edged over so that I could gaze in through the kitchen window. I could see enough. Our little black cook, a woman small in stature though full grown, was receiving a severe thrashing. I could see her writhing under the blows of a descending stick wielded by the white master of the house. I could see her face distorted with fear and agony and his with stern rage. I could see her twisting and turning as she tried to free herself from his firm grasp. I could hear her screams, as I was certain they could be heard for blocks, "Mister Sheriff! Mister Sheriff! He's killing me! Help!" Having seen and heard, I chose the better part of stuffing my fists in my ears and creeping away on trembling legs.

The thrashing of the cook was not talked about, not around me at least. Nothing was said in the family, although a strained atmosphere was present all day—a tension one came to expect whenever slight incidents of race-conflict occurred. The neighbors said nothing. Although I waited with considerable trepidation—how unnecessarily I could not know—nothing was heard from the sheriff. To my hesitant question, "What had the cook done?" I was told simply that she had been very "impudent" to her mistress; she had "answered her back."

It was not the custom for Southern white gentlemen to thrash their cooks, not by the early 1900's. But it was not heinous. We did not think so. It had once been right not so many years before. Apparently it still could be. Given sufficient provocation, it might be argued: and what recourse did a white man have? All would have assumed, and no doubt did on this occasion, that the provocation on the Negro cook's part had been very great. Few Negro sins were more reprehensible in our Southern eyes than "impudence." Small child though I was, I had learned this fact. I knew "impudence" was intolerable. In this sense I had no qualms about what I had witnessed. But in another sense I did have, and this disturbed me. Naturally I had no explanation for these mixed feelings. I could merely try to forget the thing—a child wishing to feel at one with her surroundings.

We may assume this about it. It disturbed me because I saw it. If it had been remote, if I had merely heard it as a story as one did hear of similar acts toward Negroes in my childhood, if it had thus been completely removed from all sight and sound, surely I could have felt quite pleasantly *en rapport*.

In any event, this much I know. The inevitable had happened, and what is bound to come to a Southern child chanced to come to me this way. Thereafter, I was fully aware of myself as a white, and of Negroes as Negroes. Thenceforth, I began to be self-conscious about the many signs and symbols of my race position that had been battering against my consciousness since virtual infancy.

I found them countless in number. As soon as I could read, I would carefully spell out the notices in public places. I wished to be certain we were where we ought to be. Our station waiting rooms— "For White." Our railroad coaches—"For White." There was no true occasion for a child's anxiety lest we make a mistake. It was all so plainly marked. (Said the law, it seems, " . . . in letters at least two inches high.") Trains were plain sailing. One knew the "For Colored" coach would be up next the engine, and usually but half a car, with baggage the other half. Theaters were no problem. Negroes rarely went, and in any case "their place" was only a nook railed off far up in the "buzzard's roost." Street cars were more troublesome. Here too were the signs—"White" at the forward end, "Colored" at the rear. But no distinct dividing line, no wall or rail between. How many seats we occupied depended upon our needs. Sometimes conductors must come and shift things around in the twilight zone between. If whites were standing and Negroes not, it may be the latter were told to give up their seats. Conductors were the authority. They might handle the delicate rearrangement quietly by just a tap on the shoulder and a thumb pointing back— this to a Negro; but they might be surly or even belligerent, speak in a loud rough voice so all could hear—"Move back." A little white girl would rather stand, however much she knew it was her right to be seated in place of Negroes, than have this loud-voiced notoriety; and also, I think—it is ever so faint a memory—anything rather than have a fleeting glimpse of the still, dark faces in the rear of the car, which seemed to stare so expressionlessly into space.

We knew the streets were the white man's wherever he chose to walk; that a Negro who moved out into the gutter to let us pass was in our eyes a "good darkey." I could have been hardly more than eight when a little Negro girl of our age, passing a friend and me, showed a disposition to take her half of the sidewalk. We did not give ground—we were whites! Her arm brushed against my companion's. She turned on the Negro child furiously. "Move over there, you dirty black nigger!" I know why this recollection stayed with me while others did not. It outraged us so because this partic-ular colored child did not shrink or run, but flared back at us with a stinging retort, remaining dead in her tracks, defying us, and we had no choice left us but to move on.

Less-than-proper humility from Negroes especially troubled our white consciousness. It was a danger signal and would never occur, we said, were it not for wrong policies. Nine times out of ten we linked it with education. Education was wrong. It made Negroes ambitious, impudent, wishing to "rise out of their place," we said. It was bound to result in intolerable situations.

I knew this was so. I myself had met it face to face. For example, when on Sunday mornings we would run into the line of college youths from Allen University, the Negro institution in our town. We were going to church. So were they. As was the custom for college boys and girls in my childhood, they walked to church in a line. We must cross the street they traversed on their way to church. We did not always meet them, but often we did, and there was always the possibility. What should we do? How comport ourselves? We had no precedent, save that of claiming our right to walk anywhere and Negroes to step aside. But a whole line step aside for a family group, white though it was, or hold up its march, or break its ranks? Then should we walk through it, or should we wait? We might perhaps have said politely, "Excuse me, please. May I pass?" (Of course, if they had been white students going to church. . . .) It would be awk-ward mercly to push through or try to. Suppose they did not make room. Being educated they might be "uppity"; it would be humili-ating to let an incident occur; and there was the decorum due a Sunday morning. Must we then do that most galling thing, stand waiting in our places while "darkies" passed? It did not soothe us, but just the contrary, that they were nicely dressed, for it might mean, so we said, that they thought themselves as "good" as whites; or that they were "educated," they and their professors who ac-companied them; much more than clothes, this could spell aspira-tions not encompassed in our beliefs about their "rightful place."

Often we spoke of the sin it would be to eat with a Negro. Next to "intermarriage" this was a most appalling thought. It was an un-thinkable act of "social equality." To say the words, "eat with a

Negro," stirred us disagreeably. In a sense, of course, it was no
problem. How could it arise in our protected lives, and surrounded
as we were by our racial barriers? It did, vicariously. We suspected
Northerners of doing it upon occasion, and shuddered at the
thought. We were sure Yankee teachers in Southern Negro institutions were guilty of the sin. That Republicans flaunted it was glar-
ingly confirmed when one day our newspapers were filled with
shocked accounts of President Theodore Roosevelt's entertainment
of Dr. Booker T. Washington at luncheon in the White House. It
was too much—this unpardonable "insult to the South" from the
very seat of our national government, this fomenting in high places
of "social equality." We were all aroused, on the streets, in our
homes, at recess at school. We children talked of it excitedly, echo-
ing the harshly indignant words and tones.

We often spoke of the peculiar inborn traits of this so peculiar
race. For instance, the Negro's "thieving propensities." White men
stole too, but not "as a race." We verily believed that a Negro could
not help but steal. So we acted accordingly. We must lock up our
valuables. We children should never leave the key in the food
pantry door, but turn it and put it back in its hiding place. Let
something be missing; we suspected the cook, unless it was found;
maybe even then, for she could have "got scared" and returned it.
It was not serious with us; just a disability of the race, we said, that
only we Southerners understood and took charitably. Of course in
capacity they were different. This was the essence of our sense of
difference—we superior, they inferior. But not merely that in their
mental development none could ever go beyond say a child of ten
or twelve (unless "they had white blood in them, of course"); they
were qualitatively different, somehow, though we as children could
not have explained wherein. We just used phrases such as "innately
irresponsible," "love of finery," "not to be trusted," "slovenly," and
a dozen more. To be sure, we would apply to special individuals
contradictory attributes. But this made no difficulty about general-
ization. The innate traits, we said, applied to the race. To any
doubting Thomases from the outside we had our irrefutable answer: "After all, we Southerners alone know the Negro."

At the club-forming age we children had a Ku Klux Klan. It was
natural to do it, offspring of our warm Southern patriotism. We

were happy in it for the aid and blessing it won from our adults. Our costumes, while made from worn-out sheets, were yet cut to pattern with help at home; they had fitted hoods, also, with tall peaks, and emblazoned across the front of the robes were red cheesecloth crosses. Constitution, by-laws, and ritual were something out of the ordinary. They were written, not on paper, but transcribed, as we supposed the original had been, on a long cloth scroll, at the top of which was a bright red cross. Our elders helped us write the ritual and rules and, true or not, we firmly believed that our laws and oaths were in some sense an echo from the bygone order.

It was certainly a game and fascinating as such. But it was much more besides. Its ritual, rolling off our tongues with much happy gusto, was frequently interlarded with warm exhortations to white supremacy. We held our meetings in the greatest secrecy—so we pretended—in a friend's basement near our home (our counterpart of a deep, silent forest around the hour of midnight on a moonless night). A chief topic of business when ceremonies had ended was the planning of pretended punitive expeditions against mythical recalcitrant Negroes. And while in one sense it never was real, in another it went far beyond pretense. We vented our feelings. We felt glow in us an indignant antagonism. These were real. We felt patriotic; so was this real—this warm, pulsing feeling of Southern loyalty. We told of our Cause and our Southern ideals which we were preserving. It was truly a serious game, and in a sense we were serious children bent on our ideals. We liked our clubs to have this idealistic side. Witness the fact that the club to follow our Ku Klux Klan was a "Knights of the Round Table," although it was short-lived; it broke up over sharp competition for the post of Sir Galahad.

Times would come when even we children must uphold our beliefs in a serious public way. We rejoiced to do it. It made us feel very worth while. So with me once in the sixth grade in school. Our room was divided—"Busy Bees" on one side, "Wise Owls" on the other. We were to have a debate. It was an exceedingly strange query for a Southern schoolroom: "Are Negroes Equal to White People?" It never would have been proposed if we had not had in the room a little blond Northern boy. He being a Yankee, he could with impunity be asked to serve as the straw man for the rest of us to knock down. Patently, his own side of the room could not support him, so it was all of us against one. It was a strange debate. There were just the two of us—the little Yankee boy and I who were actual participants. My debate I can see now, carefully written down in my own handwriting from the copy we had worked on with so much earnestness in my family circle. His came first—one can guess our scorn at the arguments that flowed from his Yankee home. Then I argued mine. Of course I told of our history and how the South had been saved by the courage of our fathers—we always told this. Probably I told of the Invisible Empire—we often did. Obviously, I recited all the arguments we had for Negro inferiority, and that this was why he must never be allowed to "rise out of his place." My peroration comes back to me in so many words, and how I advanced it with resounding fervor amidst a burst of applause from all the children in the room but my opponent: ". . . and the Bible says that they shall be hewers of wood and drawers of water forever!"

* * *

There came the years of 1914 and 1915. Audiences of students in our section of the nation had found themselves listening in rapt attention to a new message. Elsewhere it may have sounded before 1914. Our campus heard it in the spring of that year. It was not of heaven and hell and eternal damnation. It was not a call to repentance such as revivalists might sound. There was no "wrath of Jehovah" here, or "sins of the fathers visited unto the third and fourth generation," no hint of a vengeful Deity. It was not even a call to staid duty, to fulfill one's religious obligations to believe, and pray, and attend church services, and tithe. It came in an infinitely attractive guise. It had drawing power at a time when these same young people were beginning to feel uneasy at a world out of joint, and less secure in their surroundings and less confident in their elders. It told youth that the day of discipleship was not past. On the contrary, it said the essence of their religion, did they but know it, was old words with a new meaning—"Follow the Master," "The Kingdom of Heaven on Earth." It said God above all was a "loving Father," who was first and foremost approachable, and had infinite concern for the sons of men. As for the Son of God, he had once been Man as well; he had even been a carpenter, one who worked with his hands. Hence it was practical even in the twentieth century to call him "Master." He was a divine example, to be sure, but he could be "followed." Some might say base human nature would not change. Not the new message or the new voices. Let this religion spread, they said, and it could be potent to transform the world by changing the men who made it. To some of us at least these were little short of John-on-Patmos voices—"And I saw a new heaven and a new earth: for the first heaven and the first earth were passed away; and there was no more sea."

I was drawn into this company then and there. Nor was I any more loath than my fellows to weigh our forebears in the scales and find them wanting. We were especially prone to, who, as we supposed, had already cut loose from many of our childhood religious moorings. How, we began to wonder, as we became more and more enamored of our role, had men been so blind for all the generations of Christendom as not to see what we now perceived? How had they gone on, century after century, quarreling among themselves over theological minutiae, bothering their minds over issues of dogma, to the disregard of what all along had been the essence of our religion? Why, our minds demanded, was there still so little "brotherhood" in the world, when "brotherhood" was the very meaning of Christianity? Let enough people but be persistent enough, and "consistent" enough—this latter loomed very large in our minds who had begun to "follow the Master"—and why might not the new day mankind hoped for begin to dawn? We now had something to be and do in the admittedly very bad times in which we lived. Indeed, the further we pursued the matter, the more there appeared to be and do.

To be sure, not many continued to pursue it. Just occasional students here and there on various campuses.

For me it went on soaking into my consciousness for a year without any peculiarly eruptive consequences. But then it came. Why would it not take the form it did? I was a white Southerner living in the South. I was a young person, able blandly to assume that the Word could be made flesh and dwell among men. Except, of course, that I had never seen it in the flesh. Until I saw it, it had not remotely occurred to me what this might be thought to mean.

My college course was over, but I remained on my campus as a tutor. I was now nineteen. In late 1915 a few of us from several

Southern colleges were called to a "leadership" conference by the YWCA, the bearer on our women's campuses of the new social Christianity. The place was in North Carolina—I think, the city of Charlotte. I know it was a strictly Southern city, very Southern indeed, for presently I became exceedingly conscious of the mighty cloud of hostile witnesses that might be surrounding us. At the conference we studied and planned for a day or two. Then one of our staff leaders placed a proposal before us.

She was a Southern woman. She spoke to us as such. She assured us that she had been reared even as had we. She said that she could understand our first impulsive misgivings. Once she had stood at the crossroads we now confronted. She urged us to consider the matter. Take until morning. We could accept or reject.

The proposal was this: There was a Negro woman leader in the city then: a woman of education, a professional woman, herself belonging to the YWCA staff. It was suggested that she speak to us on Christianity and the race problem.

If our leader, in proposing it, had just called the person "*Jane* Arthur," our sense of foreboding would not have been so great. Well, surely, let a "Jane" or "Mary" speak to us, if needs must, and that could be the end of it; we could go away and forget a "Mary" or a "Jane." We had known and forgotten tens of thousands of Negro Marys and Janes. But never a "*Miss* Arthur." How forget a "*Miss* Arthur"? And must we too say: "*Miss*"? Would we be introduced and have to shake her hand and say: "*Miss* Arthur"? Shaking hands was not unheard of. Many times we had seen our people shake the hand of a "darkey" in a genuinely kindly way, asking how he was, and how was his family, and they might remark afterward, and probably would, in a spirit of warm generosity: "Now there is a *good* darkey." How could one be "good" who came to us as "*Miss*" Arthur? The only time we had ever said "Miss" or "Mrs." or "Mr." was in telling a "darkey joke," or in black-faced minstrels—"Now, *Mister* Johnson . . ." and the crowd would roar with mirth. It had always been a source of slight amusement to us, the way Negroes seemed to insist upon addressing one another as "Mr." and "Mrs." Why do such a thing, I used to wonder? To imitate white people, I supposed, in their desire to make themselves as much like us as they could. We would remark, tolerantly: "See how they try to mimic us. Queer, isn't it? But they're just like children trying to pretend they are grown up. . . ." We would smile, and not mind it in the general run of "darkies," the ignorant and humble ones. We had no such kindly sentiment toward the educated; those we knew—we had heard—always addressed one another just as we did each other; those whose dark brows seemed to grow overcast, whose countenances seemed suddenly to become strangely still and remote when a white man would say to one of them whom he met on the sidewalk: "Howdye, Jim," or "Good evening, George"—maybe a doctor, or lawyer or teacher. (Some of these had walked our streets when I was a child; we knew their alleged profession; always one thought: "How impudent . . . how presumptuous . . . !")

But see it another way. In one sense, was it so out-of-the-way for a Negro to stand before us and speak to us? There was nothing to be *scared* of. (We put scorn in the emphasis.) We were used to Negroes, weren't we? Who could be more so? How many times had we smiled at Northerners who looked at one almost with horror, and exclaimed: "How can you Southerners stand to have them fondle your children, handle your food?"—smiled at them, and said: "It only goes to show how much kindlier we Southerners feel toward the Negro than you Yankees, who are always trying to tell us how to treat them. . . . You don't understand. . . . We are their best friends. . . . They are all right in their place." But this was the wrong thought to let slip in. This really opened the door to thoughts we would like to avoid. "What would people say? What if they knew? How explain?" For to concur in what was proposed, by no stretch of our imaginations, would be other than breaking the unwritten and written law of our heritage: "Keep them in their place."

We were like a little company of Eves, who, not from being tempted—surely, we did not long to eat the fruit which up to now had been called forbidden—but by sheer force of unsought circumstance found ourselves called upon to pluck from the Tree of Life the apple that would open our eyes to see what was good and evil. But here confusion reigned. We had been taught it was wrong to eat this apple. Yet as it was put before us we felt guilty not to. Most certainly we were afraid to do it. Did we have the glimmering notion that if we did, something that hitherto had always seemed decorous and decent might, if our eyes were opened to see its naked reality, seem quite otherwise?

Why did we consent? Or perhaps put it another way: by what rationalizing means did we excuse our consent to something from which we saw no self-respecting retreat? The old Southern heritage could not be thrust aside, even momentarily, except by something insistently strong. On one side was the dictum: "In their place." Hitherto we had assumed it to be immutable and unchangeable. It carried the authority of our kind. For me it carried a special weight, which still could be felt even if much of its old glamour had slipped away, of a Lost Cause termed sacred. What could bring a counterweight and authority against this bulk, something equally reinforced by sentiment, something that could even take precedence over our assumed racial verities?

We knew what it was. Perhaps we sensed from the outset, the way the case was put, that no real choice faced us, unless we proposed to turn deserter. Before our leader let us go to think it over, she had put the matter in this wise: It was written, she read (and how many times in succeeding years did we let this story stand us in similar stead), ". . . Jesus . . . said, a certain man was going down from Jerusalem to Jericho . . . fell among robbers, who both stripped him and beat him, and departed, leaving him half dead . . . A certain priest . . . when he saw him . . . passed by on the other side . . . in like manner a Levite . . . But a certain Samaritan . . . journeyed . . . and when he saw him . . . was moved with compassion . . . bound up his wounds . . . set him on his own beast . . . brought him to an inn, and took care of him . . . Which of these three . . . was neighbor to him that fell among the robbers?" [Who was better than another here—driving home the point—the "chosen people," or the Samaritan who was despised? What, in "the Master's" lesson, made one person better than another?] Oh, for the days when nothing more than the Virgin Birth, miracles, the Trinity, pushed against one's mind as tests of credulity! But surely, we could argue, all the religious people at home, all one had ever known, would have felt even as we wanted to. Many, there came the additional passing thought, would very probably even take us sternly by the hand, saying: "We must get you out of here."

But this latter notion was not palatable. It kept coming back and we rejected it. Here we were, almost of age. "We must consider this matter for ourselves," we finally said.

In after years one might idly wonder: suppose Miss Arthur had never stood before our little group? Suppose she had been taken ill, or had broken her leg, or for any reason had been kept away? Suppose our leaders had heeded our obvious distress and decided: "We are going too fast; we must wait awhile; they will be more ready by and by." Or suppose we had said: "We just can't stomach it; maybe we should . . . but we can't live up to this test of our new Christian consistency. . . ." It was idle wondering. No doubt other occasions would have come. Of course, if they had not chanced to. . . . In any event, she did stand before us, and she was introduced as "Miss Arthur." Moreover, we were told, "She will talk to us. . . ."

What she talked about was not of such great consequence: what mattered was that she entered the door and stood before us. We told each other afterwards—could it be we felt a little gratified?— how our pulses had hammered, and how we could feel our hearts pound in our chests. Be that as it may, it was of no small moment to hear her low voice sound in the speech of an educated woman, and to have my mind let the thought flicker in, even if it disappeared again immediately—If I should close my eyes, would I know whether she was white or Negro?

In any event, when it was over, I found the heavens had not fallen, nor the earth parted asunder to swallow us up in this unheard of transgression. Indeed, I found I could breathe freely again, eat heartily, even laugh again. Back in my Georgia foothills I put it out of my mind, or better, pushed it down deep in a welter of other unwanteds. But still I would now and then find something stirring up an indefinable sense of discomfort—and then remember. Moreover, in remembering, there was just a flavor of something besides uneasiness: ever so faint exhilaration, perhaps? One of the Bible stories of my childhood which never had sat well with me, seeming to my untutored mind a punishment out of all proportion to the crime, was that of the man in the book of Samuel who broke the law forbidding any secular hand, unconsecrated and unaccustomed to minutely prescribed rules and regulations, to touch the sacred Tabernacle of Jehovah; touching it, so said the story, he was promptly stricken dead. Well, so was this tabernacle of our sacred racial beliefs untouchable. How well I knew it; how ingrained in me were the beliefs it housed, and the belief that to touch it would bring direst consequences. But I had touched it. I had reached out my hand for an instant and let my finger-tips brush it. I had done it, and nothing, not the slightest thing had happened.

Excerpted from *The Making of a Southerner* (Athens, GA, 1991 [1946]), 131–37, 187–93.

Ralph Ellison

A Party Down at the Square (ca. 1940)

Born in Oklahoma City in 1914, Ralph Ellison's arrival in Manhattan in 1936 caught the Harlem Renaissance on its way down. Employed by the New York Federal Writers Project from 1938 to 1942, Ellison published essays, reviews, and short fiction in many of the leading magazines of the day, including The New Republic *and* The Saturday Review. *During World War II, he served in the merchant marine as a cook and a baker, and began the novel* Invisible Man, *which, when it was published in 1952, took the literary world by storm and earned its author the National Book Award.*

Likely written in 1940, "A Party Down at the Square" remained unpublished in Ellison's lifetime. In this remarkable story, a young Ellison crossed the narrative color line to draw readers into the heart of a small-town lynching as seen through the eyes of an anonymous visiting white boy. A detached narrator, the child reporter presents the grisly details of organized mob violence and remarks without comment on the social composition of the crowd.

I don't know what started it. A bunch of men came by my Uncle Ed's place and said there was going to be a party down at the Square, and my uncle hollered for me to come on and I ran with them through the dark and rain and there we were at the Square. When we got there everybody was mad and quiet and standing around looking at the nigger. Some of the men had guns, and one man kept goosing the nigger in his pants with the barrel of a shotgun, saying he ought to pull the trigger, but he never did. It was right in front of the courthouse, and the old clock in the tower was striking twelve. The rain was falling cold and freezing as it fell. Everybody was cold, and the nigger kept wrapping his arms around himself trying to stop the shivers.

Then one of the boys pushed through the circle and snatched off the nigger's shirt, and there he stood, with his black skin all shivering in the light from the fire, and looking at us with a scaired look on his face and putting his hands in his pants pockets. Folks started yelling to hurry up and kill the nigger. Somebody yelled: "Take your hands out of your pockets, nigger; we gonna have plenty heat in a minnit." But the nigger didn't hear him and kept his hands where they were.

I tell you the rain was cold. I had to stick my hands in my pockets they got so cold. The fire was pretty small, and they put some logs around the platform they had the nigger on and then threw on some gasoline, and you could see the flames light up the whole Square. It was late and the streetlights had been off for a long time. It was so bright that the bronze statue of the general standing there in the Square was like something alive. The shadows playing on his moldy green face made him seem to be smiling down at the nigger.

They threw on more gas, and it made the Square bright like it gets when the lights are turned on or when the sun is setting red. All the wagons and cars were standing around the curbs. Not like Saturday though—the niggers weren't there. Not a single nigger was there except this Bacote nigger and they dragged him there tied to the back of Jed Wilson's truck. On Saturday there's as many niggers as white folks.

Everybody was yelling crazy 'cause they were about to set fire to the nigger, and I got to the rear of the circle and looked around the Square to try to count the cars. The shadows of the folks was flickering on the trees in the middle of the Square. I saw some birds that the noise had woke up flying through the trees. I guess maybe they thought it was morning. The ice had started the cobblestones in the street to shine where the rain was falling and freezing. I counted forty cars before I lost count. I knew folks must have been there from Phenix City by all the cars mixed in with the wagons.

God, it was a hell of a night. It was some night all right. When the noise died down I heard the nigger's voice from where I stood in the back, so I pushed my way up front. The nigger was bleeding from his nose and ears, and I could see him all red where the dark blood was running down his black skin. He kept lifting first one foot and then the other; like a chicken on a hot stove. I looked down to the platform they had him on, and they had pushed a ring of fire up close to his feet. It must have been hot to him with the flames almost touching his big black toes. Somebody yelled for the nigger to say his prayers, but the nigger wasn't saying anything now. He just kinda moaned with his eyes shut and kept moving up and down on his feet, first one foot and then the other.

I watched the flames burning the logs up closer and closer to the nigger's feet. They were burning good now, and the rain had stopped and the wind was rising, making the flames flare higher. I looked, and there must have been thirty-five women in the crowd, and I could hear their voices clear and shrill mixed in with those of the men. Then it happened. I heard the noise about the same time everyone else did. It was like the roar of a cyclone blowing up from the gulf, and everyone was looking up into the air to see what it was. Some of the faces looked surprised and scaired, all but the nigger. He didn't even hear the noise. He didn't even look up. Then the roar came closer, right above our heads and the wind was blowing higher and higher and the sound seemed to be going in circles.

Then I saw her. Through the clouds and fog I could see a red and green light on her wings. I could see them just for a second; then she rose up into the low clouds. I looked out for the beacon over the tops of the buildings in the direction of the airfield that's forty miles away, and it wasn't circling around. You usually could see it sweeping around the sky at night, but it wasn't there. Then, there she was again, like a big bird lost in the fog. I looked for the red and green lights, and they weren't there anymore. She was flying even closer to the tops of the buildings than before. The wind was blowing harder, and leaves started flying about, making funny shadows on the ground, and tree limbs were cracking and falling.

It was a storm all right. The pilot must have thought he was over the landing field. Maybe he thought the fire in the Square was put there for him to land by. Gosh, but it scaired the folks. I was scaired too. They started yelling: "He's going to land. He's going to land." And: "He's going to fall." A few started for their cars and wagons. I could hear the wagons creaking and chains jangling and cars spitting and missing as they started the engines up. Off to my right, a horse started pitching and striking his hooves against a car.

I didn't know what to do. I wanted to run, and I wanted to stay and see what was going to happen. The plane was close as hell. The pilot must have been trying to see where he was at, and her motors were drowning out all the sounds. I could even feel the vibration, and my hair felt like it was standing up under my hat. I happened to look over at the statue of the general standing with one leg before the other and leaning back on a sword, and I was fixing to run over and climb between his legs and sit there and watch when the roar stopped some, and I looked up and she was gliding just over the top of the trees in the middle of the Square.

Her motors stopped altogether and I could hear the sound of branches cracking and snapping off below her landing gear. I could see her plain now, all silver and shining in the light of the fire with T.W.A. in black letters under her wings. She was sailing smoothly out of the Square when she hit the high power lines that follow the Birmingham highway through the town. It made a loud crash. It sounded like the wind blowing the door of a tin barn shut. She only hit with her landing gear, but I could see the sparks flying, and the wires knocked loose from the poles were spitting blue sparks and whipping around like a bunch of snakes and leaving circles of blue sparks in the darkness.

The plane had knocked five or six wires loose, and they were dangling and swinging, and every time they touched they threw off more sparks. The wind was making them swing, and when I got over there, there was a crackling and spitting screen of blue haze across the highway. I lost my hat running over, but I didn't stop to look for it. I was among the first and I could hear the others pounding behind me across the grass of the Square. They were yelling to beat all hell, and they came up fast, pushing and shoving, and someone got pushed against a swinging wire. It made a sound like when a blacksmith drops a red hot horseshoe into a barrel of water; and the steam comes up. I could smell the flesh burning. The first time I'd ever smelled it. I got up close and it was a woman. It must have killed her right off. She was lying in a puddle stiff as a board, with pieces of glass insulators that the plane had knocked off the poles lying all around her. Her white dress was torn, and I saw one of her tits hanging out in the water and her thighs. Some woman screamed and fainted and almost fell on a wire, but a man caught her. The sheriff and his men were yelling and driving folks back with guns shining in their hands, and everything was lit up blue by the sparks. The shock had turned the woman almost as black as the nigger. I was trying to see if she wasn't blue too, or if it was just the sparks, and the sheriff drove me away. As I backed off trying to see, I heard the motors of the plane start up again somewhere off to the right in the clouds.

The clouds were moving fast in the wind and the wind was blowing the smell of something burning over to me. I turned around, and the crowd was headed back to the nigger. I could see him standing there in the middle of the flames. The wind was making the flames brighter every minute. The crowd was running. I ran too. I ran back across the grass with the crowd. It wasn't so large now that so many had gone when the plane came. I tripped and fell over the limb of a tree lying in the grass and bit my lip. It ain't well yet I bit it so bad. I could taste the blood in my mouth as I ran over. I guess that's what made me sick. When I got there, the fire had caught the nigger's pants, and the folks were standing around watching, but not too close on account of the wind blowing the flames. Somebody hollered, "Well, nigger, it ain't so cold now, is it? You don't need to put your hands in your pockets now." And the nigger looked up with his great white eyes looking like they was 'bout to pop out of his head, and I had enough. I didn't want to see anymore. I wanted to run somewhere and puke, but I stayed. I stayed right there in the front of the crowd and looked.

The nigger tried to say something I couldn't hear for the roar of the wind in the fire, and I strained my ears. Jed Wilson hollered, "What you say there, nigger?" And it came back through the flames in his nigger voice: "Will one a you gentlemen please cut my throat?" he said. "Will somebody please cut my throat like a Christian?" And Jed hollered back, "Sorry, but ain't no Christians around tonight. Ain't no Jew-boys neither. We're just one hundred percent Americans."

Then the nigger was silent. Folks started laughing at Jed. Jed's right popular with the folks, and next year, my uncle says, they plan to run him for sheriff. The heat was too much for me, and the smoke was making my eyes to smart. I was trying to back away when Jed reached down and brought up a can of gasoline and threw it in the fire on the nigger. I could see the flames catching the gas in a puff as it went in in a silver sheet and some of it reached the nigger, making spurts of blue fire all over his chest.

Well, that nigger was tough. I have to give it to that nigger; he was really tough. He had started to burn like a house afire and was making the smoke smell like burning hides. The fire was up around his head, and the smoke was so thick and black we couldn't see him. And him not moving—we thought he was dead. Then he started out. The fire had burned the ropes they had tied him with, and he started jumping and kicking about like he was blind, and you could smell his skin burning. He kicked so hard that the platform, which was burning too, fell in, and he rolled out of the fire at my feet. I jumped back so he wouldn't get on me. I'll never forget it. Every time I eat barbeque I'll remember that nigger. His back was just like a barbecued hog. I could see the prints of his ribs where they start around from his backbone and curve down and around. It was a sight to see, that nigger's back. He was right at my feet, and somebody behind pushed me and almost made me step on him, and he was still burning.

I didn't step on him though, and Jed and somebody else pushed him back into the burning planks and logs and poured on more gas. I wanted to leave, but the folks were yelling and I couldn't move except to look around and see the statue. A branch the wind had broken was resting on his hat. I tried to push out and get away because my guts were gone, and all I got was spit and hot breath in my face from the woman and two men standing directly behind me. So I had to turn back around. The nigger rolled out of the fire again. He wouldn't stay put. It was on the other side this time. I couldn't see him very well through the flames and smoke. They got some tree limbs and held him there this time and he stayed there till he was ashes. I guess he stayed there. I know he burned to ashes because I saw Jed a week later, and he laughed and showed me some white finger bones still held together with little pieces of the nigger's

skin. Anyway, I left when somebody moved around to see the nigger. I pushed my way through the crowd, and a woman in the rear
scratched my face as she yelled and fought to get up close.

I ran across the Square to the other side, where the sheriff and
his deputies were guarding the wires that were still spitting and
making a blue fog. My heart was pounding like I had been running
a long ways, and I bent over and let my insides go. Everything came
up and spilled in a big gush over the ground. I was sick, and tired,
and weak, and cold. The wind was still high, and large drops of
rain were beginning to fall. I headed down the street to my uncle's
place past a store where the wind had broken a window, and glass
lay over the sidewalk. I kicked it as I went by. I remember somebody's fool rooster crowing like it was morning in all that wind.

The next day I was too weak to go out, and my uncle kidded me
and called me "the gutless wonder from Cincinnati." I didn't mind.
He said you get used to it in time. He couldn't go out hisself. There
was too much wind and rain. I got up and looked out of the window, and the rain was pouring down and dead sparrows and limbs
of trees were scattered all over the yard. There had been a cyclone
all right. It swept a path right through the county, and we were
lucky we didn't get the full force of it.

It blew for three days steady, and put the town in a hell of a
shape. The wind blew sparks and set fire to the white-and-green-
rimmed house on Jackson Avenue that had the big concrete lions in
the yard and burned it down to the ground. They had to kill another nigger who tried to run out of the county after they burned
this Bacote nigger. My Uncle Ed said they always have to kill niggers in pairs to keep the other niggers in place. I don't know
though, the folks seem a little skittish of the niggers. They all came
back, but they act pretty sullen. They look mean as hell when you
pass them down at the store. The other day I was down to Brinkley's store, and a white cropper said it didn't do no good to kill the
niggers 'cause things don't get no better. He looked hungry as hell.
Most of the croppers look hungry. You'd be surprised how hungry
white folks can look. Somebody said that he'd better shut his damn
mouth, and he shut up. But from the look on his face he won't stay
shut long. He went out of the store muttering to himself and spit a
big chew of tobacco right down on Brinkley's floor. Brinkley said he
was sore 'cause he wouldn't let him have credit. Anyway, it didn't

seem to help things. First it was the nigger and the storm, then the plane, then the woman and the wires, and now I hear the airplane line is investigating to find who set the fire that almost wrecked their plane. All that in one night, and all of it but the storm over one nigger. It was some night all right. It was some party too. I was right there, see. I was right there watching it all. It was my first party and my last. God, but that nigger was tough. That Bacote nigger was some nigger!

In Ralph Ellison, *Flying Home and Other Stories*, ed. John F. Callahan (New York, 1996), 3–11.

Jessie Daniel Ames

Southern Women and Lynching (October 1936)

Texan Jessie Daniel Ames's career as a social activist reflected her belief that women had both the ability and the responsibility to improve race relations in the South. A suffragist and the director of the Texas branch of the Women's Committee of the Commission on Interracial Cooperation (CIC), Ames brought years of experience gained through the social Christianity movement of the late nineteenth century to the interracial movement. Galvanized by a sharp uptick in racial violence at the start of the Depression, Ames formed the Association of Southern Women for the Prevention of Lynching (ASWPL) in 1930 with two dozen "lady insurrectionists." Outraged that white men cloaked their barbarity in the name of white women, the ASWPL declared that they did not need such "protection." Turning ideals of southern honor back on white men, the ASWPL asked southern sheriffs and judges—frequently the husbands and brothers of the ASWPL members—to sign a pledge that they would uphold the law and do everything in their power to prevent a lynching. At the same time, ASWPL women, who were almost always simultaneously active in local churches and other organizations, lobbied community leaders to actively denounce mob violence. This campaign of conscience and public opinion proved remarkably effective, although it did not succeed in the passage of federal antilynching legislation, the longtime goal of the NAACP.

Conference Called

The Association of Southern Women for the Prevention of Lynching grew out of a recognized need for some central committee to assume as its sole purpose the initiative for the eradication of lynching. Although some eight years before, small groups of women in each of the thirteen Southern states had issued statements condemning lynching among a dozen or more evils afflicting the South, they set in motion no special machinery by means of which public opinion would be changed toward this one special evil. When lynchings reached a new high level in 1930, it appeared imperative to some Southern women that something should be done by them to stop or abate this particularly revolting crime. Consequently, a conference was called for November 1, 1930, in Atlanta, Georgia, to discuss what Southern women could do to stop lynching.

Favorable response to this call to confer was inspired by an increasing awareness on the part of Southern women of the claim of lynchers and mobsters that their lawless acts were necessary to the protection of women.

Participation of Women in Lynchings

Before the day set for the conference statistics were carefully gathered on the two hundred and eleven lynchings during the eight preceding years (1922–1929). When the women convened the facts about these lynchings were laid before them. Though lynchings were not all committed in the South, very little encouragement was found for stating that lynching was not sectional. Out of the two hundred and eleven persons lynched, two hundred and four had met death at the hands of Southern mobs.

Consideration of the crimes of which the victims had been charged brought further enlightenment. Less than 29% of these two hundred and eleven persons were charged with crimes against white women. Then, what, asked the women, had the 79% [should read 71%] done? Offenses of some kind against white men, they were told.

Furthermore in every lynching investigated, some attention had been paid to the mobs as well as to the victims and the crimes. Women were present in some numbers at every lynching and not infrequently they participated. Some of the women were mothers with young children. These children, members of a future generation of lynchers, were balanced precariously on parents' shoulders in order to have a better view. Young boys and girls were contributing their numbers to the mobs both as spectators and as leaders.

Repudiation of Lynching

Lynchings could no longer be considered objectively. Women everywhere must hear what happened when a mob seized control of local government. Some way must be found to arouse deep and abiding passion against lynching.

After many questions and some debate the conference came to the unanimous decision that the first and most necessary move on the part of white women was to repudiate lynching in unmistakable language as a protection to Southern women. Unless this idea of chivalry could be destroyed, lynchers would continue to use the name of women as an excuse for their crimes and a protection for themselves.

After adopting a resolution embodying their position on lynching, the conference of women voted to promote a movement of Southern white women through existing organizations, the chief purpose of which was to inform the public on the real nature of lynching.

Association Formed

The women who voted this resolution were influential officials of civic and religious organizations throughout the South. They had no authority to pledge their constituencies to any action, but they would ask the governing bodies of their organizations to support a constructive program against lynching. Before the one-day conference was over, it was clear that those connected with civic organizations did not feel that they could go farther than a personal and passive commitment.

Three Points of Agreement

Three points formed the basis of a long time program of action and education:

First, all the resources of the Council of the Association were to be directed toward the development and promotion of educational programs against lynching, leaving the field of political action to other groups.

Second, emphasis at all times was to be placed on the repudiation of the claim that lynching is necessary to the protection of white women.

Third, The Association of Southern Women for the Prevention of Lynching would be limited in organization to a Central Council and a State Council in each of the thirteen Southern States. Members of these Councils would be key women, officers or chairmen of established organizations of women who would be expected to assist in formulating policies and directing methods of procedure.

Methods of Procedure

Careful studies of lynchings indicate that mobs fall into two general classifications:

The mob that conducts a "quiet, orderly lynching," with no fanfare or publicity and without violent emotions. This type discloses debasing influences alive in the community much more dangerous to an enlightened Christian civilization than does the violently spectacular mob which, aroused to quick action through inflamed imaginations, too frequently find release only in sadistic tortures of its victim. Mobs of this second type frequently give public warning of their intention to lynch hours and even days before the capture of their suspected victim permits them to act. In these instances the Association has adopted a course of action calculated to focus public attention upon the community in which mob action threatens.

When a lynching has been committed, with or without previous public knowledge, state members of the Association inform the officers of women's organizations of the facts involved in the action of the mob. Regardless of the nature of the crime allegedly committed by the victim of the mob public condemnation is given the lynching, accompanied by the request for a rigid investigation of the mob by state and county officials.

Between Outbursts of Mob Violence

The time to prevent lynchings is before a mob forms. Investigations have disclosed that no county in the South is free from the shadow of a possible lynching. Because the county is the important unit of Government, intensive activities are planned to be carried on by women in each county seat *before a mob ever threatens.*

The Association proposes to reach every county in the South by delegating to clubs and societies at the county seat the responsibility for:

1. Interesting every organization of men and women in the county in the campaign against lynching.
2. Securing signatures of officers and members of all organizations, religious, civic, and patriotic, in the town and county.
3. Securing signatures of county officials, preachers, teachers, and laymen.

After Six Years

Twelve women! This was the number who agreed on November 1, 1930, to do what they could to stop lynching. They went home and began to work and to talk and to retell the facts as they had learned them. Nor did they forget to pray. They knew there would be opposition, and ridicule. In some places they were not allowed to speak and in others, permission was granted reluctantly and only after many cautious warnings on the things which must not be mentioned.

A conviction of the justice and the rightness of their cause and a determination to speak at all costs carried them through the first years. After six years, these twelve women have become over thirty-two thousand, living scattered over one thousand and thirty-three counties. They have secured the active co-operation of nearly seven hundred county officials in the program against lynching.

When the End of Lynching Will Arrive

The philosophy of the Association of Southern Women for the Prevention of Lynching is based on the belief that a continuous educational program, carried on day by day in the home, in the school, in the press, and in the church will end lynching by public demand.

A year will come when Tuskegee Institute will report "NO LYNCHINGS DURING ——." The actual year is the only thing about which Southern women are uncertain. But they believe that they will be able to name the year fairly accurately:

When a hundred thousand men and women pledge themselves in writing against lynching and agree to work against the crime publicly;   When every sheriff in the South pledges to uphold his oath of office—to support the Constitution without fear of bodily harm—or   When every sheriff of the South is pledged in writing to his constituents to prevent lynchings in his county;   When every Grade A college in the South makes the discussion and study of lynchings a part of classroom assignments.

In Association of Southern Women for the Prevention of Lynching Papers, Atlanta University Center, Robert W. Woodruff Library (Microfilm reel 4, #1816), *Women and Social Movements in the United States, 1600–2000,* online database accessed August 11, 2000, http://www.alexanderstreet6.com/wasm/wasmrestricted/aswpl/doc16.htm

Hollace Ransdall

Report on the Scottsboro, Alabama, Case (May 27, 1931)

In 1931, nine African American youths were arrested and accused of raping two young white women, Ruby Bates and Victoria Price, on a freight train traveling from Chattanooga to Memphis. The accused narrowly avoided a lynching and, despite flimsy evidence and the well-founded skepticism of many leading white Alabamians, were quickly convicted and sentenced to death by an all-white jury in Scottsboro, Alabama. Already engaged in significant civil rights litigation elsewhere, including the defense of alleged rapists, the NAACP decided against involvement in the Scottsboro case. Instead attorneys paid by the International Labor Defense, an affiliate of the Communist Party, stepped in and led vigorous appeals that resulted in a complex series of retrials, convictions, and ac-

quittals that spanned almost two decades. The guilty verdicts continued to roll in, despite the recantation of Ruby Bates, who testified in the second trial that no one had been raped on the train, and information gathered by Hollace Ransdall of the American Civil Liberties Union. These trials brought the injustices of common judicial practices in the South to national attention and resulted in a crucial Supreme Court ruling, Norris v. Alabama *(1935) on the racially exclusionary composition of juries. They also forced white Alabamians to ponder the possibility of consensual sex between white women and black men and the delicacy of the color line in an economic depression in which the poor of every color rode the rails looking for work and buying and selling whatever they could.*

Two Huntsville Mill Girls Hobo to Chattanooga

On March 24, 1931, two mill girls from Huntsville in Madison County, northern Alabama, dressed up in overalls and hoboed their way by freight train to Chattanooga, Tenn., about 97 miles away. The older of the two, Victoria Price, who said she was born in Fayettesville, Tenn. and gave her age as 21, planned the trip, urging the younger one, Ruby Bates, 17 years old, to go with her.

All that is known so far of this trip is what Victoria Price later told concerning it on the witness stand. No check on the truth of her story was made at the trial. Accordig to this story, the two girls arrived in Chattanooga late Tuesday, March 24, and went to spend the night at the home of Mrs. Callie Brochie, who lived, according to Victoria, several blocks off Market Street on North Seventh. Victoria said she did not know the number of the house, but found the place by asking a boy on the street where Mrs. Brochie lived. He pointed it out to the two girls, she said, and all she could say was that it was the fourth house in the block.

A thorough investigation of the neighborhood later by the attorney for the defense failed to discover either Mrs. Brochie or the house she was said to live in.

The Return to Huntsville

As the story of Victoria Price goes, the two girls spent the night with Mrs. Brochie, and set out the next morning with her to look for work in the mills. Victoria was not clear in her trial testimony as to the number and location of these mills where she said they tried to get work. Finding no jobs open, they decided to return home to Huntsville. This was around ten o'clock on the morning of March 25. Boarding an oil tanker at first, they later climbed over into a gondola, or open topped freight car used for carrying gravel. The car was partly filled with gravel. Here they met seven white boys and began talking to them. Ruby declared in a private interview later that she did not speak to them but stayed in one end of the car by herself, while Victoria was talking, laughing and singing with the white boys in the other end of the car. Victoria, however, said that both she and Ruby had talked to the boys.

As the freight neared Stevenson, less than half the way to Huntsville, Victoria testified that the 12 Negroes climbed into the gondola in which the two girls were riding with the seven white youths, walking over the top of a box car in front and jumping into the gondola. Ruby said in a personal interview later that she did not know how many colored boys were in the crowd. She said she was too frightened to count them. The Negroes gave the number of their gang as 15. Victoria maintained emphatically that there were 12.

The Alleged Rape

According to Victoria's testimony, a Negro identified at the trial as Charlie Weems came first waving a pistol, followed by the others in the crowd. A mile or two past Stevenson, Victoria said that the Negroes began fighting with the white boys, shouting "unload, you white sons-of-bitches" and forcing the white boys to jump from the freight which was moving at a fast rate of speed. One of the white boys, Orvil Gilley, who said he was afraid to jump for fear he would be killed, was allowed by the Negroes to remain. One of the Negroes testified that he pulled Gilley back upon the car as he was hanging over the edge for fear he might fall between the cars and be killed. The local papers reporting the trial, however, claimed that he was forced to remain out of viciousness to witness the alleged assault.

Victoria's story continued that while the freight was moving rapidly between Stevenson and Paint Rock, a distance of approximately 38 miles, the Negroes having driven the seven white boys from the train, attacked the two girls. Victoria Price testified that six raped her and six, Ruby Bates. Three of the ones who attacked Ruby got off before the train stopped at Paint Rock, Victoria said. She alleged that Charlie Weems was the leader and carried a pistol, but that Clarence Norris was the first one to attack her. He was followed by four others who took turns holding, she claimed, and then the leader, Weems, as the last one, was in the process of raping her when the train stopped at Paint Rock and the Negroes were captured by the posse who had been notified by telegraph from Stevenson that the Negroes were on the train.

The white gang, after having been put off the train, had informed the station master at Stevenson that the Negroes and the two white girls were on the freight. The station agent telegraphed ahead to Scottsboro, a station about 18 miles west of Stevenson, to have the train stopped, but the freight had already passed there, so Paint Rock, some 20 miles farther, was notified by telegraph.

Here nine of the Negroes were seized by an armed posse of officers and men. The other Negroes had left the train before it arrived at Paint Rock and nothing more has been heard from them. A report appeared in the press some days after the trial that two Negroes were captured and an attempt made to identify them as members of the crowd of nine Negroes in the Scottsboro case. Nothing more was said about it, so the attempt apparently fell through.

Plausibility of the Charges Questioned

The International Labor Defense, which had representatives on the scene at the time of the trial in Scottsboro, and whose attorney, George Chamlee, of Chattanooga, later made investigations of various phases of the case not brought out at the trial, claims that when the two girls were taken from the train at Paint Rock, they made no charges against the Negroes, until after they were taken into custody; that their charges were made after they had found out the spirit of the armed men that came to meet the train and catch the Negroes, and that they were swept into making their wholesale accusation against the Negroes merely by assenting to the charges as presented by the men who seized the nine Negroes.

There is no way of proving this conclusively, but from the interview I had with the two girls separately several weeks after the trial,

I would say that there is a strong possibility of truth in this statement. The talk with Victoria Price, particularly, convinced me that she was the type who welcomes attention and publicity at any price. The price in this case meant little to her, as she has no notions of shame connected with sexual intercourse in any form and was quite unbothered in alleging that she went through such an experience as the charges against the nine Negro lads imply. Having been in direct contact from the cradle with the institution of prostitution as a side-line necessary to make the meager wages of a mill worker pay the rent and buy the groceries, she has no feeling of revulsion against promiscuous sexual intercourse such as women of easier lives might suffer. It is very much a matter of the ordinary routine of life to her, known in both Huntsville and Chattanooga as a prostitute herself.

The younger girl, Ruby Bates, found herself from the beginning pushed into the background by the more bubbling, pert personality of Victoria. She was given little chance to do anything but follow the lead of Victoria, so much quicker and garrulous. When I talked with her alone she showed resentment against the position into which Victoria had forced her, but did not seem to know what to do except to keep silent and let Victoria do the talking. The general opinion of the authorities at the trial was that Ruby was slow and stupid, but that Victoria was a shrewd young woman whose testimony amounted to something because she got the point at once of what was needed to hurry the trial through so that sentence of death could be pronounced quickly. From my many talks with Judge Hawkins, who presided at the trial; with Dr. Bridges who examined the girls, and with other officials, I believe any unbiased person would have come to the conclusion that this was the basis of their judgment of the two girls as witnesses.

The Trial

About 5:45 in the morning on April 6, a picked detachment of the 167th infantry under Major Joe Stearnes, made up of 118 members of five national guard companies of Gadsden, Albertville and Guntersville, Alabama, brought the nine negroes from Gadsden and locked them in the county jail at Scottsboro until the hour of their trial. People from surrounding counties and states began arriving by car and train with the coming of dawn. Thousands had gathered by the time the trial opened at 8:30 o'clock. By ten o'clock it was estimated that a crowd of 8,000 to 10,000 swarmed in the narrow village streets of the little county seat of Scottsboro, packing the outside rim of the Square around the Courthouse with a solid mass of humanity. Armed soldiers formed a picket line to keep the mass of people out of the Square, and no one was admitted into the Courthouse without a special permit.

A Lynching Spirit

Officials and residents of Scottsboro maintained that the crowd was peaceful and showed no evidence of lynching spirit. Mrs. Ben Davis, local reporter for the Chattanooga Times, wrote that the crowd was "curious not furious" and was so pleased with her phrase that she continued to repeat it innumerable times when interviewed. Judge Hawkins, Dr. Bridges, Hamlin Caldwell, the court stenographer; Sheriff Wann and many others were emphatic in their statements that the crowd had poured into Scottsboro in the spirit of going to a circus and wanted to see the show, but were without malicious intent toward the defendants.

Chance conversation with residents of the town, however, did not tend to substantiate this view of the officials. A kind-faced, elderly woman selling tickets at the railroad station, for instance, said to me that if they re-tried the Negroes in Scottsboro, she hoped they would leave the soldiers home next time. When I asked why, she replied that the next time they would finish off the "black fiends" and save the bother of a second trial. Then she told me a lurid story of the mistreatment suffered by the two white girls at the hands of those "horrible black brutes" one of whom had had her breast chewed off by one of the Negroes.

When I called to her attention that the doctor's testimony for the prosecution was to the effect that neither of the girls showed signs of any rough handling on their bodies, it made no impression upon her. Her faith in her atrocity story which had been told to her "by one who ought to know what he was talking about," remained unshaken.

If, as the town authorities claimed, there was no lynching spirit, Major Stearnes, in charge of the soldiers called to Scottsboro, certainly did not go on this supposition. The town looked like an armed camp in war time. Armed soldiers were on guard both inside and outside the courthouse, and before Court opened, the Major gave orders to have persons in attendance at the trial searched.

Negroes Tried in Four Separate Cases

The defense did not ask for severance but was willing to have all nine negroes tried together. The State, however, demanded that they be tried in four separate cases. For the first case, two of the oldest of the boys were chosen by the prosecution. Clarence Norris, of Molina, Georgia, 19 years old, and Charlie Weems, of 154 Piedmont Avenue, Atlanta, Ga., 20 years old, were the defendants selected for the initial trial.

The chief witness for the State was the older of the two girls, Victoria Price, who told the story of the trip to Chattanooga and back from Huntsville, as given previously. She did it with such gusto, snap and wise-cracks, that the courtroom was often in a roar of laughter. Her flip retorts to the attorney for the defense, Steven Roddy, especially caused amusement. The sentiment of the courtroom was with her, ske knew it and played up to it, as can be seen by the record of the trial testimony.

The other girl, Ruby Bates, was found by the prosecution to be a "weak witness," as I was told several times by officials present at the trial. The white youth, Orvil Gilley, who remained on the train with the girls, also was considered stupid and slow-witted. The Gilley boy came from Albertville, a small village a short distance from Scottsboro. Judge Hawkins remarked to me about him, saying, "Well, we all know what his family is. His mother, for instance . . ." and he broke off as if it were too obvious for words what his mother was like. I asked if he meant that the family was feeble minded or of low mentality. "No, not that," he replied, "but . . . well we know here they are not much good." He would commit himself no farther.

From all I could gather later, it seems that the opinion of spectators and officials at the trial that both Ruby Bates and Orvil Gilley were no good because they could not make their testimony fit in with the positive identification of the Negroes and the account of events as given by Victoria on the stand. Victoria told me later that she warned the prosecutor that he had better take Ruby off the stand as she was getting mixed up and would make identifications and answers that did not coincide with those she, herself, had made. The minutes of the trial show certainly that she was the only alleged eye witness of the group on the freight train that testified at great length. Questioning of Ruby Bates and Orvil Gilley was very brief, and the other six white boys were not put on the stand at all.

Dr. M. H. Lynch, County Health Physician, and Dr. H. H. Bridges, of Scottsboro, testified at the trial that the medical examination of the girls made shortly after they were taken from the train, showed that both the girls had had recent sexual intercourse, but that there were no lacerations, tears, or other signs of rough handling; that they were not hysterical when brought to the doctor's office first, but became so later. Dr. Bridges said that Victoria had a small scratch on her neck and a small bruise or two, but nothing more serious was found. The lawyer for the defense, Mr. Roddy, inquired hesitantly and indirectly, in his cross-examination of the doctor, if it were possible to tell the difference between the spermatozoa of a white man and that of a colored male. The doctor answered that it was not possible to distinguish any difference.

Other witnesses put on the stand by the State included Luther Morris, a farmer living west of Stevenson, who testified that he had seen the girls and the Negroes on the freight train as it passed his hay loft, which he said was 30 miles away, and that he "had seen a plenty;" Lee Adams, of Stevenson, who said he saw the fight between the white and colored boys on the train, and Charles Latham, deputy who captured the Negroes at Paint Rock.

Mr. Steven Roddy, attorney for the defense from Chattanooga, was undoubtedly intimidated by the position in which he found himself. At the beginning of the trial he had asked not to be recorded as the lawyer in the case, begging the judge to leave Milo Moody, Scottsboro attorney appointed by the Judge as lawyer for the defense, on record as counsel for the Negroes with himself appearing purely in advisory capacity as representing the parents and friends of the boys in Chattanooga. He made little more than half-hearted attempts to use the formalities of the law to which he was entitled, after his motion for a change of venue made at the beginning of the trial was overruled. It might be said for him, of course, that taking the situation as it was, he felt it was hopeless for him to attempt to do anything much, except make motions for a new trial after the convictions, which he did.

The first case went to the jury Tuesday afternoon at 3 o'clock, and a verdict calling for the death penalty was returned in less than two hours. The Judge had previously warned the courtroom that no demonstration must be staged when the verdict was announced. In spite of this the room resounded with loud applause, and the mass of people outside, when the news spread to them, cheered wildly.

The next day, Wednesday, April 8, Haywood Patterson, of 910 West 19th Street, Chattanooga, 18 years old, was tried alone, as the second case. In three hours the jury returned with the death penalty verdict. It was met with silence in the courtroom.

In the third case, five of the remaining six boys were tried: Olin Montgomery, of Monroe, Georgia, 17 years old, and nearly blind; Andy Wright, of 710 West 22nd Street, Chattanooga, 18 years old; Eugene Williams, No. 3 Clark Apts., Chattanooga, Willie Robeson, 992 Michigan Ave., Atlanta, Ga., 17 years old; Ozie Powell, 107 Gilmore St., Atlanta, Ga., 16 years old.

It was brought out in this trial that Willie Robeson was suffering from a bad case of venereal disease, which would have made it painful, if not impossible for him to have committed the act of which he was accused. The case went to the jury at 4 p.m. on Wednesday, April 8, and early Thursday morning, the jury again turned in the verdict calling for the death penalty.

Judge Hawkins proceeded at once after the convictions returned against the five Negroes in the third case, to pronounce the death sentence on the eight who had been tried. He set the day of execution for July 10, the earliest date he was permitted to name under the law, which requires that 90 days be allowed for filing an appeal of a case.

In three days' time, eight Negro boys all under 21, four of them under 18 and two of them sixteen or under, were hurried through trials which conformed only in outward appearance to the letter of the law. Given no chance even to communicate with their parents and without even as much as the sight of one friendly face, these eight boys, little more than children, surrounded entirely by white hatred and blind venomous prejudice, were sentenced to be killed in the electric chair at the earliest possible moment permitted by law. It is no exaggeration certainly to call this a legal lynching.

The most shameful of the cases was left to the last. This was the trial of fourteen-year-old Roy Wright, of Chattanooga, a young brother of another of the defendants. Perhaps because of his youthfulness, the white authorities who had him at their mercy, seemed to be even more vicious in their attitude toward him than toward the older defendants. They may unconsciously have been trying to cover up a sense of uneasiness at what they were doing to a child. Several of the autorities at the trial assured me that he was really the worst of the lot and deserved no lenience on account of his youth. But for the sake of outside public opinion, the State decided to ask for life imprisonment instead of the death penalty, in view of the youth of the defendant.

At two o'clock on the afternoon of Thursday, April 9, the jury announced that they were dead-locked and could not agree on a verdict. Eleven of them stood for the death penalty and one for life imprisonment. Judge Hawkins declared a mistrial, and the child was ordered back to jail to await another ordeal at a later date. He is now in the Birmingham jail. The other eight defendants were kept a short time also in Birmingham, and then removed to Kilby prison, about four miles from Montgomery. I visited them there in their cells in the death row on May 12, locked up two together in a cell, frightened children caught in a terrible trap without understanding what it is all about.

Why the Two Girls Made the Charge?

The first of these questions can be answered only by some knowledge of the conditions of life in the mill town of Huntsville, as it affected the lives and development of the two young mill workers, Victoria Price and Ruby Bates.

Huntsville, the town seat of Madison County in northern Alabama, has within its city limits, some 12,000 inhabitants. Taking in the four mill villages which surround it, the population is about

32,000. There are seven cotton mills in and around Huntsville, the largest being the Lincoln mill made up of four units. . . . Then there are two old fashioned plants under the same management and owned by local capitalists—the Helen knitting mill and the Margaret spinning mill. It is in this last place, the Margaret Mill, that both Victoria and Ruby Bates worked before the trial and afterward.

Wages were always low and hours long in all the Huntsville Mills, but in the Margaret and Helen especially, working conditions are very bad. The workers had to bear the brunt of the competition with the modern mills, backed by outside capital and with outside connections to help them out, while the Margaret and Helen management was muddling along in the old way. Respectable citizens of Huntsville said that only the lowest type of mill worker would take a job in the Margaret and Helen Mills.

All the mills were running on short time during the period of the Scottsboro case, and had been for some months before. Most of them had cut down to two, three, and four days a week. The Margaret had its workers on shifts employed only every other week, from two to four days a week.

Mill workers found it a dreary, hopeless enough struggle making some sort of a living when times were good, so when the slump hit them, it did not take long for a large group to fall quickly below the self-sustaining line. Low standards of living were forced down still lower, and many were thrown upon the charity organizations. It is from the charity workers of Huntsville that one may get an appallingly truthful picture of what mill life in Huntsville in time of depression means to workers who are doggedly trying to live on the already meager and uncertain wages of "prosperity."

High standards of morality, of health, of sanitation, do not thrive under such conditions. It is a rare mill family that is not touched in some form by prostitution, disease, prison, insane asylum, and drunkenness. "That's the kind of thing these mill workers are mixed up with all the time," complained one social service worker. "I'm beginning to forget how decent people behave, I've been messing around with venereal disease and starvation and unemployment so long."

Under the strain of life in Huntsville, the institution of the family does not stand up very well. Charity workers grumble that too many men are deserting their families. "If they get laid off, and can't get another job they seem to think the best thing for them to do is to leave town, because then the charities will have to take care of their families," said one.

There was no father in evidence in either the families of Victoria Price or Ruby Bates.

Husbands come and go in many cases, with marriage ceremonies or without. A woman who takes in a male boarder to help out expenses is unquestionable assumed to share her bed as well as her board with him. The neighbors gossip about it, but with jealousy for her good luck in getting him, rather than from disapproval of her conduct. The distinction between wife and "whore," as the alternative is commonly known in Huntsville, is not strictly drawn. A mill woman is quite likely to be both if she gets the chance as living is too precarious and money too scarce to miss any kind of chance to get it. Promiscuity means little where economic oppression is great.

"These mill workers are as bad as the Niggers," said one social service worker with a mixture of contempt and understanding. "They haven't any sense of morality at all. Why, just lots of these women are nothing but prostitutes. They just about have to be, I reckon, for nobody could live on the wages they make, and that's the only other way of making money open to them."

It should perhaps be mentioned that there are undoubtedly very many mill families in Huntsville to whom these things just described do not apply, but is also true that there is a large group of workers to whom the conditions do apply, and Ruby Bates and Victoria, with whom this part of the report is concerned, come from this group.

* * *

Why the Boys Were Hated

Scottsboro, the county seat of Jackson county in northern Alabama, is a charming southern village with some 2,000 inhabitants situated in the midst of pleasant rolling hills. Neat, well-tended farms lie all around, the deep red of their soil making a striking contrast with the rich green of the hills. The cottages of the town stand back on soft lawns, shaded with handsome trees. A feeling of peace and leisure is in the air. The people on the streets have easy kind faces and greet strangers as well as each other cordially. In the Courthouse Square in the center of town, the village celebrities, such as the mayor, the sheriff, the lawyers, lounge and chat democratically with the town eccentrics and plain citizens.

Strolling around observing these things, it is hard to conceive that anything but kindly feelings and gentle manners toward all mankind can stir the hearts of the citizens of Scottsboro. It came as a shock, therefore, to see these pleasant faces stiffen, these laughing mouths grow narrow and sinister, those soft eyes become cold and hard because the question was mentioned of a fair trial for nine young Negroes terrified and quite alone. Suddenly these kindly-looking mouths were saying the most frightful things. To see people who ordinarily would be gentle and compassionate at the thought of a child—a white one—in the least trouble, who would wince at the sight of a suffering dog—to see these men and women transformed by blind, unreasoning antipathy so that their lips parted and their eyes glowed with lust for the blood of black children, was a sight to make one untouched by the spell of violent prejudice shrink.

The trial udge, A. E. Hawkins, a dignified, fine-looking, gray-haired Southern gentleman, who was absolutely convinced in his own mind that he had done everything to give the Negroes a fair trial, gave himself away so obviously at every other sentence he uttered, that any person with mind unclouded by the prejudice which infected him could have pointed it out. The other officials and citizens with whom I discussed the case also made it disconcertingly clear that they regarded the trial of the Negroes and the testimony given at it, not as an honest attempt to get at the truth, but as a game where shrewd tricks were to be used to bring about a result already decided upon in the minds of every one of them. They all wanted the Negroes killed as quickly as possible in a way that would not bring disrepute upon the town. They therefore preferred a sentence of death by a judge, to a sentence of death by a mob, but they desired the same result, and were impatient with anything that slowed up the conviction and death sentence which they all knew was coming regardless of any testimony.

They said that all negroes were brutes and had to be held down by stern repressive measures or the number of rapes on white women would be larger than it is. Their point seemed to be that it was only by ruthless oppression of the Negro that any white woman was able to escape raping at Negro hands. Starting with this notion, it followed that they could not conceive that two white girls found riding with a crowd of Negroes could possibly have escaped raping. A Negro will always, in their opinion, rape a white woman if he gets the chance. These nine Negroes were riding alone with two white girls on a freight car. Therefore, there was no question that they raped them, or wanted to rape them, or were present while the other Negroes raped them—all of which amounts to very much the same thing in southern eyes—and calls for the immediate death of the Negroes regardless of these shades of difference. As one southerner in Scottsboro put it, "We white people just couldn't afford to let these Niggers get off because of the effect it would have on other Niggers."

In answering the question then, of why ordinarily kind, mild people are aroused to such heartless cruelty against boys who have done them no harm, and if their case were fairly investigated quite likely would be found to have harmed nobody else either, one it brought up against the ugly fact that these pleasant people of the South, the Civil War notwithstanding, are still living on the enslavement of the Negro race. And this brings one to a second ugly fact, that when this is so, the subjugating race cannot afford to have any regard for decency, honesty, kindness, or fairness in their treatment of the black race. These traits are exclusively for relationships with their own people. The thing that stands out above everything else in their minds is that the black race must be kept down; as they put it, "The Nigger must be kept in his place." Repression, terror, and torture are the means that will do it.

* * *

"Report on the Scottsboro, Alabama Case" (New York, 1931). Accessed October 12, 2006 at http://www.law.umkc.edu/faculty/projects/FTrials/scottsboro/SB_HRrep.html.

Marion Post Wolcott

Photo of Choke-em-Down Lunchroom
(January 1939)

Photographer Marian Post Wolcott traveled the South between 1937 and 1942, documenting the Depression for the Farm Security Administration. A keen observer of social relations, Wolcott often captured Jim Crow in motion with her photographs and revealed the individual day-by-day actions and decisions necessary to keep segregation functioning. Jim Crow's absolutism was often challenged, particularly during hard times. It is unclear from this photograph if there was indoor seating in this lunchroom, or if blacks and whites were served from different windows, as was the custom throughout much of the Jim Crow South. Regardless, the lunchroom sign advertising "White and Colored Served" both welcomed black customers and warned white bigots.

Marion Post Wolcott, Choke-em-Down Lunchroom, Belle Glade (vicinity), Florida, January 1939.

Margaret Halsey

Memo to Junior Hostesses (1946)

The United Service Organization (USO) was established in February 1941 to provide safe settings in which to entertain soldiers. Civilian run and funded, the USO was staffed entirely by volunteers, most of whom were women, whose work consisted of socializing with soldiers far from home. Most canteens, following local custom and the example of the military, were segregated by race. Those that were not became targets for white southern politicians because of the possibility for interracial dancing. A significant exception to the pattern of segregated USOs was the Stage Door Canteen in midtown Manhattan, whose operating principle was that "a Negro serviceman who was good enough to die for a white girl was good enough to dance with her." The agents of this philosophy were the Junior Hostesses, young black and white women volunteers ranging in age from eighteen to twenty-five, who agreed to dance with any serviceman who asked. Despite their generally progressive politics, many of the white Junior Hostesses had racial attitudes that needed to be addressed. To this end, writer Margaret Halsey, who oversaw the Junior Hostess program, wrote and distributed a Memo to Junior Hostesses, which outlined the canteen's policy on African Americans and addressed frankly but with humor the fears of white women asked to dance with black servicemen.

* * *

When the question of the alleged specific smell of Negroes was first brought up, by a somewhat embarrassed young lady, at the all-white meeting of the Junior Hostesses, many of the hostesses were startled. But as the discussion progressed, it was observable that they were relieved and comforted to have the matter brought out into the open. Quite often, well-disposed white people are haunted by the insistent folk myths about the Negro. They do not really believe the myths, and would not defend them, but are unable wholly to forget them. Thus these white people have a nameless, indefinite feeling of constraint in their relationships with Negroes and in their thinking about the race situation. An incredible amount of literature has been written about the Negro American, so it is fairly easy to consult authorities, and healthy, candid discussion of the old wives' tales and superstitions goes a long way toward breaking their hidden power.

The meeting of the white girls on my shift had a bracing effect, but bracing effects, unfortunately, do not last forever. The following year it once again seemed advisable to remind some of the Junior Hostesses of their responsibilities, so I called a meeting of the shift, and before the meeting, I wrote and mailed to the hostesses a memorandum on the subject of dancing with Negro servicemen. My object was to save time. It seemed to me we would cover more ground at the meeting if the hostesses had the canteen's position clearly in mind before they came.

The memorandum read as follows:

Quite a few of you have asked me questions recently having to do with the Negroes at our canteen, so I think I had better explain the matter in its entirety.

The canteen's policy about Negroes is based on a quotation which runs as follows: "We hold these truths to be self-evident: That all men are created equal. . . ." I'm sure all of you know where that comes from.

The canteen's policy about Negroes is also based on the 14th and 15th Amendments to the Constitution of the United States, in which it is specifically stated that nobody is to be denied the rights, privileges and immunities of American citizenship on account of race, creed or color.

One hears a good deal of talk, in some circles, about the Reds and long-haired radicals who want to tear down the Constitution. The Reds and long-haired radicals are only spoken of as *wanting* to tear it down. The people who deny Negroes democratic equality actually *are* tearing it down.

I know that some of you on our shift are very deeply prejudiced against accepting Negroes as your social equals. You can't be blamed for having that prejudice in the first place. It was taught to you when you were too young and helpless to be critical. But you certainly can be blamed for hanging on to the prejudice when

(*a*) you are now old enough to know better;

(*b*) you are being given, in the canteen, a golden opportunity to come into contact with Negroes under the best possible circumstances and to find out what they are really like.

Let's examine the feeling that some of you have against, for instance, dancing with Negro servicemen and see what it really amounts to.

There is no scientific basis for the notion that Negroes are inferior to white people. A scientist, given a collection of human brains pickled in alcohol, cannot tell which ones belonged to Negroes and which to white people. You can check this statement in any good reference library. Intelligence depends on the number and fineness of the convolutions in the brain. It has absolutely nothing to do with the amount of pigment in the skin. If it had, you would all be much stupider when you are sunburned.

Actually, I don't believe any of you are very deeply concerned with Negro intelligence. What worries you more is the fear of rape. You unconsciously, but very arrogantly, assume that no male Negro can so much as glance at you without wanting to get you with child. The truth is, that while you are an extremely attractive group of young women, there isn't one single one of you who's *that* good. Negro males react to you no more and no less than white males. As women, you know in your hearts that men of any description respond to you pretty much as you intend them to respond. This is especially true in the canteen, which has hardly any points of resemblance at all to a lonely, moonlit shrubbery.

The real basis of prejudice against Negroes is economic and historical, not sexual or psychological. The people who talk about "keeping the niggers in their place" never admit this, because it doesn't show them in an entirely favorable light. Such people prefer to fall back on more medodramatic arguments, usually (1) the honor of their women and (2) the danger of a Negro revolt. Neither of these two arguments stands up very well under close inspection.

Revolt is a troublesome and dangerous occupation. People will put up with an awful lot before they resort to it. If the Negroes ever do rise in the night sometime and murder every white man south of the Mason and Dixon line—and perhaps some choice specimens north of it—it will be because those white men richly deserved it. But there's one way to make absolutely certain that neither the Negroes nor any other section of our population feel impelled to rebel. That is to see that they have nothing to rebel about. If Negroes have the same education, the same housing, the same jobs, the same opportunities, and the same social treatment as all the other citizens in this country—all of which things we promised them in the Declaration of Independence and again in the Constitution—they will have no more impulse to rise against us than redheads, stamp collectors, and sufferers from stomach ulcer have the impulse to rise against us.

The other argument, about the honor of our women, collapses even faster than the one about revolt. Women—ask the man who owns one—can take care of themselves a good deal better than they ever let on. The way to protect your honor is to be honorable. If white people stood, in the minds of the Negroes, for fair play and justice and real democracy, they wouldn't ever have to worry about either sexual or nonsexual assaults.

The real reason back of the refusal of some of you to mingle with Negroes at the canteen isn't nearly as romantic and dramatic as you like to think it is. The real reason has nothing to do with rape, seduction and risings in the night. The real reason can be summed up in two extremely unromantic little words: cheap labor. As long as you treat Negroes as subhumans, you don't have to pay them so much. When you refuse to dance with Negro servicemen at the canteen, you are neither protecting your honor nor making sure that white Southerners won't have their homes burned down around their ears. All you are doing is making it possible for employers all over the country to get Negroes to work for them for less money than those employers would have to pay you.

Do you find that romantic?

You don't live in a romantic age. You live in a machine age, and it's getting more machinery every day. In the old days, large groups of people could live out their entire lives without ever finding out what other large groups of people were doing. That is no longer possible. Unless you can deinvent the airplane and cause it to fall into general disuse, you are going to spend an increasing amount of your time mingling with Negroes, Russians, Chinamen, Patagonians, and all sorts of hitherto unfamiliar people this side of accredited lepers. You might as well get used to it here and now, on Sunday nights at the canteen. It will save you a lot of trouble later on.

In our world we have radios, telephones, bathtubs, air-cooling, vitamin pills and sulfa drugs, but we no longer have any group privacy. We can no longer wrap ourselves up in the comforting notion that we are better than other sorts of people. Our own inventions drop these other sorts of people right into our laps, and we either have to get along with them or watch our inventions—along with a lot of other things we hold dear—go crashing into the dust in a series of obliterating wars. There's only one possible basis for getting along with other sorts of people, and that basis is equality. Real, genuine, three-ply, copper-bottomed equality. If we have any secret yearning to think of ourselves as a Master Race, we have only to pick up a newspaper to see that nobody is giving odds on Master Races these days.*

A few words of warning before I close. Don't be surprised if you find some of the Negro servicemen sullen and unresponsive and some of them aggressive and too responsive. The war has put the Negroes in a difficult spot. We need them in the war effort, so we've been forced to give them more equality than we were ever willing to concede before. They aren't used to it, and neither are we. There are bound to be awkwardnesses and mistakes on both sides. If there are, remember that they are inevitable and take them in your stride.

Try to be a little imaginative and put yourself in the Negro's place. When you go into the canteen, nothing worse can happen to you than getting tired or being bored. When a Negro goes into the canteen, he has no reason to suppose he won't be snubbed by one of the girls on our shift or openly insulted by a white soldier whose "superiority" has not been noticeably enhanced by rye with beer chasers. Naturally, the Negroes are nervous and very possibly may not behave with Chesterfieldian calm. You wouldn't either, under the same circumstances.

The main thing to remember is this: *the Negroes aren't under any obligation to behave better than we do.* They didn't come to this country because they wanted to. We brought them here in chains. They didn't write the Declaration of Independence or the Constitution. We wrote those documents, and if we now wave them in the Negroes' faces and say, "Ha-ha! Practical joke!" we must expect to meet the customary fate of practical jokers. We kept the Negroes in official slavery until 1864 and we've kept them in unofficial slavery ever since. If you meet a Negro serviceman at the canteen whose conduct doesn't come up to your delicate and exacting standards of

*This memorandum was written in the spring of 1943.

behavior, just don't forget this one thing—whatever he is, you made him that way.

As a matter of fact, you meet plenty of white servicemen whose conduct fails to enthrall. Few outsiders realize, but all of us know, that being a Junior Hostess and and entertaining unselected strangers for three and a half hours is difficult at best. You only make it more difficult when you artificially set aside a portion of these strangers as targets for unreasonable, unscientific and undemocratic emotion. If you'd just relax and keep your pores open, there wouldn't be any "Negro problem."

From Margaret Halsey, *Color Blind: A White Woman Looks at the Negro* (New York, 1946), 52–59.

Commission on Interracial Cooperation

The Negroes and Motion Pictures, Clip Sheet (December 15, 1943)

The portrayal of African American characters and history was a concern for civil rights advocates from the birth of motion pictures. Fearful that D. W. Griffith's provocative account of Reconstruction would stir up racial violence, the NAACP tried without success to keep Birth of a Nation *out of theaters in 1917. As movie audiences skyrocketed in the 1930s and motion pictures rivaled radio in their ability to reach the masses, the black press joined the NAACP in lobbying Hollywood for more complicated and complimentary black film roles. The description of black characters contained in this 1943 report of the Commission on Interracial Cooperation suggests what they were up against.*

The Negroes and Motion Pictures

For several years Negro leaders and newspaper columnists have been conducting a campaign to change the type of roles assigned to Negroes by movie producers. They contend that since the moving picture is one of the most potent educational agencies, it can continue to preserve the stereotype of Negroes as buffoons, clowns, illiterates, fit only for inferior status in American society, or it can break this stereotype by showing cultivated, educated Negroes playing a dignified part in American life.

In the past year two all-Negro shows have been released, "Cabin in the Sky" and "Stormy Weather," the first of which on the whole has not been satisfactory to Negroes. Two other shows, "Tales of Manhattan" and "Tennessee Johnson," neither of which is a Negro film, have received harsh criticism. Other shows have been highly praised. That is, the parts assigned to Negroes have been praised. *(List of some approved films on last page)*

According to Harry Levette, writing for the Associated Negro Press from Los Angeles, although Hollywood claims to be in a state of bewilderment caused by its inability to learn what Negroes do want, this cannot be due to the failure of Negroes to express themselves. Negro spokesmen want the traditional stereotype of Negro character destroyed. They hold that the moving picture is one of the major vehicles for conveying ideas and educating the average public opinion and that as long as tradition calls for "crudity, sexuality, roughness and moronism as an illustration of the supposed Negro character", the public will continue to think of Negroes in this light.

Ted Williams, theatrical critic of the Houston *Informer*, describes the stereotype at greater length. He also tells what Negroes want in place of the stereotype.

> "The Negro has been pictured too long as a shiftless, dice-shooting individual who looks for his woman to support him. It has been the southern white man's desire to play up the fact that a Negro is either a gambler, drunkard, or a deeply religious person. They never picture the Negro church as a fine building with a highly educated minister, but rather as a store front building with an ignorant preacher who led his congregation in the rituals similar to that of the African natives. It is this that the Negro wants to erase from the minds of the other group.
>
> "The Negro wants to be pictured as he really is, hard working serious minded and learned, with fine schools, churches, and buildings. We want to be respected and not laughed at."

In answer to the almost hysterical criticism of "Cabin in the Sky" some have pointed out that there are films dealing with white

society which show up the depravity of white folk—notably "Tobacco Road." Joseph D. Bibb, disposes of this defense in one short
paragraph.

> "Unlike the folk of 'Tobacco Road'—where some of the depths and
> degradation of the poor white South were explored—there is no
> production now on the screen depicting the intelligent colored man
> and exhibiting his terrific struggle to advance himself, improve his
> status and destroy the impediments in his path."

Wallace Lee, director of the *Negro Digest* Poll sustains this opinion
in summing up a poll on this question.

> "The newest flock of films which have given bigger but not always
> better roles to Negroes has not changed the opinion of movie goers
> that the conventional portrayal of Negroes as crap shooters, water-
> melon eaters, and Stepin Fetchit is being revised."

A good test of a film about Negroes or with Negro characters is
given by Archer Winston, New York *Post* columnist. Says he:

> "A good working test of any Negro movie or single characterization
> would be whether it tends in any degree to dispel the fog of white
> misunderstanding and prejudice."

So important is this affair of Negroes and moving pictures that
the Committee on Negro Culture in War Time, sponsored by the
National Negro Council, has placed major emphasis on "the establishment of a code by Hollywood screen writers that would outlaw all derogatory references to Negro people and the appointment
of a Negro to the Hays office to act on the treatment of Negro
characters in the movies."

* * *

The South Is Responsible

After stating their case logically and fairly persuasively Negroes
look for reasons why progress in attaining their goals is not more
rapid. One reason on which all articulate leaders appear to agree

heads the list—the South. In casting Negroes in stereotype roles Hollywood is catering to the prejudices of the South. This charge is made by E. B. Rea, theatrical critic of the *Afro-American* in defense of Paul Robeson who was under attack for his role in "Tales of Manhattan." Robeson had wanted another ending in the last sequence of the play and thought he would get it. But says Rea when Robeson protested the producers refused on the grounds that it "would be out of key with the rest of the story. What the producers meant was" that the South "would not patronize a colored film unless it had the atmosphere of a minstrel show or camp meeting." Rea calls it "the Dixie theme used by Hollywood for box office in the South."

Some Films and Roles Which Negroes Approve

"Battaan"	Kenneth Spencer as Private Fesley Eaps an "expendable" soldier in the defense of the Phillipines.
"Mission to Moscow"	Leigh Whipper as Haile Selassie, "the world's most noble and heroic figure of this century, according to all estimates."
"Crash Dive"	Ben Carter, who plays another "Dorie Miller" role in the submarine fleet.
"Somewhere in the Sahara"	Rex Ingram, captor of Kurt Kruger, Nazi aviator—"second lead to Humphrey Bogart."
"Lifeboat"	Canada Lee as "Joe," steward aboard a torpedoed freighter, only Negro in lifeboat.
"Ox Bow Incident"	Anti-lynching film showing Leigh Whipper as a dignified minister of the 1880's.

"Stormy Weather" All Negro Cast	"In it, Fox put evening gowns and tails on their dancing girls and boys, depicted the Negro's ambition for a modern home and children, respected the chastity of Negro womanhood, and gave major expression to acting talent as shown by Cab Calloway and Florence O'Brien. These are landmarks which now give us an arguing point."—Phil Carter
"In This Our Life"	Albert Anderson as a Negro lawyer.

Commission on Interracial Cooperation, The Negroes and Motion Pictures, Clip Sheet, Series III, Number 11, December 15, 1943. In the Alfred H. Stone Collection, box 1, folder 6, University of Mississippi: Special Collections.

Langston Hughes

Letter to the South (July 10, 1943)

Harlem Renaissance mainstay Langston Hughes is generally recalled for his poetry and song lyrics. But he was also an editorialist. In 1942, Hughes was invited to contribute a regular column to the Chicago Defender, *a leading black weekly newspaper. Through the 1960s, black news circulated through papers like the* Pittsburgh Courier, *the* Baltimore Afro-American, *and the* Chicago Defender, *which connected disparate African American communities and fostered a sense of comradeship. As Hughes remembered, "As a child in Kansas I grew up on the* Chicago Defender *and it awakened me in my youth to the problems which I and my race had to face in America. Its flaming headlines and indignant editorials did a great deal to make me the 'race man' which I later became, as expressed in my own attitudes and in my writing."[1] In his own columns for the* Defender, *Hughes narrowed his sights on the Jim Crow*

[1] In *Langston Hughes and the* Chicago Defender: *Essays on Race, Politics, and Culture*, 1942–62, ed. Christopher C. De Santis (Urbana, 1995), 13–14.

system, commenting shrewdly on white rationales and self-deceptions as well as black criticism of the warped democracy they were fighting to participate in and uphold.

Dear Southern White Folks:

You are as much a problem to me as I am to you, I mean personally and figuratively speaking. For one thing, if it were not for you, I, Langston Hughes, might have a nice Hollywood job, like almost every other respectable American writer (who's white) has at one time or another. But you won't let Hollywood do anything decent with Negroes in pictures, so Hollywood won't hire Negro writers—not even to write about Negroes. They are afraid in Hollywood that we won't write the kind of scripts you like down South, so they won't hire us at all.

You, dear Southern white folks, are also a problem to me personally even way up here in New York. You come up here and start spreading the ugly old Jim Crowism you have down home all over Manhattan Island. You even try to get the Broadway theaters to segregate me where I have never been segregated before. You are not satisfied to keep segregation down South. Before the war, you even took it to Paris and Rome. Now, you take it abroad in the Army.

Another thing you do is bring your old prejudice about not wanting to work beside a Negro up to Jersey and Detroit and even Seattle, Washington. You start anti-Negro strikes and riots. You hold back liberal employers, and keep liberal unions from permitting me to have jobs that I might otherwise have. I have a hard enough time getting a job, without you gumming up the works from Hollywood to Hoboken.

I tell you, you are really a problem to me. Still being personal, I, as a writer, might have had many scripts performed on the radio if it were not for you. The radio stations look at a script about Negro life that I write and tell me, "Well, you see, our programs are heard down South, and the South might not like this." You keep big Negro stars like Ethel Waters and Duke Ellington off commercial programs, because the sponsors are afraid the South might not buy their products if Negro artists appear regularly on their series.

Dumbest Congressmen

You are really a problem to me, dear Southern White Folks. You send the dumbest congressmen to Congress—congressmen who don't seem to realize the world is round, or that there are human beings on the other side, too, and that we have to get along with them after the war is over. But not to speak of the other side, your congressmen don't seem to realize either that we all have to get along here at home if we are to have a peaceful and happy America. Some of them red-bait and Negro-bait and labor-bait and Roosevelt-bait so much that I don't see how they have any time left to think about the state of the nation, or your welfare.

But what I am really concerned about is them in relation to me. They keep the anti-poll tax bill from being passed, and they kill every anti-lynching bill. I really do not want to be lynched. If a law would help keep me from so being, I would like to see that law passed. But you-all don't care anything about a Negro being lynched down South, do you?

Dear Southern White Folks, your Jim Crow cars I do not like at all. I do not like your Jim Crow waiting rooms in the stations where I have to stand patiently at the ticket window until all the white folks at the opposite window are served before I can even buy a ticket. I do not like having to sit next to the baggage car and not be able to go to the diner to eat when I get hungry. I do not like the white baggage-car men and the news butchers and the conductors and any other train employees sitting in whatever extra space there may be in my Jim Crow car, smoking, spitting, and cussing in front of colored ladies.

Post-War Problem

YES, I SAID LADIES! I know you say "colored women" down your way. And I know you never address a colored man as Mr.— which I think is stupid. And I know you take pride in being just as rude and ill-bred as you can be to Negroes in public places. But I do not care so much about your manners as I care about you. Dear Southern White Folks, you are cutting off your nose to spite your face.

All the bad things you do to Negroes, Latin America knows about in spite of the censorship. Asia knows, too. Do you think your allies who are colored trust you? They do not! And in the post-war world, you are going to need that trust. You are terribly simple-minded if you think you can live on this earth by yourself.

We may be problems to each other, but for your good and mine, from Beaumont to Detroit, we ought to get together and straighten our problems out. Certainly, I personally would be willing to talk sense with you and try to come to some solution because, God knows, YOU ARE A PROBLEM TO ME, dear Southern White Folks.

In *Langston Hughes and the* Chicago Defender: *Essays on Race, Politics, and Culture, 1942–62*, ed. Christopher De Santis (Urbana, 1995), 75–76.

Part III
1945–1980

President Harry S. Truman

Assignment from the President
(December 5, 1946)

So many African Americans, but especially black veterans returning from Europe, were murdered during the summer of 1919 that NAACP leader James Weldon Johnson later dubbed it the "Red Summer." Individual black soldiers and civil rights organizations were determined to avoid a repetition of this post-World War I violence as World War II soldiers returned home in 1946. By February of that year, however, Columbia, Tennessee, had seen a riot that originated in an altercation between a white army veteran and a black navy veteran. That same month, decorated Army sergeant Isaac Woodard, still wearing the uniform of his country, was blinded and brutally beaten by a South Carolina sheriff, and Monroe, Georgia, saw a quadruple lynching whose victims included one veteran and two women. White southerners, it seemed clear, were in no mood to toy with Jim Crow. After meeting with the National Emergency Committee against Mob Violence, President Truman appointed by executive order a President's Committee on Civil Rights. Chaired by General Electric Chief Executive Officer Charles E. Wilson, the committee produced a report, published as To Secure These Rights, *that recommended the "elimination of segregation, based on color, creed, or national origin" from the armed forces, public transportation, housing, health care, and education.*

Freedom From Fear is more fully realized in our country than in any other on the face of the earth. Yet all parts of our population are not equally free from fear. And from time to time, and in some places, this freedom has been gravely threatened. It was so after the last war, when organized groups fanned hatred and intolerance, until, at times, mob action struck fear into the hearts of men and women because of their racial origin or religious beliefs.

Today, Freedom From Fear, and the democratic institutions which sustain it, are again under attack. In some places, from time to time, the local enforcement of law and order has broken down, and individuals—sometimes ex-servicemen, even women—have been killed, maimed, or intimidated.

The preservation of civil liberties is a duty of every Government—state, Federal and local. Wherever the law enforcement measures and the authority of Federal, state, and local governments are inadequate to discharge this primary function of government, these measures and this authority should be strengthened and improved.

The Constitutional guarantees of individual liberties and of equal protection under the laws clearly place on the Federal Government the duty to act when state or local authorities abridge or fail to protect these Constitutional rights.

Yet in its discharge of the obligations placed on it by the Constitution, the Federal Government is hampered by inadequate civil rights statutes. The protection of our democratic institutions and the enjoyment by the people of their rights under the Constitution require that these weak and inadequate statutes should be expanded and improved. We must provide the Department of Justice with the tools to do the job.

I have, therefore, issued today an Executive Order creating the President's Committee on Civil Rights and I am asking this Committee to prepare for me a written report. The substance of this report will be recommendations with respect to the adoption or establishment by legislation or otherwise of more adequate and effective means and procedures for the protection of the civil rights of the people of the United States.

Executive Order 9808 Establishing the President's Committee on Civil Rights

WHEREAS the preservation of civil rights guaranteed by the Constitution is essential to domestic tranquility, national security, the general welfare, and the continued existence of our free institutions; and

WHEREAS the action of individuals who take the law into their own hands and inflict summary punishment and wreak personal vengeance is subversive of our democratic system of law enforcement and public criminal justice, and gravely threatens our form of government; and

WHEREAS it is essential that all possible steps be taken to safeguard our civil rights:

NOW, THEREFORE, by virtue of the authority vested in me as President of the United States by the Constitution and the statutes of the United States, it is hereby ordered as follows:

1. There is hereby created a committee to be known as the President's Committee on Civil Rights, which shall be composed of the following-named members, who shall serve without compensation:

Mr. C. E. Wilson, chairman; Mrs. Sadie T. Alexander, Mr. James B. Carey, Mr. John S. Dickey, Mr. Morris L. Ernst, Rabbi Roland B. Gittelsohn, Dr. Frank P. Graham, The Most Reverend Francis J. Haas, Mr. Charles Luckman, Mr. Francis P. Matthews, Mr. Franklin D. Roosevelt, Jr., The Right Reverend Henry Knox Sherrill, Mr. Boris Shishkin, Mrs. M. E. Tilly, Mr. Channing H. Tobias.

2. The Committee is authorized on behalf of the President to inquire into and to determine whether and in what respect current law-enforcement measures and the authority and means possessed by Federal, State, and local governments may be strengthened and improved to safeguard the civil rights of the people.

3. All executive departments and agencies of the Federal Government are authorized and directed to cooperate with the Committee in its work, and to furnish the Committee such information or the services of such persons as the Committee may require in the performance of its duties.

4. When requested by the Committee to do so, persons employed in any of the executive departments and agencies of the Federal Government shall testify before the Committee and shall make available for the use of the Committee such documents and other information as the Committee may require.

5. The Committee shall make a report of its studies to the President in writing, and shall in particular make recommendations with respect to the adoption or establishment, by legislation or otherwise, of more adequate and effective means and procedures for the protection of the civil rights of the people of the United States.

6. Upon rendition of its report to the President, the Committee shall cease to exist, unless otherwise determined by further Executive Order.

HARRY S. TRUMAN.

THE WHITE HOUSE, *December 5, 1946.*

In *To Secure These Rights: The Report of the President's Committee on Civil Rights* (Washington, D.C., 1947), vii–ix.

President Harry S. Truman

Speech to the NAACP (June 29, 1947)

In June 1947, Harry Truman became the first American president to address the NAACP annual meeting; there were humanitarian and diplomatic reasons for Truman's speech. The excesses of Nazi Germany had shocked Truman, as they had many other Americans, into reconsidering the racial balance of power in the United States. Also, in these first shaky days of the Cold War, Truman was acutely aware of the scrutiny Jim Crow was receiving abroad. There was in addition a domestic political calculus at work. Significant numbers of southern blacks had moved north and west between 1935 and 1945, looking for work in the war industries and relief from a rigid Jim Crow society. As in the president's native border state Missouri, these northern and western blacks voted. With the Democratic Party coming unglued at the seams over the question of upholding Jim Crow, Truman became the first president since Reconstruction to openly court the black vote. In the 1948 election, which was a four-way fight between Truman and Republican Thomas E. Dewey plus "Dixiecrat" Strom

Thurmond and former vice president Henry Wallace running as a progressive,
Truman carried two-thirds of the black vote and also the day, albeit narrowly.

Mr. Chairman, Mrs. Roosevelt, Senator Morse, distinguished guests, ladies and gentlemen:

I am happy to be present at the closing session of the 38th Annual Conference of the National Association for the Advancement of Colored People. The occasion of meeting with you here at the Lincoln Memorial affords me the opportunity to congratulate the association upon its effective work for the improvement of our democratic processes.

I should like to talk to you briefly about civil rights and human freedom. It is my deep conviction that we have reached a turning point in the long history of our country's efforts to guarantee freedom and equality to all our citizens. Recent events in the United States and abroad have made us realize that it is more important today than ever before to insure that all Americans enjoy these rights.

When I say all Americans I mean all Americans.

The civil rights laws written in the early years of our Republic, and the traditions which have been built upon them, are precious to us. Those laws were drawn up with the memory still fresh in men's minds of the tyranny of an absentee government. They were written to protect the citizen against any possible tyrannical act by the new government in this country.

But we cannot be content with a civil liberties program which emphasizes only the need of protection against the possibility of tyranny by the Government. We cannot stop there.

We must keep moving forward, with new concepts of civil rights to safeguard our heritage. The extension of civil rights today means, not protection of the people against the Government, but protection of the people by the Government.

We must make the Federal Government a friendly, vigilant defender of the rights and equalities of all Americans. And again I mean all Americans.

As Americans, we believe that every man should be free to live his life as he wishes. He should be limited only by his responsibility to his fellow countrymen. If this freedom is to be more than a dream, each man must be guaranteed equality of opportunity. The only limit to an American's achievement should be his ability, his industry, and his character. These rewards for his effort should be determined only by those truly relevant qualities.

Our immediate task is to remove the last remnants of the barriers which stand between millions of our citizens and their birthright. There is no justifiable reason for discrimination because of ancestry, or religion, or race, or color.

We must not tolerate such limitations on the freedom of any of our people and on their enjoyment of basic rights which every citizen in a truly democratic society must possess.

Every man should have the right to a decent home, the right to an education, the right to adequate medical care, the right to a worthwhile job, the right to an equal share in making the public decisions through the ballot, and the fight to a fair trial in a fair court.

We must insure that these rights—on equal terms—are enjoyed by every citizen.

To these principles I pledge my full and continued support.

Many of our people still suffer the indignity of insult, the narrowing fear of intimidation, and, I regret to say, the threat of physical injury and mob violence. Prejudice and intolerance in which these evils are rooted still exist. The conscience of our Nation, and the legal machinery which enforces it, have not yet secured to each citizen full freedom from fear.

We cannot wait another decade or another generation to remedy these evils. We must work, as never before, to cure them now. The aftermath of war and the desire to keep faith with our Nation's historic principles make the need a pressing one.

The support of desperate populations of battle-ravaged countries must be won for the free way of life. We must have them as allies in our continuing struggle for the peaceful solution of the world's problems. Freedom is not an easy lesson to teach, nor an easy cause to sell, to peoples beset by every kind of privation. They may surrender to the false security offered so temptingly by totalitarian regimes unless we can prove the superiority of democracy.

Our case for democracy should be as strong as we can make it. It should rest on practical evidence that we have been able to put our own house in order.

For these compelling reasons, we can no longer afford the luxury of a leisurely attack upon prejudice and discrimination. There is much that State and local governments can do in providing positive safeguards for civil rights. But we cannot, any longer, await the growth of a will to action in the slowest State or the most backward community.

Our National Government must show the way.

This is a difficult and complex undertaking. Federal laws and administrative machineries must be improved and expanded. We must provide the Government with better tools to do the job. As a first step, I appointed an Advisory Committee on Civil Rights last December. Its members, fifteen distinguished private citizens, have been surveying our civil rights difficulties and needs for several months. I am confident that the product of their work will be a sensible and vigorous program for action by all of us.

We must strive to advance civil rights wherever it lies within our power. For example, I have asked the Congress to pass legislation extending basic civil rights to the people of Guam and American Samoa so that these people can share our ideals of freedom and self-government. This step, with others which will follow, is evidence to the rest of the world of our confidence in the ability of all men to build free institutions.

The way ahead is not easy. We shall need all the wisdom, imagination and courage we can muster. We must and shall guarantee the civil rights of all our citizens. Never before has the need been so urgent for skillful and vigorous action to bring us closer to our ideal.

We can reach the goal. When past difficulties faced our Nation we met the challenge with inspiring charters of human rights—the Declaration of Independence, the Constitution, the Bill of Rights, and the Emancipation Proclamation. Today our representatives, and those of other liberty-loving countries on the United Nations Commission on Human Rights, are preparing an International Bill of Rights. We can be confident that it will be a great landmark in man's long search for freedom since its members consist of such distinguished citizens of the world as Mrs. Franklin D. Roosevelt.

With these noble charters to guide us, and with faith in our hearts, we shall make our land a happier home for our people, a symbol of hope for all men, and a rock of security in a troubled world.

Abraham Lincoln understood so well the ideal which you and I seek today. As this conference closes we would do well to keep in mind his words, when he said,

"if it shall please the Divine Being who determines the destinies of nations, we shall remain a united people, and we will, humbly seeking the Divine Guidance, make their prolonged national existence a source of new benefits to themselves and their successors, and to all classes and conditions of mankind."

New York Times, June 30, 1947. Accessed October 13, 2006 at http://millercenter. virginia.edu/scripps/diglibrary/prezspeeches/truman/hst_1947_0629.html.

W. E. B. Du Bois

A Petition to the Human Rights Commission of the Social and Economic Council of the United Nations; and to the General Assembly of the United Nations; and to the Several Delegations of the Member States of the United Nations (1949)

It is difficult to convey the contradictory tenor of the immediate post–World War II years in the United States. Allied armies had won a hard-fought victory for democracy, which was itself the object of much discussion. What was democracy precisely? What were its defining hallmarks? Was it true, as Orson Welles declared on national radio in 1946, that "there is no room in the American century for Jim Crow?" As African Americans worked on multiple fronts to make racial equality an irrefutable attribute of democracy, anxious white supremacists reinforced the legal and social practices that had guaranteed Jim Crow for three generations. The case of Rosa Lee Ingram highlighted the injustices black southerners continued to endure. In 1947, Ingram, a sharecropper in Georgia, was convicted of murder, along with two of her sons, following the death of a neighbor who had viciously attacked her and died in the ensuing struggle. Mobilizing newly articulated international standards of human rights, African American women, including NAACP leader Mary Church Terrell, worked to bring attention to the plight of Ingram and the larger system of oppression that reigned in the region. Deeply embarrassing the United States government, a 155-page "Statement on the Denial of Human Rights to Minorities in the Case of Citizens of Negro Descent in the United States of America and an Appeal to the United Nations for Redress" was prepared under the supervision of W. E. B. Du Bois and submitted to the United Nations on October 23, 1947.

The signers of this petition wish to lay before the Assembly of the United Nations, a case of injustice done by the United States of America against its own citizens. We are bringing this case to your attention and begging you to give it your earnest thought and discussion, not because we are disloyal to this nation, but especially because we are citizens of this land and loyal to the freedom and democracy which it professes far and wide to observe.

This case of callous injustice is typical of the treatment which thousands of our fellows receive, who have slaved and toiled and fought for this country and yet are denied justice in its courts or consideration in its deeds.

In the state of Georgia alone, where this latest injustice is taking place, over 500 Negroes in the last sixty years have been publicly lynched, by mobs without trial; the latest victim being murdered this very year. Last year an election was held in the state in which the man elected governor publicly promised to break the laws of this land and deprive a million black citizens in his state of the right to vote. In this state a legal caste system is in vogue which condemns American citizens to unequal education, unequal treatment for disease, segregates them in living quarters and discriminates against them in the right to work at decent wage. The governor promised to maintain this "race segregation" "at all hazards."

In this same state of Georgia, the following incidents occurred in 1947; a Colored mother of 14 children, 12 of whom are living, lost her husband, Jackson Ingram, a share-cropper, who died in August.

With her children she tried to carry on the tilling of her farm in Schley county which was rented from C. M. Dillinger, a white man living in the town of Americus. Her neighbor was a white man named John Stratford, also a share-cropper. No fences were provided between the two farms or even between the farms and highway and often cattle strayed across the boundaries. On November

4, 1947 Stratford called the woman, cursed her and told her to drive her mules and pigs off his farm. She hurriedly left her washing and children and ran to his farm to find her stock. She found that her mules and pigs, and also stock belonging to her landlord, were on Stratford's place. As she entered his lot to drive them back, he met her, armed with a shotgun and began to pound her over the head with it. She begged him to stop and seized the gun. He kept beating her, until the blood ran, with a knife he tried unsuccessfully to open. Her two little sons 13 and 12 stood by crying and pleading, until at last a third son 16, ran from the house, seized the gun, struck Stratford over the head with it and Stratford died.

Mrs. Ingram immediately reported the death to the sheriff. She and her two oldest sons were arrested and put in jail, leaving the nine little children alone in the cottage. On January 26, 1948, she and her two sons were tried by a jury on which no Negro sat, and sentenced to be hanged for murder. Her landlord, Dillinger, seized all her stock, tools and growing crops. Colored people of the state and nation rallied to her defense ad finally, April 5, the same court which sentenced her to death, changed the sentence to life imprisonment. This sentence the three are now serving.

This crucifixion of Mrs. Rosa Lee Ingram is of one piece with Georgia's treatment of Colored women. In 1946, twenty-five white lynchers in Walton county, Georgia killed two untried colored men, and then wantonly shot their wives to death because the women recognized the murderers. No one has ever been indicted or punished for this outrage.

Thus it is clear that the part of this nation which boasts its reverence for womanhood is the part where the women of Africa were slaves and concubines of white Americans for two and a half centuries; where their daughters in states like Virginia became human brood mares to raise domestic slaves when the African trade stopped; and where their granddaughters became mothers of millions of mulattoes.

Today these colored women and their children bear the chief burden of the share-cropping system, where Southern slavery still lingers. The women work the fields for endless hours and their children are driven from their poor schools into the cotton fields under labor contracts which disgrace humanity and debar them from all franchisement by poll taxes, and make the rural Negro family the most depressed in the world. It was such a family that Mrs. Rosa Lee Ingram tried to defend and for this she toils for life in a Georgia prison camp.

Schley County has 3,000 colored and 2,000 white inhabitants, all native born and rural. Only 455 votes were cast in the county in 1942 and of these only 100 were colored. The colored people are almost totally disfranchised, hold no political offices of any kind, never share on juries, and work mostly as share-croppers on land owned by whites. Of the 750 farms 600 are worked by tenants. The money income of Negro families is probably less than $200 a year; their schools are poor and short in term. Twenty-four dollars per child is spent for white children and four dollars for colored, white school buildings are worth $1000 each and colored $600. Four Negroes have been lynched in this county without trial since 1900. It can be affirmed that in this county no Negro "has any rights which a white man is bound to respect."

In this case, we submit, every canon of law and decency, much less of justice has been violated. A boy of 16 struck an armed white man who was attacking his mother. They, mother and two teen-age sons, were tried by a jury of hostile whites, with no representative of their race. Their meager property was seized and the children are today subsisting on charity.

The federal government has made no move; the governor of Georgia has done nothing. The President of the United States, when approached by a delegation from 8 states, would not talk to them and through his secretary said he had never heard of the case. The Chief of the Civil Rights Division of the United States Department of Justice, A. A. Rosen, said: "This sort of thing is in the papers every week. It's shocking to me personally, but it is a matter to be settled internally by the State." He pleaded lack of jurisdiction and no available funds.

The formula upon which this nation rests in the ignoring and mishandling of cases like this, is the legal fiction that a sovereign government can if it will renounce all responsibility for securing justice to its citizens and leave such matters entirely in the hands of subordinate and irresponsible local corporations, even when such bodies openly transgress the law of the land. In the face of this, the

United States of America declares its practice of democracy before
the world and sits in the United Nations which has promised in its
fundamental Charter to promote and encourage "respect for human rights and for fundamental freedoms for all without distinction
as to race, sex, language or religion."

We are painfully aware that all matters of this sort, have by vote
of the General Assembly been put under the jurisdiction of the Social and Economic Council; and that this Council has established
the Commission on Human Rights to consider such cases. But the
world knows what the Commission on Human Rights has done or
rather has not done to fulfill its functions. We are nevertheless
handing this petition to the Commission which in this case as in the
past will either bluntly refuse us the right of petition, or will receive
the document and hide it in its files as though it represented treason or revolution.

* * *

We appeal in this case to the Social and Economic Council and
ask them to insist that the fundamental right of petition be affirmed
and enforced in the Human Rights Commission. And further than
this, we appeal to the General Assembly itself and to every member of it, to place on the agenda of its next meeting and publicly
discuss, the relation of democracy in the United States of America
to its citizens of Negro descent. We affirm that if the Assembly can
and should discuss at length matters affecting the fifteen million
Jews of the world, the thirteen millions of Czechoslovakia, the
seven and a half million people of Greece, the ten millions of Ara-
bia, the six millions of Austria, and the four million of Finland, it
might find a half hour to discuss fifteen million of Negro Americans without disrupting the Charter of the United Nations or af-
fronting the dignity and sovereignty of the United States.

* * *

It may seem a very little thing for 59 nations of the world to take
note of the injustice done a poor colored woman in Georgia, when
such vast problems confront them; and yet after all, is it in the end
so small a thing to "do justly, to love mercy and walk humbly" in
setting this mad world aright?

"Not by might, nor by power, but by my spirit" saith the Lord!

We Americans can send Communists to jail and drive honest citizens to suicide but can we stand before the world and defend the

life imprisonment of Mrs. Rosa Lee Ingram as an example of democracy which the United Nations is teaching?

The undersigned colored women of the United States, legal citizens, voters, wives and mothers have commissioned Dr. W. E. B. Du Bois to draw up this petition, because he has devoted much of his life to the cause of Negro equality. We endorse and subscribe to his words and urge action on the part of all nations who have signed the Charter of the United Nations.

In W. E. B. Du Bois, *Against Racism: Unpublished Essays, Papers, Addresses, 1887–1961*, ed. Herbert Aptheker (Amherst, 1987), 261–5.

Theodore G. Bilbo

False Interpretations of American Democracy (1947)

Mississippi governor and United States senator Theodore G. Bilbo was the most strident among a group of mid-century white supremacist southern Democrats who generally supported progressive social legislation but secured election through rabid race baiting. As a senator, Bilbo regularly introduced bills supporting the deportation of African Americans to Liberia, an idea he championed in Take Your Choice *as a solution to the race problem in America. Among the most vituperative of American politicians, Bilbo was loathed by African Americans and less extreme Mississippi whites but revered by plain folk Mississippians for his devotion to white supremacy and the New Deal.*

> I hold that this government was made on the white basis, by white men for the benefit of white men and their posterity forever.
> —*Stephen Douglas*

The Demands of the Negro leaders for complete political, economic, and social equality between the white and Negro races in the United States were stated in Chapter V. The doctrine of the equality of the two races upon which theory these demands are based was shown to be false in Chapter VI. Thousands of years of world history have shown that the achievements of the Caucasian race have been superior to those of the Negro race. Science has recognized physical, mental, and moral differences between the white and black races, and no amount of argument on the part of these full equality advocates can change or alter these findings. Racial differences and inequalities do exist, and they will continue to exist just as long as white women bear white children and Negro women bear Negro children.

In addition to the contention that science supports the demands for full economic, political, a social equality of the white and Negro races in the United States, the colored leaders and their white Quisling friends state that our ideals of democracy and our concepts of religion force us to grant this complete racial equality to the black race. Upon these three grounds—science, democracy, and religion—the arguments for full equality are based. We have already seen that the scientific arguments are false, and we shall now see that the other two contentions based democracy and religion are equally fallacious.

The fundamental concepts of democracy upon which the government of this Nation is based are embodied in the Declaration of Independence and the Constitution of the United States. By amendment to the Constitution, the Negroes were made citizens of this Republic, and also by constitutional amendment they were given the right to vote. The Negro, just as much as any white citizen, is entitled to the rights, privileges, and protection which are guaranteed to all American citizens. Every citizen, white and colored, is entitled to the same justice and fairness before the law and in the courts of the land.

At this point, it would be well to state the points upon which there may be said to be general agreement. The Negro leaders agree with W. E. B. Du Bois that they are seeking for the members of their race "full economic, political and social equality with American citizens, in thought, expression and action, with no discrimination based on race or color." (1) Concerning the first two demands, there is not so much dispute. All American citizens are entitled to economic equality; every man, white or black, is entitled to a job and to a wage sufficient to support himself and his family. A unified effort should be made to further the economic advancement of the Negro race in this country. This does not mean that the employer should [be] deprived of the right to select his own employees, nor does it mean that racial segregation should be abolished. (2)

Regarding the second demand, political equality, the matter becomes somewhat more complicated. No one questions the fact that Negroes have the constitutional right to qualify electors. Even in the South where Negroes heretofore did not vote in the white Democratic primaries, there was nothing to prevent them from voting in the general elections, and many [of] them did vote if they were qualified under the laws of their respective states. Whenever and wherever he can comply with the qualifications for voting as prescribed by the state in which he lives, the Negro should be permitted to vote.

It is the third demand, that of social equality, which white Americans cannot and will not grant. When the Negro leaders include social equality of the races and the abolition of all forms of racial segregation as a part of their program, they not only are asking for what they will never be freely given, but they are greatly diminishing their chances to secure the economic and political equality which they are seeking for their people. Many Southern white liberals and Southern Negro leaders have made attempts to point out how firmly the segregation of the races is established in the Southland and the dangers which will come from organized attempts to abolish segregation and establish the social equality of the races in this Nation. But the Northern and some Southern Negro leaders have refused to heed any warning.

* * *

The Negro leaders who are seeking social equality of the races and the abolition of every kind of racial segregation cannot justly claim that ideals of American democracy support their demands. They contend that democracy means "full equality" for all citizens, and they quote the Declaration of Independence as proof thereof. Discussing "Certain Unalienable Rights," Mary McLeod Bethune asks for "full American citizenship" for American Negroes. She says "As long as America offers less, she will be that much less a democracy. The whole way is the American way." (4)

There is absolutely nothing in the immortal declaration "that all men are created equal, that they are endowed by their Creator with certain unalienable rights" to support this plea for social equality of the white and black races in the United States. Any person who uses the Declaration of Independence or the Constitution to bring about the social equality of the races in this country is placing a false and dangerous interpretation on these two documents which embody the ideals of American democracy.

> To say that all men or all people or all races are equal is to assert: (a) that certain qualities exist; (b) that these qualities exist among men; (c) that each and every man has exactly the same portion. Now to discover whether there is any validity in the idea of the equality of all men, it has to be asked: What qualities, if any, are shared equally by all men? The author of the famous phrase 'all men are created equal' also wrote: 'I do not mean to deny that there are varieties in the race of man distinguished by their powers both of body and mind. I believe there are, as I see to be the case in the races of other animals.' (Notes on Virginia.) What then did Jefferson mean when he used the word *equal?* According to his own statement (Letter to Henry Lee, May 8. 1825), among his sources were 'the elementary books of public right, as Aristotle, Cicero, Locke, Sidney . . .' Now look at one of these authors, that one closest to Jefferson in time and fighting the divine right of kings exactly as Jefferson was.

* * *

It cannot be forgotten that Thomas Jefferson who wrote that "all men are created equal" also wrote the following lines concerning the Negro.

Nothing is more certainly written in the book of fate than that these people are to be free; nor is it less certain that the two races, equally free, cannot live in the same government.

Jefferson believed that the race question should be solved by colonization of the Negroes at some place outside the United States, and he devoted much time and energy to promoting such a scheme. There is no indication whatsoever that either he or any of the other Founding Fathers interpreted the words of the Declaration of Independence to destroy the racial barriers which from the very beginning of our history separated the white and black races in the United States. Practically all of these men were owners of Negro slaves, and the indications are that they never even thought of the Negro when they announced to the world that "all men are created equal."

* * *

The Negro leaders not only claim that American democracy teaches the social equality of the white and black races, but they go further and proclaim that the denial of this equality is fascism. According to Doxey A. Wilkerson, many Negroes have asked: "Why fight fascism in Germany when we have fascism right here in America?" (7) It is also contended that segregation of the races is a "Hitler-like doctrine." These social equality advocates completely overlook the fact that racial barriers existed in this Nation before the world ever heard of the fascism of modern Germany or of Adolph Hitler and his doctrines or any of his followers. Segregation of the races, racial integrity and the color line have always been the ideals of this Nation. Segregation of the white and black races is as American as any of the other well-known institutions and ideals which have come to us through the one hundred and fifty years of our national existence. Great American statesmen have proclaimed the inequalities of the white and black races all through our national history. Our illustrious leaders have advocated the segregation of the races in this country; they have warned us of the dangers of amalgamation. The present day leaders of the Negro race may attack the denial of social equality to the Negro as in accordance with the teachings of Hitler, but there is no foundation, no logic, and no reason for such a contention. Long before Hitler spoke of racial superiority and plunged the world into the greatest war in history. the Great Emancipator, Abraham Lincoln. said:

> I will say, then, that I am not, nor ever have been, in favor of bringing about in any way the social and political equality of the white and black races—that I am not, nor ever have been, In favor of making voters or jurors of negroes, nor of qualifying them to hold office, nor to inter-marry with white people; and I will say in addition to this that there is a physical difference between the white and black races which I believe will forever forbid the two races living together on terms of social and political equality. And inasmuch as they cannot so live, while they do remain together there must be the position of superior and inferior. and as much as any other man, am in favor of having the superior position assigned to the white race. (Speech at Charleston, Illinois, September 18, 1858.)

Can it be possible that the Negro leaders who today seek to destroy racial barriers would brand Abraham Lincoln as "fascist"? Do they contend that his opinions concerning the Negro race were Hitler-like? Do they contend that the Great Emancipator and war-time President was "un-American"? Of course, they dare not make such a charge. Lincoln did not believe in the social equality of the white and black races, and nowhere do we find any record to show that he believed American democracy required him or any other American to subscribe to the doctrine of complete racial equality.

* * *

How can the Negro leaders contend that it is "un-American" and "undemocratic" to preserve the government as our forefathers made it? As was once emphatically stated by Senator Robert Toombs: "This Republic was born of the soul of a race of pioneer white freemen who settled our continent and built an altar within its forest cathedral to Liberty and Progress. In the record of man, has the Negro ever dreamed this dream?" (9)

It is difficult to understand the arguments of these advocates of social equality of the races. They contend that American democracy demands that the white and Negro races mix and mingle and intermarry. Does it not occur to them that such a condition would destroy the Nation to which they claim to pledge their loyalty? Praise and acknowledgment of the power and greatness of the United States and the contention that whites and Negroes should intermarry according to individual preference are thoroughly inconsistent. Racial intermarriage would destroy the "race of pioneer white freemen" who created this Nation, and it would thus destroy the Nation itself. Who can visualize a future of progress for a Nation of octoroons? The Negro leaders either ignore this possibility, or have no objection to such a condition, or by their silence they admit that they would welcome such a future.

The colored editor of *What the Negro Wants*, R. W. Logan, pleads for the fulfilment of the democratic aims of this Nation by granting full and complete equality to the Negro race, but is not very much interested in the future of this democratic Nation when, in his plea for intermarriage, he says: "Why, we shall all be dead in 2044 and the people will do what they wish." (10) If our ancestors had been so utterly lacking in racial pride and in vision and hope for their own future and that of their posterity, we would today be a Nation of mongrels. No one except possibly the mongrels themselves would dare to contend that we would have benefitted from such a state of affairs.

At this point, there is a deplorable and sorrowful fact which should be noted by every reader. In eighteen states in this white man's country and also in the District of Columbia, where the Nation's Capitol is located, intermarriage of the races is permitted by law. This fact is a national shame, or should I say crime, against the white race of America, and I pray God that these states and the Congress of the United States, on behalf of the District of Columbia, will do something about this situation before it is too late.

> Democratic ideals among an homogeneous population of Nordic blood, as in England or America, is one thing, but it is quite another for the white man to share his blood with, or intrust his ideals to, brown, yellow, black or red men.

> This is suicide pure and simple, and the first victim of this amazing folly will be the white man himself. (11)

The Negro leaders themselves say that never in the history of the United States have the members of their race been accorded full and complete equality with the whites. And it is true that "On no aspect of the race problem are most white Americans, North as well as South, so adamant as they are on their opposition to intermarriage." (12) Then, what stronger proof than the actual practice of white Americans do we need in ascertaining how the majority of our people feel toward the demands of the Negro leaders today for the social equality of the races?

We have found that white Americans have never interpreted American democracy to mean that there would be no racial barriers between the white and black citizens of this Republic, and those who now seek to read such a meaning into the Declaration of Independence are misconstruing the immortal words which were penned by Thomas Jefferson. The social equality of the white and Negro races and the abolition of racial segregation have never been in accordance with the ideals of this Nation. Any one who advances such an argument is placing false interpretation on the meaning of American democracy, and because he is willing, either consciously or unconsciously, that the future of this Republic be destroyed, he is a traitor to his country as well as to his race.

Notes

1. Logan R. W., *What the Negro Wants*, p. 65.
2. See Chapter IV, p. 50 for a statement of equal and exact justice for negroes and whites, with the right of separation enforced at all costs.
3. Graves, John Temple, *The Fighting South* (New York: G. P. Putnam's Sons, 1943), pp. 127, 132.
4. Logan, R. W., *What the Negro Wants*, p. 255.
5. Reprinted from *What the Negro Wants* (the Publisher's Introduction p. xvi) edited by Rayford W. Logan by permission of The University of North Carolina Press. Copyright, 1944, by The University of North Carolina Press.
6. Grant, Madison, *The Passing of the Great Race*, p. xvi.
7. Logan, R. W., *What the Negro Wants*, p. 196.
8. The speech from which this quotation comes has been reprinted in: Calvin, Ira, *The Lost White Race* (Brookline, MA: Courtway-White Publications, 1944), p. 39. This speech was made by Senator Douglas at Jonesboro, Illinois, September 15, 1858.
9. Calvin, Ira, *The Lost White Race*, p. 62.
10. Logan, R. W., *What the Negro Wants*, p. 28.
11. Stoddard, Lothrop, *The Rising Tide of Color*, p. xxxii (from the Introduction by Madison Grant).
12. Logan, R. W., *What the Negro Wants*, p. 28.

Theodore G. Bilbo, *Take Your Choice: Separation or Mongrelization*, Chapter 7 (Poplarville, MS, 1947).

A Letter to a Southern Gentleman (Summer 1946)

Emboldened by the defeat of Nazi Germany and the new internationalism represented by the United Nations, white southern opponents of Jim Crow began to talk back to what many referred to as "our fascists at home." As the

Association of Southern Women for the Prevention of Lynching had done, the author of this letter connects racial and gender issues in a jovial but damning critique of the logic of Jim Crow's knights in shining armor. Printed in the liberal magazine Common Ground, *a manuscript version of this letter was also sent to actor and filmmaker Orson Welles, who used his radio commentary program on the American Broadcasting Company as a bully pulpit for racial equality.*

Dear Bill:

In your last letter you sent me a clipping about a Negro boy who criminally attacked a white woman, killed one of her children, and burned her home. On it you wrote, "Dirty, savage beasts and you want me to associate with them and give them EQUAL OPPORTUNITIES."

Your plan of basing a whole group's right to equal opportunities on the percentage of sex perverts it contains interests me and I have been doing a little research on the subject. Here are the results of some newspaper scanning I have done with your approach in mind.

First, a clipping from a Tennessee paper about a confessed murderer, white, of a forty-one-year-old Negro woman who was pregnant. He cut her throat from ear to ear and stuffed her body under a railroad bridge.

Next, there came to my mind the case of a white Epworth League friend in Ohio who went berserk one day, criminally attacked a ten-year-old girl who came to his apartment to sell benefit tickets, strangled her, and hid her body in a trunk.

Then there's the case in Detroit of the eight-year-old girl criminally attacked by a white man, and thrown down with her slit throat to die. And, of course, there's the hideous Degnan case.

Do you know, as I read and thought about these cases which occur so often in our country (not to mention the bestiality displayed by men of all races in wartorn Europe and Asia), an amazing and horrifying fact became clear. Regardless of the various colors, races, and creeds represented by our sex murderers, one thing they do have in common—so perhaps your line of reasoning does have some justification. They all appear to be male.

As a result of using your line of reasoning I am compelled to wonder just how you can bear to associate with your own sex, or—

to be even more specific—how you can endure associating with yourself? From there, this last rather simple conclusion seems inevitable—i.e., that women and children will never be safe in this world until we keep men ruthlessly segregated and suppressed and deny them any and all access to equal opportunities.

Yours for a safer world,

Mary

Common Ground (Summer 1946); in manuscript in Orson Welles Papers, Correspondence Box 3, August 12–19, 1946 folder, Lilly Library, Indiana University.

Lillian Smith

The Women (1949)

Born into a prosperous and respectable Florida family in 1897, Lillian Smith was one of the first white southern writers to openly denounce segregation and state clearly Jim Crow's social, economic, political, and moral cost. Politically progressive and active in New Deal circles, Smith's uncompromising stance on segregation distinguished her from other white southern liberals and the organizations they founded in the 1940s. In 1944, Smith gained national recognition, and regional denunciation, by publishing Strange Fruit, *a novel about love across the color line. Smith's most enduring book was* Killers of the Dream *(1949), an autobiographical investigation into the history and effects of Jim Crow. Deeply informed by Smith's reading of Freud and her own nonheterosexual orientation,* Killers of the Dream *warned that segregation corrupted the soul, alienated women from their sexuality, and erased any possibility for freedom of conscience in the South. Written as the Presidential Commission on Civil Rights went about its work,* Killers of the Dream *was self-consciously presentist in its orientation even as it detailed the past, and it provided a lucid and penetrating critique of the segregated South on the eve of the modern civil rights movement.*

---

* * *

[White southern women] climbed down from the pedestal when no one was looking and explored a bit. Not as you may think, perhaps. They were conventional, highly "moral" women, who would not have dreamed of breaking the letter of their marriage vows or, when not married, their technical chastity. But their minds went a-roaming and their sympathies attached themselves like hungry little fibers to all kinds of people and causes while their shrewd common sense kicked old lies around until they were popping like firecrackers.

These ladies went forth to commit treason against a southern tradition set up by men who had betrayed their mothers, sometimes themselves, and many of the South's children white and mixed, for three long centuries. It was truly a subversive affair, but as decorously conducted as an afternoon walk taken by the students of a Female Institute. It started stealthily, in my mother's day. Shyly, these first women sneaked down from their chilly places, did their little sabotage and sneaked up again, wrapping innocence around them like a lace shawl. They set secret time bombs and went back to their needlework, serenely awaiting the blast. They had no lady Lincoln to proclaim their emancipation from southern tradition but they scarcely needed one.

The thing was a spontaneous reaction. Mother in her old age told daughter strange truths that had gnawed on her lonely heart too long. And daughter told other women. Colored and white women stirring up a lemon-cheese cake for the hungry males in the household looked deep into each other's eyes and understood their common past. A mistress, reading the Bible to her colored maid polishing silver, would lay aside Holy Writ and talk of things less holy but of immense importance to both of them.

Insurrection was on. White men were unaware of it, but the old pedestal on which their women had been safely stowed away, was reeling and rocking. With an emotionally induced stupidity really beneath them, these men went on with their race-economic exploitation, protecting themselves behind rusty shields of as phony a moral cause as the Anglo-American world has ever witnessed. In the name of *sacred womanhood*, of *purity*, of *preserving the home*, lecherous old men and young ones, reeking with impurities, who had violated the home since they were sixteen years old, whipped up lynchings, organized Klans, burned crosses, aroused the poor and ignorant to wild excitement by an obscene, perverse imagery describing the "menace" of Negro men hiding behind every cypress waiting to rape "our" women. In the name of such holiness, they did these things to keep the affairs of their own heart and conscience and home, as well as the community, "under control." And not once did they dream their women did not believe their lies.

And then it happened. The lady insurrectionists gathered together in one of our southern cities. They primly called themselves church women but churches were forgotten by everybody when they spoke their revolutionary words. They said calmly that they were not afraid of being raped; as for their sacredness, they could take care of it themselves; they did not need the chivalry of a lynching to protect them and did not want it. Not only that, they continued, but they would personally do everything in their power to keep any Negro from being lynched and furthermore, they squeaked bravely, they had plenty of power.

They had more than they knew. They had the power of spiritual blackmail over a large part of the white South. All they had to do was drop their little bucket into any one of numerous wells of guilt dotting the landscape and splash it around a bit. No one, of thousands of white men, had any notion how much or how little each woman knew about his private goings-on. Some who had never been guilty in act began to equate adolescent fantasies with reality, and there was confusion everywhere.

This was in 1930. These women organized an Association of Southern Women for the Prevention of Lynching. Their husbands, sons, brothers, and uncles often worked by their side; many of them with sincere concern for the state of affairs, others because they had to.

It may seem incredible, but the custom of lynching had rarely been questioned by the white group. The church women's action gave a genuine shock. This was a new thing in Dixie. The ladies' valor is not diminished, I think, by reminding ourselves that the movement could not have crystallized so early had not Dr. Will Alexander, and a handful of men and women whom he gathered around him, pushed things off to a good start in 1918 with the first interracial committee in the South. There were other yeasty forces at work: A world war had squeezed and pulled the earth's people apart and squeezed them together again; the Negroes themselves, led by courageous men like Walter White of Atlanta and W. E. B.

Du Bois and their northern white friends were making our nation aware that Negroes have rights; the group around Dr. Howard Odum—whose first study of the Negro in 1910 greatly influenced social science's interest in Negro-white patterns of life—were gathering all kinds of facts concerning a region that had been for so long content with its fantasies and fears. The women's role was to bake the first pan of bread made from this rising batter, and to serve it hot as is southern custom.

After this magnificent uprising against the sleazy thing called "chivalry," these women worked liked the neat, industrious housewives they really were, using their mops and brooms to clean up a dirty spot here and there but with no real attempt to change this way of life which they dimly realized had injured themselves and their children as much as it had injured Negroes, but which they nevertheless clung to.

Of course the demagogues would have loved to call them "Communists" or "bolsheviks," but how could they? The women were too prim and neat and sweet and ladylike and churchly in their activities, and too many of them were the wives of the most powerful men in town. Indeed, the ladies themselves hated the word "radical" and were quick to turn against anyone who dared go further than they in this housecleaning of Dixie. Few of them had disciplined intellects or giant imaginations and probably no one of them grasped the full implications of this sex-race-religion-economics tangle, but they had warm hearts and powerful energy and a nice technic for bargaining, and many an old cagey politician, and a young one or two, have been outwitted by their soft bending words.

They followed a sound feminine intuition, working as "church women," leaning on the strength of Christ's teachings for support when they needed it. They worked with great bravery but so unobtrusively that even today many southerners know little about them. But they aroused the conscience of the South and the whole country about lynching; they tore a big piece of this evil out of southern tradition, leaving a hole which no sane man in Dixie now dares stuff up with public defenses. They attacked the KKK when few except the editors of the Columbus (Georgia) *Enquirer,* among white southern newspaper men, had criticized this group from whom Hitler surely learned so much.

But they were not yet done. They had a few more spots to rub out. One had to do with their own souls. They believed that the Lord's Supper is a holy sacrament which Christians cannot take without sacrilege unless they will also break bread with fellow men of other color. Believing, they put on their best bib and tucker and gathered in small groups to eat with colored women, deliberately breaking a taboo that had collected many deep fears around it.

It is difficult for those not reared as white southerners to remember how this eating taboo in childhood was woven into the mesh of things that are "wrong," how it pulled anxieties from stronger prohibitions and attached them to itself. But we who live here cannot forget. One of these church women told me of her first eating experience with colored friends. Though her conscience was serene, and her enjoyment of this association was real, yet she was seized by an acute nausea which disappeared only when the meal was finished. She was too honest to attribute it to anything other than anxiety welling up from the "bottom of her personality," as she expressed it, creeping back from her childhood training. Others have told me similar experiences: of feeling "pangs of conscience," as one put it, "though my conscience was clearly approving"; or suddenly in the night awaking, overwhelmed by "serious doubts of the wisdom of what we are doing."

The white women were not alone in these irrational reactions. Colored women also found it hard, but for different reasons. Sometimes their pride was deeply hurt that white women felt so virtuous when eating with them. They were too sensitive not to be aware of the psychic price the white women paid for this forbidden act, and yet too ignorant of the training given white children to understand why there had to be a price. And sometimes the colored women were themselves almost overcome by a break-through not of guilt but of their old repressed hatred of white people. One of the most charming, sensitive, intelligent Negro women I know, tells me that even now when she is long with white people she grows physically ill and has immense difficulty coming to terms with the resentments of her childhood.

To break bread together, each group had to force its way through thick psychological barriers, and each did it with little understanding of their own or the other group's feelings. When anxieties appeared, most of the church women, white and Negro, suppressed them firmly by laying the ponderous weight of the New Testament on them, declaring bravely that "Jesus would have done likewise."

Lillian Smith, *Killers of the Dream*, Chapter 4 (New York, 1949), 141–49.

Stetson Kennedy

Brotherhood—Union Made (1946)

Floridian Stetson Kennedy came from a family whose ancestors included two signers of the Declaration of Independence, one Confederate officer, and a Klansman. A dedicated folklorist, Kennedy traveled the South during the Depression under the auspices of the Federal Writers' Program. The people he met had not been raised, as Kennedy had, in fourteen-room houses. Dedicated to economic justice, Kennedy understood that white racial prejudice was a principal barrier to working class-solidarity. Institutionalized racism was an even greater obstacle to unity. Traditional trade unions such as those affiliated with the American Federation of Labor (AFL) were strictly all-white organizations. The Congress of Industrial Organizations (CIO), incorporated in 1938, organized industrial workers unrecognized by the AFL. Cognizant of the need to organize all the workers in interracial industries such as steel and tobacco processing and heavily influenced by Communist members already pledged to abolish segregation, the CIO adopted a formal policy of nondiscrimination. In the North, interracial CIO unions improved wages and working conditions for their members and provided educational and leadership opportunities for black and white workers alike. Between 1935 and 1945, while the NAACP pursued its legal agenda to secure individual rights, the CIO addressed economic problems and provided crucial lessons in mass action that would prove useful in the years to come.

It is within the power of the unions not only to propel the South toward economic solidity, but also along the path that leads to interracial justice and harmony.

That indispensable prerequisite to Southern progress, the unity of Southern working folk, black and white, has twice been set back for generations: first by the abolition of Reconstruction, and subsequently by the perversion of Populism. Now the mantle of responsibility and opportunity has fallen upon the unions, many of which are striving, with far-reaching success, to reawaken Southern workers to the potentialities of strength-through-unity.

But, sad to say, some unions have not accepted this opportunity and responsibility. Of the two hundred major unions in the United States, nineteen of the big craft unions have constitutional bars against Negroes and about thirty others have other excuses for not admitting Negroes. Many other unions, while not practicing outright Negro exclusion, do insist upon separate Jim Crow locals for Negroes. Such Negro locals usually are affiliated with the nearest white local and are generally dominated by it. Ten of the nineteen unions which have constitutional bars against Negroes are affiliated with the American Federation of Labor. And so it is that nearly a third of the craft and semicraft membership of the AFL, as well as the entire membership of the operating railroad brotherhoods, is limited to those who are "white, sober, and of good moral character."

In the railroad industry Negroes have been methodically squeezed out for the past several decades. This is being done through unconscionable union-company agreements—sometimes formal and sometimes tacit—to keep Negroes off the higher paid jobs without regard to seniority, and to bar Negro youths as apprentices. As a result, by 1940 only 9 per cent of the employees of the Class I railroads were Negroes, and 97 per cent of these Negroes were in the following jobs: janitors and cleaners, extra gang, section and maintenance-of-way men, laborers and helpers, baggage-room and station attendants, cooks, waiters, and train attendants. In the higher classifications, embracing 1,297,563 employees, only three tenths of 1 per cent were Negroes.

During the war there were a number of tests of the closed shop when maintained by unions which refuse to admit Negroes to membership. One such case developed at San Mateo, California, when Charles Sullivan, Negro, was denied work at the Bethlehem Shipbuilding Company because the International Association of Machinists, AFL, had a constitutional ban against Negro members. Ultimately the FEPC referred the case to President Roosevelt, who in turn called upon William Green, head of the AFL, to take appropriate action. Finally the International Association of Machinists wrote its local: "It is now our duty to advise you that there is no other course to follow than to instruct the membership of Lodge 68 to make the necessary arrangements to comply with the Executive Order of the President of the United States." However, the Negro machinist was not admitted to the union, but was merely "cleared" for work.

There can be no legitimate excuse for such behavior on the part of a union. As the Louisville (Ky.) *Courier-Journal* has observed, "Brotherhood is a term that will not be without its qualifications and contradictions as long as human beings are what they are; however, when Brotherhood denies even a minimum economic chance to a man on account of the color of his skin, it makes us think of Free Enterprise."

The International Mineworkers were the first to spade Southern soil for non-discriminatory unionism. As one Negro miner puts it, "With the union it's all the same; white or black, you're a coal digger still."

Nevertheless, in 1935, when the CIO appeared under its standard "to bring about the effective organization of the working men and women of America regardless of race, creed, color, or nationality . . ." the South of white supremacy was deeply shocked, as well it might be. The simple truth is that, to be effective in the South, unions must be non-discriminatory. Employers know this and have issued many an invitation to CIO representatives to organize their Southern plants—on a lily-white basis—but all such offers have been impolitely declined.

Southern Negroes are also well aware of the potentialities of non-discriminatory unions. As a bishop of the African Methodist Episcopal Church puts it, "When I first heard of the CIO, I asked, 'What does it stand for?' The answer I got was, 'White and colored in the same union.' When I heard that, I put on my war boots and my preachin' coat, and I been preachin' the principles of CIOism ever since!"

* * *

White Southerners, on the other hand, are learning the necessity for non-discrimination the hard way. By all odds the most effective appeal to them is that of self-interest: the prospect of wiping out the regional wage differential by first wiping out the racial wage differential. Put another way, the Southern white worker can see how bringing Negroes into the union will keep them from undercutting wages or strikebreaking. (Significantly, I can find no instance of Negroes lending themselves to strike-breaking since the CIO came South a decade ago.)

Despite the CIO's huge success in building better race relations where they are most needed, it has not discovered any magic touchstone which will instantaneously convert prejudice into brotherhood. Sometimes it has found it necessary to advance toward non-discrimination a step at a time. As one organizer pointed out to me, "You can't promote equal job rights for Negroes until you've got a union and a collective-bargaining contract."

In other words, neither Southern Negroes nor Southern whites would be helped by a union which went so far and so fast in the field of race relations that a reaction was provoked which would either prevent the formation of a local union or break up one already established. Southern Negroes are keenly aware of this fact and voluntarily conduct their activities in the unions accordingly. The CIO is not trying to impose union democracy from the top so much as it is trying to build it from the ground up. Generally speaking, this upbuilding is proceeding at the maximum speed possible without endangering the existence of the union. True, much of the initiative comes from the (duly elected) top; but for the most part it is being administered by Southerners who have risen above prejudice. As one of them said to me, "You just don't find men on the CIO pay roll who have it in their hearts to discriminate."

* * *

Whether inspired by the employer, a rival union, or other factors, prejudice is sometimes so rife that the CIO organizer must perforce—if he wishes to see a democratic union established—circumvent the race issue temporarily. One organizer recently described such a situation to me, as it developed in a Georgia plant where about 15 per cent of the employees were Negroes.

Quietly he took some of the Negro leaders aside. "Y'all know what the policy of the CIO is regarding racial discrimination," he told them, "but y'all also know how the whites in this plant feel. If I start right in organizing you fellows, I won't have a chance with them, and then nobody will have a union. So I'm asking you people to stand fast, and, when the time comes, vote for the union."

Then he went to work with the whites. When the election was finally held, the majority voted for the union, despite violent opposition from the employer. Now the organizer was in a position to say to the white members, "The colored have helped us by voting for the union. Without their votes we would have been licked. Now, as you know, the CIO is opposed to racial discrimination. Furthermore, the NLRB says the union has got to represent *all* employees in the plant. On top of that, the plant's contracts with the government specify that there be no discrimination. We're in for some hard sledding in the postwar period, and we can't expect the Negroes to stick by us if we don't give them a square deal. And so no matter how you look at it, it's up to us to take the colored in."

By that time the whites were sufficiently converted to unionism to put aside their prejudices—and thus another non-discriminatory Southern union was born. Short of a democratic revolution, this would seem to be one of the devious paths which democracy-in-evolution must take in the South.

* * *

The influence of the CIO's policy of non-discrimination is by no means confined to the union, but carries over into community life. As a result of their working relationship on the job and in the union, white and Negro members are in a position to approach their common community problems on a basis of friendship instead of prejudice, and understanding instead of misunderstanding. . . . Too, the CIO exerts its influence for non-discrimination directly upon community agencies; whenever any of the welfare bodies solicit contributions from the CIO, the union's prime condition is: "The fund must be expended without discrimination."

Anti-union forces have striven mightily to create a public impression that the CIO is dedicated to a revolutionary program for bringing about "social equality." In clarifying the practical application of the CIO's resolution against discrimination, director George L. P. Weaver, of the union's Committee to Abolish Discrimination, reported in 1945: ". . . the phrase 'social equality' has always been used to create confusion. To illustrate, the following public services are often included within its scope: Equal access to all residential areas, to all public transportation, public recreation, hotels, restaurants, public schools and other facilities used by the public and supported wholly or in part by public funds. These services must be removed from the realm of private social activities and considered as public facilities to be equally enjoyed by all citizens.

"Private social activities may be defined as the right of individuals or groups to make purely arbitrary selections, such as marriage, friendships, home entertainment, and participation in organizations concerned with social uplift. To attempt to regulate or dictate to an individual in this sphere would be a violation of his constitutional rights and outside the scope of our jurisdiction."

While the CIO has thus condemned compulsory segregation, it has not sought any overnight revolution against the laws and practices of segregation which exist in the South. Within its own ranks, however, the CIO is doing what it can to discourage segregation in the South. What it can do varies within geographical (and psychological) boundaries. For example, in Alabama and Georgia, I have seen Negro delegates segregate themselves on one *side* of the hall at state CIO conventions. On the other hand, at a Tennessee convention there was no segregation, although one individual white delegate did take the trouble to inform me that "This section has been reserved for the colored." However, I have not encountered any instance of a CIO staff member insisting upon segregation, while many have actively discouraged it. The position of the majority is, "We don't have anything to say about it; the Negroes segregate themselves."

A related question has to do with the recreational activities of mixed unions in the South. I have attended such affairs in Georgia. White members served the Negro members refreshments and then served themselves. There was a tendency on the part of both groups to sit apart while eating. Whatever talent there was in the union, white and Negro, took turns performing. Whenever there was music for dancing, either the white couples danced at one end of the hall and the Negroes at the other or the two races took turns dancing alternately. Throughout the entire proceedings there was an evident spirit of comradeship, and there were no incidents or friction. I describe these events here, not because either the CIO or I regard them as ideal, but because they are significant mileposts marking the South's transition from white supremacy to democracy.

Another such milepost, whose significance lies largely in its symbolism, is the manner in which the abhorrent "etiquette" of white supremacy is gradually being discarded by the CIO's white Southern members. As a single example of this, I recall what took place after a Negro delegate to a recent Alabama CIO convention had delivered a stirring speech. Several white staff members shook the Negro's hand in congratulation. Slowly a few white delegates moved forward to do likewise.

"You goin' to shake his hand?" I heard a white delegate apprehensively ask his companion behind me.

"I don't know," came the answer cautiously.

"Come on," said the other, "everybody else is. I don't care if he is colored; he made the best union speech of the convention."

And so the white brothers shook hands with their darker brother; and the walls didn't come tumbling down; and the union and the South were stronger.

* * *

From Stetson Kennedy, *Southern Exposure* (New York, 1946), 302–12.

Supreme Court of California

Decision in *Perez v. Lippold* (October 1, 1948)

Racially restrictive marriage laws (antimiscegenation laws) both rested on and supported the laws of racial identity that undergirded the entire system of Jim Crow. In 1948, thirty out of the 48 states of the Union prohibited marriage between whites and nonwhites, variously defined. That year, California's antimiscegenation law was challenged by two residents of Los Angeles, Andrea Perez and Sylvester Davis. In a landmark 4–3 decision that found the California law too vague to enforce because of the state's lack of definition of any of the racial groups (such as "mulattoes") forbidden to marry "whites," the California Supreme Court also ruled that racially restrictive marriage laws violated the equal protection clause of the Fourteenth Amendment. Although the decision in the Perez *case applied only to California, Justice Roger J. Traynor's ringing endorsement of equal marriage rights, adopted belatedly by the U.S. Supreme Court in 1967, emboldened civil rights activists and caused consternation among those dedicated to preserving Jim Crow. At the same time, Justice John W. Shenk's dissent, which noted, among other things, the* Perez *decision's radical departure from precedent, highlighted the continuing power of scientific racism far beyond Dixie.*

Justice Traynor

In this proceeding in mandamus, petitioners seek to compel the county clerk of Los Angeles County to issue them a certificate of registry and a license to marry. In the application for a license, petitioner Andrea Perez states that she is a white person and petitioner Sylvester Davis that he is a Negro. Respondent refuses to issue the certificate and license, invoking Civil Code section 69, which provides: 'no license may be issued authorizing the marriage of a white person with a Negro, mulatto, Mongolian or member of the Malay race.'

Civil Code section 69 implements Civil Code section 60, which provides: 'All marriages of white persons with negroes, Mongolians, members of the Malay race, or mulattoes are illegal and void.' This section originally appeared in the Civil Code in 1872, but at that time it prohibited marriages only between white persons and Negroes or mulattoes. It succeeded a statute prohibiting such marriages and authorizing the imposition of certain criminal penalties upon persons contracting or solemnizing them. Since 1872, Civil Code section 60 has been twice amended, first to prohibit marriages between white persons and Mongolians and subsequently to prohibit marriages between white persons and members of the Malay race.

* * *

The regulation of marriage is considered a proper function of the state. It is well settled that a legislature may declare monogamy to be the 'law of social life under its dominion,' even though such a law might inhibit the free exercise of certain religious practices. If the miscegenation law under attack in the present proceeding is directed at a social evil and employs a reasonable means to prevent that evil, it is valid regardless of its incidental effect upon the conduct of particular religious groups. If, on the other hand, the law is discriminatory and irrational, it unconstitutionally restricts not only religious liberty but the liberty to marry as well.

The due process clause of the Fourteenth Amendment protects an area of personal liberty not yet wholly delimited. 'While this court has not attempted to define with exactness the liberty thus guaranteed, the term has received much consideration and some of the included things have been definitely stated. Without doubt, it denotes not merely freedom from bodily restraint but also the right of the individual to contract, to engage in any of the common occupations of life, to acquire useful knowledge, to marry, establish a home and bring up children, to worship God according to the dictates of his own conscience, and, generally, to enjoy those privileges long recognized at common law as essential to the orderly pursuit of happiness by free men.' Marriage is thus something more than a civil contract subject to regulation by the state; it is a fundamental right of free men. There can be no prohibition of marriage except for an important social objective and by reasonable means.

No law within the broad areas of state interest may be unreasonably discriminatory or arbitrary. The state's interest in public education, for example, does not empower the Legislature to compel school children to receive instruction from public teachers only, for it would thereby take away the right of parents to 'direct the upbringing and education of children under their control.' Again, the state's vital concern in the prevention of crime and the mental health of its citizens does not empower the Legislature to deprive 'individuals of a right which is basic to the perpetuation of a race the right to have offspring' by authorizing the sterilization of criminals upon an arbitrary basis of classification and without a fair hearing.

The right to marry is as fundamental as the right to send one's child to a particular school or the right to have offspring. Indeed, 'We are dealing here with legislation which involves one of the basic civil rights of man. Marriage and procreation are fundamental to the very existence and survival of the race.' Legislation infringing such rights must be based upon more than prejudice and must be free from oppressive discrimination to comply with the constitutional requirements of due process and equal protection of the laws.

I.

Since the right to marry is the right to join in marriage with the person of one's choice, a statute that prohibits an individual from marrying a member of a race other than his own restricts the scope of his choice and thereby restricts his right to marry. It must therefore be determined whether the state can restrict that right on the basis of race alone without violating the equal protection of the laws clause of the United States Constitution.

'Distinctions between citizens solely because of their ancestry are by their very nature odious to a free people whose institutions are founded upon the doctrine of equality. For that reason, legislative classification or discrimination based on race alone has often been held to be a denial of equal protection. In the Hirabayashi case the United States Supreme Court held that despite the fact that under the Constitution of the United States 'racial discriminations are in most circumstances irrelevant and therefore prohibited, it by no means follows that, in dealing with the perils of war, Congress and the Executive are wholly precluded from taking into account those facts and circumstances which are relevant to measures for our national defense and for the successful prosecution of the war, and which may in fact place citizens of one ancestry in a different category from others. The adoption by Government, in the crisis of war and of threatened invasion, of measures for the public safety, based upon the recognition of facts and circumstances which indicate that a group of one national extraction may menace that safety more than others, is not wholly beyond the limits of the Constitution and is not to be condemned merely because in other and in most circumstances racial distinctions are irrelevant. The fact alone that attack on our shores was threatened by Japan rather than another enemy power set these citizens apart from others who have no particular association with Japan.' Whether or not a state could base similar measures on the peril caused by a national emergency in the face of the equal protection of the laws clause of the United States Constitution, which does not apply to the federal government, it clearly could not make such a distinction based on ancestry in the absence of an emergency.

A state law prohibiting members of one race from marrying members of another race is not designed to meet a clear and present peril arising out of an emergency. In the absence of an emergency the state clearly cannot base a law impairing fundamental rights of individuals on general assumptions as to traits of racial groups. It has been said that a statute such as section 60 does not discriminate against any racial group, since it applies alike to all persons whether Caucasian, Negro, or members of any other race. The decisive question, however, is not whether different races, each considered as a group, are equally treated. The right to marry is the right of individuals, not of racial groups. The equal protection clause of the United States Constitution does not refer to rights of the Negro race, the Caucasian race, or any other race, but to the rights of individuals. In construing the equal protection of the laws clause of the Constitution, the United States Supreme Court has declared that the constitutionality of state action must be tested according to whether the rights of an individual are restricted because of his race. Thus, in holding invalid state enforcement of covenants restricting the occupation of real property on grounds of race, the Supreme Court of the United States declared: 'The rights created by the first section of the Fourteenth Amendment are, by its terms, guaranteed to the individual. It is, therefore, no answer to these petitioners to say that the courts may also be induced to deny white persons rights of ownership and occupancy on grounds of race or color. Equal protection of the laws is not achieved through indiscriminate imposition of inequalities.' In an earlier case, where a Negro contended that the state's failure to give him equal facilities with others to study law within the state impaired his constitutional rights under the equal protection clause, the court rejected any consideration of the difference of the demand for legal education among white persons and Negroes, stating: 'Petitioner's right was a personal one. It was as an individual that he was entitled to the equal protection of the laws, and the State was bound to furnish him within its borders facilities for legal education substantially equal to those which the State there afforded for persons of the white race, whether or not other negroes sought the same opportunity.' Similarly, with regard to the furnishing of sleeping, dining, and chair car facilities on trains, the Supreme Court of the United States has held that even though there was less demand for such facilities among Negroes than among whites, the right of a member of the Negro race to substantially equal facilities was a right of the individual and not of the racial group: 'It is the individual who is entitled to the equal protection of the laws, and if he is denied by a common carrier, acting in the matter under the authority of a state law, a facility or convenience in the course of his journey which, under substantially the same circumstances, is furnished to another traveler, he may properly complain that his constitutional privilege has been invaded.' In these cases the United States Supreme Court determined that the right of an individual to be treated without discrimination because of his race can be met by separate facilities affording substantially equal treatment to the members of the different races. A holding that such segregation does not impair the right of an individual to ride on trains or to enjoy a legal education is clearly inapplicable to the right of an individual to marry. Since the essence of the right to marry is freedom to join in marriage with the person of one's choice, a segregation statute for marriage necessarily impairs the right to marry.

In determining whether the public interest requires the prohibition of a marriage between two persons, the state may take into consideration matters of legitimate concern to the state. Thus, disease that might become a peril to the prospective spouse or to the offspring of the marriage could be made a disqualification for marriage. Such legislation, however, must be based on tests of the individual, not on arbitrary classifications of groups or races, and must be administered without discrimination on the grounds of race. It has been suggested that certain races are more prone than the Caucasian to diseases such as tuberculosis. If the state determines that certain diseases would endanger a marital partner or offspring, it may prohibit persons so diseased from marrying, but the statute must apply to all persons regardless of race. Sections 60 and 69 are not motivated by a concern to diminish the transmission of disease by marriage, for they make race and disease the disqualification. Thus, a tubercular Negro or a tubercular Caucasian may marry subject to the race limitation, but a Negro and a Caucasian who are free from disease may not marry each other. If the purpose of these sections were to prevent marriages by persons who do not have the qualifications for marriage that the state may properly prescribe, they would make the possession of such qualifications the test for members of all races alike. By restricting the individual's right to marry on the basis of race alone, they violate the equal protection of the laws clause of the United States Constitution.

II.

The parties, however, have argued at length the question whether the statute is arbitrary and unreasonable. They have assumed that under the equal protection clause the state may classify individuals according to their race in legislation regulating their fundamental rights. If it be assumed that such a classification can validly be made under the equal protection clause in circumstances besides those arising from an emergency, the question would remain whether the statute's classification of racial groups is based on differences between those groups bearing a substantial relation to a legitimate legislative objective. Race restrictions must be viewed with great suspicion, for the Fourteenth Amendment 'was adopted to prevent state legislation designed to perpetuate discrimination on the basis of race or color' and expresses 'a definite national policy against discrimination because of race or color.' Any state legislation discriminating against persons on the basis of race or color has to overcome the strong presumption inherent in this constitutional policy. 'Only the most exceptional circumstances can excuse discrimination on that basis in the face of the equal protection clause.' We shall therefore examine the history of the legislation in question and the arguments in its support to determine whether there are any exceptional circumstances sufficient to justify it.

* * *

Civil Code section 60, like most miscegenation statutes, prohibits marriages only between 'white persons' and members of certain other so-called races. Although section 60 is more inclusive than most miscegenation statutes, it does not include 'Indians' or 'Hindus'; nor does it set up 'Mexicans' as a separate category, although some authorities consider Mexico to be populated at least in part by persons who are a mixture of 'white' and 'Indian.' Thus, 'white persons' may marry persons who would be considered other than white by respondent's authorities, and all other 'races' may intermarry freely.

The Legislature therefore permits the mixing of all races with the single exception that white persons may not marry Negroes,

Mongolians, Mulattoes, or Malays. It might be concluded there from that section 60 is based upon the theory that the progeny of a white person and a Mongolian or Negro or Malay are inferior or undesirable, while the progeny of members of other different races are not. Nevertheless, the section does not prevent the mixing of 'white' and 'colored' blood. It permits marriages not only between Caucasians and others of darker pigmentation, such as Indians, Hindus, and Mexicans, but between persons of mixed ancestry including white. If a person of partly Caucasian ancestry is yet classified as a Mongolian under section 60 because his ancestry is predominantly Mongolian, a considerable mixture of Caucasian and Mongolian blood is permissible. A person having five-eighths Mongolian blood and three-eighths white blood could properly marry another person of preponderantly Mongolian blood. Similarly, a Mulatto can marry a Negro. Under the theory that a Mulatto is a person having one-eighth or more of Negro ancestry, a person having seven-eighths white ancestry could marry a Negro. In fact two mulattoes, each of four- eighths white and four-eighths Negro blood, could marry under section 60, and their progeny, like them, would belong as much to one race as to the other. In effect, therefore, section 60 permits a substantial amount of intermarriage between persons of some Caucasian ancestry and members of other races. Furthermore, there is no ban on illicit sexual relations between Caucasians and members of the proscribed races. Indeed, it is covertly encouraged by the race restrictions on marriage.

Nevertheless, respondent has sought to justify the statute by contending that the prohibition of intermarriage between Caucasians and members of the specified races prevents the Caucasian race from being contaminated by races whose members are by nature physically and mentally inferior to Caucasians.

Respondent submits statistics relating to the physical inferiority of certain races. Most, if not all, of the ailments to which he refers are attributable largely to environmental factors. Moreover, one must take note of the statistics showing that there is a higher percentage of certain diseases among Caucasians than among non-Caucasians. The categorical statement that non-Caucasians are inherently physically inferior is without scientific proof. In recent years scientists have attached great weight to the fact that their segregation in a generally inferior environment greatly increases their liability to physical ailments. In any event, generalizations based on race are untrustworthy in view of the great variations among members of the same race. The rationalization, therefore, that marriage between Caucasians and non-Caucasians is socially undesirable because of the physical disabilities of the latter, fails to take account of the physical disabilities of Caucasians and fails also to take account of variations among non-Caucasians. The Legislature is free to prohibit marriages that are socially dangerous because of the physical disabilities of the parties concerned. The miscegenation statute, however, condemns certain races as unfit to marry with Caucasians on the premise of a hypothetical racial disability, regardless of the physical qualifications of the individuals concerned. If this premise were carried to its logical conclusion, non-Caucasians who are now precluded from marrying Caucasians on physical grounds would also be precluded from marrying among themselves on the same grounds. The concern to prevent marriages in the first category and the indifference about marriages in the second reveal the spuriousness of the contention that intermarriage between Caucasians and non-Caucasians is socially dangerous on physical grounds.

Respondent also contends that Negroes, and impliedly the other races specified in section 60, are inferior mentally to Caucasians. It is true that, in the United States, catalogues of distinguished people list more Caucasians than members of other races. It cannot be disregarded, however, that Caucasians are in the great majority and have generally had a more advantageous environment, and that the capacity of the members of any race to contribute to a nation's culture depends in large measure on how freely they may participate in that culture. There is no scientific proof that one race is superior to another in native ability. The date on which Caucasian superiority is based have undergone considerable re-evaluation by social and physical scientists in the past two decades. Although scientists do not discount the influences of heredity on the ability to score highly on mental tests, there is no certain correlation between race and intelligence. There have been outstanding individuals in all races, and there has also been wide variation in the individuals of all races. In any event the Legislature has not made an intelligence test a prerequisite to marriage. If respondent's blanket condemnation of the mental ability of the proscribed races were accepted, there would be no limit to discrimination based upon the purported inferiority of certain races. It would then be logical to forbid Negroes to marry Negroes, or Mongolians to marry Mongolians, on the ground of mental inferiority, or by sterilization to decrease their numbers.

Respondent contends, however, that persons wishing to marry in contravention of race barriers come from the 'dregs of society' and that their progeny will therefore be a burden on the community. There is no law forbidding marriage among the 'dregs of society,' assuming that this expression is capable of definition. If there were such a law, it could not be applied without a proper determination of the persons that fall within that category, a determination that could hardly be made on the basis of race alone.

Respondent contends that even if the races specified in the statute are not by nature inferior to the Caucasian race, the statute can be justified as a means of diminishing race tension and preventing the birth of children who might become social problems.

It is true that in some communities the marriage of persons of different races may result in tension. Similarly, race tension may result from the enforcement of the constitutional requirement that persons must not be excluded from juries solely on the ground of color, or segregated by law to certain districts within a city. In *Buchanan v. Warley*, the Supreme Court of the United States declared unconstitutional a statute forbidding a 'white person' to move into a block where the greater number of residences were occupied by 'colored persons' and forbidding a 'colored person' to move into a block where the greater number of residences were occupied by 'white persons.' The contention was made that the 'proposed segregation will promote the public peace by preventing race conflicts.' The court stated in its opinion that desirable 'as this is, and important as is the preservation of the public peace, this aim cannot be accomplished by laws or ordinances which deny rights created or protected by the federal Constitution.'

The effect of race prejudice upon any community is unquestionably detrimental both to the minority that is singled out for discrimination and to the dominant group that would perpetuate the prejudice. It is no answer to say that race tension can be eradicated through the perpetuation by law of the prejudices that give rise to the tension. Nor can any reliance be placed on the decisions of the United States Supreme Court upholding laws requiring segregation of races in facilities supplied by local common carriers and schools, for that court has made it clear that in those instances the state must secure equal facilities for all persons regardless of race in order that no substantive right be impaired. In the present case, however, there is no redress for the serious restriction of the right of Negroes, Mulattoes, Mongolians, and Malays to marry; certainly there is none in the corresponding restriction of the right of Caucasians to marry. A member of any of these races may find himself barred by law from marrying the person of his choice and that person to him may be irreplaceable. Human beings are bereft of worth and dignity by a doctrine that would make them as interchangeable as trains.

* * *

The rationalization that race discrimination diminishes the contacts and therefore the tensions between races would perpetuate the deprivation of rights of racial minorities. It would justify an abridgment of their privilege of holding office, of jury service, of entering the professions. The courts have made it clear that these privileges are not the prerogatives of any race.

* * *

Respondent maintains that Negroes are socially inferior and have so been judicially recognized, and that the progeny of a marriage between a Negro and a Caucasian suffer not only the stigma of such inferiority but the fear of rejection by members of both races. If they do, the fault lies not with their parents, but with the prejudices in the community and the laws that perpetuate those prejudices by giving legal force to the belief that certain races are inferior. If miscegenous marriages can be prohibited because of tensions suffered by the progeny, mixed religious unions could be prohibited on the same ground.

There are now so many persons in the United States of mixed ancestry, that the tensions upon them are already diminishing and are bound to diminish even more in time. Already many of the progeny of mixed marriages have made important contributions to the community. In any event the contention that the miscegenation laws prohibit inter-racial marriage because of its adverse effects on the progeny is belied by the extreme racial intermixture that it tolerates.

Careful examination of the arguments in support of the legislation in question reveals that 'there is absent the compelling justification which would be needed to sustain discrimination of that nature.' Certainly the fact alone that the discrimination has been sanctioned by the state for many years does not supply such justification.

III.

Even if a state could restrict the right to marry upon the basis of race alone, sections 60 and 69 of the Civil Code are nevertheless invalid because they are too vague and uncertain to constitute a valid regulation. A certain precision is essential in a statute regulating a fundamental right. 'It is the duty of the lawmaking body in framing laws to express its intent in clear and plain language to the end that the people upon whom it is designed to operate may be able to understand the legislative will.' In re Alpine, 203 Cal. 731, 736, 737, 265 P. 947, 949, 58 A.L.R. 1500; cases collected 50 Am.Jur. 484., 'it is a fundamental rule of law that no citizen should be deprived of his liberty for the violation of a law which is uncertain and ambiguous.'

* * *

Section 60 of the Civil Code declares void all marriages of white persons with Negroes, Mongolians, members of the Malay race or Mulattoes. In this section, the Legislature has adopted one of the many systems classifying persons on the basis of race. Racial classifications that have been made in the past vary as to the number of divisions and the features regarded as distinguishing the members of each division. The number of races distinguished by systems of classification 'varies from three or four to thirty four.' The Legislature's classification in section 60 is based on the system suggested by Blumenbach early in the nineteenth century. Blumenbach classified man into five races: Caucasian (white), Mongolian (yellow), Ethiopian (black), American Indian (red), and Malayan (brown). Even if that hard and fast classification be applied to persons all of whose ancestors belonged to one of these racial divisions, the Legislature has made no provision for applying the statute to persons of mixed ancestry. The fact is overwhelming that there has been a steady increase in the number of people in this country who belong to more than one race, and a growing number who have succeeded in identifying themselves with the Caucasian race even though they are not exclusively Caucasian. Some of these persons have migrated to this state; some are born here illegitimately; others are the progeny of miscegenous marriages valid where contracted and therefore valid in California. The apparent purpose of the statute is to discourage the birth of children of mixed ancestry within this state. Such a purpose, however, cannot be accomplished without taking into consideration marriages of persons of mixed ancestry. A statute regulating fundamental rights is clearly unconstitutional if it cannot be reasonably applied to accomplish its purpose. This court therefore cannot determine the constitutionality of the statute in question on the assumption that its provisions might, with sufficient definiteness, be applied to persons not of mixed ancestry.

The only reference made in the statute to persons of mixed ancestry is the prohibition of marriages between a 'white person' and a 'mulatto.' Even the term 'mulatto' is not defined. The lack of a definition of that term leads to a special problem of how the statute is to be applied to a person, some but not all of whose ancestors are Negroes. The only case in this state attempting to define the term 'mulatto' in section 60 of the Civil Code leaves undecided whether a person with less than one-eight Negro blood is a 'mulatto' within the meaning of the statute. Even more uncertainty surrounds the meaning of the terms 'white persons,' 'Mongolians,' and 'members of the Malay race.'

* * *

To determine that a person is a Mongolian or Malayan within the meaning of the statute because of any trace of such ancestry, however slight, would be absurd. If the classification of a person of mixed ancestry depends upon a given proportion of Mongolians or Malayans among his ancestors, how can this court, without clearly invading the province of the Legislature, determine what the decisive proportion is? Nor can this court assume that a predominance in number of ancestors of one race makes a person a Caucasian, Mongolian, or Malayan within the meaning of the statute, for absurd results would follow from such an assumption. Thus, a person with three-sixteenths Malay ancestry might have many so-called Malay characteristics and yet be considered a white person in terms of his preponderantly white ancestry. Such a person might easily find himself in a dilemma, for if he were regarded as a white person under section 60, he would be forbidden to marry a Malay, and yet his Malay characteristics might effectively preclude his marriage to another white person. Similarly, a person having three-eighths Mongolian ancestry might legally be classed as a white person even though he possessed Mongolian characteristics. He might have little opportunity or inclination to marry any one other than a Mongolian, yet section 60 might forbid such a marriage. Moreover, if a person were of four-eighths Mongolian or Malayan ancestry and four-eighths white ancestry, a test based on predominance in number of ancestors could not be applied.

Section 69 of the Civil Code and section 60 on which it is based are therefore too vague and uncertain to be upheld as a valid regulation of the right to marry. Enforcement of the statute would place upon the officials charged with its administration and upon the courts charged with reviewing the legality of such administration the task of determining the meaning of the statute. That task could be carried out with respect to persons of mixed ancestry only on the basis of conceptions of race classification not supplied by the Legislature. 'If no judicial certainty can be settled upon as to the meaning of a statute, the courts are not at liberty to supply one.'

In summary, we hold that sections 60 and 69 are not only too vague and uncertain to be enforceable regulations of a fundamental right, but that they violate the equal protection of the laws clause of the United States Constitution by impairing the right of individuals to marry on the basis of race alone and by arbitrarily and unreasonably discriminating against certain racial groups.

Let the peremptory writ issue as prayed. Gibson, C. J., and Carter, J., concur.

Justice Shenk, dissenting

I dissent.

The power of a state to regulate and control the basic social relationship of marriage of its domiciliaries is here challenged and set at naught by a majority order of this court arrived at not by a concurrence of reasons but by the end result of four votes supported by divergent concepts not supported by authority and in fact contrary to the decisions in this state and elsewhere.

It will be shown that such laws have been in effect in this country since before our national independence and in this state since our first legislative session. They have never been declared unconstitutional by any court in the land although frequently they have been under attack. It is difficult to see why such laws, valid when enacted and constitutionally enforceable in this state for nearly one hundred years and elsewhere for a much longer period of time, are now unconstitutional under the same constitution and with no change in the factual situation. It will also be shown that they have a valid legislative purpose even though they may not conform to the sociogenetic views of some people. When that legislative purpose appears it is entirely beyond judicial power, properly exercised, to nullify them.

This proceeding, therefore, involves a most important state function long since recognized as such. Indeed as late as June 7, 1948, it has been recognized by the Supreme Court of the United States 'that the regulation of the incidents of the marital relation involves the exercise by the States of powers of the most vital importance.' Because of the far-reaching effect of an order of this court in connection with this basic social relationship the subject is worthy of somewhat extended discussion in support of our statutes.

* * *

Courts are neither peculiarly qualified nor organized to determine the underlying questions of fact with reference to which the validity of the legislation must be determined. Differing ideas of public policy do not properly concern them. The courts have no power to determine the merits of conflicting theories, to conduct an investigation of facts bearing upon questions of public policy or expediency, or to sustain or frustrate the legislation according to whether they happen to approve or disapprove the legislative determination of such questions of fact. The fact that the finding of the Legislature is in favor of the truth of one side of a matter as to which there is still room for difference of opinion is not material.

What the people's legislative representatives believe to be for the public good must be accepted as tending to promote the public welfare. It has been said that any other basis would conflict with the spirit of the Constitution and would sanction measures opposed to a republican form of government.

Text and authorities which constitute the factual basis for the legislative finding involved in the statute here in question indicate only that there is a difference of opinion as to the wisdom of the policy underlying the enactments.

Some of the factual considerations which the legislature could have taken into consideration are disclosed by an examination of the sources of information on the biological and sociological phases of the problem and which may be said to form a background for the legislation and support the reasoning found in the decisions of the courts upholding similar statutes. A reference to a few of those sources of information will suffice.

On the biological phase there is authority for the conclusion that the crossing of the primary races leads gradually to retrogression and to eventual extinction of the resultant type unless it is fortified by reunion with the parent stock. In September, 1927, in an article entitled, "Race Mixture," which appeared in *Science*, Vol. 66, page X. Dr. Charles B. Davenport of the Carnegie Foundation of Washington, Department of Experimental Evolution, said: 'In the absence of any uniform rule as to consequences of race crosses, it is well to discourage it except in those cases where, as in the Hawaiian-Chinese crosses, it clearly produces superior progeny,' and that the Negro-white and Filipino-European crosses do not seem to fall within the exception.

In Volume 19 of the Encyclopedia Americana (1924), page 275, it is said: 'The results of racial intermarriage have been exceedingly variable. Sometimes it has produced a better race. This is the case when the crossing has been between different but closely allied stocks. Prof U. G. Weatherly writes: 'It is an unquestionable fact that the yellow, as well as the negroid peoples possess many desirable qualities in which the whites are deficient. From this it has been argued that it would be advantageous if all races were blended into a universal type embodying the excellencies of each.

But scientific breeders have long ago demonstrated that the most desirable results are secured by specializing types rather than by merging them.

"The color line is evidence of an attempt, based on instinctive choice, to preserve those distinctive values which a racial group has come to regard as of the highest moment to itself."

* * *

W. E. Castle, Bussey Institution, Harvard University, in an article entitled "Biological and Social Consequences of Race Crossing" printed in Volume 9, *American Journal of Physical Anthropology* (April, 1926), states on page 152: 'If all inheritance of human traits were simple Mendelian inheritance, and natural selections were unlimited in its action among human populations, then unrestricted racial intercrossing might be recommended. But in the light of our present knowledge, few would recommend it. For, in the first place, much that is best in human existence is a matter of social inheritance, not of biological inheritance. Race crossings disturb social inheritance. That is one of its worst features.' This then leads to a consideration of the sociological phase.

The writings of Father John LaFarge, S.J., are typical of many who have considered the subject of race-crosses from a sociological standpoint. Reference has been made to his work "The Race Question and the Negro" (1943). Under the heading "The Moral Aspect," he writes: '[T]here are grave reasons against any general practice of intermarriage between the members of different racial groups. These reasons, where clearly verified, amount to a moral prohibition of such a practice.

'These arise from the great difference of condition which is usually experienced by the members of the respective groups. It is not merely a difference of poverty or riches, of lesser or greater political power, but the fact that identification with the given group is far-reaching and affects innumerable aspects of ordinary daily life. * * *

'Where marriage is contracted by entire solitaries, such an interracial tension is more easily borne, but few persons matrimonially inclined are solitaries. They bring with them into the orbit of married life their parents and brothers and sisters and uncles and aunts and the entire social circle in which they revolve. All of these are affected by the social tension, which in turn reacts upon the peace and unity of the marriage bond.

'When children enter the scene the difficulty is further complicated unless a complete and entirely self-sacrificing understanding has been reached beforehand. And even then the social effects may be beyond their control. * * *

'In point of facts as the Negro group becomes culturally advanced, there appears no corresponding tendency, to seek intermarriage with other races.'

The foregoing excerpts from scientific articles and legal authorities make it clear that there is not only some but a great deal of evidence to support the legislative determination (last made by our Legislature in 1933) that intermarriage between Negroes and white persons is incompatible with the general welfare and therefore a proper subject for regulation under the police power. There may be some who maintain that there does not exist adequate data on a sufficiently large to enable a decision to be made as to the effects of the original admixture of white and Negro blood. However, legislators are not required to wait upon the completion of scientific research to determine whether the underlying facts carry sufficient weight to more fully sustain the regulation. * * *

Ralph McGill

The Story of Dr. Ralph Bunche (1954)

When American president Franklin Roosevelt, British prime minister Winston Churchill, and Soviet premier Joseph Stalin met at Yalta in February 1945 to negotiate the future of post–World War II Europe, they agreed to the creation of the United Nations (UN), an international peacekeeping organization. The UN would welcome all nations as members, though the charter reserved exceptional powers for the Security Council, whose permanent members would be made up of representatives from the Allied Powers. In 1948, the General Assembly of the UN adopted the Universal Declaration of Human Rights, which included a provision asserting that racial discrimination was a violation of the declaration. The United States' participation in World War II had ushered it into a new era of international prominence, cooperation, and international surveillance. The lethal racism of Japan and, especially, Germany had cast racial iniquities in the United States in high relief and made some southerners uneasy about the realities and the future of the Jim Crow South. Ralph McGill, the editor and publisher of the Atlanta Constitution, *cautiously mounted a modest critique of Jim Crow through consideration of the accomplishments of Ralph Bunche, a black political scientist and outstanding diplomat who negotiated the 1949 armistice between Israel and the Arab states and who in 1950 became the first African American to win the Nobel Peace Prize.*

In September, 1948, Count Folke Bernadotte, Swedish nobleman, was murdered in Jerusalem by gangsters who thought they might thereby precipitate the United Nations' occupancy of Palestine.

The job being done by the Swedish nobleman was transferred to an American Negro, grandson of a Texas slave. This man, Dr. Ralph Johnson Bunche, took over the task of negotiating peace, not merely in the Holy Land, but also in the Middle, or Near, East.

No diplomatic enterprise since the end of the war has been so successful. The results of it pushed Dr. Bunche into an international spotlight. The following years have failed to reveal any flaw in the man.

The story of Dr. Bunche begins with his birth in Detroit in 1904. When the boy was ten years old, his father, a barber, took the family to Albuquerque, New Mexico. His mother died there. The family then moved to Los Angeles in 1917 and put down roots which have kept it there ever since. The grandmother, "Nana," was a strong influence in the lives of the boy and his sisters, as one may see and feel from hearing his story of those days.

From the time he was about fourteen years of age, this young boy was pretty much on his own. He worked as a messenger boy in the Los Angeles *Times* office and later in its press room, handling metal. He worked in a dye works and as a waiter on a coastal vessel.

The record runs on to show he was given an athletic scholarship at the University of California, where he played on three championship basketball teams and won letters in three years of college baseball.

He did jobs such as early-morning cleaning and mopping of stores to make additional money. These were followed by work in the library. He graduated in 1927 and on a scholarship proceeded to Harvard to take a master's degree. A Rosenwald fellowship enabled him to study and travel in Europe, and to earn a Doctor of Philosophy degree at Harvard. Employed by a social-science research council he studied colonial problems in East Africa, Malaya, and the Dutch East Indies. He had a year in economics at the University of London. After this he taught political science at Swarthmorc and Howard Colleges.

Aided by a grant from the Carnegie Foundation he studied the problems of his own race in America. He married a teacher, and they have a son and two daughters.

This, in brief, is a history of the man who became, within the span of a year, one of the best known and most widely respected Americans in Europe and the Near East. He is one of our top diplomats, one of our most valuable citizens.

In May, 1949, he accepted the award of the American Association for the United Nations, and in discussing the problem of the Negro in this country, he said:

> In this regard, as an American and a Negro, I cannot avoid reminding my fellow Americans that all of us who have a sense of justice and fair play must contribute to the solution of a problem on our doorstep which is perhaps more baffling than the Palestine problem, if our own great country is to be enabled fully to live up to the principles of the Charter to which all of the United Nations are solemnly pledged.

No observer or student of the problem can fail to be grateful for the achievements of the man and for his statement that the problem in America is "more baffling than the Palestine problem."

It is. The fact that there have been so many who attempted to present it as a problem confounded only by the ill will of the South, or problem which could be solved overnight if only it were not for "Southern bigots" and "reactionaries," has, of course, added to its complexity. The bigots, the reactionaries, the processes in Georgia and other states, our density of population, our lack of jobs, our general poverty, our ancient prejudices—all these have served, singly or in combination, to obscure the real problem and to make it difficult to approach. They have persisted as continual skirmishes, avoiding the real campaign.

Slowly, but nevertheless surely, the population has shifted. The Negro has become a political power in many northern states and is becoming so in some of those in the South. The Negro has flocked to industrial cities, to employ a southern phrase, like martins to their gourds. The problem was always a national one. Now few dispute or fail to recognize this fact.

Today more and more Southerners are seeing not merely that the Negro has been too often deprived of some fundamental rights and denied political and economic opportunity, but that such a policy has been morally wrong and economically costly.

We see that what the policy has done is to deprive us of the best intelligence and contributions the Negro has had to offer, while leaving us with a large part of the worst.

Certainly all of us who have a sense of justice and fair play must contribute to the solution of it. For many—too many, indeed—the first contribution must be an awareness of it. And an admission of it. This means seeing it not in terms of farm or industrial labor, but also in terms of what an intelligence and an ability such as those exhibited by Dr. Bunche could contribute if allowed to develop and to be employed where they are most needed. Segregation no longer fits today's world.

In *The Fleas Come with the Dog* (New York, 1954), 118–20.

Zora Neale Hurston

Letter Deploring the *Brown* Decision (August 11, 1955)

Folklorist and author Zora Neale Hurston was born in Alabama in 1891 and raised in Eatonville, Florida, one of the first all-black towns established after the Civil War. As a student at Barnard College in the mid-1920s, Hurston studied with anthropologists Franz Boas and Ruth Benedict, who inspired her to collect African American stories and other folklore. During the 1930s, Hurston worked with the Federal Writers' Project in the South. Best known for her 1937 novel Their Eyes Were Watching God, *Hurston has been credited with having captured the voice and interior life of rural blacks, a group ignored by more urbane African American writers. A supporter of Marcus Garvey and his all-black United Negro Improvement Association (UNIA), the largest pre–World War II African American organization, Hurston eschewed the leftist politics that characterized many of her fellow authors of the Harlem Renaissance. A firm Cold War anti-Communist and staunch believer in race pride, Hurston denounced the* Brown *decision as insulting to African Americans and, like many white critics of the Supreme Court's decision, as Communist-inspired and likely to result in more intimate forms of association than those formed on the playground. The following comments appear in a letter she wrote to the Orlando (Florida)* Sentinel.

I PROMISED GOD and some other responsible characters, including a bench of bishops, that I was not going to part my lips concerning the United States Supreme Court decision on ending segregation in the public schools of the South. But since a lot of time has passed and no one seems to touch on what to me appears to be the most important point in the hassle, I break my silence just this once. Consider me as just thinking out loud.

The whole matter revolves around the self-respect of my people. How much satisfaction can I get from a court order for somebody to associate with me who does not wish me near them? The American Indian has never been spoken of as a minority and chiefly because there is no whine in the Indian. Certainly he fought, and valiantly for his lands, and rightfully so, but it is inconceivable of an Indian to seek forcible association with anyone. His well-known pride and self-respect would save him from that. I take the Indian position.

NOW A GREAT CLAMOR will arise in certain quarters that I seek to deny the Negro children of the South their rights, and therefore I am one of those "handkerchief-head niggers" who bow low before the white man and sell out my own people out of cowardice. However, an analytical glance will show that that is not the case.

If there are not adequate Negro schools in Florida, and there is some residual, some inherent and unchangeable quality in white schools, impossible to duplicate anywhere else, then I am the first to insist that Negro children of Florida be allowed to share this boon.

But if there are adequate Negro schools and prepared instructors and instructions, then there is nothing different except the presence of white people.

For this reason, I regard the ruling of the United States Supreme Court as insulting rather than honoring my race. Since the days of the never-to-be-sufficiently-deplored Reconstruction, there has been current the belief that there is no greater delight to Negroes than physical association with whites. The doctrine of the white mare. Those familiar with the habits of mules are aware that any mule, if not restrained, will automatically follow a white mare. Dishonest mule-traders made money out of this knowledge in the old days.

* * *

Lead a white mare along a country road and slyly open the gate and the mules in the lot would run out and follow this mare. This ruling being conceived and brought forth in a sly political medium with eyes on '56, and brought forth in the same spirit and for the same purpose, it is clear that they have taken the old notion to heart and acted upon it. It is a cunning opening of the barnyard gate with the white mare ambling past. We are expected to hasten pell-mell after her.

It is most astonishing that this should be tried just when the nation is exerting itself to shake off the evils of Communist penetration. It is to be recalled that Moscow, being made aware of this folk belief, made it the main plank in their campaign to win the American Negro from the 1920's on. It was the come-on stuff. Join the party and get yourself a white wife or husband. To supply the expected demand, the party had scraped up this-and-that off of park benches and skid rows and held them in stock for us. The highest types of Negroes were held to be just panting to get hold of one of these objects. Seeing how flat that program fell, it is astonishing that it would be so soon revived. Politics does indeed make strange bedfellows.

* * *

But the South had better beware in another direction. While it is being frantic over the segregation ruling, it had better keep its eyes open for more important things. One instance of government by fiat has been rammed down its throat. It is possible that the end of segregation is not here and never meant to be here at present, but the attention of the South directed on what was calculated to keep us busy while more ominous things were brought to pass. The stubborn South and the Midwest kept this nation from being dragged farther to the left than it was during the New Deal.

But what if it is contemplated to do away with the two-party system and arrive at government by administrative decree? No questions allowed and no information given out from the administrative department? We could get more rulings on the same subject and more far-reaching any day. It pays to weigh every saying and action, however trivial, as indicating a trend.

In the ruling on segregation, the unsuspecting nation might have witnessed a trial balloon. A relatively safe one, since it is sectional and on a matter not likely to arouse other sections of the nation to the support of the South. If it goes off fairly well, a precedent has been established. Government by fiat can replace the Constitution. You don't have to credit me with too much intelligence and penetration, just so you watch carefully and think.

* * *

Meanwhile, personally, I am not delighted. I am not persuaded and elevated by the white mare technique. Negro schools in the State are in very good shape and on the improve. We are fortunate in having Dr. D. E. Williams as head and driving force of Negro instruction. Dr. Williams is relentless in his drive to improve both physical equipment and teacher quality. He has accomplished wonders in the 20 years past and it is to be expected that he will double that in the future.

It is well known that I have no sympathy nor respect for the "tragedy of color" school of thought among us, whose fountainhead is the pressure group concerned in this court ruling. I can see no tragedy in being too dark to be invited to a white school social affair. The Supreme Court would have pleased me more if they had concerned themselves about enforcing the compulsory education provisions for Negroes in the South as is done for white children. The next 10 years would be better spent in appointing truant officers and looking after conditions in the homes from which the children come. Use to the limit what we already have.

Them's my sentiments and I am sticking by them. Growth from within. Ethical and cultural desegregation. It is a contradiction in terms to scream race pride and equality while at the same time spurning Negro teachers and self-association. That old white mare business can go racking on down the road for all I care.

Orlando *Sentinel*, August 11, 1955. Reprinted in the *Richmond Times-Dispatch*, August 22, 1955.

Grass Roots League

Flyer Reprint of 1928 Negro Program of Communist Party (March 25, 1956)

The Communist Party USA (CPUSA) played a defining role in the development of the industrial labor movement in the first half of the twentieth century. During the Depression, African Americans were drawn to the Communists by their support of black rights and their willingness to engage issues of racial discrimination and oppression in the workplace. The Party courted black farmers and workers throughout the 1930s; Communist influence in the Congress of Industrial Organizations (CIO) was behind the CIO's opposition to racial discrimination. The willingness of the International Labor Defense (ILD), the legal arm of the Communist Party, to take on the defense of the Scottsboro Boys earned the Party the gratitude if not necessarily the political allegiance of many American blacks. In the 1950s, at the height of McCarthyism, opponents of integration, such as the Grass Roots League, circulated the CPUSA's 1928 party platform reproduced in flyers in an effort to equate support of civil rights with Communism.

Here's Proof of the Red Pro-Negro Plot Against South & USA

Started 1920:

". . . the Communist negro drive was started in the United States in 1920. (According to James W. Ford, negro Communist Party leader, as stated in the House Un-American Activity Committee report of July 21, 1947).

NAACP Penetrated by Reds:

In 1925 "the official report of the Communist Party's 4th national convention stated that the Party had penetrated the NAACP." (The Red Network)

1928 Negro Program of Communist Party

XII. Oppression of the Negroes

American white imperialism oppresses in the most terrific way the ten million Negroes who constitute not less than one-tenth of the total population. White capitalist prejudice considers the Negroes a "lower race," the born servants of the lofty white masters. The *racial caste system* is a fundamental feature of the social, industrial and political organization of this country. The Communist Party declares that it considers itself not only the party of the working class generally but also the champion of the Negroes as an oppressed race, and especially the organizer of the Negro working-class elements. *The Communist Party is the party of the liberation of the Negro race from all white oppression.*

There is a "new Negro" in process of development. The social composition of the Negro race is changing. Formerly the Negro was the cotton farmer in the South and domestic help in the North. The industrialization of the South, the concentration of a new Negro working-class population in the big cities of the East and North, and the entrance of the Negroes into the basic industries on a mass scale have changed the whole social composition of the Negro race. *The appearance of a genuine Negro industrial proletariat creates an organizing force for the whole Negro race*, furnishes a new working-class leadership to all Negro race movements, and strengthens immensely the fighting possibilities for the emancipation of the race.

Demands

1. Abolition of the whole system of race discrimination. Full racial, political, and social equality for the Negro race.

2. Abolition of all laws which result in segregation of Negroes. Abolition of all Jim Crow laws. The law shall forbid all discrimination against Negroes in selling or renting houses.

3. Abolition of all laws which disfranchise the Negroes.

4. Abolition of laws forbidding intermarriage of persons of different races.

5. Abolition of all laws and public administration measures which prohibit, or in practice prevent, Negro children or youth from attending general public schools or universities.

6. Full and equal admittance of Negroes to all railway station waiting rooms, restaurants, hotels, and theatres.

7. Federal law against lynching and the protection of the Negro masses in their right of self-defense.

8. Abolition of discriminatory practices in courts against Negroes. No discrimination in jury service.

9. Abolition of the convict lease system and of the chain gang.

10. Abolition of all Jim Crow distinctions in the army, navy, and civil service.

11. Immediate removal of all restrictions in all trade unions against the membership of Negro workers.

12. Equal opportunity for employment, wages, hours, and working conditions for Negro and white workers. Equal pay for equal work for Negro and white workers.

Grass Roots League, reprint of 1928 Negro Program of Communist Party, Plank XII, "Oppression of the Negroes" in flyer, "Here's Proof of the Red Pro-Negro Plot against South & USA," March 25, 1956. From E. A. Holt Papers, #3551, f. 12, Southern Historical Collection, University of North Carolina, Chapel Hill.

Herbert Ravenel Sass

Mixed Schools and Mixed Blood (1956)

A white southern gentleman of the old school, Herbert Ravenel Sass was born in turn-of-the-century Charleston and published widely in every conceivable literary genre. His works included novels and stories as well as his thoughts on South Carolina history, local flora and fauna, and questions of broader concern

to his region and his nation. In this article, Sass puts forward a common argu-
ment against school desegregation: that integrated schools would, inevitably, lead
to interracial marriage, which would in turn lead to inferior mixed-race children
unable to defend America from her enemies. This argument was ridiculed by
supporters of Brown v. *Board of Education, who pointed out that the races*
mixed freely during slave times and that the Nazi experience had discredited
master-race theories. But concerns about hybridization and white racial purity
resonated with large numbers of Americans, and fear of interracial marriage un-
derlay a significant portion of white southern resistance to school desegregation.

1

What may well be the most important physical fact in the story of
the United States is one which is seldom emphasized in our history
books. It is the fact that throughout the three and a half centuries
of our existence we have kept our several races biologically distinct
and separate. Though we have encouraged the mixing of many different strains in what has been called the American "melting pot,"
we have confined this mixing to the white peoples of European ancestry, excluding from our "melting pot" all other races. The result
is that the United States today is overwhelmingly a pure white nation, with a smaller but considerable Negro population in which
there is some white blood, and a much smaller American Indian
population.

* * *

These facts are well known. But now there lurks in ambush, as it
were, another fact: we have suddenly begun to move toward abandonment of our 350-year-old system of keeping our races pure and
are preparing to adopt instead a method of racial amalgamation
similar to that which has created the mixed-blood nations of this
hemisphere; except that the amalgamation being prepared for this
country is not Indian and white but Negro and white. It is the deep
conviction of nearly all white Southerners in the states which have
large Negro populations that the mingling or integration of white
and Negro children in the South's primary schools would open the
gates to miscegenation and widespread racial amalgamation.

This belief is at the heart of our race problem, and until it is realized that this is the South's basic and compelling motive, there can be no understanding of the South's attitude.

* * *

2

The South has had a bad time with words. Nearly a century ago the word slavery, even more than the thing itself, did the South irreparable damage. In a strange but real way the misused word democracy has injured the South; its most distinctive—and surely its greatest—period has been called undemocratic, meaning illiberal and reactionary, because it resisted the onward sweep of a centralizing governmental trend alien to our federal republic and destructive of the very "cornerstone of liberty," local self-government. Today the word segregation and, perhaps even more harmful, the word prejudice blacken the South's character before the world and make doubly difficult our effort to preserve not merely our own way of life but certain basic principles upon which our country was founded.

Words are of such transcendent importance today that the South should long ago have protested against these two. They are now too firmly imbedded in the dialectic of our race problem to be got rid of. But that very fact renders all the more necessary a careful scrutiny of them. Let us first consider the word segregation.

Segregation is sometimes carelessly listed as a synonym of separation, but it is not a true synonym and the difference between the two words is important.

Segregation, from the Latin *segregatus* (set apart from the flock), implies isolation; separation carries no such implication. Segregation is what we have done to the American Indian—whose grievous wrongs few reformers and still fewer politicians ever bother their heads about. By use of force and against his will we have segregated him, isolated him, on certain small reservations which had and still have somewhat the character of concentration camps.

The South has not done that to the Negro. On the contrary, it has shared its countryside and its cities with him in amity and understanding, not perfect by any means, and careful of established folk custom, but far exceeding in human friendliness anything of the kind to be found in the North. Not segregation of the Negro race as the Indian is segregated on his reservations—and as the Negro is segregated in the urban Harlems of the North—but simply *separation* of the white and Negro races in certain phases of activity is what the South has always had and feels that it must somehow preserve even though the time-honored, successful, and completely moral "separate but equal" principle no longer has legal sanction.

Until the Supreme Court decision forbidding compulsory racial separation in the public schools, the South was moving steadily toward abandonment or relaxation of the compulsory separation rule in several important fields. This is no longer true. Progress in racial relations has been stopped short by the ill-advised insistence of the Northern-directed Negro leadership upon the one concession which above all the white South will not and cannot make—public school integration.

Another word which is doing grave damage to the South today is prejudice, meaning race prejudice—a causeless hostility often amounting to hatred which white Southerners are alleged to feel in regard to the Negro. Here again the South, forgetful of the lessons of its past, has failed to challenge effectively an inaccurate and injurious word. Not prejudice but preference is the word that truth requires.

Between prejudice and preference there is vast difference. Prejudice is a preconceived unfavorable judgment or feeling without sound basis. Preference is a natural reaction to facts and conditions observed or experienced, and through the action of heredity generation after generation it becomes instinctive. Like separateness, it exists throughout the animal kingdom. Though the difference between two races of an animal species may be so slight that only a specialist can differentiate between them, the individuals of one race prefer as a rule to associate with other individuals of that race.

* * *

Hence it is nonsense to say that racial discrimination, the necessary consequence of race preference, is "un-American." Actually it is perhaps the most distinctively American thing there is, the reason why the American people—meaning the people of the United

States—are what they are. Today when racial discrimination of any kind or degree is instantly denounced as both sinful and stupid, few stop to reflect that this nation is built solidly upon it.

The truth is, of course, that there are many different kinds and degrees of racial discrimination. Some of them are bad—outdated relics of an earlier time when conditions were unlike those of today, and these should be, and were being, abolished until the unprecedented decree of the Supreme Court in the school cases halted all progress. But not all kinds of racial discrimination are evil—unless we are prepared to affirm that our forefathers blundered in "keeping the breed pure."

* * *

[A] fantastic perversion of scientific authority has been publicized in support of the new crusade. Though everywhere else in Nature (as well as in all our plant breeding and animal breeding) race and heredity are recognized as of primary importance, we are told that in the human species race is of no importance and racial differences are due not to heredity but to environment. Science has proved, so we are told, that all races are equal and, in essentials, identical.

Science has most certainly not proved that all races are equal, much less identical; and, as the courageous geneticist, Dr. W. C. George of the University of North Carolina, has recently pointed out, there is overwhelming likelihood that the biological consequences of white and Negro integration in the South would be harmful. It would not be long before these biological consequences became visible. But there is good hope that we shall never see them, because any attempt to force a program of racial integration upon the South would be met with stubborn, determined, and universal opposition, probably taking the form of passive resistance of a hundred kinds. Though secession is not conceivable, persistence in an attempt to compel the South to mingle its white and Negro children in its public schools would split the United States in two as disastrously as in the sixties and perhaps with an even more lamentable aftermath of bitterness.

For the elementary public school is the most critical of those areas of activity where the South must and will at all costs maintain separateness of the races. The South must do this because, although it is nearly universal instinct, race preference is not active in the very young. Race preference (which the propagandists miscall race prejudice or hate) is one of those instincts which develop gradually as the mind develops and which, if taken in hand early enough, can be prevented from developing at all.

Hence if the small children of the two races in approximately equal numbers—as would be the case in a great many of the South's schools—were brought together intimately and constantly and grew up in close association in integrated schools under teachers necessarily committed to the gospel of racial integration, there would be many in whom race preference would not develop. This would not be, as superficial thinkers might suppose, a good thing, the happy solution of the race problem in America. It might be a solution of a sort, but not one that the American people would desire. It would inevitably result, beginning with the least desirable elements of both races, in a great increase of racial amalgamation, the very process which throughout our history we have most sternly rejected. For although to most persons today the idea of mixed mating is disagreeable or even repugnant, this would not be true of the new generations brought up in mixed schools with the desirability of racial integration as a basic premise. Among those new generations mixed matings would become commonplace, and a greatly enlarged mixed-blood population would result.

* * *

There are other cogent reasons for the white South's stand: the urgent necessity of restoring the Constitution and our federal form of government before they are permanently destroyed by the Court's usurpation of power; the equally urgent necessity of reestablishing law and precedent instead of sociological and psychological theory as the basis of the Court's decisions; the terrible damage which racial integration would do to the South's whole educational system, black as well as white. These and other aspects have been fully and effectively explored and need not be touched upon here.

But the underlying and compelling reason for the South's refusal to operate mixed schools—its belief that mixed schools will result in ultimate racial amalgamation—has been held virtually taboo and if mentioned in the North is not examined at all but is summarily dismissed as not worthy of consideration. The amalgamation "bogey," it is said, is not really believed by intelligent Southerners but is a smoke screen used to hide the South's real motives, which are variously described, ranging from plain sadism to a shrewd determination to deprive the Negro of education so that he can never displace the Southern white man. Besides, it is confidently alleged, the Negro does not wish to destroy the identity of his race by merging it with the white race.

Both those statements are incorrect. As already pointed out, the fear that mixed schools in the South would open the way to racial amalgamation is not a bogey or a smoke screen or a pretense of any kind but the basic animating motive of the white South in resisting the drive of the N.A.A.C.P. and its supporters. The second statement is as erroneous as the first. The Negro leaders do want racial amalgamation; they not only want the right to amalgamate through legal intermarriage but they want that right to be exercised widely and frequently.

It is only natural and human that they should feel this way. The truth is that these ambitious, intelligent, often amalgamated, and often genuinely dedicated Negro men and women feel about this matter exactly as white men and women would feel if they were similarly constituted and circumstanced—fusion of the two races would solve the Negro's problem at once. How much of the Negro rank and file consciously seeks amalgamation is a question; to the Southern Negro in particular the thought of intermarriage is still new and strange. As for the Northern leaders of the movement, some of them make no bones about it, and when they do evade the question they do so only for reasons of strategy.

But actually it does not matter much whether or not intermarriage is the admitted aim of the N.A.A.C.P. strategists. To suppose that, proclaiming the virtual identity of the races, we can promote all other degrees of race mixing but stop short of interracial mating is—if I may use an overworked but vivid simile—like going over Niagara Falls in a barrel in the expectation of stopping three fourths of the way down. The South is now the great bulwark against intermarriage. A very few years of thoroughly integrated schools would produce large numbers of indoctrinated young Southerners free from all "prejudice" against mixed matings.

It is because there the adolescent and "unprejudiced" mind can be reached that the integrationists have chosen the Southern schools as their primary target; and it is precisely because the adolescent and therefore defenseless mind would there be exposed to brain-washing which it would not know how to refute that the white South will not operate integrated public schools. If the South fails to defend its young children who are not yet capable of defending themselves, if it permits their wholesale impregnation by a propaganda persuasive and by them unanswerable, the salutary instinct of race preference which keeps the races separate, as in Nature, will be destroyed before it develops and the barriers against racial amalgamation will go down.

This is the new and ominous fact which, as was said at the beginning of this article, lurks in ambush, concealed like a viper in the school integration crusade. Success of that crusade would mean that after three and a half centuries of magnificent achievement under a system of racial separateness and purity, we would tacitly abandon that system and instead would begin the creation of a mixed American race by the fusion of the two races which, as H. G. Wells expressed it, are at opposite extremes of the human species.

Many well-meaning persons have suddenly discovered that the tenets of the Christian religion and the professions of our democratic faith compel us to accept the risks of this hybridization. No one who will face up to the biological facts and really think the problem through can believe any such thing or see the partial suicide of the white race in America (and of the Negro race also) as anything other than a crime against both religion and civilization.

Atlantic Monthly, November 1956. Reprinted as pamphlet by Georgia Commission on Education (no date).

The Reverend James F. Burks

Integration or Segregation (May 30, 1954)

Two weeks after the Brown v. Board of Education *decision was announced, the Reverend James F. Burks, pastor of Bayview Baptist Church in*

Norfolk, Virginia, preached on the topic, "Integration or Segregation." Setting aside theories of racial hierarchy, Burks pitted the Bible against the Supreme Court's interpretation of the Constitution. This sermon represents a conscious effort to distance opponents of desegregation such as Burks from the Klan and other far-right organizations springing up across the South. At the same time, through its appropriation of scriptural authority for racial segregation, the sermon offered divine backing to opponents of black civil rights. Burks's sermon was reproduced and distributed widely across the South.

Before entering upon the subject itself, there are certain general observations that should be made:

1. I would not speak upon such a far-reaching matter unless the spirit of God seemed to be leading.
2. The question of racial equality or racial superiority is absolutely NOT the subject under discussion.
3. Any individual who feels that one group of society is entitled to more privileges and more liberties than another disqualifies himself for the honor of American citizenship. There is nothing in God's economy that entitles one man to more rights than another.
4. The true issue before us is whether or not the three basic races of mankind should be intermixed and integrated.
5. The Constitution of the United States of America does not demand the integration of races, but merely guarantees equal rights and privileges to all American people. Granting equal facilities and equal appropriations for both Negro and White populations meets this requirement. In fact, it seems to be somewhat more unconstitutional to force a mixture of races than to permit—on a basis of equality—the segregation of these peoples.
6. The present trend seems to be an effort—consciously or unconsciously I cannot say—to legislate righteousness. This cannot be done successfully.
7. The issue of segregation or non-segregation has been turned into a major problem because of the tactics and brainwashings by liberal clergymen, the National Council of Churches, and an admixture of modern-day philosophy foreign to the Word of

God, that thrives on the abandonment of restraint and high moral standards.

8. If integration of races is based upon the contention that men are all "one in Christ," then the foundation is not secure. The idea of "Universal Fatherhood of God and Brotherhood of Man" is MAN'S concoction and contradicts the Word of God. Only those who know Jesus Christ as personal Saviour in the forgiveness of sins through His Precious Atoning Blood are Children of God and "one in Christ." Furthermore, those who are "one in Christ" are such through a spiritual union and certainly not physical. Therefore, if this "oneness in Christ" is the basis of integration, then it is to be applied ONLY to born-again believers. Realizing this, the spiritual "oneness" of believers in the Lord Jesus Christ actually and ethically has nothing to do with the problem before us.

9. The practice of segregation in NO sense violates the doctrine of equal rights and liberties of the races. Nor does it prohibit one race from coming to the aid and assistance of the other when a particular need arises. It is the practice of a sustained or perpetual integration that is being proposed, as well as being opposed.

10. We are interested—finally and absolutely—in what the Word of God teaches about the races of men, and not in the changeable, fallible ideas of modern man.

And so, to our subject. There is absolutely neither a feeling of animosity in my heart nor an attitude of inferiority as regards the colored race. They have made their contribution to the world, and unless the white race legislates and forces the practice of integration upon them—thereby robbing them of their distinctive—they will continue to make their contribution. But no one appreciates a tinted white or a faded black.

My first charge is that the amalgamation of races is part of the spirit of antichrist. The Lord God has Providentially divided the races of men, and, according to Deuteronomy 32:8, "the Most High divided to the nations their inheritance, when he separated the sons of Adam." And in Acts 17:26 we read that God made the nations of men and has determined "the bounds of their habitation." The

Word of God is the surest and only infallible source of our facts of Ethnology, and when man sets aside the plain teachings of this Blessed Book and disregards the boundary lines God Himself has drawn, man assumes a prerogative that belongs to God alone. The Anti-Christ will consumate this attitude by opposing and exalting Himself above God (II Thess: 2) [.]

What does the Word of God say? We go to Genesis 9:18, 19. (Read). We should recognize the fact that today certain areas of modern education and higher Criticism laugh at the integrity of the Genesis Record. But we should also remind ourselves that so-called "higher criticism", which is based upon the theory of Naturalism (rejecting anything of old that does not still occur today) also rejects anything in the Bible that is miraculous, supernatural, or that cannot be explained in terms of man's wisdom. Consequently, we shall certainly not reject the Genesis Record—any jot or tittle of it—because the modern critic raises his brow at it. The instigators and propagators of the Documentary Theory (still a theory) will NOT rob us of our avowed faith in the authenticity of the Genesis Record in its entirety.

Genesis 9:19 teaches that, following the Deluge, the earth's population sprang from the three sons of Noah, namely: Shem, Ham, and Japheth. Immediately following in this record is the account of an incident in the life of Noah that resulted in a significantly time-proved prophecy. Noah, drunk from intoxicating drink, lay uncovered in his tent. Ham saw him in this condition, apparently rejoiced in what he saw, and reported the same to his brethren, undoubtedly with an undermining purpose in mind. While some liberal, rejecting theological minds accuse Noah of being but a primitive and drunken man, speaking his vehement anathemas thoughtlessly, he actually spoke under the impulse of the prophetic Spirit in his threefold pronouncement: (1). Cana[a]n's curse, (2). Shem's blessing, and (3). Japheth's enlargement.

Even if one does not care to accept in simple faith, the record "as is," he finds it difficult to reject the annals of secular history, for history has borne out the integrity of Noah's pronouncement. CANAAN was to be a "servant of servants," a servant reduced to the lowest plane of servitude. Subsequent events reveal that the Canaanites were subjugated in the time of Joshua (Joshua 9:27;

Judges 1:28) and partly reduced to the lowest form of slavery by Israelites, who came from Shem. Of those remaining, some were conquered in the time of Solomon, (I Kings 9:20, 21) and, still later, the people of Carthage and Egypt,—all descendants of Ham— were taken by Macedonians, Romans, and Persians, who came from Japheth.

The lineage of Shem was to furnish spiritual blessings to the world. This they did in the Lord Jesus Christ. The lineage of Japheth would furnish a race that would make up the great populators and colonizers of the world. However, the descendants of Ham through Canaan—the Egyptians, Assyrians, Ethiopians, and Phoenicians—though not necessarily in a lower political position, have been conquered by the children of Japheth and Shem, and have handed down the great things of their civilization—their wealth and achievements—to Northern, Western, and Eastern peoples. These lines still mark the Lord's division of the races of men. As Arthur W. Pink has so ably written: "Who but He who knows the end from the beginning could have outlined the whole course of the three great divisions of the postdiluvian race so tersely and so accurately!"

The whole problem of race relations has arisen again in our day because the minds of natural men refuse to accept the pronouncements of the only Omniscient, Omnipotent God!

My second charge is simply this: In the Bible, wherever we find the integration of these three races trouble resulted. We shall observe a few examples from the pages of the Scriptures.

(1). Sodom and Gomorrah were within the border of the Canaanites, who were descendants from Ham. Lot, a descendant of Shem, took his belongings and attempted to settle among them. His residence in Sodom got him into serious trouble, God's judgment was finally visited upon Sodom.

(2). The detrimental result of mixing races is further seen in the experience of Abraham, a descendant of Shem, whose son Ishmael was born to his Egyptian Slavewoman, Hagar. The result was the Arab, of whom it is prophesied in Genesis 16:12 . . . (Read).

(3). When Israel was delivered from the land of Egypt, a mixed multitude of Egyptians went out of the land with them. (Ex. 12:38; Lev. 11:4–6). This mixed multitude was a constant source of weakness and division among the people. This was a physical mixing of races which resulted in social and spiritual weakness. The outcome in the wilderness at Kadesh-Barnea was that, because of unbelief, the older generation was sentenced to die in that wilderness. (Num. 14:13, 23).

(4). Upon entering the Land of Promise, (Josh. 23:4, 7, 12, 13.) Israel found the Land usurped by Canaanites. Israel had received commandment from the Lord to maintain their own social purity—they were not to intermix or intermarry. Against this commandment they eventually rebelled. They thus wandered away into idolatry, and were carried away into the captivities.

(5). In Nehemiah's Day—the Restoration Period—one of the chief causes of spiritual decline—making revival necessary—was social integration of the races. (Neh. 10:29, 30; 13:3).

In the THIRD place, we take one look at a situation just south of us, in SOUTH AMERICA. In places on that continent, there has been an intermixing of races for four centuries. First there was the mixing of the Spanish and Indian races, which produced a mongrel race. Then with the coming of the negro slaves, the Spanish whites mixed freely with them, producing the mullatoe. Today, one of the major problems facing our missionaries is the problem of mixed races of people—though under the domination of the Roman Catholic Church for 4 centuries—who know almost nothing of marriage and the sanctity of home life. No one can deny the vigorous expansiveness of North America as contrasted with the puny, restricted, backward poverty that dominates a large percentage of South American people.

We would all do well to take note of the fact that America's greatness over these past 3 centuries, and especially during the past century, has developed during a period when segregation has been the law in our Section.

While we are looking at one of our Mission Fields, we might make another observation. We have, for many years, known that our best job of Foreign Missions is in training a native ministry. All of our major Foreign Mission Boards know this is true. And WHY is it so? Simply because each can work best with his own race of people. The basic principle underlying all is the principle of God's own Providential division of the races of men. We dare not overstep the boundary lines God has drawn.

We are investing thousands of our missionary dollars in Theological schools in foreign lands for the purpose of training a native ministry to work among their own people. This same underlying principle has its application at home as well as abroad.

Again, our text. (Acts 17:26: Deut. 32:8). Since the segregation of races is God's Work; since the integration of major races has generally proved a detriment wherever tested; since there is visible evidence of the detrimental result of racial integration in the world of today, THERE ARE CERTAIN LESSONS WHICH WE MAY SAFELY DRAW IN CONCLUSION.

(1). Disregarding the basic principle of segregation will ultimately lead to the mingling of the tides of life, mongrelizing of the bloodstreams of men, and will eventually weaken rather than strengthen America. (High school students in Norfolk are already expressing their approval of mixed social activities and marriage). Once this begins, no power on earth can stop it. We had better beware. If I were black, I would praise the Lord for it, and would not want to make myself anything else contrary to what God made me to be. THIS IS MERELY A CLARION CALL TO THE OLD-FASHIONED FACT OF RACIAL SELF-RESPECT.

(2). Social integration is not the answer to America's problems. We need to be reminded that God's Cause is not dependent upon the federation of large numbers. God's call today is not to federation, but to separation. The Cause of the Lord Jesus Christ is best served by the purity of its component parts. And that purity cannot be absolutely maintained by the social integration of those serving the Lord.

(3). Spurning and rejecting the plain Truth of the Word of God has always resulted in the Judgment of God. Man, in overstepping the boundary lines God has drawn, has taken another step in the direction of inviting the Judgment of Almighty God. This step of racial integration is but another stepping stone toward the gross immorality and lawlessness that will be characteristic of the last days, just preceding the Return of the Lord Jesus Christ.

(4). The issue has become a problem because modern-day Churchianity has substituted a social Gospel for the Blood-purchased

Gospel of Christ, "which is the power of God unto salvation for everyone" . . .

General Correspondence, Executive Papers, Gov. Thomas B. Stanley (1954–1958) Typescript, folder 1, box 100. (Library of Virginia, Richmond)

Presbyterian Church U.S.A.

The Church and Segregation (May 3, 1954)

The scriptural arguments for Jim Crow were approached from a different angle in this publication of the Presbyterian Church, USA. Anticipating both the Court's ruling in Brown v. Board of Education *and public, but particularly Presbyterian, reaction to it, the denomination's Council on Christian Relations prepared a report demonstrating the spiritual and theological rightness of desegregation.*

In its report to the approaching General Assembly the Council on Christian Relations says:

"Behind every code of ethics is a concept of God so that ultimately every human relationship, whether it be voluntary or prescribed by statute, is determined by what a man believes about God. It will be a sad day for the church . . . if our belief in a personal God should permit us to foster a relationship inferior to that which impersonal law demands."

Then it recommends:

1. That the General Assembly affirm that enforced segregation of the races is discrimination which is out of harmony with Christian theology and ethics and that the church, in its relationship to cultural patterns, should lead rather than follow.

2. That the General Assembly . . . especially urge:

(1) That the trustees of institutions of higher education belonging to the General Assembly adopt a policy of opening the doors of these institutions to all races.

(2) That the synods consider earnestly the adoption of a similar recommendation to trustees of institutions under their control.

(3) That the governing bodies of the various conferences throughout the church consider the adoption of a similar policy.

(4) That the sessions of local churches admit persons to membership and fellowship in the local church on the scriptural basis of faith in the Lord Jesus Christ without reference to race.

(5) That in this time of crisis and concern, we commend to all individuals in our communion and especially to all leaders of our churches the earnest cultivation and practice of the Christian graces of forbearance, patience, humility and persistent goodwill.

The Church and Segregation

The 93rd General Assembly placed in the hands of the Council of Christian Relations a resolution offered by the Rev. Jack W. Ewart relative to segregation in church-controlled institutions. The General Assembly directed that the Council study the resolution and report to the 94th General Assembly. The resolution reads as follows:

"1. That the General Assembly in carrying out the implications of this section (adoption of Section III, Race Relations, report of Division of Christian Relations) shall direct the trustees of all its institutions of higher education to open its doors to all races;

"2. That the General Assembly strongly recommends the same action to synods and presbyteries;

"3. That the local churches be directed to examine their own life, and practice no discrimination within its fellowship or outreach."

After careful study the Council of Christian Relations offers this report with recommendations. The report consists of three parts; namely:

1. The Bible and Human Relationships
2. Racial Integration
3. The Position of the Church

I. The Bible and Human Relationships

Any study of relationship involving people of different cultural and racial background is essentially a study of human relationships. It is important in such a study to recognize the authority of Scripture.

Attention is called to the following basic truths relevant to our study which are taught in Scripture:

1. The Sovereignty of God

The first of these truths is that God is one and he is ruler over all creation. His will is right and shall be done in heaven and in earth. This truth is set forth in striking terms by John on the Isle of Patmos when he had a vision of God's judgment upon the evil forces of the world:

> "And I heard as it were the voice of a great multitude, and as the voice of many waters and as the voice of mighty thunderings, saying, Alleluia: for the Lord God omnipotent reigneth."—Revelation 19:6.

God being sovereign ruler of the universe, "Man's chief end is to glorify God and enjoy him forever."

2. The Dignity of Man

A second basic truth found in Scripture relevant to our study is that every person is of infinite value and has infinite possibilities. This truth is set forth principally in the doctrine of creation; in the doctrine of the incarnation; and in the doctrine of redemption. Scripture teaches that man was created *in the image of God*. It is believed that this has reference to man's capacity to think, to feel, to will—a spiritual being who can know God, love him and communicate with him.

The dignity of man is further set forth in the incarnation of Jesus Christ. Said the writer of the Fourth Gospel:

> "And the Word was made flesh, and dwelt among us, and we beheld his glory, the glory as of the only begotten of the Father, full of grace and truth."—John 1:14.
>
> In Jesus we behold the perfect man, "the image of the invisible God." In him we see God's ideal for man.

The infinite value of every person is finally and completely demonstrated in the sacrificial death of Jesus Christ.

> "For God so loved the world, that he gave his only begotten Son, that whosoever believeth in him should not perish, but have everlasting life."—John 3:16.

3. The Oneness of Mankind

A third basic truth is the oneness of mankind. This truth is supported in Scripture by five facts. The first of these is *the fact of creation*. The story of creation as given in the Book of Genesis shows the common origin of man.

The second fact in support of man's oneness is the Providence of God. The Hebrew people were chosen by God not because they were better than other peoples, but that he might use them in revealing himself to the world. His blessings are poured out upon all people. It is significant that in Scripture the usual division between peoples has to do with the two groups, Jews and Gentiles, or believers and non-believers.

The third fact is that God's plan of redemption applies to all people alike. The circumstances of one's birth do not affect God's will to redeem that individual. It is God's will that all should come to a knowledge of the truth. Said the Apostle Peter:

> "Of a truth I perceive that God is no respecter of persons: but in every nation he that feareth him, and worketh righteousness, is accepted with him."—Acts 10:34, 35.

The fourth fact is that God's law for human relationships, the law of love, applies to all people alike. Jesus in the Parable of the Good Samaritan indicates that one's cultural and racial background is not to be determinative in the application of this law. The Christian law of love transcends the barrier of race.

The fifth fact supporting the oneness of mankind is that God's judgment upon people is impartial. His judgment is based upon moral principles and not upon externalities. In the Parable of the Judgment, Jesus warned that all nations would be gathered before the Son of Man to be judged. The basis of the judgment would be their relationship to him manifested in their behavior toward their fellowmen.

Conclusions

Five conclusions concerning human relationships are reached from a careful study of the Bible:

1. God is the sovereign ruler over all creation. Man's chief end, therefore, is to glorify him.

2. God in his concern for, and in his dealing with man, is no respecter of persons. The people of Israel were chosen for his instrument in the salvation of all people which points up this truth. Since Christ died for all, Christians are constrained to look upon all people as those for whom Christ died, even as the Apostle Paul said:

"Henceforth know we no man after the flesh."—II Corinthians 5:16a.

3. Every person is of infinite value, and therefore of equal value in the sight of God. In his sight there is no "superior race." Rather, all people have been created in his image and are to be treated as such.

4. People, while differing in outward appearance, are essentially *one*. They have fundamentally the same needs, aspirations, hopes and fears. God in Christ is the goal of their life and their souls are restless till they repose in him.

5. It is God's will that the law of Christian love be operative in all human relationships. Guided by this law Christians recognize and meet need apart from the circumstances of one's birth and culture.

People are to be looked upon and treated as people. Whatever injures or prevents the growth of human personality is contrary to the law of love. The Christian's conduct toward others must be guided by the law of neighborliness which seeks the welfare and happiness of all people.

* * *

III. The Position of the Church

Since segregation of the white and Negro people continues to diminish it is time to determine the church's relationship to this trend. This state of flux is due to two dynamic forces at work, the Federal Constitution and the Christian conscience, the one legal and the other spiritual; the one finding expression in statutes and court decisions, and the other in personal conduct, in the voice and policies of the church. If it be judged that segregation is not merely the separation of two peoples, but the subordination of one people to another, we can, on good evidence, observe that the courts have shown more sympathy toward the Negro than has the church. The church would then find itself in the embarrassing position of having to adjust its sense of morality to measure up to the morals of the state. This would belie its pristine nature. Our Christ was and still is ahead of the times; the customs, traditions, and laws of it. The church must strive to keep apace of its Master or become bereft of his spirit.

Our religious convictions form the dynamic for the making, amending and repealing of laws.

We recognize three levels of relationship, the legal, the ethical, and the spiritual. A law is the least common denominator of human behavior. It is a restraint so generally acceptable that it can be enforced without curtailing freedom. Behind every set of laws is a code of ethics which contains the unwritten laws of corporate life.

Unwritten laws, as they become generally taught and observed, are subsequently codified. Behind every code of ethics is a concept of God so that ultimately every human relationship, whether it be voluntary or prescribed by statute, is determined by what a man believes about God.

It will be a sad day for the church if these three levels of relationship should be inverted, that is, if our belief in a personal God should permit us to foster a relationship inferior to that which impersonal law demands.

If this should happen, the church would lose its status as the conscience of society, its intangible, controlling and quickening force.

With special reference to the resolution placed in the hands of the Council of Christian Relations by the 93rd General Assembly for study and recommendations the Council recognizes that in Presbyterian procedure, the General Assembly does not *direct* that certain changes in educational and cultural patterns be adopted. On the other hand, the Council understands that the General Assembly may properly *urge* the adoption of such changes in the practices of the church. In keeping with this procedure, therefore, the following recommendations are offered:

1. That the General Assembly affirm that enforced segregation of the races is discrimination which is out of harmony with Christian theology and ethics and that the church, in its relationship to cultural patterns, should lead rather than follow.

2. That the General Assembly, therefore, submit this report for careful study throughout the church, and that it especially urge:

(1) That the trustees of institutions of higher education belonging to the General Assembly adopt a policy of opening the doors of these institutions to all races.

(2) That the synods consider earnestly the adoption of a similar recommendation to trustees of institutions under their control.

(3) That the governing bodies of the various conferences held throughout the church consider the adoption of a similar policy.

(4) That the sessions of local churches admit persons to membership and fellowship in the local church on the scriptural basis of faith in the Lord Jesus Christ without reference to race.

(5) That in this time of crisis and concern, we commend to all individuals in our communion and especially to all leaders of our churches the earnest cultivation and practice of the Christian graces of forbearance, patience, humility and persistent goodwill.

Presbyterian Outlook, 136, no. 17 (May 3, 1954).

American Nationalist Flyer *Total Integration Means . . . Total Mongrelization (ca. 1956)*

This flyer was produced and sent through the mail by the American Nationalist, one of a number of far-right associations opposed to integration. Its goal was to stir up resistance to implementation of school desegregation. The organizations assailed by the authors—the NAACP, the Ford Foundation, the National Council of Churches, and the National Conference of Christians and Jews—all supported the Brown v. Board of Education *decision. Testifying to the ability of civil rights advocates to capture the moral high ground, the authors of this flyer refuse to concede the authority of Christianity to those who insist that "the brotherhood of man knows no races," and offer an alarmist picture of the results of flawed interpretations of scripture.*

Three Steps To Mongrelization

A BLUEPRINT FOR THE DESTRUCTION OF OUR CHRISTIAN-AMERICAN CIVILIZATION

MIX THE SCHOOLS

Every race agitator and every professional race mixing organization knows that the first step toward racial mongrelization is the "integrated" school. They know that if the growing child can be exposed to an inter-racial atmosphere early enough in life, and can be conditioned in a Negroidal environment from kindergarten on, it will never develop racial pride or racial self respect.

Accordingly, the integrationists are seeking to transform the educational process into an instrument of mass mongrelization; they are fanatically determined to mix Negroes and whites in our public schools at all costs. In Little Rock they tried to do it with bayonets. In New York City they are using school buses to import Negroes into all-white schools. In other areas they are utilizing court injunctions, coercion and propaganda to gain their ends. Their immediate goal is the integration of our schools; their ultimate objective is the bastardization of the white race . . .

TEACH THEM "TOLERANCE"

The second important step toward total mongrelization of our white youth with "tolerance" propaganda. This means that at all times the maturing child must be impressed with the notion that all races are equal, and that "science" has never proven one race to be superior to another. At no time is criticism of the Negro race to be tolerated, but is to be instantly branded as a show of racial "prejudice." At the same time the Negro must always be portrayed as a victim of white "bigotry." A constant repetition of the latter theme serves a double purpose: it arouses Negroes to a fever pitch of racial militancy and aggressiveness, and it instills a sense of guilt in the white Christian child. Thus by inciting Negroes to a hypersensitive awareness of race, and by destroying or watering down the very concept of race among whites, "tolerance" propaganda serves as a double edged weapon in the hands of the integrationists. That is why they are always so anxious to teach racial "tolerance" in our schools . . .

INTEGRATE THE CHURCHES

The third major step toward the universal mongrelization and destruction of our white Christian-American heritage is the integration of the churches—a project dear to the heart of a great many of our social gospel clergymen. In many ways the NAACP crowd regard church integration as their most important goal, for it breaks down the moral barriers against miscegenation in the same way that school integration breaks down the intellectual barriers. They know, to begin with, that the mere presence of Negroes in white churches will eventually result in interracial marriages—all the more so if children are warned repeatedly from the pulpit that racial "discrimination" is a cardinal sin, and "un-Christian." In short, if the child is taught in church and in Sunday school that all the races are "children of God," and that race mixing is a high Christian virtue, it is unreasonable to expect that interracial attachments will not result. Once the churches have been transformed into an instrument for popularizing and encouraging racial mongrelization, there is little hope of preserving our civilization . . .

THESE ARE THE PRODUCTS OF INTEGRATION . . .

This girl, on honeymoon with her Negro husband, will make her parents proud someday—with mulatto grandchildren.

These white girls, all of whom have married Negroes, have obviously taken racial "tolerance" seriously—as they were taught to do.

Experience has already shown that there is no such thing as just a little integration. Negroes cannot be integrated in the classroom, but segregated at the school party; they cannot be treated as "equals" in the school lunch room, but as inferiors at the junior prom. It's all or nothing; the line cannot be drawn halfway . . .

These are the products of integration—the inevitable consequence of throwing Negroes and whites into the same schools, churches and social environment. Once integration is achieved on a mass scale, mongrelization on a mass scale can be expected to follow.

Flyer, n.d. (ca. 1956), Miscellaneous Papers–Race Relations, #517-38a, f.2, Southern Historical Collection, University of North Carolina, Chapel Hill.

Langston Hughes

How to Integrate without Danger of Intermarriage (November 26, 1955)

African American advocates of integration and black voting rights frequently tried to defuse the explosive power of white anxiety about intermarriage by ridiculing what Langston Hughes elsewhere called the "ballot box to the bedroom" logic of opponents of black civil rights. In this editorial, written for a black audience, Hughes cuts straight to the heart of white men's sexual anxiety about desegregation by noting that white women have ultimate power over white racial "purity." At the same time, Hughes makes a quiet argument for freedom of marriage for individual adults.

One of the things about integration that seems to most worry some white American citizens is intermarriage. They seem to think that if colored and white children attend the same schools when young, they will intermarry when old. There is one sure way to prevent this. Let us take for example a little dark boy and little blond girl sitting across the aisle from each other in the third grade in Jackson, Mississippi[.] Suppose the little brown boy says to the little blond girl, "When I grow up I would like to marry you. Will you marry me?" How can such a marriage be prevented[?] That's the question.

Let us take another example from a field other than education, that of housing. Suppose Negroes and whites live in neighboring apartments in a federal, state, or municipal housing project. And suppose a Negro family and a white family develop a speaking acquaintance as neighbors. Suppose a little farther—there is a teenage girl in the Negro family, and there is a teenage boy in the white family. Suppose the white boy asks the colored girl for her hand in marriage. How can this be stopped? I know, and will tell you.

Again, let us take a case that might develop from the Fair Employment Practice, should such a practice become really national. Suppose a white man and a colored woman in Memphis are working side by side in a factory at the same machines opposite each other. And suppose they find they have interests in common, such as raising chickens, or listening to bop music. Suppose one fine day the white man asked the colored woman to marry him. How can consummation of his request for matrimony be prevented. I will tell you in a word in a moment.

But first let us consider another area of possible integration, the area of Civil Rights. Suppose all the hotels all over America admitted Negro guests, all the trains dropped their Jim Crow cars, all the street cars and busses in the South discarded their COLORED and WHITE signs separating the races, and all public facilities everywhere were open fairly and equally to everybody, black or white. Let us imagine then a colored youth in Atlanta spotting a white maiden on a street car and wishing in his heart so desperately to take her to himself as a bride that he writes her a note proposing, "Will you be mine?" How could such a proposal be successfully thwarted? It is really no problem.

One more area should be considered before an answer is given, that of the purely social. Let us imagine that all clubs, fraternities, sororities, festivals, parties, socials, and dances from coast to coast all over the U. S. A. were open to colored participants as well as white. And a colored boy and girl found themselves dancing together in Birmingham so smoothly that they liked it. But the boy liked it so much that the urge to dance through life with the girl caused him to gather up enough courage to ask her, "Will you marry me?" What should that girl do? How could she stop him from marrying her? How could such legal miscegenation be prevented?

These are questions troubling the minds of many white people in the South today as the word "integration" invades the news and the national consciousness more and more. In some white minds "integration" and "intermarriage" are almost synonymous. They don't want the former much—but the latter they don't want at all.

They seem to think, too, that intermarriage would present a mass problem, a broad social challenge, and a general catastrophe with which the whole white race could hardly cope. I see the problem, on the other hand, as being of no such enormous proportions. I do not see where it would call for the participation of millions to solve it all. Marriage really involves only two people. And consent to marry actually concerns but one—the woman who must first give her consent. So the answer to the problem to me seems extremely simple. The way to integrate without intermarriage is for the girl to decline to get married. If a man, white or colored, says to a woman, colored or white, "Will you marry me?" all the woman has to do to prevent marrying the man, is say, "No."

Why anything so simple should cause so much discussion, I cannot, for the life of me, understand. Can you?

Editorial, *Chicago Defender*, November 26, 1955.

White Citizens Council of Greater New Orleans
Anti-Rock and Roll Flyer (ca. 1956)

While their parents were organizing against the Brown v. Board of Education *decision, white teenagers were listening to black rock and rollers like Little Richard and Chuck Berry and to the white artists like Elvis Presley and Buddy Holly who flourished alongside. Both forms of rock and roll were denounced nationwide by white adults who considered rock music an assault on middle-class American values. In the South, the parental campaign against rock and roll became bound up with the broader contemporaneous defense of Jim Crow. Alabama Ku Klux Klan leader and George Wallace speechwriter Asa Carter denounced "sensuous Negro music" that eroded "the entire moral structure of man, Christianity, of spirituality in Holy marriage," and accused the NAACP of using music to integrate and hence corrupt the nation's young people. Segregating the air waves was much more difficult than segregating the buses, however, and so was policing the consumer patterns of whites.*

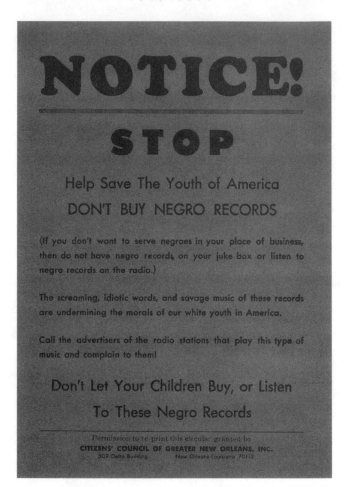

Charles L. Black, Jr.

The Lawfulness of the Segregation Decisions
(January 1960)

On May 17, 1954, Chief Justice Earl Warren spoke for a unanimous Supreme Court on the issue of segregation. "In the field of public education, the doctrine of separate but equal has no place. Separate educational facilities are inherently unequal." The decision was intentionally narrow and did not constitute an attack on Jim Crow in general. It nonetheless provoked a firestorm of protest from the South. Lawyers and jurists faulted the constitutional merits of the decision and ridiculed the justices' reliance on sociological and historical information. The Brown v. Board of Education *decision triggered the formation of organizations such as the White Citizens' Councils, whose members intimidated local officials favoring compliance with the law. Southern state legislatures set out to destroy the NAACP; it had sponsored the case and its chief litigator, Thurgood Marshall, had argued the case before the Court. In this climate of mounting violence and persecution, and with even liberal academics doubting the legal justification of the desegregation decision, Charles Black, the Henry R. Luce Professor of Jurisprudence at the Yale Law School, offered a defense of the decision and its successor, commonly known as* Brown II *(1955). Black's voice was hardly disinterested—he had contributed briefs for the first* Brown *decision—but he spoke with the authority of a white man raised in Jim Crow Texas.*

If the cases outlawing segregation were wrongly decided, then they ought to be overruled. One can go further: if dominant professional opinion ever forms and settles on the belief that they were wrongly decided, then they will be overruled, slowly or all at once, openly or silently. The insignificant error, however palpable, can stand, because the convenience of settlement outweighs the discomfort of error. But the hugely consequential error cannot stand and does not stand.

There is pragmatic meaning then, there is call for action, in the suggestion that the segregation cases cannot be justified. In the long run, as a corollary, there is practical and not merely intellectual significance in the question whether these cases were rightly decided. I think they were rightly decided, by overwhelming weight of reason, and I intend here to say why I hold this belief.

My liminal difficulty is rhetorical—or, perhaps more accurately, one of fashion. Simplicity is out of fashion, and the basic scheme of reasoning on which these cases can be justified is awkwardly simple. First, the equal protection clause of the fourteenth amendment should be read as saying that the Negro race, as such, is not to be significantly disadvantaged by the laws of the states. Secondly, segregation is a massive intentional disadvantaging of the Negro race, as such, by state law. No subtlety at all. Yet I cannot disabuse myself of the idea that that is really all there is to the segregation cases. If both these propositions can be supported by the preponderance of argument, the cases were rightly decided. If they cannot be so supported, the cases are in perilous condition.

As a general thing, the first of these propositions has so far as I know never been controverted in a holding of the Supreme Court. I rest here on the solid sense of *The Slaughterhouse Cases* and of *Strauder v. West Virginia*, where Mr. Justice Strong said of the fourteenth amendment:

> It ordains that no State shall make or enforce any laws which shall abridge the privileges or immunities of citizens of the United States (evidently referring to the newly made citizens, who, being citizens of the United States, are declared to be also citizens of the State in which they reside). It ordains that no State shall deprive any person of life, liberty, or property, without due process of law, or deny to any person within its jurisdiction the equal protection of the laws. What is this but declaring that the law in the States shall be the same for the black as for the white; that all persons, whether colored or white, shall stand equal before the laws of the States, and, in regard to the colored race, for whose protection the amendment was primarily designed, that no discrimination shall be made against them by law because of their color? The words of the amendment, it is true, are prohibitory, but they contain a necessary implication of a positive immunity, or right, most valuable to the colored race,—the right to exemption from unfriendly legislation against them distinctively as colored,—exemption from legal discriminations, implying inferiority in civil society, lessening the security of their enjoyment of the rights which others enjoy, and discriminations which are steps towards reducing them to the condition of a subject race.

If *Plessy v. Ferguson* be thought a faltering from this principle, I step back to the principle itself. But the *Plessy* Court clearly conceived it to be its task to show that segregation did not really disadvantage the Negro, except through his own choice. There is in this no denial of the *Slaughterhouse* and *Strauder* principle; the fault of *Plessy* is in the psychology and sociology of its minor premise.

The lurking difficulty lies not in "racial" cases but in the total philosophy of "equal protection" in the wide sense. "Equal protection," as it applies to the whole of state law, must be consistent with the imposition of disadvantage on some, for all law imposes disadvantage on some; to give driver's licen[c]es only to good drivers is to disadvantage bad drivers. Thus the word "reasonable" necessarily finds its way into "equal protection," in the application of the latter concept to law in general. And it is inevitable, and right, that "reasonable," in this broader context, should be given its older sense of "supportable by reasoned considerations." "Equal" thereby comes to mean not really "equal," but "equal unless a fairly tenable reason exists for inequality."

But the whole tragic background of the fourteenth amendment forbids the feedback infection of its central purpose with the necessary qualifications that have attached themselves to its broader and so largely accidental radiations. It may have been intended that "equal protection" go forth into wider fields than the racial. But history puts it entirely out of doubt that the chief and all-dominating purpose was to ensure equal protection for the Negro. And this intent can hardly be given the self-defeating qualification that necessity has written on equal protection as applied to carbonic gas. If it is, then "equal protection" for the Negro means "equality until a tenable reason for inequality is proferred." On this view, Negroes may hold property, sign wills, marry, testify in court, walk the streets, go to (even segregated) school, ride public transportation, and so on, only in the event that no reason, not clearly untenable, can be assigned by a state legislature for their not being permitted to do these things. That cannot have been what all the noise was about in 1866.

What the fourteenth amendment, in its historical setting, must be read to say is that the Negro is to enjoy equal protection of the laws, and that the fact of his being a Negro is not to be taken to be a good enough reason for denying him this equality, however "reasonable" that might seem to some people. All possible arguments, however convincing, for discriminating against the Negro, were finally rejected by the fourteenth amendment.

It is sometimes urged that a special qualification was written on the concept of "equality" by the history of the adoption of the amendment—that an intent can be made out to exclude segregation from those legal discriminations invalidated by the requirement of equality, whether or not it actually works inequality. This point has been discussed and documented by Professor Alexander Bickel, who, though he finds convincing arguments for the conclusion that school segregation was not among the evils the framers of the amendment intended for immediate correction, suggests that they intended at the same time to set up a general concept for later concrete application. Other recent writers take somewhat similar views. The data brought forward by Professor Bickel do not seem to me as persuasive, on his first point, as they do to him. But in supporting his second point he develops a line of thought tending to establish that the legislative history does not render the segregation decisions improper, and I am glad to join him in that practical conclusion. I would add only one point: The question of the "intent" of the men of 1866 on segregation *as we know it* calls for a far chancier guess than is commonly supposed, for they were unacquainted with the institution as it prevails in the American South today. To guess their verdict upon the institution as it functions in the midtwentieth century supposes an imaginary hypothesis which grows more preposterous as it is sought to be made more vivid. They can in the nature of the case have bequeathed us only their generalities; the specifics lay unborn as they disbanded. I do not understand Professor Bickel to hold a crucially different view.

Then does segregation offend against equality? Equality, like all general concepts, has marginal areas where philosophic difficulties are encountered. But if a whole race of people finds itself confined within a system which is set up and continued for the very purpose of keeping it in an inferior station, and if the question is then solemnly propounded whether such a race is being treated "equally," I think we ought to exercise one of the sovereign prerogatives of philosophers—that of laughter. The only question remaining (after we get our laughter under control) is whether the segregation system answers to this description.

Here I must confess to a tendency to start laughing all over again. I was raised in the South, in a Texas city where the pattern of segregation was firmly fixed. I am sure it never occurred to anyone, white or colored, to question its meaning. The fiction of "equality" is just about on a level with the fiction of "finding" in the action of trover. I think few candid southerners deny this. Northern people may be misled by the entirely sincere protestations of many southerners that segregation is "better" for the Negroes, is not intended to hurt them. But I think a little probing would demonstrate that what is meant is that it is better for the Negroes to accept a position of inferiority, at least for the indefinite future.

But the subjectively obvious, if queried, must be backed up by more public materials. What public materials assure me that my reading of the social meaning of segregation is not a mere idiosyncrasy?

First, of course, is history. Segregation in the South comes down in apostolic succession from slavery and the *Dred Scott* case. The South fought to keep slavery, and lost. Then it tried the Black Codes, and lost. Then it looked around for something else and found segregation. The movement for segregation was an integral part of the movement to maintain and further "white supremacy"; its triumph (as Professor Woodward has shown) represented a triumph of extreme racialist over moderate sentiment about the Negro. It is now defended very largely on the ground that the Negro as such is not fit to associate with the white.

History, too, tells us that segregation was imposed on one race by the other race; consent was not invited or required. Segregation in the South grew up and is kept going because and only because the white race has wanted it that way—an incontrovertible fact which in itself hardly consorts with equality. This fact perhaps more than any other confirms the picture which a casual or deep observer is likely to form of the life of a southern community—a picture not of mutual separation of whites and Negroes, but of one in-group enjoying full normal communal life and one out-group that is barred from this life and forced into an inferior life of its own. When a white southern writer refers to the woes of "the South," do you not know, does not context commonly make it clear, that he means "white southerners"? When you are in Leeville and hear someone say "Leeville High," you know he has reference to the white high school; the Negro school will be called something else—Carver High, perhaps, or Lincoln High to our shame. That is what you would expect when one race forces a segregated position on another, and that is what you get.

Segregation is historically and contemporaneously associated in a functioning complex with practices which are indisputably and grossly discriminatory. I have in mind especially the long-continued and still largely effective exclusion of Negroes from voting. Here we have two things. First, a certain group of people is "segregated." Secondly, at about the same time, the very same group of people, down to the last man and woman, is barred, or sought to be barred, from the common political life of the community—from all political power. Then we are solemnly told that segregation is not intended to harm the segregated race, or to stamp it with the mark of inferiority. How long must we keep a straight face?

Here it may be added that, generally speaking, segregation is the pattern of law in communities where the extralegal patterns of discrimination against Negroes are the tightest, where Negroes are subjected to the strictest codes of "unwritten law" as to job opportunities, social intercourse, patterns of housing, going to the back door, being called by the first name, saying "Sir," and all the rest of the whole sorry business. Of course these things, in themselves, need not and usually do not involve "state action," and hence the fourteenth amendment cannot apply to them. But they can assist us in understanding the meaning and assessing the impact of state action.

"Separate but equal" facilities are almost never really equal. Sometimes this concerns small things—if the "white" men's room has mixing hot and cold taps, the "colored" men's room will likely have separate taps; it is always the back of the bus for the Negroes; "Lincoln Beach" will rarely if ever be as good as the regular beach. Sometimes it concerns the most vital matters—through the whole history of segregation, colored schools have been so disgracefully inferior to white schools that only ignorance can excuse those who have remained acquiescent members of a community that lived the Molochian child-destroying lie that put them forward as "equal."

Attention is usually focused on these inequalities as things in themselves, correctible by detailed decrees. I am more interested in their very clear character as *evidence* of what segregation means to the people who impose it and to the people who are subjected to it. This evidentiary character cannot be erased by one-step-ahead-of-the-marshal correction. Can a system which, in all that can be measured, has practiced the grossest inequality, actually have been "equal" in intent, in total social meaning and impact? "Thy speech maketh thee manifest . . ."; segregation, in all visible things, speaks only haltingly any dialect but that of inequality.

Further arguments could be piled on top of one another, for we have here to do with the most conspicuous characteristic of a whole regional culture. It is actionable defamation in the South to call a white man a Negro. A small proportion of Negro "blood" puts one in the inferior race for segregation purposes; this is the way in which one deals with a taint, such as a carcinogene in cranberries.

The various items I have mentioned differ in weight; not every one would suffice in itself to establish the character of segregation. Taken together they are of irrefragable strength. The society that has just lost the Negro as a slave, that has just lost out in an attempt to put him under quasi-servile "Codes," the society that views his blood as a contamination and his name as an insult, the society that extralegally imposes on him every humiliating mark of low caste and that until yesterday kept him in line by lynching—this society, careless of his consent, moves by law, first to exclude him from voting, and secondly to cut him off from mixing in the general public life of the community. The Court that refused to see inequality in this cutting off would be making the only kind of law that can be warranted outrageous in advance—law based on self-induced blindness, on flagrant contradiction of known fact.

I have stated all these points shortly because they are matters of common notoriety, matters not so much for judicial notice as for the background knowledge of educated men who live in the world. A court may advise itself of them as it advises itself of the facts that we are a "religious people," that the country is more industrialized than in Jefferson's day, that children are the natural objects of fathers' bounty, that criminal sanctions are commonly thought to deter, that steel is a basic commodity in our economy, that the imputation of unchastity is harmful to a woman. Such judgments, made on such a basis, are in the foundations of all law, decisional as well as statutory; it would be the most unneutral of principles, improvised *ad hoc*, to require that a court faced with the present problem refuse to note a plain fact about the society of the United States—the fact that the social meaning of segregation is the putting of the Negro in a position of walled-off inferiority—or the other equally plain fact that such treatment is hurtful to human beings. Southern courts, on the basis of just such a judgment, have held that the placing of a white person in a Negro railroad car is an actionable humiliation; must a court pretend not to know that the Negro's situation there is humiliating?

I think that some of the artificial mist of puzzlement called into being around this question originates in a single fundamental mistake. The issue is seen in terms of what might be called the metaphysics of sociology: "Must Segregation Amount to Discrimination?" That is an interesting question; someday the methods of sociology may be adequate to answering it. But it is not our question. Our question is whether discrimination inheres in that segregation which is imposed by law in the twentieth century in certain specific states in the American Union. And that question has meaning and can find an answer only on the ground of history and of common knowledge about the facts of life in the times and places aforesaid.

Now I need not and do not maintain that the evidence is all one way; it never is on issues of burning, fighting concern. Let us not question here the good faith of those who assert that segregation represents no more than an attempt to furnish a wholesome opportunity for parallel development of the races; let us rejoice at the few scattered instances they can bring forward to support their view of the matter. But let us then ask which balance-pan flies upward.

The case seems so onesided that it is hard to make out what is being protested against when it is asked, rhetorically, how the Court can possibly advise itself of the real character of the segregation system. It seems that what is being said is that, while no actual doubt exists as to what segregation is for and what kind of societal pattern it supports and implements, there is no ritually sanctioned way in which the Court, as a Court, can permissibly learn what is obvious to everybody else and to the Justices as individuals. But surely, confronted with such a problem, legal acumen has only one proper task—that of developing ways to make it permissible for the Court to use what it knows; any other counsel is of despair. And, equally surely, the fact that the Court has assumed as true a matter of common knowledge in regard to broad societal patterns, is (to say the very least) pretty far down the list of things to protest against.

I conclude, then, that the Court had the soundest reasons for judging that segregation violates the fourteenth amendment. These reasons make up the simple syllogism with which I began: The fourteenth amendment commands equality, and segregation as we know it is inequality.

Let me take up a few peripheral points. It is true that the specifically hurtful character of segregation, as a net matter in the life of each segregated individual, may be hard to establish. It seems enough to say of this, as Professor Pollak has suggested, that no such demand is made as to other constitutional rights. To have a confession beaten out of one might in some particular case be the beginning of a new and better life. To be subjected to a racially differentiated curfew might be the best thing in the world for some individual boy. A man might ten years later go back to thank the policeman who made him get off the platform and stop making a fool of himself. Religious persecution proverbially strengthens faith. We do not ordinarily go that far, or look so narrowly into the matter. That a practice, on massive historical evidence and in common sense, has the designed and generally apprehended effect of putting its victims at a disadvantage, is enough for law. At least it always has been enough.

I can heartily concur in the judgment that segregation harms the white as much as it does the Negro. Sadism rots the policeman; the suppressor of thought loses light; the community that forms into a mob, and goes down and dominates a trial, may wound itself beyond healing. Can this reciprocity of hurt, this fated mutuality that inheres in all inflicted wrong, serve to validate the wrong itself?

Finally it is doubtless true that the *School Segregation Cases*, and perhaps others of the cases on segregation, represented a choice between two kinds of freedom of association. Freedom from the massive wrong of segregation entails a corresponding loss of freedom on the part of the whites who must now associate with Negroes on public occasions, as we all must on such occasions associate with many persons we had rather not associate with. It is possible to state the competing claims in symmetry, and to ask whether there are constitutional reasons for preferring the Negroes' desire for merged participation in public life to the white man's desire to live a public life without Negroes in proximity.

The question must be answered, but I would approach it in a way which seems to me more normal—the way in which we more usually approach comparable symmetries that might be stated as to all other asserted rights. The fourteenth amendment forbids inequality, forbids the disadvantaging of the Negro race by law. It was surely anticipated that the following of this directive would entail some disagreeableness for some white southerners. The disagreeableness might take many forms; the white man, for example, might dislike having a Negro neighbor in the exercise of the latter's equal right to own a home, or dislike serving on a jury with a Negro, or dislike having Negroes on the streets with him after ten o'clock. When the directive of equality cannot be followed without displeasing the white, then something that can be called a "freedom" of the white must be impaired. If the fourteenth amendment commands equality, and if segregation violates equality, then the status of the reciprocal "freedom" is automatically settled.

I find reinforcement here, at least as a matter of spirit, in the fourteenth amendment command that Negroes shall be "citizens" of their States. It is hard for me to imagine in what operative sense a man could be a "citizen" without his fellow citizens' once in a while having to associate with him. If, for example, his "citizenship" results in his election to the School Board, the white members may (as recently in Houston) put him off to one side of the room, but there is still some impairment of their freedom "not to associate." That freedom, in fact, exists only at home; in public, we have to associate with anybody who has a right to be there. The question of our right not to associate with him is concluded when we decide whether he has a right to be there.

I am not really apologetic for the simplicity of my ideas on the segregation cases. The decisions call for mighty diastrophic change. We ought to call for such change only in the name of a solid reasoned simplicity that takes law out of artfulness into art. Only such grounds can support the nation in its resolve to uphold the law declared by its Court; only such grounds can reconcile the white South to what must be. *Elegantia juris* and conceptual algebra have here no place. Without pretending either to completeness or to definitiveness of statement, I have tried here to show reasons for believing that we as lawyers can without fake or apology present to the lay community, and to ourselves, a rationale of the segregation decisions that rises to the height of the great argument.

These judgments, like all judgments, must rest on the rightness of their law and the truth of their fact. Their law is right if the equal protection clause in the fourteenth amendment is to be taken as stating, without arbitrary exceptions, a broad principle of practical equality for the Negro race, inconsistent with any device that in fact relegates the Negro race to a position of inferiority. Their facts are true if it is true that the segregation system is actually conceived and does actually function as a means of keeping the Negro in a status of inferiority. I dare say at this time that in the end the decisions will be accepted by the profession on just that basis. Opinions composed under painful stresses may leave much to be desired; it may be that the per curiam device has been unwisely used. But the judgments, in law and in fact, are as right and true as any that ever was uttered.

Yale Law Journal 69, no. 3 (January 1960): 421–38.

Virginia Foster Durr

Letter (March 2, 1956)

Raised a child of privilege in Birmingham, Alabama, Virginia Durr first became involved in black civil rights during the 1930s, when her New Deal husband Clifford Durr took the family to Washington, D.C. A founding member of the Southern Conference for Human Welfare (SCHW), Durr labored tirelessly through the war years for the National Committee to Abolish the Poll Tax. In 1951, the Durrs returned to Alabama and settled in Montgomery, where Clifford Durr practiced law. Among those he represented was an acquaintance of Virginia's, NAACP member Rosa Parks, whose arrest for failing to heed a segregation statute on December 5, 1955, was the opening move in what became the Montgomery Bus Boycott. Two months later, Autherine Lucy became the first African American to attend the University of Alabama. After several thousand whites rioted, Lucy was suspended by the board of trustees "for her own safety." Nonconformist whites who failed to appreciate the wisdom of this course were targeted by the White Citizen's Council, which enforced Jim Crow orthodoxy through economic pressure and private intimidation. This letter to English writer Jessica Mitford suggests the excitement of the moment and the capacity of political issues to divide families and friends, quite apart from the efforts of the White Citizens' Council.

March 2, 1956
Dearest Dec: . . .

I saw Mrs. Parks yesterday and she has gotten enough money for herself to relieve her own personal difficulties and she thinks that the women should now turn their efforts towards raising money for the Protest (they are not calling it a Boycott any more since they were indicated for boycotting) and if they can work with the Preachers that will be fine and make it broader and more dynamic. It takes a lot of money to keep it going in terms of gas for the cars and after all there are forty or fifty THOUSAND that are involved and while tremendous numbers of them walk—still some of them simply have to be transported and all of that takes money, and then too there is the money for the trials and the legal fees and the court costs and the bail, etc. Also the expressions of support and unity are wonderful and help keep up their spirit and it is this feeling that the country and the Negro community is behind them that helps to keep up their wonderful spirit . . .

I agree that this is far more than just a local protest. It is bigger than Montgomery and involves the conscience of the whole country, and the fact that the Negroes have been so brave and so calm and good natured and determined and above all so UNITED shows what they can do. The bus Company is losing about $1500 a day and they can't keep in business here indefinitely at that loss, and they have privately told the Negroes that as far as they are concerned they are willing to meet their demands for equal seating but the City Commission stands in the way of course, but IF the Bus Company would only let their position be known publicly then I think the City Commission might come to terms. The City Commission does not want to have to take on the Bus Company when it is losing money at this rate, and it may end with having no bus service at all, which a great many people here will accept for the keeping of the principle of segregation. I cannot tell you how incredible they are, they have no . . . idea of how they appear to the rest of the country, they think they are heroes standing by the

Confederate Flag and the more awful they are the prouder they are of themselves. I am sorry in a way for Cliff to be so disillusioned about his own people and mine too but after all disillusionment is the beginning of wisdom. There are a few, a very few that are wonderful. But it is really hard for Cliff to accept the low down skullduggery of which expelling Miss Lucy is the latest—on the part of the leading citizens of the State. Then too his own family while they stay silent for the most part when we are around are heart and soul with the other side and his Aunt who is completely outspoken about the "niggers" thinks they should all be sent back to Africa. She told Mary who bathes her, rubs her back, cleans up after her . . . feeds her, nurses her when she's sick . . . that "you niggers are not citizens of this country, you ought to go back to Africa if you don't like it here." And Mary with her eyes simply snapping said "Well when the Lord wants to send me back just let him send a chariot to take me, but when he takes us all back to Africa I don't know who is goin' to look after the white folks." That is what makes the whole thing so completely and obviously and wholeheartedly ridiculous that the White South rests on the Black South and now the Alabama Senate is trying to get the Negroes to "move to the West" (as they did the Indians), [and] they are simply pulling out (but only in words) the foundations of the economy, but I must say that reason has flown out of the window and nothing is left but hysteria—pure hysteria. My only hope is that like a bursting abscess it might clear up the body politic, but then on the other hand it might infect the rest of the country and there will be a meeting of the Racists and the Anti-Reds and we will go to Hell in a bucket. I think it is terribly important that the rest of the country be aroused and try to get as much white support as you can and the politicians put on record and an issue be made of it. Because if these two forces in our lives coalesce, then Fascism will cease to be a word and become a reality . . .

Thanks a lot and lots of love and encourage your women out there to begin putting the politicians on the spot and get it in writing and make it an issue and especially that low down SOB [Richard] Nixon.

In *Freedom Writer: Virginia Foster Durr, Letters from the Civil Rights Years*, ed. Patricia Sullivan (New York, 2003), 110–12.

Harry L. Golden

How to Solve the Segregation Problem
(1956–1958)

"A Northerner living in the South, a Jew in the most Gentile community on the continent, [and] an integrationist among white supremacists," as he described himself, Harry Golden was in a minority position no matter where he stood in the civil rights–era South. In his Charlotte newspaper The Carolina Israelite, *published from 1942 to 1968, Golden printed nostalgic stories about Jewish life in New York and approached southern social conventions through his own experience as a Jew in a Christian world. Aware of Jewish proscriptions on socializing with non-Jews, it is likely that Golden was familiar with a common rabbinic rationale for the prohibition of Jews eating with non-Jews. As one rabbi put it, "It's not the eating and drinking—it's what might happen between courses!" Understanding that white worries about interracial sociability supported much of the resistance to school desegregation, Golden offered a number of tongue-in-cheek suggestions on how to integrate without intimacy.*

The Golden Vertical Negro Plan in Operation

Four "Dime" stores, in as many great Southern cities have put the Golden Vertical Negro Plan into operation, as an effective means of ending racial segregation. This is being accomplished without the slightest trouble or even the hint of controversy. In each of these stores they had never served Negroes at their snack bars; but when they read of the Golden Vertical Negro Plan, they removed their stools, and now the "whites" and the Negroes stand up at the bars, eating and drinking like mad and everybody's happy about the whole thing.

And one follows the other. Take for instance High Point, North Carolina. There, Woolworth's does not serve Negroes at the snack counter, whereas Kress' does. The reason of course is that Kress' took out the stools. Some folks have sent a petition to Woolworth's urging them to take out the stools so that folks can come and go as free citizens in a happy city.

The interesting thing about the Golden Vertical Negro Plan is that it works just as well in Atlanta as it does in High Point.

The stools of course will come back—gradually. Maybe at first the Negroes can just lean against the seat in a sort of half-standing position; and by such easy stages finally get to a forty-five-degree angle without stirring up anything.

The Golden Carry-the-Books Plan

This may help toward the final solution of the "integration" problem of the South, implementing the several Supreme Court decisions to end racial segregation in the public schools.

There is no vertical segregation. But neither is there "45-degree-angle" segregation if the "sitting" or "leaning" Negro is a servant, a domestic, or a chore-boy of some kind.

Therefore the Negro parents of the South should make this proposition to their local school boards: that they will allow their children to carry the books for their "white" classmates. A system can easily be worked out whereby the Negro boy, (going to an integrated school), can meet a "white" classmate at a convenient corner, a block or so away from the school, and carry the "white" boy's books into the school building. And if there are sixteen Negro students in a school of four hundred "whites", an alternating system can be worked out so that by the end of the semester, each "white" boy will have had his books carried into the school building by a Negro student, at least once.

The Negro girls would not have to participate in this "Golden Carry-the-Books-Plan." The girls should wear a sort of miniature apron over their street dresses, and this would settle everything once and for all. Everybody would be satisfied. Eventually, I suspect, the "white" girls may even adopt those cute little aprons themselves, but they will have served their purpose.

I know I am calling on the Negroes to make a considerable sacrifice, but it is worth it because this would settle the matter even for the most outspoken "white supremacists." If it became known throughout the South that the Negro boys were toting books for the "whites," and that Negro girls were wearing aprons to school, all the school kids could go on with their work without any further

disturbance from segregationist mobs, National Guardsmen, or
Federal troops.

Golden Out-of-Order Plan in Operation

One of the great retail chain stores has put the Golden "Out-of-
Order Plan" into operation and with considerable success. They
placed an "Out-of-Order" sign on the "white" drinking fountain in
most of their stores in the "Upper" south. Within six weeks everybody was drinking the "colored" water without any bad effects,
physical or emotional; and all the signs came off, "Out-of-Order,"
"white" and "colored." There is a problem however. In most of
these stores they made this experiment in the "Basement," and naturally they could not put an "Out-of-Order" sign simultaneously
on the other floors. The whole idea would have been given away
and made matters worse. I understand they intend to stagger the
"Out-of-Order" signs from now on. They'll put them up on the second and fourth floors and then double back to the main and third
floors. This thing has to be done—gradually.

You throw a tiny pebble into a stream and you never really know
the extent of the ripples.

In a seminar on education in Tennessee I suggested to the Negro
parents to make sure that their children study French immediately
upon entering high school. We know of course, that there is no vertical segregation, but if the vertical Negro suddenly begins to talk
French, he can even sit down without creating any serious emotion
among the "whites." I had a fellow try this out on the cashier's line
at the A&P store. He suddenly asked the cashier about some product in French, and the "white" folks ahead of him actually broke
ranks to give him priority.

Of course there could be too much of a good thing. If the Negroes of the South follow my suggestion it is possible that within
twenty years they'll all be talking French; it would no longer be a
novelty. But by that time there may not be need for any more
"Golden Plans."

The Carolina Israelite, (May–June, 1956—May–June, 1958)

Stetson Kennedy

Jim Crow Guide to the U.S.A.: The Laws, Customs and Etiquette Governing the Conduct of Nonwhites and Other Minorities as Second-Class Citizens (1959)

Filled with a loathing of bigotry and small-mindedness, during the 1940s writer Stetson Kennedy became, in his own words, a "dissident at large." When the Ku Klux Klan revived in the immediate postwar years, Kennedy infiltrated an Atlanta klavern. Convinced that secrecy was vital to the Invisible Empire's appeal, Kennedy conspired to broadcast the Klan's passwords and secret rituals and hierarchy as widely as possible. The producers of The Adventures of Superman *radio show were happy to oblige: With Hitler, Mussolini, and Hirohito defeated, the show needed new villains to vanquish. Over the course of four weeks, the muscular defender of truth, justice, and the American way took on the Klan over the air waves, baring its leaders, exposing its inner workings, and eroding the mystique of the white-robed white men. In this spoof of the standard tourist guide, Kennedy used mockery, irony, exposure, and humor, as he had against the Klan, to promote human rights and attack Jim Crow.*

Open to All (Whites)

If you think any law-abiding orderly person can enter any restaurant, hotel, cinema, auditorium, park, playground, golf-course, swimming pool, bathing beach, or other such place of public accommodation in the U.S.A. regardless of race, you've got another think coming. . . .

Not since 1883, when the U.S. Supreme Court invalidated the Civil Rights Act of 1875, has there been any national law against racial discrimination in public places.

During the 12 years of its existence, that law assured all persons in the U.S.A. full and equal access to hotels, common carriers, theatres, and other places of amusement, subject only to such regulations as applied to *everyone alike.*

In those bygone days if you were denied admission because of your race you could file a complaint in Federal court, which would impose a heavy fine and sentence against the proprietor, and award you substantial cash damages.

About that same time the Reconstruction legislatures of five former Confederate states—Louisiana, Florida, South Carolina, Arkansas, and Mississippi—adopted similar civil rights laws (this was, of course, before the poor whites and Negroes were disfranchised by the Klan terror). But with the exception of Louisiana, all these laws were repealed when the democratic white-Negro régimes were overthrown by the oligarchic white planters. The Louisiana law, an Act of 1869, is still on the books; but it has long since been forgotten, and should you seek to claim your rights under it, you should be prepared for fireworks.

Today in more than half of the 48 states of the U.S.A. there are no laws prohibiting racial and religious discrimination in places of public accommodation. Those state civil rights laws which do exist are of varying degrees of comprehensiveness and are inadequately enforced. For instance, on March 1, 1953, Kenneth Brush, a barber of Waterloo, New York, finally consented to give a haircut to Clyde (Butch) Williams, an 8-year-old Negro lad, only after the boy's mother sent a letter to the *Waterloo Observer* complaining that previous refusals by the shop had made it necessary to take her son 40 miles to Syracuse to have his hair cut.

* * *

The effect of such exclusionist laws and regulations is rough on the nonwhites. As one young Southern nonwhite girl has put it: "I didn't think so much about things I couldn't do till one day I went downtown and stopped by a movie house to look at the picture outside, and I thought I'd like to see it, and I looked for a sign for the colored entrance, but there wasn't any; just a sign for the white, so I knew I couldn't go. I have to go all the way to Greensboro to see the movies, just because I'm colored."

Come and Bring Your Lunch

Both in and out of the segregated territory, the refusal of hotels catering to whites to admit nonwhites costs the proprietors considerable sums in their inability to play host to interracial conventions.

For example, when the National Education Association met in a New Orleans hotel, the management installed a step-ladder at a side window and suggested that Negro delegates use it rather than the main entrance and lobby—whereupon the Negroes refused to attend.

In the same way, on those rare occasions when the Atlanta Biltmore Hotel has permitted an interracial conference to be held in its conference rooms, it has refused to serve meals to the Negro delegates, even in the privacy of the conference room. Consequently, the Negro delegates had to bring their lunches with them, or make the long journey to that section of the city where they could obtain a meal.

Those hotels which refuse to accommodate Negroes generally will not accept whites and Negroes who may be travelling together, as Presidential candidate Henry A. Wallace and the Negro baritone Paul Robeson discovered in Illinois and elsewhere in 1948.

* * *

Appearances are more important in such matters than citizenship status. For example, in Decatur, Illinois, Dr. Bidhan Chandra Roy, personal physician of the late Mohandas Ghandi and former Mayor of Calcutta, and five of his countrymen were refused service in a restaurant while travelling on an official mission for the Government of India. The restaurant operator said later that she had presumed that the party consisted of American Negroes. Because of such incidents, many visiting dignitaries of dark complexion feel obliged to wear some distinguishing article of their native dress, rather than American-style clothes.

Even in the civil rights territory, the laws are quite generally circumvented by a variety of devices and subterfuges. If you are non-white, or are travelling in "mixed company," the hotel clerk may insist that he has no vacancies, even though you may hold an advance reservation.

In restaurants, the head waiter may insist that all vacant tables are "reserved," or he may seat you out of sight or near a hot kitchen, or you may be allowed to sit indefinitely without service, or you may be served food too salty to eat, etc.

* * *

Where Not to Go

Virtually all of the public swimming areas in the segregated territory have been reserved for whites only, including those which have been purchased and operated with tax money.

This means that if you are nonwhite you are precluded from entering the surf at Miami Beach or any of the South's other famous beaches. In a few instances you will find that some remote and relatively inaccessible and undeveloped spot has been made available to nonwhite bathers. However, if you are a female nonwhite, you can enter a white beach if you are accompanied by a white infant who is under your care.

* * *

Tax-supported swimming pools are another public facility which have long been reserved for whites only, both in and out of the segregated territory.

In St. Louis, Missouri, young whites beat up Negroes when an attempt was made on June 21, 1949, to open the pool on a nondiscriminatory basis.

In York, Pennsylvania, the City Council kept the municipal pool closed for two years rather than admit Negroes, and in 1949 finally sold it to a private operator who would be free to discriminate.

In New York City, extra-legal exclusion is accomplished in public pools on the upper East Side by Italians, who through terrorism force Puerto Ricans as well as Negroes to swim in the polluted East River.

You Can't Worship Together

Racial segregation is at its peak throughout the U.S.A. every Sunday at 11 a.m., the hour when millions of Americans congregate to worship the God who "hath made of one blood all nations of men" and the Christ who "is our peace, who hath made both one and hath broken down the middle wall of partition between us."

Before the abolition of Negro chattel slavery in the U.S.A., Negro slaves were sometimes admitted to a "reserved" section or gallery of white churches.

This practice varied with the individual slave-owner, there being a difference of opinion as to whether the teachings of Christianity would promote submissiveness or rebellion.

The National Council of Churches has reported that over 90 per cent of Negro churchgoers are affiliated with all-Negro denominations. Of the 5 per cent who belong to *interracial denominations*, 95 per cent attend racially *separate churches*.

The number of white churches in the segregated territory which will admit Negro worshippers may be counted upon the fingers of one hand.

The exception to this rule comes when the Negro janitor of a white church dies after long years of faithful service, whereupon the funeral service may be conducted in the white church, with white and Negro mourners carefully segregated.

* * *

The Civil War-wrought breach between the Southern and Northern branches of the Protestant denominations has not been narrowed in recent years, despite all proposals and plans for re-union. Militant declarations by the Northern branches, such as the dedication of the Presbyterians in 1948 to an "unsegregated church in an unsegregated society," have scarcely been published in the South.

That same year the National Council of Churches adopted by a large majority a recommendation that all of its affiliated denominations abolish separate churches for whites and Negroes; but even after a decade this resolution had not had any noticeable effect upon church segregation in the South.

The World Council of Churches, meeting in Chicago in 1950, condemned racial prejudice as anti-Christian, but refrained from going on record against racial segregation inside churches or out.

Outside the South, some progress toward desegregation in worship has been made in a few spots. For instance, when in 1957 the neighbourhood surrounding the Normandie Avenue Methodist Church in Los Angeles had become 60 per cent Negro, the Bishop sent in a Negro pastor, Nelson Higgins, Jr., whereupon the lily-white congregation quit in a body.

"I have no objection to the new minister, except that he's black," said John Henry Seal, a laundryman.

Pastor Higgins stuck to his post, however, and eventually drew a mixed congregation to him.

Generally speaking, you will find that Protestant denominations in the segregated territory make few apologies for practising racial exclusiveness. Many, in fact, are inclined to quote the Scriptures in justification, asserting that all nonwhite races are under a curse visited by God upon the "sons and daughters of Ham."

Stetson Kennedy, *Jim Crow Guide to the U.S.A.*, Chapter 13, (London, 1959), 190–98.

The Dictates of Racist Etiquette

In many sections of the U.S.A. the ordinary rules of etiquette do not apply when you are dealing with persons of another race.

In such circumstances you are supposed to forget what you have been taught is proper behaviour in human relations—much of it is altogether taboo in interracial relations.

* * *

But on the whole, regional variations in interracial etiquette conform more or less to the institutionalized forms of racial segregation in the area. The dictates of the etiquette are therefore most stringent in the territory long segregated by law, diminishing progressively in the border areas and relatively free territory.

* * *

Thou Shalt Not Sup Together

One of the most stringent commandments of the interracial etiquette is that you shall not partake of food with a person of the other race.

Should some sort of emergency arise in which it appears necessary to eat with the other race, the etiquette requires that everything possible be done to indicate that it is not being done on a basis of equality. Wherever possible you are supposed to sit at separate tables, preferably with some article of furniture between the tables to further symbolize the segregation. Whites are supposed to be served first.

Here's how one group lived up to the etiquette under difficult circumstances. Four Southern white fishermen, together with a nonwhite man whom they had hired to row their boat, found themselves in the middle of a lake at lunchtime. Before partaking of food they required the nonwhite to sit in the bow of the boat, and laid a fishing pole laterally across the boat to segregate him from them.

There are precious few situations in which the bar against co-racial eating is lowered in the segregated territory.

However, if you are a nonwhite nursemaid and wish to consume an ice-cream cone or soda pop along with the white child in your custody, you are permitted by the etiquette to do so, provided you take the refreshment with you—that is, you cannot sit at a table, use utensils, or have a drink of water (except in a paper cup).

If you are male, you are free under the etiquette to drink intoxicating liquors with males of the other race. In formulating this etiquette, the whites have swallowed their pride in this instance in order to swallow nonwhites' liquor.

However, if a white man should offer you a drink, he will hardly expect you to drink from the bottle after the manner of his white fellow workers, but rather to find a receptacle of some kind. On the other hand, should you offer a white man a drink from your bottle, he may drink from it if there is no receptacle at hand, and rationalize his behaviour by assuming that the alcohol will sterilize the germs which nonwhites are supposed to monopolize.

In either situation, if a new, unopened bottle of liquor is involved, the etiquette recommends that all white men be allowed to drink from it first, before the remains are passed around among nonwhites.

As for smoking, if you are male you may also feel free to indulge with males of the other race.

But if you are female, you are not thus privileged. Under the *mores* of the segregated territory, white women would still regard it as highly presumptuous if a nonwhite woman were to drink or smoke in their presence. However, it is permissible to partake of snuff in the presence of white women.

Warning: If you are a nonwhite male, you are not under any circumstances supposed to offer to light a cigarette for a white female in segregated territory (this is regarded as an intimate gesture reserved for white males only).

Sex Can Be Dangerous

If you are a white man, good interracial etiquette requires only that you be discreet in having sexual relations with a nonwhite woman.

In segregated territory, it is imperative that the relationship, if more than casual, be no more than concubinage. Such relationships continue quite common, and many are common knowledge in the community. It is often possible to indulge in such a relationship, and yet retain the respect of the white community.

* * *

Interracial etiquette's sanction of sexual intercourse between white men and nonwhite women extends also to children born of such intercourse, so that in many Southern communities the white father can contribute more or less openly to their support.

On the other hand, sexual intercourse between white women and nonwhite men may not even be discussed in white circles. The mere idea of any degree of mutuality or reciprocity in such relationships is ruled out as unthinkable by the white community. Consequently, whenever such a case comes to light, it is automatically interpreted as rape.

* * *

How to Avoid White Women

If you are a nonwhite man, your very life may depend upon your ability to keep a safe distance from white women in segregated territory.

Generally speaking, it can be dangerous to get within arm's reach of one.

In fact, the farther you stay away from them, the safer you will be.

This is most true of the segregated territory, but you will find it hazardous to associate with white women anywhere in the U.S.A.

You need not harbour any amorous intentions to get into serious trouble. For instance, Eugene Talmadge (later Governor of Georgia) once publicly flogged a Negro chauffeur for eating candy out of the same paper bag with his Northern white woman employer while driving through Georgia. Others have been lynched for allegedly winking or whistling at white women (hence, you may want to avoid whistling, or blinking in any manner that might be construed as a wink, in the presence of a white woman).

Any unnecessary physical contact may also prove fatal, including accidental bumping. Even if you are employed as a chauffeur you are not supposed to offer physical assistance to a white woman to alight from an automobile, unless she is infirm.

* * *

It is even dangerous to approach a white man's house to ask for a drink of water; white housewives have been known to scream hysterically at the unexpected sight of a nonwhite man, with dire consequences for the latter.

There are special risks associated with being alone with a white woman. Offers of affection from a white woman are often subject to sudden retraction. Should the relationship be discovered by white persons, the odds are very great that she would accuse you of rape in order to save her own face. The perils of such relationships are so great that many nonwhite men in the segregated territory are inclined to give white women, especially those who wax amorous, the widest possible berth.

Love is no excuse for making love with someone of the other race. In fact, it is the worst possible excuse in the eyes of the white community.

* * *

Hand-Shaking Is Taboo

Under no circumstances does interracial etiquette permit you to shake hands with a person of the other race anywhere in segregated territory.

This taboo is primarily designed to prevent nonwhite men from coming into physical contact with white women; but you will find it applies almost as rigorously to hand-shaking between men.

* * *

The importance attached to this taboo against hand-shaking is illustrated by an event which took place at Columbus, Georgia. Three teen-age Negro boys, Robert Ford, Matthew Brown, and Ernest Chester, were kidnapped at gunpoint on the city's streets by five white men. After being driven to a secluded spot, the boys were asked whether the white speakers who had appeared at the Negro high school during Brotherhood Week had shaken hands with the school's Negro Principal. When the boys insisted they didn't know, they were stripped naked, severely flogged, and forced to run for their lives while the men took pot-shots at their heels.

* * *

How to Address the Other Race

Compulsory modes of address are another traditional means whereby interracial etiquette seeks to achieve its purpose of maintaining a master-servant relationship between the white and Negro races in the segregated territory.

Reduced to essentials, here's what the etiquette of interracial address requires:

1. If you are white, *never* say "Mr.," "Mrs.," "sir," or "ma'am" to nonwhites, but always call them by their first names.

2. If you are nonwhite, *always* say "Mr.," "Mrs.," "sir," or "ma'am" to whites, and never call them by their first names.

The forms of interracial address carry over to references to third persons. For example, if you are nonwhite, whites will insist that you refer to other whites as "Mr." or "Mrs." Conversely, if in a conversation with whites you refer to other nonwhites, you are expected to do so by their first names, or, at most, by calling them "Brother Smith" or "Sister Jones."

Should you, in a conversation with a white, refer to a nonwhite as "Mr.," the white person is likely to say: "Who? I never heard of him." Should you persist in the same form of address, the white is likely to say eventually, "Oh, you mean that nigger, Sam Smith. Why didn't you say so?"

If you are a nonwhite house-servant, even though you may have suckled, bathed, and fed the children of your white employer since their birth, you will be expected to address them as "Mr. Bob" or "Miss Jean" just as soon as they reach puberty.

When you as a nonwhite have occasion in segregated territory to address a white man whose name is unknown to you, you are expected to call him "Bossman," "Captain," or some other title of respect.

The plural form, to be used in addressing more than one white, is "white-folks."

If you spend any length of time in segregated territory you will undoubtedly learn how it sounds to be addressed as "nigger." The most you can hope for by way of respectful public address from most white persons in this region is to be called by your last name rather than by your first.

Regardless of your age, class, distinction, or education, you are apt to frequently be called "boy" or "girl." However, if your hair is actually grey you are more likely to be called "uncle" or "auntie." If you maintain a professional-class appearance, you are likely to be called "Doctor," "Professor," or "Parson," regardless of your real profession. Such titles are approved by the interracial etiquette as "salutations without prejudice."

The sanctions and taboos governing interracial address apply with full force to telephone conversations, although, of course, there is the difficulty of ascertaining the race of the person to whom you are speaking. The spread of public education with its effect upon dialect is intensifying this problem. It is expected, therefore, if you are employed as a maid in segregated territory, that in answering your employer's telephone you will hasten to say "sir" or "ma'am" so that the caller will know to speak to you as a nonwhite. Should you neglect to do this, you will find that many callers will ask, "Is this the maid?" before proceeding with the conversation.

The interracial etiquette has also evolved a formula whereby whites, in telephoning nonwhites, can avoid saying "Mr." or "Mrs." For example:

"Hello. . . . Is this the residence of James Smith, the coloured doctor? . . . Well, I want to speak to his wife."

If you are nonwhite you may also come up against the etiquette in placing long-distance telephone calls inside the segregated territory; operators have been known to refuse to handle calls for nonwhites if they insist upon identifying themselves as "Mr." or "Mrs."

You are also expected to abide by the etiquette in conducting written correspondence with persons of the other race. If you are white and have occasion to write a nonwhite, etiquette prescribes that you omit "Mr." or "Mrs." in addressing the letter, and refrain from saying "Dear" in the salutation, but simply begin "John" or "Mary."

You will find that newspapers in the segregated territory scrupulously observe the usages of interracial address. For instance, when the celebrated contralto Miss Marian Anderson visited the region, some papers referred to her as "Anderson," while others simply said "Marian."

* * *

You Can't Say That

There are a few simple rules nonwhites are supposed to observe in conversing with whites:
  1. Never assert or even intimate that a white person may be lying.
  2. Never impute dishonourable intentions to a white person.
  3. Never suggest that the white is of an inferior class.
  4. Never lay claim to, or overtly demonstrate, superior knowledge intelligence.
  5. Never curse a white person.
  6. Never laugh derisively at a white person.
  7. Never comment upon the physical attractiveness of a white person of the opposite sex.

* * *

How to Talk Back and Live

If you are nonwhite there are not many ways whereby you, acting as an individual, can talk back to whites in the segregated territory and live.

* * *

The whole principle of reciprocity in human relationships—for example, "If he curses me, I'll curse him"—is ruled out if you are a nonwhite and the other person is white.

If you have a grievance you feel obliged to voice directly to the responsible person, the acceptable method is to do it in the form of a non-belligerent question, such as, "Do you think that's the right way to treat anybody?"

* * *

The traditional form of protest which nonwhites have found to be acceptable to the whites of the segregated territory is song. Complaints and petitions which would never be tolerated in prose form are not only condoned, but are sometimes laughed at and even given some consideration when put to song.

Here are some samples:

Slave-Gang

White man kill muscogee duck;
Give the nigger the bones to suck.
A cold cup of coffee and the meat's mighty fat;
White folks growl if we eats much of that.
White man in the dinin'-room, eatin' cake and cream;
Nigger in the kitchen, eatin' them greasy greens.
A aught's a aught, a figger's a figger—
All for the white man, and none for the nigger.

* * *

Work-Gang

Some of these days
   (About twelve o'clock)
This old world
   Am gonna reel and rock.
Me and my buddies
   And maybe two-three more
Gonna raise hell
   Around the payhouse door.

* * *

When Not to Wear Your Hat

If you are a nonwhite man in segregated territory you are required to remove your hat while talking with white persons, regardless of their sex. If you fail to remove your hat in talking with a white man, you will be told to do so; if the party to whom you are speaking is a white woman, some white man may knock off your hat.

* * *

Some nonwhites have, however, evolved certain evasive tactics in connection with this custom:

1. If they see the white person coming soon enough, they can remove the hat before he reaches them, thus avoiding the significance of the gesture.

2. If a white person engages a nonwhite in conversation unexpectedly, the nonwhite can remove his hat and wipe his brow, as though motivated solely by the heat.

3. A nonwhite man can refrain from wearing a hat.

Inside segregated territory there are a number of places where whites may keep their hats on, while nonwhites are expected to remove theirs. This includes hotel lobbies, office buildings, and the like.

Outside segregated territory many elevators now display signs urging men to keep their hats on to save space. Not so in segregated territory, however. The reason for this rigidity in elevator etiquette lies not in the tradition of Southern courtesy, but rather in the conviction that nonwhites must be required to remove their hats in the presence of whites, no matter what the extenuating circumstances.

* * *

Racial Etiquette on the Road

There was a time—before many nonwhites owned automobiles of their own—when the rules of the road were applied equally to them, it being assumed that the vehicles they drove were owned by whites.

But as soon as nonwhites began to acquire cars (often at great sacrifice, to escape segregation in public transportation), white motorists began to insist upon a right-of-way based on whiteness.

Of course the rules of the road as set forth in the traffic regulations of the states and communities of the U.S.A. ostensibly apply to all motorists equally, regardless of race. But, in segregated territory especially, you will often find that traffic laws are superceded by interracial etiquette when the motorists involved are of different race.

* * *

If the other motorist or pedestrian is white, he may claim right-of-way regardless of any traffic regulations to the contrary; and if you fail to grant him right-of-way, you may have to suffer the consequences.

* * *

You are most likely to get into trouble at intersections, while seeking to make a left turn. Although the laws of most states say that you are supposed to signal and then complete the turn after the *first* oncoming car has cleared the intersection, many white motorists will run right over that law, and you too if you fail to wait until *all* oncoming whites have passed. The theory here is that it is intolerable for a nonwhite to deliberately delay a white.

The guiding principle of interracial etiquette, on the road as elsewhere, is "Whites first."

So real is this that nonwhites all over the segregated territory tell the story of the nonwhite driver who, upon being haled into traffic court for driving through a red light, explained to the judge that he had seen white folks going ahead on the green light, and naturally assumed that the red light meant it was time for nonwhites to go.

* * *

Keep Moving

On the sidewalk as on the road, interracial etiquette is all-pervasive.

If you are a white pedestrian, the etiquette requires nonwhite motorists waiting at an intersection for a green light to give you all the time you care to take in getting out of the street after the light changes.

But on the other hand, if you are a nonwhite pedestrian, you had better leap for the kerb the instant waiting white motorists get even a yellow caution light indicating that the signal is changing to green. Making nonwhite pedestrians leap for their lives is a favourite sport of many Southern white motorists.

* * *

Where to Shop

If you are nonwhite you will find that many business establishments, both inside and outside the segregated territory, will not welcome you as a customer.

Department, clothing, and millinery stores are especially inclined to cater to white only, or to nonwhites grudgingly if at all.

A prominent Jewish woman residing in New Orleans was mistakenly thought to be a Negro by a clerk in one of the city's large department stores, and so was denied the right to try on a hat. The woman sued and collected substantial damages.

Due to the reluctance of nonwhites to trade where they are not wanted, a thriving business of catering to them in stores in nonwhite neighbourhoods has developed. Some of the whites who operate these stores are wont to save face by explaining, "Their money will spend too, won't it?" These merchants are also inclined to charge exorbitant prices for inferior merchandise.

If you prefer to take your chances in the big uptown stores of the South and border territories, you may:

1. Be ejected.
2. Be insulted.
3. Be served only after all whites have been served.
4. Be intercepted by a shopwalker whose job it is to direct all nonwhites to basement counters.
5. Be denied the privilege of trying on clothes.
6. Be required to try on clothing in the privacy of your own home.
7. Be required to put on a cloth skullcap before trying on millinery.

* * *

Alarum and Excursion

It goes without saying—the author's tongue-in-cheek having more than once slipped and betrayed his indignation—that this has been a mock guide, couched in the jargon of tourism, simply to point out the Way of White Supremacy in all its ugliness. And so wherever it says "you should," of course you should not; for racism is the obverse of morality.

Some may say this book presents a one-sided picture. And so it does.

An entire literature harping upon the other side already exists. To be sure, great progress has been made—but by reaction too. The author confesses to being not so impressed by what has been done as he is oppressed by all that remains to be done. Hence this book.

* * *

Some may say I have been over-critical of America, but it is precisely because I love my country so much that I want her to live up to the best that is in her.

Some may even say I lack faith in America, while in fact the book is a testimonial to the infinite faith of countless Americans (this one included) and their determination to translate that faith into ever more finite forms.

Of course, the Klan says I am "White outside, black inside"; when in truth I am not at all white in their sense of the word. And yet it is as an ostensibly-white Southerner and American that I say racism hurts my people too. Prejudice has ever blighted its subject even more than its object. Egoism, no less than altruism, bids us abjure the doctrine of white supremacy.

* * *

No doubt about it: we Americans have a rocky road to travel before we can enter into the promised land of liberty and justice for all.

Behind Little Rock there stands a Stone Mountain of prejudice. And yet a faith like ours can move any mountain.

What happened to that republic which our forefathers conceived in liberty and dedicated to the proposition that all men are created equal? What has that new birth of freedom envisioned by Lincoln at Gettysburg been waiting for?

That noble heritage, which ought to be ours by birthright, has been denied us by mean men of little faith but much greediness, who will leave us, if we let them, an America cast in their own image.

It is now evident that if we wish to reclaim our birthright for ourselves, for our children, and our children's children, we have got to fight for it once more.

The time has passed—if indeed it ever existed—for compromising with those who would compromise the American ideal.

In the days, months, and years immediately ahead, the danger of regionwide race rioting against Negroes—of mass massacres of innocent men, women, and children—is real and imminent.

In this situation we must prevail upon our Government to serve notice that the law of the land is going to be inexorably enforced against all transgressors, whether they be high or low, few or many.

If we fail in this, we may not be able to avoid the ultimate national tragedy and disgrace of race war.

Even if we succeed, it is not enough. The order of our day must be: Popular escorts where possible; military escorts where necessary!

The call here is for decent white Southerners to step into the breach and do their manifest duty.

More, the call is for Negro Southerners to seek out those white Southerners who are in the habit of mouthing that word "brotherhood"—churchfolk, trade unionists, Masons, Rotarians, Boy Scouts. Corner them in their cloisters! Shake them by the collar! Shout out, loud enough for all the world to hear, that the hour has struck for them to put up or shut up for evermore!

For unless we Southerners, white and Negro, get together and go arm-in-arm to the schools, polls, parks, buses, and every place else we have an equal right to go, the day will go to those who thirst for our blood in the streets.

As the Negro miner said to his coal-blackened white brothers-in-the-union, "If we're ever going to get anywhere, we've got to get there together!"

Stetson Kennedy, *Jim Crow Guide to the U.S.A.*, Chapter 14 (London, 1959), 203–30.

Robert Williams

Excerpt from *The Crusader* (August 15, 1959)

Born in 1925 into a family that remembered African American voting and resistance to the imposition of Jim Crow, Robert Williams was a straight-shooting spokesman for black civil rights in mid-twentieth century America. After serving in World War II, Williams returned to the small town of Monroe, North Carolina, determined to organize the flagging local branch of the NAACP and to resist white violence and oppression. The achievement of the first goal magnified the controversy stirred by Williams's remarks concerning the second. After an all-white jury acquitted a local white man accused of assaulting and attempting to rape a pregnant black woman in 1959, Williams declared that black southerners "cannot rely on the law" and that it was time to "meet violence with violence." With school desegregation on the horizon and Klan violence on the rise, Williams's call for armed self-defense was both practical and provocative. Repudiated by the national NAACP, Williams continued to organize local protests against Jim Crow. In 1961, persecuted by the FBI, Williams fled the United States for Cuba. He and his wife Mabel broadcast a news and music radio program, "Radio Free Dixie," from Havana ("where integration is an ac-complished fact") and published The Crusader, *a weekly newsletter. Habit-ually at odds with the mainstream civil rights organizations (he debated the merits of nonviolence with Martin Luther King, Jr., at the 1959 NAACP na-tional conference), Williams's writings on African American armed self-reliance were influential with the coming generation of black power leaders.*

Much is being said on the subject of violence across the nation to-day. The way self righteous eyebrows are being lifted at the mention of the word, one would think that violence is something new under the sun. Why is violence in self defense so unthinkable by white moderates, liberals and Negro parrots of white gradualist. Knowl-edge begotten of history proves that physical resistance to brutality, oppression and tyranny is the most powerful weapon in the arsenal of liberation. Civil strife is the one manifestation of social ills that governments cannot afford to look upon with indifference.

A society where constituted government pleads for oppressed factions of the populace to be patient and forego human rights that are tantamount to human dignity, for the sake of domestic tran-quility, is a society of hypocrites, moral weaklings and prostitutes of the rights of man. When law fails in its duty to protect the citizen, what other course is there left but for the citizen to protect himself. Violence is as old as mankind itself. [T]his nation was founded on the proposition of violence. Violence immortalized such places as Valley Forge, Lexington and Concord.

If the Negro musters enough courage to fight back against his vi-olent oppressors in America, the day will be hastened when he will be free and respected. A great many submissive Negroes maintain that to fight back violently offers an excuse for the white suprem[ac]ist to exterminate the colored race. Did anyone ever hear of people as filled with blind hate as the racist ever needing an excuse to exterminate a race? Chauvinist[s] are very prolific in for-mulating excuses to justify genocide and pogr[o]ms. Hitler is an ex-ample of how far these racists will go. When Hitler's tyranny threatened the world, especially the white world, we did not hear very much about how immoral it is to meet violence with violence. If passive resistance is as powerful as it is claimed to be, why did not

the armies of the Allies resort to non-violence instead of violent resistance? Even the Christian Church was willing to "Praise The
Lord and Pass The Ammunition," and by so doing we all stayed
free.

The white supremacist is overjoyed at the thought that the
Negro is willing to be killed in a cringing, submissive manner. Our
government will do nothing to protect us, so long as we show a willingness to die without troubling our murderers. Other races of men
are willing to resist their oppressors to the death. What is so special
about the Negro that he thinks he is too precious to die for anything
as noble as a just cause? Negroes shudder from the thought of a
righteous death delivered by a white man a hundred times more
than death at the hands of another Negro over some trifle. It is foolish to think of the American white man wiping out 20 million of
their fellowmen. A man cannot wipe out what is a part of him without exterminating himself. Deathe is no more than death whet[h]er
delivered by Negro or white. The struggle for Negro liberation is
certainly going to cost some blood. The question is whether the Negro is willing to pay on a long drawn installment plan or a lump
sum. A lump sum cash payment will seem expensive, but will be
cheaper in the long run because the carrying charge will be absent.

The white liberals and moderates of today sit like self appointed
Gods having the divine authority of saying how long and how
much freedom during gradual periods of transition the Negro
should have. They offer to help us so long as we allow them to dictate the methods and the means to be used. Their advice revolves
around stock phrases of long suffering patience and gradualism. If
they had to daily suffer the indignities and pain of the Negro's oppression, I wonder how patient they would be?

They say we should wait for a change in the hearts of the good
Christian, southern gentlemen? Why is it that these same people
advocate armies instead of a long patient wait for a change in the
hearts of the leaders of the Communist World? Those who pretend
to be shocked by the possibility of the Negro fighting back are not
half as shocked by the brutal conditions that force the Negro to
even consider fighting back. I have no desire to kill or be killed at
home nor abroad, by a Russian, a Negro or a white Christian gentleman—nay not even by God, but I can for[e]see times when this

type of violence may become necessary in a society where constituted law and moral conscience falters. A government encourages anarchy when it recoils from the responsibility of equally dispensing justice.

Robert F. Williams Papers (Bentley Historical Library, University of Michigan, Ann Arbor), microfilm reel 10.

Julian Mayfield

Challenge to Negro Leadership: The Case of Robert Williams (April 1961)

Pacifist Bayard Rustin, a chief interpreter of Gandhian nonviolence for American civil rights leaders, once noted that "protest becomes effective to the extent that it elicits brutality and oppression from the power structure." The 1961 Freedom Rides illustrated Rustin's point beautifully. Orchestrated by the Congress of Racial Equality (CORE) to challenge segregation in interstate travel, which the Supreme Court ruled unconstitutional in 1960, the Freedom Riders were first assaulted in South Carolina and then famously mauled in Anniston, Alabama. Those riders and those who came after, are credited with having forced the hand of the Kennedy administration, which until 1961 had kept its distance from the civil rights movement. Robert Williams's challenge to the NAACP, and his stand on armed self-reliance, occurred in this highly charged atmosphere of competition for leadership in the movement and disputation over how and when to meet white violence.

There is one, and only one, issue in the Robert Williams case. That single issue is: Shall the National Association for the Advancement of Colored People endorse the advocacy by a local NAACP officer of stopping "lynching with lynching" or "meeting violence with violence"?

—from *The Single Issue*, a pamphlet distributed at the NAACP national convention in New York, July 1959.

For some time now it has been apparent that the traditional leadership of the American Negro community—a leadership which has been largely middle class in origin and orientation—is in danger of losing its claim to speak for the masses of Negroes. This group is being challenged by the pressure of events to produce more substantial and immediate results in the field of civil rights or renounce the position it has long held. The dramatic Tuskegee and Montgomery boycotts, the rash of student sit-ins—none was inspired by the National Association for the Advancement of Colored People, the Urban League, or the established Negro church denominations, but it is to their credit that they hurriedly gave the boycotts and sit-ins their blessing and, as with the NAACP, much needed financial help. They were thereby able to present a united front to their common enemy, the system of white supremacy.

But the challenge to middle-class Negro leaders—including the newer type like Martin Luther King—remains. It is inherent in the rapid growth of the militant, white-hating Muslim movement among working-class Negroes. It can be heard in the conversations of black intellectuals and students from the South who regard the efforts of the NAACP, the Urban League, and most religious and civic leaders with either disdain or despair, in the belief that they are doing too little, too timidly and too late.

Probably nothing more clearly illustrates this challenge, however, than the case of *Wilkins vs. Williams*. Robert F. Williams is the president of the Union County, North Carolina, branch of the NAACP. *Wilkins vs. Williams* was a hearing before the board of directors of the NAACP in New York City, which grew out of three criminal cases that were disposed of in one day by the Superior Court in Monroe, the seat of Union County.

Before this court on May 5, 1959, stood James Mobley, B. F. Shaw, and Louis Medlin. Mobley, a mentally retarded colored man, was charged with assault with intent to commit rape on a white woman. (He admitted he had caught her wrist during an argument.) Shaw, a white man, was charged with assault on a Negro chambermaid who claimed he had kicked her down a flight of stairs in the hotel where she worked. The case of the other white defendant, Medlin, was the most inflammatory. He was accused of having entered the home of a Negro woman, eight months pregnant, of attempting to rape her, and, when she resisted and tried to flee across a field, of brutally assaulting her and her six-year-old son. A white woman neighbor had witnessed the assault and summoned the police.

The Union County branch of the NAACP is the only one of its kind now in existence. Its members and supporters, who are mostly workers and displaced farmers, constitute a well-armed and disciplined fighting unit. Union County Negroes have had more than their share of ugly race relations, and by 1959, their experience—which we shall examine in detail later—had taught them to rely on their own resources in their dealings with the white community. After Medlin was arrested, their first impulse was to mount an assault against the Monroe jail, seize the prisoner, and kill him. It was Robert Williams who restrained them. He pointed out that murdering Medlin would place them in the position of the white men who, shortly before, had dragged Mack Charles Parker from a jail in Poplarville, Mississippi, and lynched him. Besides, Williams argued, so much national and international attention was focused on Monroe that the judge and juries would be forced to punish the white men.

But Williams was wrong. Impervious to world opinion, the court freed both Shaw and Medlin, and committed the mentally retarded Negro to prison for two years. (Only the last-minute discovery by his attorney of a technicality, which reduced the charge from rape to assault, prevented the judge from handing down a thirty-year sentence.) On the steps of the courthouse, Williams issued an angry statement to a UPI reporter:

> We cannot take these people who do us injustice to the court and it becomes necessary to punish them ourselves. In the future we are going to have to try and convict them on the spot. We cannot rely on the law. We can get no justice under the present system. If we feel that injustice is done, we must right then and there, on the spot, be prepared to inflict punishment on the people.

> Since the federal government will not bring a halt to lynching in the South, and since the so-called courts lynch our people legally, if it's necessary to stop lynching with lynching, then we must be willing to resort to that method.

Roy Wilkins, executive secretary of the NAACP, called Williams from New York to ask about the statement. Williams confirmed it

as his and said he intended to repeat it that afternoon for several radio and television stations eager to interview him. He would make
it clear, he assured Wilkins, that he was not speaking for the
NAACP but for himself, though he would stress that his views represented the prevailing feeling of the colored people in Union
County. Wilkins replied that it would be virtually impossible for the
general public to separate Williams's statement from the policies of
the NAACP since he would be identified as an officer of the organization. Williams then made his scheduled appearances, and the
next day, May 7, Wilkins sent a telegram directing him to suspend
his activities as a local officer pending consideration of his status at
a meeting of the Association's board of directors. Williams answered that he would attend the meeting with counsel.

Thus the stage was set for a contest between a highly respected
leader of a distinguished national organization and a relatively unknown young Southerner capable of issuing rash statements on the
steps of a courthouse. *Wilkins vs. Williams* aroused heated discussions in nearly every Negro community in the country, but it was
obvious from the beginning that Williams was bound to lose. At a
closed hearing in June, before the Committee on Branches,
Williams, represented by Conrad Lynn, a veteran civil-rights attorney, asserted that his statement had been made under emotional
duress, and that he had not meant to imply that Negroes should exercise anything more than their legal right to self-defense and the
right to come to the defense of another party against criminal attack. The committee upheld the action of its executive secretary
and suspended Williams for six months. A few weeks later, the delegates to the Association's fiftieth annual convention voted 764 to
14 against Williams and in favor of suspension.

The one-sided vote should have settled the matter, with Williams
returning to obscurity. But the questions raised by *Wilkins vs.
Williams* are profound, and still far from settled. A close examination of relevant documents and newspaper files, and interviews
with some of the principals involved, leads one to conclude that the
real issue was never raised, and that Williams was slapped on the
wrist for having stated publicly what many of his fellow Negroes,
even those on the board of directors of the NAACP, felt but did not

think it politic to express. Indeed, a statement issued by Roy Wilkins on May 6, 1959, deploring Williams's statement might well have been written by Williams himself.

> At the same time it must be recognized that the mood of Negro citizens from one end of the nation to the other is one of bitterness and anger over the lynching [of Mack Parker] in Poplarville, Miss., April 25, and over numerous instances of injustice meted out to Negroes by the courts in certain sections of the South. They see Negroes lynched or sentenced to death for the same crimes for which white defendants are given suspended sentences or set free. They are no longer willing to accept this double standard of justice.

If Negroes were no longer willing to accept the double standard of justice, *what were they to do about it?* Wilkins did not say, but one paragraph in the brief Williams submitted to the Committee on Branches provides the answer which he has been expounding ever since and which daily finds wider and wider acceptance:

> He [Williams] believes the message of armed self-reliance should be spread among Negroes of the South. He is convinced that a somnolent national government will only take action when it is made aware that individual Negroes are no longer facing the mobs in isolation but are acquiring the habit of coming to the aid of their menaced brothers.

But this was precisely the position which the NAACP could not publicly support. The organization was already being subjected to constant harassment by the Southern states. And to have advocated Williams's position would have exposed the NAACP to widespread criticism from many of the people who now warmly support it, those who, for the most part, prefer the legalistic or pacifist approach to American race relations. Moreover, the possible resulting violence could have shaken the nation to its very foundation, and caused it intense embarrassment in the conduct of its diplomacy with a largely non-white world. But the situation in the South that provoked Williams's statement and the ensuing controversy remains unchanged. The NAACP's rejection of Williams's position only postponed the crisis facing Negro leadership; it did not eliminate it.

* * *

One evening I asked Williams a question I thought he might not answer. What truth was there in the rumor that had been circulated during the NAACP convention that his men were not only armed (in the South, after all, a surprisingly large number of people keep guns) but that they were in fact a small army, drilled and disciplined, with access to an arsenal?

He laughed. "Hell, man, that's no secret, and I don't know why it should frighten the board of directors of the NAACP. Everybody in Monroe knows what we have, that we know how to use it, and that we are willing to use it. The Mayor and the Chief of Police know, and so does the Klan. Come to Monroe when you get back to the States and see for yourself." This was the same kind of invitation that had taken me to Cuba and two months later I was in Monroe, North Carolina.

Some Southern towns are lovely, with great old houses that slumber on broad streets beneath spreading, ancient trees. In such towns even a Negro writer on a hurried visit can perceive that, although *his* ancestors only supplied the labor under the ante-bellum system of caste and privilege, at least there was a comprehensive society in which everyone had a place; and, dimly, he can understand why the Southern aristocracy fought so desperately to retain the cruel and dehumanizing system that was slavery. Here, at least, social relations had a symmetry wherein the dark, ugly things were hidden away, in the slave quarter or on the backstairs of the big house.

But Monroe is not such a town. It is ugly. There is little distinction in the architecture of its finest houses; and although it is built on hills, there is a dreary flatness about it. Worse, it is a composite town. Unpainted one-room Negro shacks, which rent for an inflated ten dollars a month, sit within a stone's throw of the tiny, neat, unimaginative bungalows of the white middle class. One can drive three blocks in any direction and see the graphic reality of race relations in Union County. The Northern visitor, keenly aware that violence always simmers beneath the seeming tranquility, wonders that anybody, black or white, would want to fight over this place.

In the days of the steam engine Monroe was a prosperous railroad maintenance town. A generation ago Robert Williams's father, along with a significant number of Monroe's colored men, serviced the trains and earned a steady living at it. They bought their own homes in the colored section called Newtown, sent their children to the colored school most of the year, and saw in their youngsters the hope of a better future. If they were not a genuine middle class, they were better off than the tenant farmers and sharecroppers in the county's rural population. But the Diesel engine supplanted steam, and the depression and mechanization displaced most of the tenant farmers and sharecroppers; and, though Monroe did not die, it was left severely crippled.

By the time Williams had grown to adolescence, unemployment was a chronic problem in Newtown. He served a hitch in the army, somehow squeezed in three years of college at West Virginia State and Johnson C. Smith College in nearby Charlotte, and then enlisted in the Marine Corps for a tour of duty. On returning to Monroe, he entered the lists of the letters-to-the-editor columns of the Charlotte newspapers and seems to have spent most of his time incensing the local whites by debunking their notions of white supremacy. During this period he married Miss Mable Robinson, a sturdy, tall, attractive woman with whom he has had two children. He worked at his trade of machinist while he wrote his provocative letters to the newspapers. It is possible that no one outside of North Carolina would ever have heard of Williams if the Supreme Court had not ordered school desegregation in 1954.

It is still difficult to imagine the impact of the Court's decision on small Southern towns. Intercourse between the races—that is, social intercourse during the Southern day which, as James Baldwin has pointed out, is quite different from the guilt-ridden, integrated Southern night—was the function of the local white officials and businessmen, and colored ministers and other self-appointed spokesmen who purported to represent the views of their fellow Negroes. White lawyers in Monroe often defended Negroes who were in trouble (not too vigorously, to be sure) and were paid by the NAACP chapter. There was an understanding, a working relationship, between the whites who ran the town and the colored ministers. The whites would try to control their extremists, and in return, the black men of God helped to keep the black population in its place.

But suddenly, one Monday in 1954, a long held tradition was struck a death-blow. The NAACP, which had never claimed to be anything but a moderate organization, became the ogre of the Southland. Acknowledged membership in it could mean the loss of job, credit, and physical security. Negro doctors, lawyers, undertakers—whoever had to be licensed by the state—promptly withdrew from membership. When the Union County chapter was apparently in its last throes (with only six members), Robert Williams was drafted for the presidency. ("You're the only fool left," said one of those who urged him to accept the position.) Somewhat innocently, Williams set about trying to recruit members among the respectable middle class, and, needless to say, he failed absolutely. In desperation he turned to the lower class of the Negro community. He likes to tell of the day he walked into a pool parlor and asked if anyone there wanted to join the NAACP. The players looked at him in astonishment: "Man, do you mean *we* can belong to that organization?" From that time on, Williams has had as many members as he could manage, sometimes more. He says of that period, "I made an important discovery. The woman earning ten, fifteen dollars a week as a domestic, the sharecropper, the ditch-digger—they were more loyal to the NAACP than the Negroes who were much better off. They would stick under pressure, probably because they had less to lose and we were the only fighting organization they had."

As the Union County branch of the NAACP grew, so did the Ku Klux Klan, which had renewed its activity soon after the Supreme Court decision. Most of the Klan's wrath was directed against Dr. A. E. Perry, one of the six who had remained in the chapter when Williams assumed leadership. The popular young physician, who was fairly prosperous, had built an attractive, ranch-style home overlooking a new highway. The Klan considered the house an affront, and it believed that Perry contributed large sums of money to the NAACP chapter. It publicly announced its intention of running him out of the county.

"When we heard over the radio," Williams says, "that a Klan meeting had drawn 8,000 people, we figured it was time to take a stand. You see, there are only 13,000 people in the county." (Klansmen from surrounding counties were swelling the attendance.) The colored men of Monroe armed themselves with the heaviest weapons available, and set up an alarm system that would summon them instantly to the scene of any trouble. A regular night guard was established around Dr. Perry's home. Trenches were dug, Molotov cocktails prepared, and gas masks and helmets were distributed. At one point during this troubled period the police attempted to seize the weapons, but desisted when Williams and Perry threatened a law suit. (Nothing in the laws of North Carolina and of most Southern states restricts or contravenes the constitutional right "to keep and bear arms, and be secure in one's person.")

A Klan motorcade, sixty cars strong, invaded Newtown on the evening of October 5, 1957. As was their custom, the robed Klansmen fired at the homes of the Negroes as they drove past. Near Dr. Perry's home they were confronted with the sustained fire of several scores of men who had been instructed by Williams not to injure anyone if it could be helped. At the first sign of resistance the Klan motorcade dissolved into chaos. Panicky Klansmen fled in every direction, some of them wrecking their automobiles. There have been no Klan motorcades in Monroe since.*

It is interesting to speculate on why this significant event received so little publicity. Monroe Chief of Police Mauney admitted to the Associated Press the next day that there had been a motorcade—he knew because it had included several police cars—but he denied that there had been an exchange of gunfire. Williams invited the press to Newtown to view the bullet-scarred houses and the wrecked automobiles whose owners did not care to come to claim them. Nevertheless, few people outside the state knew that the clash had taken place, and that the Klan had sustained a decisive defeat. Compare this with the nationwide news coverage and wide applause given the Indians in nearby Lumberton County, when they routed a Klan meeting with gunfire a few weeks later. About this Williams says, "It's as if they were afraid to let other Negroes know what we have done here. We have proved that a hooded man who thinks a white life is superior to a black life is not so ready to

---

*Dr. Perry has been driven out of Union County. The county's leading Catholic layman, he was arrested in 1958 and indicted on charges of performing an abortion on a white woman. Sole evidence submitted against him was her uncorroborated statement. He was convicted, sent to prison, and barred from Union County. Denied the right to practice medicine, he now works as an assistant to an undertaker in Durham.

risk his white life when a black man stands up to him." He recalls proudly that in Monroe they have had their sit-ins and wade-ins, but none of their boys and girls has been the victim of violence from racist hoodlums. "They know, don't you see, that we are not passive resisters."

The morale of the Negroes in Union County is high. They carry themselves with a dignity I have seen in no other Southern community. Largely vanished are the slouching posture, the scratching of head, and the indirect, mumbled speech that used to characterize the Negro male in the presence of whites. It is as if, in facing up to their enemies, they have finally confronted a terrible reality and found it not so terrible after all.

But they have had to pay a price for their new self-respect! Paternalism has been destroyed in Union County. The leftover food that the colored maid could once carry home is now consigned instead to the garbage pail, and the old clothes that found their way to the colored section are now either sold or burned. The intimate communication that used to pass from mistress to maid, master to workman (seldom in the reverse direction) has largely disappeared. Negroes suspected of belonging to the NAACP are told "Let Williams feed you!" and "Let Williams find you a place to live!" as they are fired from their jobs and evicted from their homes. Northern owners of the new factories, by agreement with the city fathers, hire no Negroes but import white workers from Charlotte, twenty-five miles away. It would almost appear that the rulers of Monroe society had determined to strengthen the Union County NAACP and Williams's influence on the colored community; and, in fact, that is what they have done.

But what role is Williams likely to play in the future? Although he has shown great personal courage and demonstrated effective leadership ability in Monroe, he can claim no large following outside his own county. True, he has a scattering of fervent supporters in the United States, Europe, and Latin America, who subscribe to *The Crusader*, the weekly newsletter in which he flays not only white supremacists but Negro moderates who accommodate themselves to the system. But he is in danger of being driven out of Monroe where his standard of living is close to penury. (No one will employ him in any capacity in Union or nearby counties.) Certainly the present national leadership of the NAACP does not fear that Williams will undermine their position in the near future. The organization is still the most effective civil rights force in the country, and few of its members have shown any inclination to abandon it.

But sooner than anyone now supposes, three factors may create a social climate in the South in which a Robert Williams will play a leading role. They are the growing militancy of Negro students; the intransigence of the Southern white oligarchy; and the depressed Negro working class and peasantry. The students and the white ruling groups of the South are locked in a struggle that has greater ramifications than perhaps even they realize. At stake is not whether a black child shall sit beside a white child in a schoolroom or at a lunch counter; it is not even whether a black *boy* sits beside a white *girl* and one day marries her. At stake is the very existence of the Southern oligarchy, its entrenched power and traditional privileges which rest on a non-democratic political system and an economy based on a plentiful supply of cheap, unorganized labor. Ultimately the struggle in the South will determine who will represent the states and the Congressional districts in Washington, who will sit in the legislatures, the city halls, and the courts, who will operate the industries and the arable land. As the real issue becomes more apparent, two developments seem certain. First, those who now wield power will refuse to yield beyond a minimum of token desegregation and will retaliate, often violently and in defiance of federal law; and second, the students will abandon the technique of passive resistance as it proves ineffectual in seriously disturbing the power structure of Southern society.

The most decisive factor in the conflict will probably be the Negro laboring class, heretofore unheard from. These are the great masses of the unskilled, who belong to no labor unions or civic organizations, whose churches are more concerned with leading their flocks to heaven than to a fuller share of democracy on earth, whose only fraternity is that of the millions of neglected and untrained who have nothing to barter in the labor market but their willingness to work. Only yesterday the man of this class could pick the cotton, run the elevator, pack the crate, but now the machine can do it better and displaces him. Government statistics hardly suggest how great his number is, much less what he is feeling and thinking, but we know he is everywhere. (The industrialization programs of the South almost always exclude him. Fourteen per cent of the black labor force is now unemployed as opposed to 7 per cent for the nation as a whole.) A casual walk through any colored section of a Southern town or city will reveal him, standing on the corner, lounging near the bar, slouched on the doorstep, staring into the uncertainty that is his future. The "they" in his life, those who make decisions that vitally affect him, are not only the governments, federal, state, and local, the captains of industry and finance, but even the Negro middle class and the striking students, all of whom seem to be going someplace without him. It is not *his* children that all of the school desegregation furor is about; he is lucky if he can keep them in the colored school. No one can presently claim to speak for this man, not church, union, nor NAACP; and just as he does not yet clearly understand the social forces arrayed against him, neither do *they* understand *him* or the various stimuli to which he is likely to respond.

Predictions are risky at best, but it seems safe to say that as these forces come into sharper conflict in what is essentially an attempt to overthrow an entrenched political and economic power, the Negro leadership class will be faced with a crisis, for its purely legalistic (or passive resistance) approach will clearly not be able to control the dynamics of the Negro struggle. Then to the fore may come Robert Williams, and other young men and women like him, who have concluded that the only way to win a revolution is to be a revolutionary.

Commentary, April 1961

President Lyndon B. Johnson

To Fulfill These Rights (June 4, 1965)

Texan Lyndon Baines Johnson became America's thirty-sixth president when President John F. Kennedy was assassinated on November 22, 1963. Elected in his own right in 1964 by the largest popular majority in American history,

Johnson was perfectly situated to address social and political issues that had pre-occupied him since he entered Congress during the New Deal. In a commencement speech at the University of Michigan in May 1964, Johnson announced an ambitious plan to create a "Great Society," in which poverty and racial injustice would be eradicated. The Democrat-dominated 89th Congress passed important civil rights legislation, including the Civil Rights Act of 1964 and the Voting Rights Act of 1965. Congress also followed the president's lead by funneling huge sums of money into education, health care, and programs created to serve the nation's poorest citizens. Although many Americans benefited from Great Society programs, the effectiveness of these programs was limited almost from the first by the war in Vietnam, which became more costly in monetary as well as human terms with each passing year. In 1965, however, prospects were bright. The speech reprinted here, given at a Howard University commencement, paid homage to the 1947 report of the Presidential Commission on Civil Rights, "To Secure These Rights." In it, Johnson links human and civil rights and suggests that there is a role for government as well as individuals to play in achieving both.

Dr. Nabrit, my fellow Americans:

I am delighted at the chance to speak at this important and this historic institution. Howard has long been an outstanding center for the education of Negro Americans. Its students are of every race and color and they come from many countries of the world. It is truly a working example of democratic excellence.

Our earth is the home of revolution. In every corner of every continent men charged with hope contend with ancient ways in the pursuit of justice. They reach for the newest of weapons to realize the oldest of dreams, that each may walk in freedom and pride, stretching his talents, enjoying the fruits of the earth.

Our enemies may occasionally seize the day of change, but it is the banner of our revolution they take. And our own future is linked to this process of swift and turbulent change in many lands in the world. But nothing in any country touches us more profoundly, and nothing is more freighted with meaning for our own destiny than the revolution of the Negro American.

In far too many ways American Negroes have been another nation: deprived of freedom, crippled by hatred, the doors of opportunity closed to hope.

In our time change has come to this Nation, too. The American Negro, acting with impressive restraint, has peacefully protested and marched, entered the courtrooms and the seats of government, demanding a justice that has long been denied. The voice of the Negro was the call to action. But it is a tribute to America that, once aroused, the courts and the Congress, the President and most of the people, have been the allies of progress.

Legal Protection for Human Rights

Thus we have seen the high court of the country declare that discrimination based on race was repugnant to the Constitution, and therefore void. We have seen in 1957, and 1960, and again in 1964, the first civil rights legislation in this Nation in almost an entire century.

As majority leader of the United States Senate, I helped to guide two of these bills through the Senate. And, as your President, I was proud to sign the third. And now very soon we will have the fourth—a new law guaranteeing every American the right to vote.

No act of my entire administration will give me greater satisfaction than the day when my signature makes this bill, too, the law of this land.

The voting rights bill will be the latest, and among the most important, in a long series of victories. But this victory—as Winston Churchill said of another triumph for freedom—"is not the end. It is not even the beginning of the end. But it is, perhaps, the end of the beginning."

That beginning is freedom; and the barriers to that freedom are tumbling down. Freedom is the right to share, share fully and equally, in American society—to vote, to hold a job, to enter a public place, to go to school. It is the right to be treated in every part of our national life as a person equal in dignity and promise to all others.

Freedom Is Not Enough

But freedom is not enough. You do not wipe away the scars of centuries by saying: Now you are free to go where you want, and do as you desire, and choose the leaders you please.

You do not take a person who, for years, has been hobbled by chains and liberate him, bring him up to the starting line of a race and then say, "you are free to compete with all the others," and still justly believe that you have been completely fair.

Thus it is not enough just to open the gates of opportunity. All our citizens must have the ability to walk through those gates.

This is the next and the more profound stage of the battle for civil rights. We seek not just freedom but opportunity. We seek not just legal equity but human ability, not just equality as a right and a theory but equality as a fact and equality as a result.

For the task is to give 20 million Negroes the same chance as every other American to learn and grow, to work and share in society, to develop their abilities—physical, mental and spiritual, and to pursue their individual happiness.

To this end equal opportunity is essential, but not enough, not enough. Men and women of all races are born with the same range of abilities. But ability is not just the product of birth. Ability is stretched or stunted by the family that you live with, and the neighborhood you live in—by the school you go to and the poverty or the richness of your surroundings. It is the product of a hundred unseen forces playing upon the little infant, the child, and finally the man.

Progress for Some

This graduating class at Howard University is witness to the indomitable determination of the Negro American to win his way in American life.

The number of Negroes in schools of higher learning has almost doubled in 15 years. The number of nonwhite professional workers has more than doubled in 10 years. The median income of Negro college women tonight exceeds that of white college women. And there are also the enormous accomplishments of distinguished individual Negroes—many of them graduates of this institution, and one of them the first lady ambassador in the history of the United States.

These are proud and impressive achievements. But they tell only the story of a growing middle class minority, steadily narrowing the gap between them and their white counterparts.

A Widening Gulf

But for the great majority of Negro Americans—the poor, the unemployed, the uprooted, and the dispossessed—there is a much grimmer story. They still, as we meet here tonight, are another nation. Despite the court orders and the laws, despite the legislative victories and the speeches, for them the walls are rising and the gulf is widening.

Here are some of the facts of this American failure.

Thirty-five years ago the rate of unemployment for Negroes and whites was about the same. Tonight the Negro rate is twice as high.

In 1948 the 8 percent unemployment rate for Negro teenage boys was actually less than that of whites. By last year that rate had grown to 23 percent, as against 13 percent for whites unemployed.

Between 1949 and 1959, the income of Negro men relative to white men declined in every section of this country. From 1952 to 1963 the median income of Negro families compared to white actually dropped from 57 percent to 53 percent.

In the years 1955 through 1957, 22 percent of experienced Negro workers were out of work at some time during the year. In 1961 through 1963 that proportion had soared to 29 percent.

Since 1947 the number of white families living in poverty has decreased 27 percent while the number of poorer nonwhite families decreased only 3 percent.

The infant mortality of nonwhites in 1940 was 70 percent greater than whites. Twenty-two years later it was 90 percent greater.

Moreover, the isolation of Negro from white communities is increasing, rather than decreasing as Negroes crowd into the central cities and become a city within a city.

Of course Negro Americans as well as white Americans have shared in our rising national abundance. But the harsh fact of the matter is that in the battle for true equality too many—far too many—are losing ground every day.

The Causes of Inequality

We are not completely sure why this is. We know the causes are complex and subtle. But we do know the two broad basic reasons. And we do know that we have to act.

First, Negroes are trapped—as many whites are trapped—in inherited, gateless poverty. They lack training and skills. They are shut in, in slums, without decent medical care. Private and public poverty combine to cripple their capacities.

We are trying to attack these evils through our poverty program, through our education program, through our medical care and our other health programs, and a dozen more of the Great Society programs that are aimed at the root causes of this poverty.

We will increase, and we will accelerate, and we will broaden this attack in years to come until this most enduring of foes finally yields to our unyielding will.

But there is a second cause—much more difficult to explain, more deeply grounded, more desperate in its force. It is the devastating heritage of long years of slavery; and a century of oppression, hatred, and injustice.

Special Nature of Negro Poverty

For Negro poverty is not white poverty. Many of its causes and many of its cures are the same. But there are differences—deep, corrosive, obstinate differences—radiating painful roots into the community, and into the family, and the nature of the individual.

These differences are not racial differences. They are solely and simply the consequence of ancient brutality, past injustice, and present prejudice. They are anguishing to observe. For the Negro they are a constant reminder of oppression. For the white they are a constant reminder of guilt. But they must be faced and they must be dealt with and they must be overcome, if we are ever to reach the time when the only difference between Negroes and whites is the color of their skin.

Nor can we find a complete answer in the experience of other American minorities. They made a valiant and a largely successful effort to emerge from poverty and prejudice.

The Negro, like these others, will have to rely mostly upon his own efforts. But he just cannot do it alone. For they did not have the heritage of centuries to overcome, and they did not have a cultural tradition which had been twisted and battered by endless years of hatred and hopelessness, nor were they excluded—these others—because of race or color—a feeling whose dark intensity is matched by no other prejudice in our society.

Nor can these differences be understood as isolated infirmities. They are a seamless web. They cause each other. They result from each other. They reinforce each other.

Much of the Negro community is buried under a blanket of history and circumstance. It is not a lasting solution to lift just one corner of that blanket. We must stand on all sides and we must raise the entire cover if we are to liberate our fellow citizens.

The Roots of Injustice

One of the differences is the increased concentration of Negroes in our cities. More than 73 percent of all Negroes live in urban areas compared with less than 70 percent of the whites. Most of these Negroes live in slums. Most of these Negroes live together—a separated people.

Men are shaped by their world. When it is a world of decay, ringed by an invisible wall, when escape is arduous and uncertain, and the saving pressures of a more hopeful society are unknown, it can cripple the youth and it can desolate the men.

There is also the burden that a dark skin can add to the search for a productive place in our society. Unemployment strikes most swiftly and broadly at the Negro, and this burden erodes hope. Blighted hope breeds despair. Despair brings indifferences to the learning which offers a way out. And despair, coupled with indifferences, is often the source of destructive rebellion against the fabric of society.

There is also the lacerating hurt of early collision with white hatred or prejudice, distaste or condescension. Other groups have felt similar intolerance. But success and achievement could wipe it away. They do not change the color of a man's skin. I have seen this uncomprehending pain in the eyes of the little, young Mexican-American schoolchildren that I taught many years ago. But it can be overcome. But, for many, the wounds are always open.

Family Breakdown

Perhaps most important—its influence radiating to every part of life—is the breakdown of the Negro family structure. For this, most of all, white America must accept responsibility. It flows from centuries of oppression and persecution of the Negro man. It flows from the long years of degradation and discrimination, which have attacked his dignity and assaulted his ability to produce for his family.

This, too, is not pleasant to look upon. But it must be faced by those whose serious intent is to improve the life of all Americans.

Only a minority—less than half—of all Negro children reach the age of 18 having lived all their lives with both of their parents. At this moment, tonight, little less than two-thirds are at home with both of their parents. Probably a majority of all Negro children receive federally-aided public assistance sometime during their childhood.

The family is the cornerstone of our society. More than any other force it shapes the attitude, the hopes, the ambitions, and the values of the child. And when the family collapses it is the children that are usually damaged. When it happens on a massive scale the community itself is crippled.

So, unless we work to strengthen the family, to create conditions under which most parents will stay together—all the rest: schools, and playgrounds, and public assistance, and private concern, will never be enough to cut completely the circle of despair and deprivation.

To Fulfill These Rights

There is no single easy answer to all of these problems.

Jobs are part of the answer. They bring the income which permits a man to provide for his family.

Decent homes in decent surroundings and a chance to learn—an equal chance to learn—are part of the answer.

Welfare and social programs better designed to hold families together are part of the answer.

Care for the sick is part of the answer.

An understanding heart by all Americans is another big part of the answer.

And to all of these fronts—and a dozen more—I will dedicate the expanding efforts of the Johnson administration.

But there are other answers that are still to be found. Nor do we fully understand even all of the problems. Therefore, I want to announce tonight that this fall I intend to call a White House conference of scholars, and experts, and outstanding Negro leaders—men of both races—and officials of Government at every level.

This White House conference's theme and title will be "To Fulfill These Rights."

Its object will be to help the American Negro fulfill the rights which, after the long time of injustice, he is finally about to secure.

To move beyond opportunity to achievement.

To shatter forever not only the barriers of law and public practice, but the walls which bound the condition of many by the color of his skin.

To dissolve, as best we can, the antique enmities of the heart which diminish the holder, divide the great democracy, and do wrong—great wrong—to the children of God.

And I pledge you tonight that this will be a chief goal of my administration, and of my program next year, and in the years to come. And I hope, and I pray, and I believe, it will be a part of the program of all America.

What Is Justice?

For what is justice?

It is to fulfill the fair expectations of man.

Thus, American justice is a very special thing. For, from the first, this has been a land of towering expectations. It was to be a nation where each man could be ruled by the common consent of all—enshrined in law, given life by institutions, guided by men themselves subject to its rule. And all—all of every station and origin—would be touched equally in obligation and in liberty.

Beyond the law lay the land. It was a rich land, glowing with more abundant promise than man had ever seen. Here, unlike any place yet known, all were to share the harvest.

And beyond this was the dignity of man. Each could become whatever his qualities of mind and spirit would permit—to strive, to seek, and, if he could, to find his happiness.

This is American justice. We have pursued it faithfully to the edge of our imperfections, and we have failed to find it for the American Negro.

So, it is the glorious opportunity of this generation to end the one huge wrong of the American Nation and, in so doing, to find America for ourselves, with the same immense thrill of discovery which gripped those who first began to realize that here, at last, was a home for freedom.

All it will take is for all of us to understand what this country is and what this country must become.

The Scripture promises: "I shall light a candle of understanding in thine heart, which shall not be put out."

Together, and with millions more, we can light that candle of understanding in the heart of all America.

And, once lit, it will never again go out.

Commencement address at Howard University, June 4, 1965. In Ira Katznelson, *When Affirmative Action Was White* (New York, 2006), 173–81.

Calvin C. Hernton

And You, Too, Sidney Poitier! (1966)

Trained in sociology at Talladega College and Fisk University, Calvin Hernton was an author and professor, most notably at Oberlin College, where he was writer-in-residence for over thirty years. Although he identified primarily as a poet, Hernton was best known for his nonfiction books, especially Sex and Racism in America *(1965), which laid bare the racist sexual assumptions of blacks as well as whites and argued for freedom of marriage as a basic right in a democratic society. Here, Hernton comments on the disinclination of Hollywood to create complicated and sexually aware African American characters, and on the complicity of black writers and actors in this two-dimensional portrayal.*

I remember the first time I went to the movies, or as they called it in those days, the "picture show." One Friday my stepfather and my mother took my younger brother and me down the main street in the Negro section of Chattanooga, Tennessee, past pawnshops and liquor stores, poolrooms and beer joints, past hordes of swarthy Negroes leaning on corners and thronging the littered pavement, to where a long line of colored folks stood outside a great crumbling structure with neon signs flashing on and off. In-side, on the screen, a young beautiful woman, dressed in the most elegant gown, who looked like she was not of the colored race, sang "tick-a-tock-tick-a-tock." Another young woman, very brown and somehow motherly looking, cried and sang softly as she hugged a man's shirt while it hung drying on the washline. A very handsome light-skinned man with long straight black hair, wearing a very loose-fitting suit, pranced and glided across the screen while his hair flopped about his head and face, singing "hi-di-hi-di-ho!"

I learned later that one woman was Lena Horne, the other, Ethel Waters, and the man, the indomitable and flamboyant Cab Cal-loway. They were Negro personalities that down-South colored folks could be and indeed were proud of. It was all so thrilling. But, somehow, some way, even as a child who knew nothing about act-ing, I felt that something was lacking in their performance. Despite their great singing and dancing and cooing, and definitely despite their prettiness, they did not strike me as being as *real* in what they were doing as, say, the Negroes I had passed that evening on the street. Although I had enjoyed what I had seen, I was left a little confused.

From that time on I made a point of seeing films in which there were Negroes. Eventually I learned the names of the more promi-nent film personalities: Ralph Cooper, Herb Jeffries, Mantan Moreland, Stepin Fetchit, Canada Lee, Juan Hernandez, Roch-ester, Bo-jangles, Noble Sissle, and the rest. All of them entertained me greatly. In fact, that's all most of them were, entertainers. By this I mean they were either clowns and buffoons with big rolling eyes and invariably afraid of haunted houses, or they were maids and butlers and musicians and singers and tap dancers and band leaders. The few who did not conform to the above stereotypes were poor mimics of white gangsters (Ralph Cooper) and white cowboys (Herb Jeffries); or they struck me as "foreign" black men with strange accents (Hernandez and Lee) who had never lived in America, at least not in the America I knew.

By this time I was fully aware of what had perplexed me as a small boy that day my mother had taken me to see *Stormy Weather*. There had been too much artificiality. It was the absence of the *re-ality* of Negroes as men and the absence of the *reality* of Negroes as *dramatic* individuals, as I knew them to be in everyday life. In too many instances, it was the negation of the Negro's very humanity in terms of the authentic portrayal of his personality as an entire integrity rather than a fractionary dysfunction. The integrated complexity of the Negro's personality never came to bear upon any one or a variety of situations. Only singular aspects of the Negro—his dancing, or musical, comic, religious, bellicose, or sly character-istics, to name a few—were portrayed, as if they represented the whole of his emotional wellspring.

The first film I saw in which the Negro did not appear as a com-plete- or semi-caricature was *Home of the Brave*, starring James Ed-wards. At that time the name of James Edwards was unknown and until his appearance I had begun to grow fearful that perhaps Ne-groes really did lack the capacity for dramatic portrayal. It was as if they had a deep psychological block, stemming from their racial ex-periences, that prevented them from performing as straight human beings rather than as mere entertainers. But my fear was dispelled or at least mitigated when I saw James Edwards play the role of a Negro soldier in foreign combat who not only became a hero be-cause of his bravery against the enemy, but who also showed manly prowess in regard to the prejudice of his white comrades. James Edwards was not the best actor I had dreamed of. He was a little too stiff and somewhat slow on cues. Yet he played a proud role in which not merely one but many aspects of his personality (as a *hu-man being* who was a Negro) came through. To me this was a defi-nite sign that Negroes were not necessarily inferior performers. It gave me hope that one day, if Negroes fought diligently, America would have to let black men appear on the screen like bonafide ac-tors with complete integrity regarding their humanity and the es-sential realism of the situations they might portray.

As is evident now, my hope was not without some degree of re-alization. There is at least one Negro who has pounced on the American screen and, like a jet, has soared to fame and stardom. What is important here is that Sidney Poitier is not an entertainer, not a singer or a comedian or a musician. Rather, he is strictly an *actor*.

When I first saw him on the screen I was shocked, dumbfounded and delighted. I believe it was around 1955, and Poitier starred in a television drama called *A Man Is Ten Feet Tall*. The story was about a Negro dock worker, a foreman as a matter of fact, who befriends a timid and very insecure white worker against the brutes and roughnecks of the dock, and especially against the southern-born, racist head foreman. The head foreman, of course, hates Poitier because of his color. Moreover, he hates him for his manly attitude in that Poitier does not play the usual role of "Uncle Tom." Envying the friendship between Poitier and the timid white worker, the head foreman proceeds to take out his venom on the white worker whom Poitier defends, ultimately, by way of a hook duel in which the foreman unfairly kills Poitier. In the end the timid worker gains courage and avenges Poitier's death first by beating the foreman, and then by breaking the "silent code" of the docks and literally dragging the murderer to the authorities. The play was later made into a movie entitled *Edge of the City*.

Since that movie Poitier has played, always with great skill and dignity, a variety of starring roles, so that he has become, by all standards, one of America's best actors. His winning of the Academy Award indubitably marked a historic occasion in the annals of Hollywood. What is important about all this is not so much that a Negro has finally won an Academy Award—not this alone; rather, it is the fact that Hollywood and the general public (both white and black) have accepted the *kind* of Negro that Poitier characteristically portrays on the screen. First of all, he is *all* Negro. He is black, his features are markedly Negroid, his body is long and regal, his hands are large and dexterous, his hair is rather "nappy," and he has thick, agile lips. In combination these features make Poitier an unusually powerful figure on the screen. Secondly, his style of acting has involved the entire range of Negro behavior and personality characteristics vehicled by what is known as the "method" technique. Invariably, his role interpretations are rugged, bold, and without the slightest suggestion of "Uncle Tomism," which is to say that everything about his projections definitely lets one know Poitier is authentically Negro. He is no caricature, no stereotyped colored man acting out one or several fractionalized aspects of the Negro personality which whites usually demand of black actors.

* * *

I have stated that the thing that troubled me about most Negroes in movies was that they, for all of their entertainment value, never seemed real in what they were doing in comparison to the way they are in actual life. I said, something was missing. Sidney Poitier does seem, at first scrutiny, very much real. Yet, when one probes deeply into all the films in which he has played, for every coefficient of Negro life as that life is lived in the real world, one discovers something frightening and terrible. There is something systematically missing, the absence of which turns Poitier, no matter how brilliantly he performs, into a caricature of the Negro that is as artificial and dehumanizing, if not more so, as all the other Hollywood vulgar negations of the black man as a complex, integral human being.

I am talking about the absence, in *all* the Poitier movies, of the primeval emotion, and of that deep psyche-physical yearning to mate with the opposite sex. Why can't Sidney Poitier, since he is such a superb actor, make love in the movies?

No amount of argument can convince me that Poitier is incapable of effectively portraying an amorous involvement on the screen. Neither is it reasonable to say that Poitier is the wrong "type" to make love in the movies. After all, as I have pointed out, Poitier and Paul Newman are the same type of actors, and Newman makes love on the screen constantly. Newman is white. And now we are getting close to the problem—Poitier's blackness, his "Negroness."

The fact that Poitier cannot or does not make love in the movies is a manifestation of American racism as it relates to the sexuality of the Negro. Elsewhere I have written that by and large white America conceives of the Negro as sexually vulgar and repulsive; to see a Negro kiss or pet on the screen would send large numbers of white people, throughout the United States, cringing and recoiling in prurient disgust or excitement. It would be too much for the sexual insecurity and anxiety that the majority of American whites have, not only about the Negro, but about themselves as well. Therefore, the black man in mass media, the cinema especially, must be desexed. And by desexing the Negro, America is denying him his manhood, which ultimately means the negation of his very humanity. This is precisely what Hollywood has done and is doing to, ironically (or is it quite naturally?), the only Negro who has won an Academy Award.

Sidney Poitier and Paul Newman, along with Diahann Carroll and Joanne Woodward, were the stars in a movie called *Paris Blues*. As the story goes, Poitier and Newman are jazz musicians in Paris. One night, after their performance they meet a couple of girls outside the supper club. The two couples confront each other and Diahann Carroll, the colored girl, seems to be fascinated by Paul Newman. For a quick moment it appears as if the foursome is going to pair off interracially. Suddenly Miss Carroll, as if something snaps in her or, better yet, as if on cue from the director, rejects Newman and comes on to her black brother, Poitier.

While there are numerous scenes showing Newman and Miss Woodward hugging, petting, kissing, and even lying around in bed together, there are "equivalent" scenes of Poitier and Miss Carroll walking around Paris, stopping here and there, taking in the sights, and *discussing the race problem*. At one "high" point Poitier *actually* gets a chance to touch Miss Carroll's hand. That's all, brother, that's all.

What is so false and artificial about the entire story is that Poitier, a jazz musician, gets involved, no, gets *associated* with a middle-class, nice-nice, sexually rigid Negro woman who is hung-up about living up to some kind of "race pride." And she convinces Poitier to come back "home" and be a "shining knight" for his people. What a joke! Everybody knows, and I do mean everybody, including Hollywood and the NAACP, that no jazz musician is *that* "nice." There are plenty of Negro women like the one portrayed by Miss Carroll, but you will seldom, if ever, find a jazz musician giving one of them a second thought. Yet I know, we all know, why the pairing-off did not happen interracially. It probably would have caused a riot on Broadway and a slaughter in Alabama. In essence, by denying Poitier the right to make love with either of the women, Hollywood endeavored to play up to the fears of white America, on the one hand, and make the Negro "presentable" to black people, on the other. On both accounts they succeeded only in telling the public a lie. And, incidentally, the movie was the lousiest Poitier film I have seen.

In *The Long Ships* Poitier plays a dashing Moorish prince with not only a beautiful wife but an entire pavilion of pretty girls. He is respected throughout his kingdom. He fights well, and people bow down in his presence. He is the dashing black prince! But for all of that, he is more interested in some golden bell than he is in his most attractive and love-starved wife. In one scene the wife actually begs him and pulls on his arm (nothing else) to stay with her, to give her some of his affection. The black prince stands there rigid like a eunuch; he pushes her aside and runs off looking for gold.

On the other hand, Richard Widmark comes from another land and runs amuck with the women of Poitier's court. Widmark, a white man, ultimately seduces the very wife of the black prince, while the black prince is sitting in a tent talking "intrigue" with Widmark's wife.

All of this is so telling. The sexual stereotypes of black and white are completely reversed: the Negro is "impotent," the white man is "virile." It is not beyond imagination that there might have been some Moorish kings who were homosexuals or "faggots," or what have you. But why did Hollywood have to make such a *point* of this? Why, for instance, did they not put less stress on this aspect, or omit it altogether? I assert that it was no accident. While it may not have been consciously deliberate, it represents a pattern, a systematic attempt to castrate Sidney Poitier in the movies. This signifies, insofar as Poitier in the movies must be a symbolic representation of America's concept of the Negro in general, the outright denial of manhood with reference to all black Americans.

The most "immaculate" version of the desexing of Poitier as an actor is, of course, the role which won him the Academy Award. To me *Lilies of the Field* is a pitiful joke. Picture this—here is a tall, regal, young black man in tight white pants that reveal his every muscle, jumping and running around with a group of nuns. (Incidentally, they are foreigners.) He even shows his naked bulging chest. He is *sexy*, nobody can deny that. One need not belabor the twisted psychological subtleties of this movie. Yet I am compelled to point out that white America can let its imagination run wild, secure in the knowledge that nothing can really happen between that sexy black boy and those white nuns.

* * *

But why talk only about racists and so-called white liberals. Negroes tend to adhere to the same systematic model of desexing themselves in the cinema just as whites do and just as the American public seems bent on demanding. Of course, Negroes who do not adhere to the practice of sterilizing themselves in the visual arts are apt to find that their works will lie around unproduced, or, if produced, will be killed at the box office. But when a few Negroes who have independent means still conform to the same protocol as do the white writers and producers, it means that Negroes have sufficiently internalized the racist concept of, among other things, their sexuality and therefore are ashamed of their nature, and are participating in the denial of one of the bases of their very humanity.

Sidney Poitier does not have the opportunity to act out love emotions even in an all-Negro movie, because, as it were, the Negro author (the late Lorraine Hansberry) of *A Raisin in the Sun* did not choose to emphasize love and tenderness between men and women as vital aspects of Negro life. And where these aspects are brought up in other all-Negro movies, such as in *The Cool World* and *Nothing but a Man*, the treatment of them is so skimpy and glossed over that one gets the impression that if the moviemakers were to treat sexual emotions of and between black people in America in an authentic and human fashion, all hell would break loose. No doubt it would.

To recognize the *human validity* of Negro sexuality is one of the necessary ways of affirming the Negro's essential manhood. This would constitute a tumultuous psychological revolution with ramifications no less significant than the changes resulting from current civil rights activities.

In Calvin C. Hernton, *White Papers for White Americans* (Garden City, NY, 1966), 465–75.

Loving v. Virginia, 388 U.S. 1 (1967)

In the fall of 1963, Mrs. Mildred Jeter Loving wrote a letter to Robert Kennedy, at that time the attorney general of the United States. The letter concerned Mrs. Loving's marital status. Mildred Loving and her husband Richard had grown up down the road from each other in Caroline County, Virginia, during and after World War II. Although this was the age of segregation, neither Richard nor Mildred lived in a black-white world, either physically or imaginatively. Richard's father worked as a truck driver for a wealthy black farmer. Addicted to NASCAR, Richard formed a highly successful integrated drag-racing team. In this context, nobody paid much attention when in 1958 Richard married young Mildred Jeter, who traced her family along a bumpy genealogical road that included ancestors from three continents. Arrested almost immediately, the Lovings relocated to Washington, D.C., where their marriage was recognized at law. Mildred Loving's 1963 letter to the attorney general was passed along to the local branch of the American Civil Liberties Union, which challenged the Lovings' original conviction in 1965 and lost. The lawyers appealed to the Supreme Court, which agreed to hear the case in 1966. This in itself was a significant victory—the Court had been ducking the interracial sex issue since Brown v. Board of Education *had been decided in 1954. On the far side of the civil rights movement in 1967,* Loving v. Virginia *decided the last remaining question of fundamental rights denied by Jim Crow.*

Virginia's statutory scheme to prevent marriages between persons solely on the basis of racial classifications held to violate the Equal Protection and Due Process Clauses of the Fourteenth Amendment. Pp. 4–12.

206 Va. 924, 147 S. E. 2d 78, reversed.

Bernard S. Cohen and Philip J. Hirschkop argued the cause and filed a brief for appellants. Mr. Hirschkop argued pro hac vice, by special leave of Court.

R. D. McIlwaine III, Assistant Attorney General of Virginia, argued the cause for appellee. With him on the brief were Robert Y. Button, Attorney General, and Kenneth C. Patty, Assistant Attorney General.

William M. Marutani, by special leave of Court, argued the cause for the Japanese American Citizens League, as amicus curiae, urging reversal.

Briefs of amici curiae, urging reversal, were filed by William M. Lewers and William B. Ball for the National Catholic Conference for Interracial Justice et al.; [388 U.S. 1, 2] by Robert L. Carter and Andrew D. Weinberger for the National Association for the Advancement of Colored People, and by Jack Greenberg, James M. Nabrit III and Michael Meltsner for the N. A. A. C. P. Legal Defense & Educational Fund, Inc.

T. W. Bruton, Attorney General, and Ralph Moody, Deputy Attorney General, filed a brief for the State of North Carolina, as amicus curiae, urging affirmance.

MR. CHIEF JUSTICE WARREN delivered the opinion of the Court.

This case presents a constitutional question never addressed by this Court: whether a statutory scheme adopted by the State of Virginia to prevent marriages between persons solely on the basis of racial classifications violates the Equal Protection and Due Process Clauses of the Fourteenth Amendment. For reasons which seem to us to reflect the central meaning of those constitutional commands, we conclude that these statutes cannot stand consistently with the Fourteenth Amendment.

In June 1958, two residents of Virginia, Mildred Jeter, a Negro woman, and Richard Loving, a white man, were married in the District of Columbia pursuant to its laws. Shortly after their marriage, the Lovings returned to Virginia and established their marital abode in Caroline County. At the October Term, 1958, of the Circuit Court [388 U.S. 1, 3] of Caroline County, a grand jury issued an indictment charging the Lovings with violating Virginia's ban on interracial marriages. On January 6, 1959, the Lovings pleaded guilty to the charge and were sentenced to one year in jail; however, the trial judge suspended the sentence for a period of 25 years on the condition that the Lovings leave the State and not return to Virginia together for 25 years. He stated in an opinion that:

> "Almighty God created the races white, black, yellow, malay and red, and he placed them on separate continents. And but for the interference with his arrangement there would be no cause for such marriages. The fact that he separated the races shows that he did not intend for the races to mix."

After their convictions, the Lovings took up residence in the District of Columbia. On November 6, 1963, they filed a motion in the state trial court to vacate the judgment and set aside the sentence on the ground that the statutes which they had violated were repugnant to the Fourteenth Amendment. The motion not having been decided by October 28, 1964, the Lovings instituted a class action in the United States District Court for the Eastern District of Virginia requesting that a three-judge court be convened to declare the Virginia antimiscegenation statutes unconstitutional and to enjoin state officials from enforcing their convictions. On January 22, 1965, the state trial judge denied the motion to vacate the sentences, and the Lovings perfected an appeal to the Supreme Court of Appeals of Virginia. On February 11, 1965, the three-judge District Court continued the case to allow the Lovings to present their constitutional claims to the highest state court.

The Supreme Court of Appeals upheld the constitutionality of the antimiscegenation statutes and, after [388 U.S. 1, 4] modifying the sentence, affirmed the convictions. The Lovings appealed this decision, and we noted probable jurisdiction on December 12, 1966, 385 U.S. 986.

* * *

Virginia is now one of 16 States which prohibit and punish marriages on the basis of racial classifications. Penalties for miscegenation arose as an incident to slavery and have been common in Virginia since the colonial period. The present statutory scheme dates from the adoption of the Racial Integrity Act of 1924, passed during the period of extreme nativism which followed the end of the First World War. The central features of this Act, and current Virginia law, are the absolute prohibition of a "white person" marrying other than another "white person," a prohibition against issuing marriage licenses until the issuing official is satisfied that [388 U.S. 1, 7] the applicants' statements as to their race are correct, certificates of "racial composition" to be kept by both local and state registrars, and the carrying forward of earlier prohibitions against racial intermarriage.

I.

In upholding the constitutionality of these provisions in the decision below, the Supreme Court of Appeals of Virginia referred to its 1955 decision in Naim v. Naim, 197 Va. 80, 87 S. E. 2d 749, as stating the reasons supporting the validity of these laws. In Naim, the state court concluded that the State's legitimate purposes were "to preserve the racial integrity of its citizens," and to prevent "the corruption of blood," "a mongrel breed of citizens," and "the obliteration of racial pride," obviously an endorsement of the doctrine of White Supremacy, Id., at 90, 87 S. E. 2d, at 756. The court also reasoned that marriage has traditionally been subject to state regulation without federal intervention, and, consequently, the regulation of marriage should be left to exclusive state control by the Tenth Amendment.

While the state court is no doubt correct in asserting that marriage is a social relation subject to the State's police power, Maynard v. Hill, 125 U.S. 190 (1888), the State does not contend in its argument before this Court that its powers to regulate marriage are unlimited notwithstanding the commands of the Fourteenth Amendment. Nor could it do so in light of Meyer v. Nebraska, 262 U.S. 390 (1923), and Skinner v. Oklahoma, 316 U.S. 535 (1942). Instead, the State argues that the meaning of the Equal Protection Clause, as illuminated by the statements of the Framers, is only that state penal laws containing an interracial element [388 U.S. 1, 8] as part of the definition of the offense must apply equally to whites and Negroes in the sense that members of each race are punished to the same degree. Thus, the State contends that, because its miscegenation statutes punish equally both the white and the Negro participants in an interracial marriage, these statutes, despite their reliance on racial classifications, do not constitute an invidious discrimination based upon race. The second argument advanced by the State assumes the validity of its equal application theory. The argument is that, if the Equal Protection Clause does not outlaw miscegenation statutes because of their reliance on racial classifications, the question of constitutionality would thus become whether there was any rational basis for a State to treat interracial marriages differently from other marriages. On this question, the State argues, the scientific evidence is substantially in doubt and, consequently, this Court should defer to the wisdom of the state legislature in adopting its policy of discouraging interracial marriages.

Because we reject the notion that the mere "equal application" of a statute containing racial classifications is enough to remove the classifications from the Fourteenth Amendment's proscription of all invidious racial discriminations, we do not accept the State's contention that these statutes should be upheld if there is any possible basis for concluding that they serve a rational purpose. The mere fact of equal application does not mean that our analysis of these statutes should follow the approach we have taken in cases involving no racial discrimination where the Equal Protection Clause has been arrayed against a statute discriminating between the kinds of advertising which may be displayed on trucks in New York City, Railway Express Agency, Inc. v. New York, 336 U.S. 106 (1949), or an exemption in Ohio's ad valorem tax for merchandise owned by a nonresident in a storage warehouse, Allied Stores of Ohio, [388 U.S. 1, 9] Inc. v. Bowers, 358 U.S. 522 (1959). In these cases, involving distinctions not drawn according to race, the Court has merely asked whether there is any rational foundation for the discriminations, and has deferred to the wisdom of the state legislatures. In the case at bar, however, we deal with statutes containing racial classifications, and the fact of equal application does not immunize the statute from the very heavy burden of justification which the Fourteenth Amendment has traditionally required of state statutes drawn according to race.

* * *

There can be no question but that Virginia's miscegenation statutes rest solely upon distinctions drawn according to race. The statutes proscribe generally accepted conduct if engaged in by members of different races. Over the years, this Court has consistently repudiated "[d]istinctions between citizens solely because of their ancestry" as being "odious to a free people whose institutions are founded upon the doctrine of equality." Hirabayashi v. United States, 320 U.S. 81, 100 (1943). At the very least, the Equal Protection Clause demands that racial classifications, especially suspect in criminal statutes, be subjected to the "most rigid scrutiny," Korematsu v. United States, 323 U.S. 214, 216 (1944), and, if they are ever to be upheld, they must be shown to be necessary to the accomplishment of some permissible state objective, independent of the racial discrimination which it was the object of the Fourteenth Amendment to eliminate. Indeed, two members of this Court have already stated that they "cannot conceive of a valid legislative purpose . . . which makes the color of a person's skin the test of whether his conduct is a criminal offense." McLaughlin v. Florida, supra, at 198 (STEWART, J., joined by DOUGLAS, J., concurring).

There is patently no legitimate overriding purpose independent of invidious racial discrimination which justifies this classification. The fact that Virginia prohibits only interracial marriages involving white persons demonstrates that the racial classifications must stand on their own justification, as measures designed to maintain White Supremacy. We have consistently denied [388 U.S. 1, 12] the constitutionality of measures which restrict the rights of citizens on account of race. There can be no doubt that restricting the freedom to marry solely because of racial classifications violates the central meaning of the Equal Protection Clause.

II.

These statutes also deprive the Lovings of liberty without due process of law in violation of the Due Process Clause of the Fourteenth Amendment. The freedom to marry has long been recognized as one of the vital personal rights essential to the orderly pursuit of happiness by free men.

Marriage is one of the "basic civil rights of man," fundamental to our very existence and survival. Skinner v. Oklahoma, 316 U.S. 535, 541 (1942). See also Maynard v. Hill, 125 U.S. 190 (1888). To deny this fundamental freedom on so unsupportable a basis as the racial classifications embodied in these statutes, classifications so directly subversive of the principle of equality at the heart of the Fourteenth Amendment, is surely to deprive all the State's citizens of liberty without due process of law. The Fourteenth Amendment requires that the freedom of choice to marry not be restricted by invidious racial discrimiations. Under our Constitution, the freedom to marry, or not marry, a person of another race resides with the individual and cannot be infringed by the State.

These convictions must be reversed.

It is so ordered.

Charles Marsh

Douglas Hudgins: Theologian
of the Closed Society

Most books about the struggle for racial equality emphasize the central role that religion played in bringing down Jim Crow. Historians have noted the deep religious faith of many civil rights leaders and supporters, the influence of religious language and ideals on the movement, and the importance of the religiosity of both black and white southerners in structuring their views in favor of civil rights. A small but growing number of scholars have studied the religious beliefs of those who defended Jim Crow. In this selection from God's Long Summer, *set in Mississippi in 1964, Charles Marsh explains why segregationists thought God was on* their *side of the civil rights struggle, and why white southern churches played such a minor role in the central political struggle of their day.*

* * *

In his 1965 essay, "Mississippi: The Fallen Paradise," the novelist Walker Percy held up "the wacky logic of white supremacy" to critical analysis (the phrase is not Percy's but William Faulkner's). Percy—who was born in Alabama and raised in Greenville, Mississippi, by his uncle William Alexander Percy—reached the conclusion that in the attempt to reconcile increasingly contradictory claims about social life under Jim Crow, segregationists had forged a discourse wherein all assertions became both equally true and equally false, "depending on one's rhetorical posture." Percy explained, "When Senator Eastland declares, 'There is no discrimination in Mississippi,' and 'All who are qualified to vote, black or white, exercise the right of suffrage,' these utterances are received by friend and foe alike with a certain torpor of spirit. It does not matter that there is very little connection between Senator Eastland's utterances and the voting statistics of his home county: that of a population of 31,020 Negroes, 161 are registered to vote." A disconnection is made between language and reality: arguments advanced in support of the status quo create in turn their own logic and credibility. As a result, the prevailing syllogism goes as follows:

"1. There is no ill-feeling in Mississippi between the races; the Negroes like things the way they are; if you don't believe it, I'll call my cook out of the kitchen and you can ask her. 2. The trouble is caused by outside agitators who are Communist-inspired. 3. Therefore, the real issue is between atheistic Communism and patriotic, God-fearing Mississippians." How did it happen, Percy asks, that a fairly decent people has become so completely deluded about itself, "that it is difficult to discuss the issues with them, because the common words of the language no longer carry the same meanings?"

One large piece of the puzzle was indisputably theological. In the sermons and Bible studies delivered zealously from the pulpits and fellowship halls of the white Protestant churches, the disjunction between language and reality gained powerful reenforcement. A certain deracinated piety created a strange, new world (pearly clean and tidy) that resided in but not of the old world (where darkness, difference, and clutter prevailed). No better illustration of the theology that shaped this world can be found than in the career of the state's preeminent Southern Baptist preacher, Douglas Hudgins, who presided over the congregation of First Baptist Church in Jackson from 1946 until his retirement from the ministry in 1969.

First Baptist Church, which occupied an entire city block near the state capital building, was the single most powerful religious institution in Mississippi during the civil rights years. Among its well-known members was Ross Barnett, vociferous supporter of white supremacy as governor of the state from 1960 to 1964 and long-time teacher of the Men's Sunday school class. Barnett had made international headlines in 1962 by arrogantly defying the Justice Department's order that the black student James Meredith be enrolled at Ole Miss. "We will not drink from the cup of genocide," Barnett had proclaimed. Also at First Baptist were Thomas and Robert Hederman. Owners of the two largest newspapers, the militantly segregationist *Clarion Ledger* and *Jackson Daily News*, the Hedermans were the church's leading patrons. Hodding Carter, Jr., the Pulitzer-prize-winning and iconoclastic editor of the *Greenville Delta Democrat-Times*, once described the Hedermans as a homegrown product of Jim Crow racism and Christian fundamentalism. Hodding Carter III, who had written an undergraduate thesis at Princeton on white resistance to civil rights in Mississippi, was even more candid than his father in his assessment. "The Hedermans were to segregation what Joseph Goebbels was to Hitler. They were cheerleaders and chief propagandists, dishonest and racist. They helped shape as well as reflect a philosophy which was, at its core, as undemocratic and immoral as any extant." Not to be overlooked among the church's members was Tom Etheridge, the *Daily News*'s main political columnist and savage interpreter of the civil rights movement to the paper's 100,000 readers.

Doug Hudgins, or "Mister Baptist" as one Jackson columnist called him, took full advantage of his influential pulpit, winning a wide range of civic and political honors: he was chaplain of the Mississippi Highway Safety Patrol, director of the Jackson Chamber of Commerce, member of both the Masonic order and the Chamber of Commerce, and president of the Jackson Rotary Club (in 1961). As the shepherd of First Baptist's highly influential congregation, Hudgins preached a gospel of individual salvation and personal orderliness, construing civil rights activism as not only a defilement of social purity but even more as simply irrelevant to the proclamation of Jesus Christ as God. The cross of Christ, Hudgins explained at the conclusion of a sermon in late 1964, has nothing to do with social movements or realities beyond the church; it's a matter of individual salvation. The congregation at First Baptist knew exactly what Hudgins meant. Had he stated the matter more explicitly, he might have said that the cross has nothing to do with the civil rights of black Mississippians. On the other hand, the cross ought to inspire decent white people toward the preservation of the purity of the social body. And it certainly did.

Douglas Hudgins was the premier theologian of the closed society. He articulated in his sermons, Bible studies, and occasional writings, and embodied in his church leadership, an austere piety that remained impervious to the sufferings of black people, as well as to the repressive tactics of the guardians of orthodoxy, many of whom were lodged in his own congregation. Hudgin's faith contained elements of traditional Southern Baptist theology, anti-modernist fundamentalism, and republican civil religion, but these were put in the service of his distinctive emphasis on personal and spiritual purity. In Hudgin's view, the important matters of faith were discovered in the interior dimensions of the soul's journey to perfection.

He proclaimed in a televised sermon in the early years of the civil rights era, "Now is the time to shift the emphasis from the material to the spiritual." The greatest influence on Hudgins, the Baptist theologian E. Y. Mullins, once wrote, "The Bible places nothing between the individual soul and God." Sadly, the fair-minded Mullins had no way of knowing the various misuses awaiting his peculiar Southern mysticism when he declared a generation earlier: "Soul competency means to me that I find truth when I am furthest removed from the distractions and contingencies of people and things and authorities—again, when truth takes forms which are unique to me and my understanding of the Bible."

An Uncluttered Life

Doug Hudgins was born on May 4, 1905, in Estill Springs, Tennessee, which he once described as "a little wide place in the road, but primevally beautiful." He counted among his forbears the colonial settlers of King and Queen County in Virginia, where his paternal grandfather Henry S. Hudgins was born. Henry Hudgins eventually became one of the pioneer settlers of Tennessee and a planter in the Rock Creek settlement near Tullahoma. Hudgins's father, William Douglas, worked as a merchant, a farmer, and a cattleman until the Baptists established an encampment in Estill Springs in 1908. That was the year he sold his business interests and "surrendered" to full-time religious work with the Sunday School Board and the Baptist Young Person's Union in the Tennessee Baptist convention. His "six-step program" toward establishing a successful Sunday school was frequently cited throughout the state as an effective, brass-bolts strategy for a certain increase in numbers. The elder Hudgins instructed: "1. Find 'em. 2. Fetch 'em. 3. Fix 'em. 4. Fasten 'em. 5. Follow 'em. 6. Finish 'em." Hudgins's mother, Lelia Barrow Hudgins, was the daughter of a Baptist minister in Kentucky, a faithful member of the Women's Missionary Union, and a woman fully committed to raising her two sons in the faith.

The traditional Southern Baptist culture in which Hudgins was raised nurtured a distinctive moral and religious sensibility. In historian Ted Ownby's words, this culture offered a life "without chance or risk . . . where permanent values and moral development held worldly excitements in check." Just as faith's purity required protection from all forms of foreign corruption—including, as the Alabama Baptist newspaper maintained, the "vainglorious scholarship" of "German born vagaries" who were corrupting Holy Scriptures through historical-critical research—so should the body and mind be protected against moral impurity. Even Scripture itself existed as a kind of pure body, thus needing to be guarded with unceasing vigilance. A fierce sectarian self-consciousness shaped domestic and moral etiquette and equally influenced patterns of religious feeling and understanding. In defiance of outside threats to Southern culture, evangelicals placed an almost exclusive emphasis on individual regeneration and the competency of the soul before God. One Southern Baptist pastor of the 1920s noted that "having considered the matter, [he was] convinced that the religion existing among the whites of the South was of a purer form than that existing in the North." The individual soul and body were the proving ground of salvation's efficacy.

Agitation could very likely assume the form of libidinous forces plaguing the self. In the world of Hudgins's Southern Baptist childhood, many preachers blamed contemporary fashions in women's dress for unsettling men's fragile concentration on things spiritual. Reverend John W. Porter, editor of the *American Baptist* and pastor in Kentucky, mourned that "scant dress is usually accompanied by scant morals. . . . If some of the dresses continue the same ratio for the next twenty-five years that they have maintained for the past ten years, they will be exactly fifteen feet above the head." Not surprisingly, motion pictures took an equally hard shot from the Southern Baptist moralists. In 1926, the convention announced its "uncompromising disfavor for the salacious and character-destroying [motion] pictures produced and shown the public." Cinemas invited men and women to enjoy the cool comforts of a darkened room and then bombarded them with "vulgar styles of dress (or undress)" and "the shameless exposure of female nakedness," and with images "utterly putrid, indecent, vulgar, saturated with sex," all the while leaving "an indelible blot upon the minds" of the viewers.

If moving pictures stirred up impure desires, imagine the possibilities of the dancing female body. Southern preachers did, and what they saw was not pretty: "waltz, turkey trot, grizzly bear, bunny hug, buzzard lope and the shimmy, ad nauseam ad infinitum," intoned the Reverend Porter. Not only was dancing simply too much fun, as Ownby surmised, displaying a wild disregard for evangelical values of serenity and introspection, but it exhibited a veritable feast of sexual debauchery. The worries of one Georgia minister were shared by many: "the close relations into which the sexes are thrown are such as to inflame the animal passions to a very high degree." The Southern Baptist Social Service Commission offered the appropriate conclusion to the issue of secular entertainment by declaring that dancing, "accompanied, as it is, by immodest dress, by close physical contact of the sexes, and by its lack of restraint, is undoubtedly doing much to undermine the morals of the young people."

With all this worry about personal purity, it was no wonder that little attention was given to the concrete application of Christian teachings to racial and economic issues. An attempt at a meaningful social analysis published in the Georgia Baptist newspaper illustrates the degree of the difficulty: "The majority of the poor, 'the submerged tenth,' the begrimed masses who swarm in the slums and wretched tenement houses of our large cities, some of whom are also found in the smaller towns and even in the country, are dissipated, vicious, wicked, and immoral. Many reformers of the day teach that, if you improve their surroundings and educate them, you can lift them up. . . . But what these people need is to be made over again. There is but only one power in the world that can do this, and that is the gospel of the Son of God." The Southern Baptist Convention of 1921 resolved that "nothing but the power of the gospel in regeneration of individual men in large numbers can ever make the world safe for the highest happiness and most real peace." As one Baptist minister declared, "The best thing men can do is spread the Bible and to get it read and obeyed. This would be the end of hard times, of poverty, of unemployment, of injustice, or wrong, or war [sic].'" As Hudgins himself preached two decades later, "America's Imperative Need is a soul-stirring, like-changing, God-sent, spirit-filled prayed-down revival of religion." A steady concentration on the soul's regeneration and an attentiveness to the body's concomitant tidiness were enough to concern the righteous man. Everything else was clutter.

Of course, simmering fears of racial contamination heightened white anxieties. The dangers of impurity connected with each other in all sorts of intricate ways. Not only was racial homogeneity necessary in maintaining the clean blue lines of Anglo-Saxon gene pools, it was also ordained by God as part of his design for the created order. The protection of the soul's purity depended, in large part, on the preservation of racial homogeneity. The story of the "curse of Ham" added much-needed theological reinforcement to the more general speculations about God's creation of separate races.

As the story goes, Noah lay in a stupor after a long night of drinking. Ham—Noah's son—saw his father's nakedness. He told his two brothers what he had seen, but Shem and Japheth, unlike Ham, did not look upon his body but instead placed a garment over him. When Noah awoke, he was filled with anger toward Ham and declared of Canaan, the son of Ham, "Cursed be Canaan, a servant of servants shall he be unto his brother." That is the end of the story, an unlikely source indeed for the fantastic racial readings that followed. What actually angered Noah is unclear from the narrative, thin as it is on detail. The most plausible conjecture is that the son committed an act which, in his father's eyes, was regarded as a sexual abomination, a violation of sanctioned sexual etiquette.

Yet by the early 1900s many Southern Baptists had come to read the story as a convincing account of the origin of the black race, condemned to a legacy of perpetual servitude. (Noah's intemperate response to a humiliation of his own doing was never questioned.) In its most bizarre configuration, an additional racist component to the Genesis account was developed to show that blacks and other dark-skinned people were created before Adam and Eve, on the day God created animals. The account claimed that when Eve was tempted in the Garden, Satan did not assume the form of a serpent but that of a "negro gardener." As if this were not enough, theologians further pondered the existence of "pre-Adamite negroes" who inhabited the Land of Nod (where Cain went and fathered children), making the cursed son of Ham the first amalgamationist. Accordingly, the mother of all sins, the sin that brought on the calamitous flood and all things invidious and corrupt, was miscegenation. Mongrelization was the root of all evil after all.

Even aside from the popular influence of the Ham theory, racial separation most commonly meant white superiority. In 1912 the Home Mission Board of the Southern Baptist Convention—the agency in charge of religious instruction for minorities and the poor— called on white Christians to help blacks reach their full potential as a separate race, for in so doing, the report stated, "we shall save Anglo-Saxon supremacy." Far less charitable was the writer of an article in Mississippi's *Baptist Record*, who argued that God intended for the white race to rule supreme over blacks, because "a race whose mentality averages on borderline idiocy" is quite obviously bereft of any divine blessing. (The writer's stab at biblical exegesis was no compliment to the capabilities of white "mentality": "Christ would not that the inferior mind should rule, for he said to the disciples who wished a superior place that if they were able to drink the cup with him, they would be granted the petition. The black race is not able to drink the cup of authority with success.") White supremacy was the "divine law," intoned the *Laurel Leader Call*, "enacted for the defense of society and civilization."

When white Christians feared that blacks wanted more than their natural lot warranted—and were seeking to drink "the cup of authority"—any means to preserve Anglo-Saxon supremacy was justified on broad religious and moral grounds, including lynching. Writing in a Mississippi Baptist publication, the minister P. I. Lipsey defended the barbarous practice as "the wholesome desire to maintain the inviolability of the home." "Nothing stirs the blood of white men like a wrong committed upon a white woman by a negro," wrote Livingston Johnson in the *Biblical Recorder*. The ideal of personal purity had to be defended at all costs, mandated as it was by God for maintaining creation's harmony and coherence.

* * *

Hudgins began pastoring churches during his undergraduate years, preaching in towns like Bull's Gap and Lenoir City—towns scattered throughout the hollows of Loundon County. After marrying Blanche Jones in 1927, a trained musician and vocalist who "bears out the Tennessee tradition of beautiful women," Hudgins worked on the staff of Knoxville's Fifth Avenue Baptist Church and soon became senior minister at First Baptist, La Follette, Tennessee.

But in 1931 he left the pastorate to begin studies at the Southern Baptist Theological Seminary in Louisville, Kentucky, the largest Protestant seminary in the world and the most academically demanding in the Southern Baptist Convention.

Southern Seminary had taken a moderate view on the race issue. Though the founding fathers of the school had uncritically accepted the practices of racial separation in antebellum South Carolina (where the seminary was established in 1859), a racist ideology had never prevailed in the life of the school. The aristocratic James P. Boyce, a founder and first president of the seminary, described himself as "an ultra-proslavery man," but later confessed, "I feel that our sins as to this institution have cursed us . . . and I fear that God is going to sweep [it] away." By the time Douglas Hudgins arrived in Louisville in 1931, courses on race relations had been part of the curriculum since 1918, taught first by the remarkable Charles Spurgeon Gardner, and then by the racial progressive Jesse B. Weatherspoon. In his classes, Gardner had taught the brotherhood of humanity in Jesus Christ as the basis of any adequate Christian moral thought. He once responded to a student's question of whether blacks would go to heaven by saying, "In my judgment the Negroes have a much better chance than a preacher who would raise such a question." Jesse Weatherspoon, whose course on "Christianity and Race Relations" provoked intense debate among the seminarians, would soon become a leader in race reform both at Southern Seminary and in the Southern Baptist Convention. Not only did he espouse a biblical ethic of racial equality in the tradition of his predecessor Gardner, but he also encouraged his students to think about concrete political solutions to social issues, and called for full voting rights for blacks, equally distributed educational funding, fair economic policies, and the elimination of all discriminatory laws. In 1950, Weatherspoon fought successfully for the integration of the seminary and later, in 1954, he provoked the wrath of Baptist segregationists throughout the nation by lobbying (also successfully) for the support of *Brown vs. Board of Education* at the annual Southern Baptist Convention, just weeks after the Supreme Court decision.

* * *

Civil Rights Distractions

Ten years before the Summer Project tried to force Mississippi's hand on desegregation, the state's most renowned Baptist minister—and a budding leader in the Southern Baptist Convention—found himself forced to speak publicly on racial politics. Hudgins would have preferred avoiding the matter of *Brown vs. Board of Education* altogether, but a sequence of events made it impossible for him to remain silent.

The Supreme Court decision came to public debate at the 1954 Southern Baptist Convention in St. Louis, less than a month after the May 17 ruling. By a surprisingly overwhelming majority, the messengers to the Convention voted in favor of a report advanced by the progressive Christian Life Commission supporting the Supreme Court decision. The report stated the *Brown vs. Board* was "in harmony with the constitutional guarantee of equal freedom to all citizens, and with the Christian principles of equal justice and love of all men." The Christian Life Commission also pledged Southern Baptist support to the public school system as a whole, calling it "one of the greatest factors in American history for the maintenance of democracy and our common culture" and urging continued support of public schools as "one of the foundations of our democracy." Messengers at the convention—not only pastors but lay people with differing educational backgrounds and professions—not only accepted the Supreme Court decision, but encouraged fellow Baptists to apply a "Christian spirit" to the hard task of working out the implications of the new law. Although the report praised the high court's delay of the decision's effective date, the Southern Baptist Convention had decisively put its support of *Brown vs. Board of Education* into the public record.

And it put Douglas Hudgins into the national spotlight, testing his hitherto unmitigated loyalty to Baptist life and denominational service. How would he explain his congregation's (and his own) disapproval of the Supreme Court decision—thus pleasing his constituents and saving his job—and also maintain good standing with his denominational peers? Hudgins quit the convention before the vote was cast. He left behind a vote in opposition to the report, hoping to spare himself conspicuous attention on the convention floor.

However, his vote was read to the messengers by Jay Storer, the president of the Southern Baptist Convention. And it was read after two men—both denominational unknowns—acrimoniously voiced their opposition to the report. One W. M. Nevins, a pastor of a small, firebrand church in Lexington, Kentucky, took to the microphone to warn the convention that "soon . . . some of you who sit in this audience today will have grandchildren with mixed blood." Next came Arthur Hay, a dentist from Albuquerque, New Mexico, who held forth on the perils of amalgamation, quoting a variety of Bible verses and offering anecdotes about "white girls dating Negro men, and Negro girls dating white men" at a local university. He finished his comments by declaring that he was "a friend of the Negro" but that "Negroes are descendants of Ham," and "we whites must keep our blood pure." It was an embarrassing moment, even to most of the messengers in the audience who held similar views.

Without even so much as acknowledging these two opinions, Professor J. B. Weatherspoon rose to the occasion, and the racial progressive from Southern Seminary explained to the convention, in his melodic baritone, the reasons Southern Baptists should affirm the report. Directing the convention's attention to the large banner above the speakers' platform, where the words "Forward in Christ Jesus" were emblazoned in red, Weatherspoon told the messengers, "We're not going to shut our eyes to the fact that ours is a critical period, our nation needs men of faith, men who believe in Jesus Christ . . . to understand what is the most Christian thing to do in a most difficult time." He urged the convention to support the Christian Life Commission report and register its support of *Brown vs. Board of Education*. A vote was then taken, and fewer than one hundred of the ten thousand messengers voiced opposition to the report.

Hudgins's hopes for a graceful exit were dashed when his name appeared alongside those of Nevins and Hay in numerous media accounts of the convention, prompting him to break with routine and speak directly to the issue on his first Sunday back at First Baptist Church in Jackson. (At the conclusion of Weatherspoon's remarks, Jay Storer abruptly announced that his "very good friend Doug Hudgins" had left behind a vote against the report.) In his comments to the church, Hudgins appealed first to the issue of congregational autonomy so basic to the faith and practice of Baptist churches. He reminded his people that the Christian Life Commission report, even though it had passed overwhelmingly at the St. Louis convention, had no binding authority on the local church. "If, perhaps, you are not familiar with Baptist church polity," he said, "let me remind you that every Baptist congregation in the world—if it be truly Baptist in its position—is a democratic entity, and is responsible to no other body or individual, but is under the leadership of the Lord." The decisions of convention reports and resolutions are "actions of subjective co-operation. They are not authoritarian nor disciplinary." He added that the report had a "very large disagreeing vote," referring to what he considered a large number of nonvoting messengers. But the heart of Hudgins's remarks was his claim that the Supreme Court decision was "a purely civic matter" and thus "not appropriate nor necessary before a religious body."

His concluding statement cast in theological language the sentiment of his instructions for furnishing the pulpit: "Brethren, a church, in our interpretation of the New Testament, is a group of baptized believers, equal in rank and privilege; but a study of the New Testament further reveals that a church is a fellowship. If the fellowship of the church be broken, the idealism of the first is very definitely retarded." Intercourse with other, outside realities cheapens the church's serene repose, threatening her purity, her unbroken fellowship.

As the 1964 Summer Project took shape and rumors of "outside agitators" invading Mississippi increased, Jacksonians were treated to daily harangues in the local media against the civil rights leaders and volunteers. First Baptist parishioner, Tom Etheridge, in his column "Mississippi Notebook" in the *Clarion Ledger*, never disappointed his readers. "It is logical to assume," he wrote, "that Communists may have some sort of active role in the so-called Mississippi Summer Project, which reportedly will bring hundreds of leftist students and many potential troublemakers to our state before long." The *Jackson Daily News* warned: "We are presently under attack as no state has ever been." The Hederman paper further observed: "It appears to be more than coincidence that racial disorders always seem to develop somewhere in the South at the very time Communism takes another step forward in the Caribbean area at this country's doorstep." Not to be outdone, the Citizens' Council circulated numerous cautionary leaflets and flyers. One of its open letters encouraged white Mississippians to show special support for the local police, for "the coming violence in the name of 'civil rights' appears to be the climax of the Communist takeover of the United States. Washington has been taken over by Communist influences and for all practical purposes the communists are in working control of the federal government."

In the summer and fall of the previous year, the civil rights movement, which had hitherto existed well outside the immaculate lawn of First Baptist Church, appeared on the front steps of Hudgins's cavernous sanctuary in the form of students from Tougaloo College, a private black school in Jackson. Under the leadership of Jackson civil rights leader Medgar Evers and the college chaplain, Reverend Ed King, the Tougaloo group sought permission to worship with the regular members of First Baptist Church, just as they had sought to do in their numerous visits to other white churches in the city. From Hudgins's perspective, these visits (like the *Brown* decision) "imposed some difficult problems on the First Baptist Church," but it still remained a political concern and warranted no pastoral consideration. Hudgins would not meet with Evers or the students, nor would he meet Ed King, whose custom it was to discuss the intent of the visits with the white ministers. The church visitors posed only a strategic nuisance, and the matter was promptly turned over to the deacons for resolution.

On June 9, 1963, one week after the first confrontation with the students from Tougaloo and two days before the murder of Medgar Evers (and the night of Mrs. Hamer's torture in Winona), the lay leadership of the church proposed a resolution to the congregation that was later adopted by a unanimous standing vote. The resolution lamented "the present social unrest brought about by agitators who would drive a wedge of hate and distrust between white and colored friends." However, it would be necessary for the First Baptist Church to "confine its assemblies and fellowships to those other than the Negro race, until such time as cordial relationships could be reestablished." The disingenuous notion that cordial relationships would be reestablished once the agitators were gone bears some explanation. The last black members of the church—former slaves—had been expelled in 1868 as white Southerners responded to Reconstruction fears of black enfranchisement. The church's in-house historian justified the expulsion by reference to the fundamental difference in black and white styles of worship—and the need to preserve the solemn eloquence of white religion. "There was a great deal of rejoicing," he wrote, "creating a loud noise and otherwise conducting themselves in a manner that did not meet the approval of the members of the church." Suffice it to say that the singing and praying of the church visitors on the front steps nearly a century later met with equal disapproval. The church visitors were turned away with the threat that arrests and jail sentences would result from further attempts to sully Hudgins's sanctuary.

In the deacons' meeting on June 11, 1963 (hours before Medgar Evers was murdered less than a mile from First Baptist), the shared sense was that the worst had passed. As the minutes indicate: "The Pastor spoke briefly of our church's problems and asked for the Board's continuing prayers. He also announced that he and Mrs. Hudgins were planning on having the Deacons and their wives over to their new home on June 25." Hudgins called for "loyalty to the Church's worship and other services, in spite of and even because of the tensions which might be in our city." The meeting was then turned over to the Property and Maintenance Committee, which discussed its progress report on the construction of an elevator and the cleaning of the sanctuary. No mention was made of the decision to withdraw the church's annual $1,500 contribution to a local colored seminary.

After the start of the summer project, Hudgins was visited by an old acquaintance and classmate, H. Hansel Stembridge, Jr. The two had enjoyed theological discussions and social outings together during their student years at the Southern Baptist Theological Seminary, though they had not maintained strong ties since graduation in 1934. Hudgins and Stembridge would exchange courtesies if they saw each other at the annual Southern Baptist Convention, but the dramatically different directions their ministries had taken made it difficult for the two to find common ground.

Stembridge had become increasingly drawn to a faith that fostered racial justice; his tenure at churches in Georgia, Tennessee, Kentucky, North Carolina, and Virginia was always fragile, and sometimes shortened by his unwillingness to keep quiet on controversial issues. In 1961, while pastor at the First Baptist Church of Lynchburg, Virginia, Stembridge welcomed into the Sunday morning service a group of black students from the local Lynchburg Seminary. At the end of the service, church leaders complained to Stembridge about his decision. They emphasized to him the congregation's complete support of the church's closed-door policy: blacks would not be allowed to enter the church. After a week of soul searching, Stembridge explained in a sermon the following Sunday that if a segregated church was what parishioners wanted, then he could not continue as their pastor. Aside from the support of a local rabbi and Catholic priest—which heightened evangelical resentment—Stembridge stood alone with his theological convictions. The church leaders encouraged a speedy resignation.

The Lynchburg experience solidified Stembridge's growing awareness that ministry in a mainline Southern Baptist church was incompatible with his understanding of faith. To be sure, the denomination counted among its members courageous clergymen like Clarence Jordan, T. B. Maston, Will D. Campbell, and Stembridge's close friend, Carlyle Marney, but the difficulties of sustaining a pastorate in a traditional setting seemed to be insurmountable. Although the Southern Baptist Convention had voiced support of *Brown vs. Board of Education* in 1954, segregation continued to be widely accepted as God's good design for humanity. And in Lynchburg, segregation was preached with cavalier assurance by the town's Protestant clergy, including the young Jerry Falwell, whose newly founded Thomas Road Baptist Church adhered to strict closed-door policies. (In these years, Falwell stated in no uncertain terms his opposition to any meddling of Christians in political matters: "Nowhere are we commissioned to reform the externals. We are not told to wage war against bootleggers, liquor stores, gamblers, murderers, prostitutes, racketeers, prejudiced persons, or institutions, or any other existing evil as such.")

Stembridge and his wife took up residence in San Francisco. There he attended classes at the Baptist Seminary in the Graduate

Theological Union in Berkeley and began changing affiliation from the Southern Baptist Convention to the more liberal American Baptist Convention. He continued to support civil rights causes, largely through his daughter, Jane Stembridge, who had recently left her organizational post with SNCC in Atlanta to help develop a field office in Greenwood, Mississippi. (In 1960, Jane had interrupted her own theological studies at Union Seminary in New York and come south.). Stembridge admired his daughter's commitments; he and his wife had always encouraged her to think about the social dimensions of faith. But the parents' fears for their daughter's safety were difficult to bear. With the Klan killings of Schwerner, Chaney, and Goodman and the national media coverage of intensified anti-civil rights violence, Stembridge decided to travel to Mississippi. There he would spend time with his daughter and see first hand the situation reported almost daily on television and in newspapers in the bay area. He also would visit his old seminary classmate and encourage Hudgins to use his influence by preaching against violence and racism.

In July of 1964, with the financial support of a parishioner in his new congregation in Daly City, California, Stembridge flew to Mississippi on what he called a "tour of reconciliation." On the first day of his visit, Stembridge and his daughter drove northwest of Jackson toward Yazoo City to observe the ruins of a bombed black church—where still-smoldering foundations were all that was left of the building. The church was located in a settlement several miles off the main highway, reached only by a narrow dirt road that ended just beyond the church. While Stembridge surveyed the tragedy—this was his first close-hand look at Klan terrorism—Jane talked to her father about the movement and about her hopes for the Summer Project. She talked about the three missing civil rights workers. "No one else should die down here. Nobody should die anymore," she wanted her father to know. But the sudden roaring of engines put a quick end to her reflections. As several cars and pickup trucks pulled into the church parking lot, a group of young white men, with their wives and children, proceeded to get out of their vehicles and walk toward the church. Stembridge and his daughter headed directly to their rental car, locked the doors, and began driving cautiously toward the road, their eyes straight ahead, purposefully avoiding eye contact with any of the men. The crowd stood their ground for one terrifying moment, but then moved slowly aside, allowing the minister and his daughter to drive back to the main highway and then on to Jackson.

That night Stembridge and his daughter visited Douglas Hudgins and his wife. They were served coffee in the Hudgins's living room, and talked politely about seminary and denominational affairs. Then in his gentle, almost naive way, Stembridge asked Hudgins the question (in the same kind of pained, brotherly manner he had asked a Birmingham minister after the Klan bombing of a church had killed four black girls in their Sunday school class): "How can it be, Doug, that you are here in this town preaching the Gospel and there's all this hatred and violence?" Hudgins was momentarily silent. Then he said, "You simply don't understand. You know Baptists have no business tinkering in political matters." Hudgins invoked the familiar claim that civil rights for blacks has nothing to do with the Gospel.

Stembridge came away from his meeting in despair, with the sad feeling that Hudgins was a man who "wanted to be blind." But even more, it appeared to Stembridge that Hudgins had developed a "Messianic complex"; he had deceived himself with the arrogant belief that white Mississippians were the last to save the Southern Way of Life—"even to save America itself." Hudgins was unmoved by the visit. He simply refused to see how Stembridge's worries had anything to do with his responsibility as a preacher of the Gospel. Stembridge concluded, "At least I ascertained who the Freedom Workers could depend upon and whom they couldn't." His old seminary friend could not be counted among the former.

Anti-civil rights violence did not subside at the end of Freedom Summer. Klan terrorism became more random and unpredictable in the three years following. Moderate whites and blacks became targets of violent attacks and harassment. Increasingly, the Klan directed terrorist campaigns against Jewish Mississippians—not just Jewish civil rights workers—who emerged in the Klan's paranoid imagination as the driving force behind the civil rights movement.

Shortly before Thanksgiving of 1967, a bomb ripped through the home of Rabbi Perry Nussbaum, just weeks after his Temple Beth Israel's newly constructed building had been greatly damaged by a Klan bombing. The explosion destroyed the kitchen, dining room, living room, and parts of a bedroom. Miraculously, neither Rabbi Nussbaum, who publicly supported desegregation, nor his wife was harmed; both had been asleep in their back bedroom. When firemen, reporters, police officers, and neighbors arrived at the scene, Arene Nussbaum, the rabbi's wife, was found standing beside the rubble of the explosion, crying hysterically, picking splinters of glass from her hair, face, and clothing. As journalist Jack Nelson tells the story, Nussbaum stood beside his wife in his bathrobe, saying over and over that while this was the work of Ku Klux Klan, the "atmosphere of violence" was the work of Christian leaders who did nothing to change it. His first thought turned to Douglas Hudgins. Go call Hudgins, Nussbaum said to Reverend Ken Dean, a neighbor who had been awakened by the explosion. Tell Hudgins that he needs to make a public statement against all this violence.

When Dean called the First Baptist pastor early the next morning, Hudgins told him he resented his call and was capable of taking care of his own business. He should never call him again. Dean explained that Rabbi Nussbaum simply wanted Hudgins to use his influence to condemn the Klan violence, but Hudgins hung the phone up without replying.

Less than an hour later Dean returned to the Nussbaum's house, and was surprised to find Hudgins and Nussbaum standing on a pile of scorched two by fours that had once been the back porch. Alongside Nussbaum and Hudgins stood Governor Paul Johnson and Lucian Harvey, Jr., a friend of Hudgins and current president of the Jackson Rotary Club who often described his friend and pastor as a man "well-liked by Jew and Gentile." While Charles Quinn from NBC filmed the scene, Nussbaum waved his finger in Hudgins' face and shouted: "If you had spoken out from your pulpit after the synagogue was bombed and told your people it was wrong to have done that, this wouldn't have happened!" Hudgins tried to tell Nussbaum he was deeply sorry about what had happened, but Nussbaum was not interested in pastoral platitudes. He continued, "Don't tell me now how sorry you are. Those sons-of-a-gun attacked me and my family! They've attacked my house! I don't want to hear how sorry you are!" Hudgins was shocked, as were the governor and Mr. Harvey, that Rabbi Nussbaum would dare "deliver such an attack on Mississippi's most prominent religious figure." But Nussbaum was not finished. "Doug, if you're really sorry about this," he said, "get on the pulpit Sunday and tell your people this is wrong. Talk to those segregationists that fill up your church."

With that he turned to Ken Dean, who as the director of the Mississippi Council on Human Relations had always considered himself allies with Nussbaum in a common struggle against racial prejudice. Nussbaum exclaimed, "You're a white Christian—a Baptist, the worst kind for Jews. You've got a responsibility for what happened too. It's the Sunday-school lessons from the New Testament in Baptist churches that lead people to commit such terrible acts."

On the Sunday morning after the bombing, Nussbaum listened by radio to Hudgins's weekly broadcast of the worship service at the First Baptist Church. The sermon was a typical example of Hudgins's otherworldly piety. He made a general reference to the terrorist attack, saying it was regrettable that houses were bombed and wrong to bomb another man's house. He did not mention Nussbaum by name, nor did he mention that the house bombed most recently had been the rabbi's. "The Lord works in mysterious ways," the minister concluded on the subject, before turning to an exposition of a scriptural text. Nussbaum found Hudgins's words outrageous.

In his cryptic remark, Hudgins was not exactly saying that Klan violence had a divine though inscrutable purpose. More than anything else, Hudgins was retreating to a piety that disconnected language from reality, which fashioned a serene, self-enclosed world, undisturbed by the sufferings of blacks and Jews.

A Piety of the Pure Soul

The writer Lillian Smith once described the religion of her southern childhood as one "triangulated on sin, sex and segregation." There was a God in heaven who loved the world and gave his son as a sacrifice for its sins; but this same God would consume in eternal flames anyone who displeased him. Then there were parts of the body that must be separated from touch and curiosity, honored but feared. The lesson on segregation seemed only "a logical extension" of the lessons on the erotic body and the inscrutable God. Smith wrote, "The banning of people and books and ideas did not appear more shocking than the banning of our wishes which we learned so early to send to the Darktown of our unconscious." Purity held everything together. If the encumbrances of the flesh were allowed to agitate the soul's equanimity, then the delicate balance of communion with God would be disturbed—and the individual soul would collapse into chaos and despair.

Douglas Hudgins's piety of the pure soul betrayed this kind of anxious need to save the individual from incoherence and disintegration. The Christian life is about personal union with the saving God, secured in one decisive but continually repeated encounter with the risen Jesus. Nothing else matters. If the Christian admits other concerns into the event of salvation—like good works, doctrinal or creedal confession, or mediations like church tradition and hierarchy—then the purity of the soul's intimacy with God becomes threatened. The impure soul, like the defiled body of the white women (and like the integrated church) signals more than the tragic consequence of sin—it represents the fraying of the self's unbroken union with God, nothing less than the disintegration of the self.

The imprimatur of the Baptist theologian E. Y. Mullins is clearly present in Hudgins's understanding of personal regeneration. Like many of his generation, Hudgins came of age theologically under the influence of Mullins's austere theology. Mullins had been president of the Southern Baptist Theological Seminary until his death in 1928, and was widely regarded as one of the denomination's seminal minds.

Here is Mullins's description of the competency of the soul in communion with God, from his landmark book, *The Axioms of Religion:*

> Observe then that the idea of the competency of the soul in religion excludes at once all human interference, such as episcopacy, and infant baptism, and every form of religion by proxy. Religion is a personal matter between the soul and God. The principle is at the same time inclusive of all particulars. . . . It must include the doctrine of separation of Church and State because State churches stand on the

assumption that civil government is necessary as a factor in man's life in order to [sic] a fulfillment of his religious destiny; that man without the aid of the State is incompetent in religion. Justification by faith is also included because this doctrine is simply one detail in the soul's general religious heritage, from Christ.

Justification asserts man's competency to deal directly with God in the initial act of the Christian life. Regeneration is also implied in the principle of the soul's competency because it is the blessing which follows close upon the heels of justification or occurs at the same time with it, as a result of the soul's direct dealing with God.

On the basis of his definition of the Christian life, Mullins developed his famous "Six Axioms of Religion":

1. The theological axiom: The holy and loving God has a right to be sovereign.
2. The religious axiom: All souls have an equal right to direct access to God.
3. The ecclesiastical axiom: All believers have a right to equal privileges in the church.
4. The moral axiom: To be responsible man must be free.
5. The religio-civic axiom: A free Church in a free State.
6. The social axiom: Love your neighbor as yourself.

For his part, Hudgins revised the list to a neater threefold definition: "The New Testament is Our Only Rule of Faith and Practice," "Individuality in Matters of Religion," and "The Autonomy of the Local Church." These three "principles" stem from the fact that faith's chief concern is "the soul's competency before God."

What does it mean for the New Testament to be "our only rule of faith and practice"? Hudgins emphasized that Baptists have no creed or "ecclesiastical mold or tradition"—no authority or edicts—that might impose "regulatory and compulsory power over the individual church." Just as the individual is alone competent in matters of faith, so "the relationship of pastor and people is one between him and the local church." No outside group has any right to intrude upon this intimate union of shepherd and flock. No ecumenical agency or worldwide religious association dare suggest to the individual congregation how it should structure its beliefs and practices. Everything hangs on the person's regeneration in the experience of inviting Jesus to come into his heart. The only standard against which soul competency can be judged is the witness of the New Testament—understood not as a book of doctrine but as the life and breath of the spirit, kindling the soul's passion for perfect union with the Lord.

If everything hangs on personal regeneration, any trace of what Hudgins calls "sacramentarianism" vanishes. When salvation is interiorized to the soul's competency before God, every reality outside this encounter, which is to say all worldly reality, is stripped clean of sacramental consequence. There are then no sacraments in the church, but only what Hudgins grimly called the two "ordinances" of baptism and "the memorial supper." But these ordinances bring no grace: to those who go down into the saving waters or eat the bread and drink the wine (or the Welch's grape juice), no real presence of God is touched and received. Hudgins calls the ordinances "symbolic" (without regard for how the term was used by many theological modernists to divest Christian doctrine of its literal sense). If one were to consider baptism and the "memorial supper" sacraments, then one would not only steer perilously close to the Roman Catholic mistake, but also cheapen the purity of the ordinances. For the ordinances, Hudgins warns, should be observed with "reverence, dignity and beauty"; they dare not be "practiced loosely, carelessly, shoddily or hurriedly." The pastor must approach their practice with "unhurried gentleness," "simplicity," "quiet dignity," and "precision." A solemn vigilance must guard these tranquil silences from looseness and contamination. Yet even aside from the ordinances, it is equally important to emphasize that there is nothing in the texture of worldly experience—in love or charity, desire or sorrow—that radiates a sacramental light. You will not find, feel, or experience God in compassionate acts or in life with others; you will not find, feel, or experience God anywhere but in the solitude of your own walk with Jesus in your private spiritual garden.

Hudgins's second principle is "Individuality in Matters of Religion." This principle is really first in order of theological importance, though it is certainly understandable why Hudgins would want to begin with the New Testament as the basic rule of faith.

Hudgins does not intend to model Christian faith on individual experience as such. This would entail a concession to relativism or pragmatism that Hudgins dare not make (the inevitable concession to a gnostic detachment is far more encompassing and unavoidable), even though every single aspect of his religious thought threatens to end in relativistic or pragmatic reductions. His intentions notwithstanding, to him the individual context of religious experience governs all church teachings and polity, and the authority of scripture as well. Quoting the theologian Mullins, Hudgins explains, "The individual, not man en masse, is the primary object of God's love. 'God loves the whole world, but the whole is reached by contacting individuals one by one.' Individuals do not respond to God as a part of a group; each acts on his own responsibility. Each must act in his own sovereign power of choice. 'The individual not only must act for himself; he is the only one who can. God has made him competent.'" What matters spiritually and above all is that individuals or sovereign entities act for themselves alone. "A man's relationship to God is his own responsibility," Hudgins asserts.

The autonomous, local church thus becomes an extension of individual souls and their interior walks with Christ. By analogy, no one can tell my particular congregation how it ought to conduct its business. This is the third principle, the lesson of "The Autonomy of the Local Church." "No conference, presbyter, diocese, council, association, or convention has any right of dictation to the individual church or its membership," Hudgins says. The local church is free to do its own thing—as long as the spirit leads. But since there is "a direct relationship between the Spirit and the individual," and since congregational polity best accommodates this relationship, there is no external body or authority to judge decisions made by particular congregations. Thus the Holy Spirit, in the form of the Board of Deacons, inevitably shapes the congregation in its own image. Importantly, this kind of autonomy put extraordinary pressure on Baptist ministers throughout the South to maintain the status quo; if a minister rubbed the congregation the wrong way on the race issue, or any other matter, he would be promptly dismissed. The polity structure that promised maximum individual freedom ironically proved to suffocate individual freedom by group consensus.

The question Hudgins could not answer, and did not ask, is what exactly the individual does in the experience of personal regeneration. Does he confess a creed? No, Baptists have no creed. Does he make a covenant with God for the salvation of his family? No, there is "no such thing as family or proxy faith." Does he do good works? Of course not; this is papist nonsense. What then does one do to be saved? In the end, no one can tell the believer what he or she should do; the salvation experience is pieced together from whatever fragments of desires, prejudices, and dreams one brings to the event. Hudgins writes, "If the individual is responsible to God for himself, then there must be an experience of personal commitment to the saving grace of God before he can be received into the fellowship of other equally transformed individuals." Other equally transformed individuals will bring from their solitary encounters a common conviction and a common identity.

But what creates commonality here? In good Baptist form, Hudgins admits that infants and small children cannot be part of the church; they are simply not yet equipped with the spiritual tools necessary for personal regeneration. Is there anything then left of the church, of the spiritual community's interrelatedness or worldly presence, not to speak of the Pauline doctrine of the church as the mystical body of Christ? It seems unlikely. What could link together these spiritual atoms in a common identity and shared conviction? Hudgins is left with the accidents of race, class, and custom. Add to this a final problem. In his insightful book on American religion, Harold Bloom shows that such spiritual architectures as the one bequeathed by Mullins ironically and inevitably lead to the conclusion that the interiority of the soul's communion with God precedes all religious authority, including not only Roman Catholic hierarchy but even quite possibly the infallible Bible itself. Bloom writes, "If one's undying spirit accepts the love of Jesus, walks with the resurrected Jesus, knows what it is to love Jesus in return, alone with Jesus in the only permanent and perfect communion that ever will be, then there can be no churchly authority over me. As for the authority of Scripture, even it must yield to the direct encounter with the resurrected Jesus." The Spirit blows most vigorously when the shackles of hierarchy and ecumenism are removed; conviction comes down to a fellowship of one.

The will to pure freedom betrays an all-too-typical Baptist quandary. The soul that breaks free from the authorities of scriptural interpretation, hierarchy, and state, not to mention from the demands of justice and mercy, cannot tolerate the limitlessness of its possibilities. (Klansman Sam Bowers and his insatiable drive for world historical greatness prove an exception here.) So the church is created as a depository of shared feeling—local and autonomous—determined by whatever traditions and customs prevail. To be sure, Hudgins would not concede this point for a minute. As he writes, "The only church the New Testament projects is a local, autonomous, independent body, functioning under the leadership of the Holy Spirit." Yet although Hudgins (for obvious theological reasons) must locate final authority in the individual congregation as governed by the Holy Spirit, and not in the individual person, the cards are stacked against the move. Final authority on matters of Christian faith and practice resides in the individual's soul competency before God, configured in community by the historical and social contingencies of the self. The theological content of personal regeneration vaporizes under close scrutiny. All that is left of the experience is the individual's inchoate longing for holiness, a holiness which, in Hudgins's case, approximates the Southern Way of Life.

It bears repeating that the forces threatening piety and holiness are forces that absorb individuality into anonymous collectives. Of the federal government, Hudgins would say, "No one but a moron could fail to see the insidious trend in the last thirty years toward a continuous centralization of government." Hudgins would address political concerns to the extent to which these appear to infringe upon individual competency. In fact, it is surprising how often Hudgins did address political matters, his clearly drawn lines of demarcation between church and state notwithstanding. The cross of Jesus may have nothing to do with social movements like civil rights, but it seems altogether pertinent to states' rights, not to mention moral issues like promiscuity and alcohol and the playing of cards. As the uncensurable Mississippi newspaper editor, Hodding Carter, once said, "It is reasonably certain that if a reincarnated General Sherman were to run for governor of Mississippi as a prohibitionist and Marse Robert E. Lee opposed him as an advocate

of repeal, General Sherman would be elected, because more than
seventy-five per cent of our population are Baptists, who are committed ideologically to an eleventh commandment: 'Thou shalt not
drink'—an admonition which has not prevented dry Mississippi
from consuming illegally more whiskey per capita than do the adjoining wet states of Arkansas, Louisiana, and Alabama." The
point clarifies Hudgins's concerns. When the "wild and socialistic
fanaticism" of "the group" intrudes upon the integrity of the individual, Christianity does indeed have social relevance, if only to
point out that God is on the side of sobriety, wholesomeness, and
individual initiative.

Take the case of "minority groups." Hudgins declares, "Minority groups—and there are many of them—with shrewd planning
and political pressure, thrust their wills upon the great majority and
those of us who do not wish so to be manipulated are maligned,
caricatured and despised." That these groups were often represented by religious persons only emphasizes the insidiousness of the
problem. Hudgins bemoaned the pronouncement of "philosophi-
cal sophistries" by ministers who seemed more concerned with
"Thus saith the people" than "Thus saith the Lord." The fact is:
you either rally around the "brotherhood of man" and "ecumenical acceptance" or you rally around "new life in Christ" and the
true faith. Those who want to change the social order inevitably put
their trust in Washington rather than in God's "regeneration of the
individual." Thus reliance on the federal government to solve problems amounts to a betrayal of faith in God (that is, in individual
soul competency). Unless the social order mirrors the spiritual order—arranged in autonomous, individual, self-determining units—
the potential for danger reaches the whole way down to the
individual's spiritual freedom.

Here is exposed the two competing themes of Hudgins's theology: the interiorized experience of the saving Jesus and the articulation of that experience in social existence. Hudgins cavalierly
presumes in his sermons and public discourse that these two themes
fit together, or rather that the latter follows from the former, or in
any case, that there is a quality of evidence in biblical faith that not
only legitimates but demands the values of the closed society—that

is, states' rights, decentralized government, and the like. But as we have seen, the core experience of salvation—the soul's direct encounter with God—is individual in essence. It cannot graduate into larger corporate or covenantal forms. As Hudgins says, without any recognition of the consequences for church life, "the 'competency of the individual soul' sets the policy and the polity of Baptists." Still, since personal regeneration remains essentially spiritual and asocial, what accounts for Hudgins's ideas about the church views on race and civil rights? Are they taken simply from available cultural and social traditions? Obviously, this is true in part. But not in full.

The experience of personal regeneration does give a certain shape to social existence. The experience is unbroken, unmediated, seamless: it is virginal in texture, guarded against intrusion from external powers. Not to be overlooked is that unmediated harmony with God—the soul's marriage to its heavenly bride—commands powerful racial meanings. The notion of lives triangulated on God, the body, and social purity turns racial homogeneity into a theological—if not a metaphysical—necessity. This is the sad legacy of the Baptist doctrine of "soul competency" as it played itself out in the career of Douglas Hudgins.

The Interior Battle

Like Sam Bowers, terrorist and high priest of the White Knights of the Ku Klux Klan, Hudgins saw the present historical moment as the field of a cosmic battle between spiritual and material forces. "As was the case with the disciples—OUR FUTURE IS NOW! The world in which we will live tomorrow depends on what we do today," Hudgins urged. Resting on the promises of God to save from eternal damnation, Christians "must face the compelling responsibilities of the immediate present." Whatever these responsibilities may involve in exact detail, they are in any case "staggering," requiring nothing less than "the reshaping of the concepts of a pagan world." Hudgins preached, "Worship must change into work; adoration must turn into action; fear must give way to faith; security must be supplanted by self-abandonment. THE FUTURE must give way to the PRESENT!"

Hudgins agreed with Bowers that Christians must prepare themselves for combat, but the battlefield, as Hudgins saw it, remained
largely interiorized and incorporeal. "Our greatest enemy is not
flesh and blood," he said, "it is the intangibles," the "rulers of the
darkness of this world," the "spiritual wickedness in high places."
The "things" that matter most cannot be won through material
struggle or through mortal combat. For the spiritual world reigns
supreme over the quotidian matters of our earthy toil. "We deal
with [worldly] things," lamented Hudgins, "but place too little
value on things of the soul. We have unlocked many secrets of the
material world about us . . . but in spiritual conquest we have little
experienced the wonder-working constructive power of God made
effective by the reality of personal prayer." Herein lies the real
landscape of spiritual warfare. When the preacher must speak
against the impurities of the day, he does so almost regretfully, certainly hesitantly, because what matters most, and what ultimately
matters solely, is that "you, dear friend, individually become a
Christian, a follower of the Son of God, a new and transformed
person through the spiritual alchemy of regeneration by means of
faith in Jesus Christ as your Savior."

Hudgins offered America the chance to repent. (We know by
now that Sam Bowers would never extend the possibility of forgiveness to the heretics.) Those sins America ought confess, when
they reached some sort of social expression, were nonetheless
highly individualized or carnal in nature. "Barbarism, butchery
and the concentration camp are not our greatest tragedies." "Pa-
ganized materialism" needs to go, as do the more pervasive sins of
"promiscuous sex indulgence," "the rise in perversion," "the mania
for gambling," and "the wild abandon in revolt against authority."
In this manner, sin could take shape in massive powers and institutions but only in ways that threatened the individual's quest for purity: powers like communism and ecumenism, and institutions like
the federal government or even, at times, the agencies of the Southern Baptist Convention, especially the Christian Life Commission.

In his widely circulated speech on the "Decade of Destiny,"
Hudgins forecast the "soaring sixties" as America's pivotal moment. "What is achieved, or not achieved, by the people of God in
this ten-year period immediately ahead of us will determine, in my

judgment, the continuation of our Christian witness to a needy
world, or the deterioration and decay of our citizenship as a nation." Recall Sam Bowers's prediction in early 1964 that "the
events which will occur in Mississippi this summer may well determine the fate of Christianity for centuries to come," and the two
men both seem eerily posed to seize the world historical moment
for all its immense promise. But again, while the forecasts for the
future looked very much alike, the theological responses differed
dramatically. Hudgins's retreat to a spirituality unspoiled by intercourse with the civil rights movement shies away from the kinds of
assaults against authority encouraged by Bowers. If God wishes to
bring judgment and retribution against the heretics, he will have to
do it himself. And, of course, God will if America continues unre-
pentently down the path of sinfulness and impiety. But even more
importantly, Hudgins urged his listeners to prepare themselves for
the "decade of destiny"—for combat with "idolatry and evil"—by
nurturing "a Christian concept of moral integrity" that places "the
individual soul in harmonious fellowship with a redeeming God."
The best way to counter the rulers and powers of the present darkness is to cultivate the inner disciplines of the spiritual life. Only in
this way can Christians hope to provide the solutions to problems
facing America in the "soaring sixties."

Hudgins's proposal for social change surely would not win him
the respect of the White Knights of Ku Klux Klan, who in 1964
began waging violent war against blacks and civil rights workers.
For Hudgins never failed to remind his listeners and readers that
the best way to be about the business of the soul's competency with
God was through faithful attendance of worship services and various other church activities. "The neglect of public worship, family
prayer, and Bible study are greater enemies than any armed force,"
he said. Wholesomeness was of the essence. Although Hudgins did
not want to turn faith into morality, as he imagined the social
gospel theologians doing (those modernist liberals in Boston and
New York who threatened the faith's miraculous inner sense), he
did not avoid reducing the visceral intensity of the faith—with the
bleeding body of the Lord at the center   to the cultivation of character and social refinement. In other words, faith in the cross of Jesus must inspire wholesome living, civic responsibility, and all

around niceness. "Our standard of morals must be lifted; our social conduct must be elevated," he says. This is an important point. Hudgins would never suggest that the piety of the pure soul underwrites any sort of asceticism. God forbid the insinuation of a monkish renunciation of the world. Rather, Hudgins was convinced that the individualized nature of the person's relationship with God emphasized in turn the social value of individual initiative and purity as well as the goods associated with these values. The church was responsible for the preaching of the Gospel and the nurturing of the soul's perfection, but the preaching of the Gospel ought to make people industrious, thrifty, and wholesome.

As pastor of a congregation ever eager to grow in membership and budget, there was also, of course, an undeniable savvy in his contention. By the year 1964 the membership of First Baptist significantly declined to the middle 4,000s from a high of 5,556 in 1952. Hudgins needed to get people back into the pews of his sanctuary, and back to his downtown church from the suburbs. Certainly, he would not for a moment have suggested that regular church participation was tantamount to genuine religion. Church membership represented the proper and indeed the only context for nurturing the individual soul's fellowship with God and the attainment of "new and higher standard of morality and personal character." But by calling the faithful away from civil rights and social existence, Hudgins was able to preserve the purity of the closed church and the closed society for the sake of the closed Gospel. It is no exaggeration to say that one can simply not understand white indifference to black suffering and liberation during the civil rights movement without understanding the religion of William Douglas Hudgins.

* * *

In *God's Long Summer: Stories of Faith and Civil Rights* (Princeton, 1997), 82–115.

Glenda Elizabeth Gilmore

Diplomatic Women

Black men may have been barred from the polls in Jim Crow North Carolina but that does not mean that African Americans were politically powerless, particularly in an age of blooming civic volunteerism. Already locked out of the masculine world of party politics, middle-class black women belonged to a wide variety of organizations that had white counterparts. These nonpartisan women's groups played an ever-larger role in drafting public policy. Through these associations, historian Glenda Gilmore argues, black women became "diplomats to the white community" and forged crucial links between African American activists and the Progressive-era state.

After disfranchisement, "the Negro," white supremacists were fond of saying, was removed from politics. But even as African American men lost their rights, the political underwent a transformation. As state and local governments began to provide social services, an embryonic welfare state emerged. Henceforth, securing teeter-totters and playgrounds, fighting pellagra, or replacing a dusty neighborhood track with an oil-coated road would require political influence. Thus, at the same time that whites restricted the number of voters by excluding African Americans, the state created a new public role: that of the client who drew on its services. Contemporaries and historians named this paradoxical period the Progressive Era.

From the debris of disfranchisement, black women discovered fresh approaches to serving their communities and crafted new tactics designed to dull the blade of white supremacy. The result was a greater role for black women in the interracial public sphere. As long as they could vote, it was black men who had most often brokered official state power and made interracial political contacts. After disfranchisement, however, the political culture black women had created through thirty years of work in temperance organizations, Republican Party aid societies, and churches furnished both an idcological basis and an organizational structure from which black women could take on those tasks. After black men's banishment from politics, North Carolina's black women added a network of women's groups that crossed denominational—and later party—lines and took a multi-issue approach to civic action. In a nonpolitical guise, black women became the black community's diplomats to the white community.

In the first twenty years of the century, the state, counties, and municipalities began to intervene in affairs that had been private in the past. Now, government representatives killed rabid dogs and decided where traffic should stop. They forced bakers to put screens on their windows and made druggists stop selling morphine. They told parents when their children could work and when their children must go to school. As they regulated, they also dispensed. Public health departments were formed, welfare agencies turned charity into a science, and juvenile court systems began to separate youthful offenders of both sexes from seasoned criminals. Public education expanded exponentially and became increasingly uniform across the state. The intersection of government and individual expanded from the polling place to the street corner, from the party committee meeting to the sickbed.

Black women might not be voters, but they could be clients, and in that role they could become spokespeople for and motivators of black citizens. They could claim a distinctly female moral authority and pretend to eschew any political motivation. The deep camouflage of their leadership style—their womanhood—helped them remain invisible as they worked toward political ends. At the same time, they could deliver not votes but hands and hearts through community organization: willing workers in city cleanup campaigns, orderly children who complied with state educational requirements, and hookworm-infested people eager for treatment at public health fairs.

Southerners at the time called themselves "progressives," but historians have been loath to allow that name to stick. For those who championed a static history of the region, the "Progressive Era" ran counter to their continuity arguments. Moreover, those who found the roots of northern progressivism twining amid urban growth and rapid immigration saw only a stunted transplant on southern soil that remained comparatively rural and isolated. Finally, southern progressive solutions seemed a pale imitation of those in the North. If southerners reformed at all, historians judged their programs to be too little, too late.

Even for those who claimed to locate a southern Progressive Era, the juxtaposition of African Americans losing ground and whites "progressing" remained problematic. In a period when the country moved from an administrative government that maximized free enterprise toward an interventionist state, the white South busily invented and embellished segregation and drove black men away from the polls. White southern Democrats applied a pernicious ingenuity to the task of expanding state services in a society divided by the color line, and they allocated government money in increasingly unequal racial divides. C. Vann Woodward termed it "Progressivism—for Whites Only." J. Morgan Kousser went further, attaching an additional caveat: "Progressivism—for Middle Class Whites Only." Southern progressivism lived but, according to these readings, without the participation of blacks, poor whites, or women.

After Woodward, Anne Firor Scott, searching for southern progressivism, discovered white women at its center. Social reform enabled women to claim a privileged knowledge in civic affairs and to exercise power prior to suffrage, even in the South, where middle-class white women faced a stereotype of helpless gentility. White women fought child labor, ran settlement houses, and assumed responsibility for municipal housekeeping in growing New South cities. Working-class southern white women used progressive ideas and programs to shake the South's confidence in its grossly unfair wage system and to condemn its anti-union virulence, thus challenging the familiar notion that social control was the raison d'être for reform.

But even if southern progressivism included women, was it reserved for whites? The answer is that whites intended for it to be, and it would have been even more racist, more exclusive, and more oppressive if there had been no black women progressives. Black women fought back after disfranchisement by adapting progressive programs to their own purposes, even while they chose tactics that left them invisible in the political process. As southern African American women began this task, they were further away from southern white women than ever before. Since black men could not vote, white women dropped appeals to black women to influence their male family members. Many white women had chosen race over gender in the white supremacy campaigns and had gained their first electoral experience under a racist banner.

Given the distance between white and black women, the point is not that black women simply contributed to progressive welfare work and the domestication of politics, although, of course, they did. In comparing black women's progressivism to white women's progressivism, one must be cautious at every turn because black and white women had vastly different relationships to power. To cite just one example, white middle-class women lobbied to obtain services *from* their husbands, brothers, and sons; black women lobbied to obtain services *for* their husbands, brothers, and sons.

Black women's task was to try to force those white women who plunged into welfare efforts to recognize class and gender similarities across racial lines. To that end, they surveyed progressive white women's welfare initiatives and political style and found that both afforded black women a chance to enter the political. They had two purposes in mind. First, they would try to hold a place for African Americans in the ever-lengthening queue forming to garner state services. Second, they would begin to clear a path for the return of African Americans to the ballot box.

As confused and obfuscating as the term "progressive" is, one might wonder if it even applies to black women activists at all. Considering black women as progressives, however, demonstrates how gender and race as tools of historical analysis can enrich traditional political history. In this case, they lead us to rethink progressivism's periodization, roots, and results. Certainly, one can only apply the term "progressive" to this time and in these circumstances with a profound sense of irony. But it is important to make an explicit attempt to reclaim "progressivism," to stroll among the dismembered corpses of other historians' definitions and gather up some limbs, a hank of hair here, a piece of bone there. Then, like Dr. Frankenstein, perhaps we might build a new progressivism, this one a little less monstrous than some of those other hulks that still walk among us.

Given the expansion of the public sphere and whites' attempts to exclude African Americans from new state and municipal programs, black women's religious work took on new meaning. In the wake of disfranchisement, African American men and women turned to their churches for solace and for political advice. Yet many black men now feared the potentially explosive mixture of politics and religion in turbulent times. Ministers of all denominations began to circumscribe their own discourse and to monitor their flocks' debate. A Baptist minister declared that such "perilous times" made even "preaching of the pure gospel embarrassing, if not dangerous."

Using women's church organizations to press for community improvement incurred less risk than preaching inflammatory sermons on civil rights. The church remained, in the words of John Dancy, "an organized protest," but the nature of that protest transformed itself from arguments at Republican conventions and good turnouts at the ballot box into a flanking movement. While white political leaders kept their eyes on black men's electoral political presence and absence, black women organized and plotted an attack just outside of their field of vision. They began by transforming church missionary societies into social service agencies.

This is not to say that the political intentions of denominational women's groups were apparent to insiders or even omnipresent in the beginning. Initially, the groups did three things: they focused church attention away from spiritual debate and toward social conditions; they taught women to be organized managers; and they offered a slim ray of hope for community improvement in the midst of political disaster. Henry Cheatham, who had been recorder of deeds in Washington, D.C., prior to Dancy's assumption of the post, deplored African Americans' "political misfortunes" and gloomily predicted that civil rights might be lost forever. Cheatham argued that the "one thing" that remained for African Americans was the work women did in Sunday schools to build better homes, to educate the children, and to improve the community in general. In effect, he implored North Carolina Baptist women to use church work as a parapolitical tool.

African American women needed little urging. They understood their new role in community life and their unique ability to execute it. One Baptist home missionary, Sallie Mial of Raleigh, put it this way: "We have a peculiar work to do. We can go where you can not afford to go." Mial's "peculiar work" was social welfare reform. The tasks of black women's home missionary societies read like a Progressive Era primer. They organized mothers' clubs and community cleanup days. They built playgrounds and worked for public health and temperance. Marshaling arguments from the social purity and social hygiene movements, they spoke on sexual dangers outside of marriage. To achieve their goals, southern black women entered political space, appearing before local officials and interacting with white bureaucrats.

Even as they undertook this "peculiar work," black women knew that they must avoid charges of political interference. As a black woman, Mial could go where black men could no longer afford to go—into public space—for two reasons. First, her presence could not be misconstrued as a bid for sexual access to white women, as the Democrats so cunningly characterized black men's exercise of citizenship. Second, Mial could enter the realm of politics as a client, as an interpreter of social needs for families whom she represented to a state that had pledged something to her. Mial and thousands of other southern black women set about expanding on the state's amorphous promise, even as the growing bureaucracy tried to find practical ways to exclude African Americans from its largesse.

Sallie Mial would have never openly characterized her work as political, even though she may have understood it to be. Indeed, her success depended upon remaining invisible in the political process, a posture that contributes to historians' difficulties in recovering her experience. Taking a lesson from the high price of black men's former public presence, capitalizing on the divisions among whites over the allocation of new services to African Americans, and concerned about gender politics among African Americans, black women reformers depended on not being seen at all by whites who would thwart their programs and not being seen as political by whites who would aid them. They used their invisibility to construct a web of social service and civic institutions that remained hidden from and therefore unthreatening to whites.

Women's organizations within religious bodies were not new, but they became more important, expanded, and reordered their priorities after disfranchisement. For example, the Women's Baptist Home Mission Convention of North Carolina began in 1884, primarily as an arm for evangelical work. At the turn of the century, the group employed Mial as a full-time missionary in the state. In this capacity, she organized local women's groups and founded Sunshine Bands and What-I-Can Circles for girls. Mial explained her work to the African American Baptist men this way: "We teach the women to love their husbands, to be better wives and mothers, to make the homes better." At the same time, church workers taught Baptist women lobbying and administrative skills. One woman remembered, "From this organization we learn[ed] what is meant to be united." Another observed, "Many of our women are being strengthened for the Master's use." Along the way, the organization began calling itself the Baptist State Educational Missionary Convention.

Making "the homes better" covered a wide range of community activities. Good homes rhetoric was, of course, promulgated by whites to justify white supremacy; southern educational reformers used depictions of debasement, for example, to justify industrial education. Black women could use this discourse for their own purposes, and they grasped the opportunity it gave them to bargain for the state services that were beginning to improve whites' lives but were denied to African Americans. As Margaret Murray Washington put it, "Where the homes of colored people are comfortable and clean, there is less disease, less sickness, less death, and less danger to others [that is, whites]." Good homes, however, required good government. "We are not likely to [build good homes] if we know that the pavements will be built just within a door of ours and suddenly stop," Washington warned. Turning from the ballot box to the home as the hope of the future was canny political strategy that meshed nicely with the new welfare role of the state, and it explicitly increased women's importance at a time when women across the nation campaigned to extend their influence through volunteer activities and the professionalization of social work.

The elevation of the home to the centerpiece of African American life sprang from several sources. Certainly it resonated with a nationwide Progressive Era movement for better homes, particularly among immigrant enclaves in crowded northern cities. But among North Carolina's African Americans, the movement's roots reached closer to home. Religious convictions that had inspired nineteenth-century black women who did church work continued to serve as moral imperatives to bring families to godly lives. African American women tried to eliminate grist for the white supremacy mill by abolishing the images of the immoral black woman and the barbaric black home. Moreover, now that voting required literacy, education was political, and it began at home. Able to tap into the larger context of rhetoric on better homes and the importance of literacy, black women expanded their roles, first in the church, then in the community as a whole.

Some men felt threatened by this new activity, even though most women made it clear that their goal was not to preach or to rise within the formal church hierarchy, as, for example, Mary Small had done in the African Methodist Episcopal (AME) Zion Church in the 1890s. William F. Fonvielle, a supporter of coeducation at Livingstone College, had called repeatedly on women to work for racial uplift. But in 1900, he complained that there were too many women delegates at the AME Zion general conference. He came away from the experience completely opposed to women representatives, even though "some of them are good friends of mine. . . . It looks like a bad precedent." Many black Baptist men questioned the expenditures for home missions. When Baptist women implored men to "Give us a push," the men wondered if they should not push the women out of the limelight altogether. Unlike the AME Zion convention, by 1900 Baptist men and women met separately, and women often found themselves fending off attempts to abolish the Baptist Educational and Missionary Convention. Even those who did not want to sweep away the women's structure were determined to insure its control by men. They advocated solving the problem "by appointing an advisory committee each year to attend the Women's Convention and to advise with them in their deliberations, and [send] . . . an annual report to this body."

Women did their best to reassure men by stressing their solidarity with them. "We are your sisters, your wives, your mothers. We have not outgrown you. We have been given to you to help you. We dare not leave you. You have opened your hearts, and given us increased privileges in the churches," Sallie Mial told the men's Baptist convention. Roberta Bunn, another paid missionary, said that the women's relationship with the men's convention was "indestructible" but that women had an important place to fill that men could not. She quoted Scripture: "I sought for a man among them that should make up the hedge, and stand in the gap before me." She reminded the brothers that when God could find no man to fill the gap, two women stood in. Over the years, the debate over the power of women's organizations among North Carolina Baptists escalated. By 1917, women insisted that "it behooves us to think of and discuss the great questions confronting us as citizens of this great nation," while the men reiterated that the women needed "intelligent supervision" and directed them to turn their funds over to the men's convention.

The growth of women's organizations in the AME Zion Church demonstrates women's desire to carve out a distinct space for themselves within the denomination. After the turn of the century, AME Zion women created a formal, hierarchical, and separate women's structure and changed the thrust of their work from evangelism to education and social service. When Sarah Dudley Pettey served as treasurer and then secretary of the Woman's Home and Foreign Missionary Society, the organization's primary activity was fundraising for African missions. She began the "Woman's Column" in the *Star of Zion* during her term as secretary, and her writing revealed her personal concerns more than it represented the society. In the 1890s, society officers met only once every four years at the regular convention, and all were wives of bishops.

The structure of the Woman's Home and Foreign Missionary Society changed radically between 1900 and 1915, and the women moved from integration with the men to performing separate functions within the church. In 1901, while Dudley Pettey still edited the "Woman's Column," the society persuaded the *Star of Zion* to allow Marie Clay Clinton, George Clinton's new wife, to write a "missionary" column. That column eventually grew into a separate women's newspaper, the *Missionary Seer*. At the 1904 convention, Woman's Christian Temperance Union (WCTU) activist Annie Blackwell demanded that women operate the Woman's Home and Foreign Missionary Society autonomously, and a women's convention began meeting the next year. An independent executive board oversaw the society's business, and by 1912, the board dealt with the issue of bishops' wives monopolizing the board by making them nonvoting members. The women's convention began electing the *Star*'s "Woman's Column" editor in 1912. The term "missions" came to be broadly interpreted to mean social service work among African American neighbors.

Two North Carolina women, Marie Clinton and Victoria Richardson, founded youth educational departments within the society. Clinton had arrived in Charlotte in 1901 when she married widower George Clinton, and by the following year, she became fast friends with Victoria Richardson of Livingstone College. Richardson's uncles were the famous Harris brothers who had founded the Fayetteville graded school during Reconstruction. Legend had it that Victoria's parents sent her from Ohio to North Carolina to save her from making an unsuitable early marriage. After a brief stint as Charles Chesnutt's colleague at the Charlotte graded school in the 1870s, Richardson went to teach at Livingstone College when it opened in 1880. She stayed a lifetime, teaching music and building the library. With her warm friend Mary Lynch, Richardson set an example of "finer womanhood" for Livingstone's women students. "Saved" from love, Victoria Richardson never married.

In 1904, Marie Clinton established the Buds of Promise within the Woman's Home and Foreign Missionary Society. "Blooming All for Jesus," the Buds functioned as an educational service club for AME Zion children aged three to twelve. In 1909, Victoria Richardson began the Young Woman's Home and Foreign Missionary Society for teenaged girls. The group took on social service work, nursed the sick, visited the elderly, and presented public health programs. By 1912, the officers of the Woman's Home and Foreign Missionary Society had years of social service experience behind them and an organization that could channel women's energies from the cradle to the grave. Annie Blackwell served as corresponding secretary, and elder Mary Small presided.

These African American women's denominational groups created a vast network throughout the South, virtually invisible to whites. It is helpful to see the groups as cells through which information and ideas could pass quickly. The invisibility of black women's work suited them. They did not want to antagonize their husbands by making a power play within their denominations—the men in the church were already uneasy about their activities. They did not want to endanger their families by drawing attention to themselves. They did not want to risk interference from whites by being overtly political. Better to call social work "missionary work";

better to gather 100,000 Baptist women in a movement to produce good homes. If such activities resulted in organizing the community to lobby for better schools, swamp drainage, or tuberculosis control, no white could accuse them of meddling in politics.

From these bases, women forged interdenominational links. North Carolinian Anna Julia Cooper, by then living in Washington, D.C., was present at the creation of the National Association of Colored Women's Clubs in 1896. Delegates to that first meeting represented a wide range of women's denominational organizations, interdenominational unions such as the WCTU and the King's Daughters, and secular civic leagues. In her capacity as North Carolina's state WCTU president, Mary Lynch attended the first national convention in 1897; she became national corresponding secretary at the second. The Biddle University Club of Charlotte was a charter member. North Carolina black women founded a statewide federation of clubs in 1909 and elected Marie Clinton president.

In addition to the women's clubs, the WCTU survived as an organizational home for black women after the white WCTU women found their work overtaken by the male Anti-Saloon League. By 1901, the national organization was paying a state organizer, and Lucy Thurman, national superintendent of "Colored Work," visited North Carolina regularly. Marie Clinton was an active member, and she helped direct WCTU work toward efforts to help children. Victoria Richardson served as state president of the Loyal Temperance League, an organization that encouraged youngsters to sign the temperance pledge and sponsored oratorical contests denouncing strong drink. Their work left telling memories. At eighty-four, Abna Aggrey Lancaster recalled her excitement on the day in 1914 when Mary Lynch visited her Sunday school class. Seven-year-old Lancaster returned home for Sunday dinner proudly boasting that she would never allow alcohol or tobacco to touch her lips. Decades later, George Lincoln Blackwell, Annie Blackwell's nephew, still savored his victory in a Loyal Temperance League oratorical contest as one of the proudest moments of his childhood. Almost every large city in the state had a WCTU chapter. Lynch marveled at the organization's progress: "It seems a long time since that sultry day in July when in Salisbury we launched our little bark upon the waves of opposition."

Activist black women also met at frequent regional sociological conferences. The Progressive Era trend toward organization, discussion, and investigation blossomed in these huge confabulations. Mary Lynch went to the Negro Young People's Christian and Educational Congress in Atlanta in 1902, where she delivered the address, "The Woman's Part in the Battle against Drink." There she met Charlotte Hawkins, a young Boston student who had just moved to Sedalia, North Carolina, and banker Maggie L. Walker of Richmond. She also renewed ties with Lucy Thurman of the national WCTU and Josephine Silone-Yates, president of the National Association of Colored Women's Clubs. The Woman's Day theme was "No race can rise higher than its women."

As women were building vast voluntary networks, public school teaching was becoming an increasingly feminized profession. In 1902, the number of black women teachers and black men teachers was almost the same: 1,325 women and 1,190 men. The percentage of black women teachers exactly matched that of white women teachers: 52 percent. By 1919, 78 percent of black teachers were women, and 83 percent of the white teachers were women. The growing number of black women teachers did not escape notice. At the 1903 meeting of the Negro State Teachers Association, more than half of the delegates were women, including Sarah Dudley Pettey's sisters, Nannie and Catherine. Men had abandoned the profession, one speaker complained, because "they cannot compete with [women] teachers who are willing to work for low wages."

But that analysis leaves black women taking the rap for the white supremacists. White women flocked to public teaching at the same time as black women, yet their salaries rose because politics determined educational allocations on the state level. It was black men's exclusion from the political sphere, not black women's willingness to work for low wages, that caused African American teachers to be poorly compensated. In some counties, salaries for black teachers actually declined after the fusion government ended. Generally, however, throughout the state in the first two decades of the century, black teachers' wages crept upward, even as they continued to fall further behind white teachers' salaries. The statewide average salary in 1905 was $156 for whites and $107 for African Americans. Fourteen years later, whites averaged $353 and blacks $197. The increasing number of black women teachers was a result, not a cause, of declining wages. In addition to driving black men from the profession, low wages contributed to a difference in the marital status of white and black women teachers. White women teachers were almost always single. Many black women teachers were married women who remained partially dependent upon their husbands' income.

The most staggering statistic was the growth in the number of white teachers: from a total of 5,472 in 1902 to 11,730 in 1919, a 214 percent increase. During the same period, the number of black teachers rose from 2,515 to 3,511, a 139 percent increase. White teachers' numbers grew at the expense of black education. The white North Carolina Normal and Industrial College at Greensboro graduated large numbers of white women teachers at the same time that the state eliminated four black normal schools and banned women from the North Carolina Agricultural and Technical College. Black women had a much harder time than white women formally preparing to teach, and fewer jobs awaited them after they graduated.

Those who did succeed were likely to be active members of church women's organizations, involved in the WCTU, and participants in their city's literary societies and civic leagues. The black woman teacher had to withstand the scrutiny of white superintendents on the lookout for moral failings at the same time that she had to vanquish intense competition among dozens of aspirants for a single position. She had to be so unselfish, so dedicated, and so above reproach that no gossip could touch her. Teachers' organizational connections protected and nurtured them. Conversely, they took their organizations' goals into their classrooms.

Even without their own progressive agenda, African American women teachers would have found schools to be an increasingly politicized setting. After 1900, the importance of literacy for voting and the movement toward industrial education commanded the attention of both the black and white community, and perennial battles over allocating taxes for education turned the black schoolhouse into a lightning rod, propelling female teachers into the political sphere, for better or for worse. The disfranchisers split among themselves over black public education after the amendment passed. Alfred Moore Waddell, ever the bumbling misanthrope, once chose a commencement address as a platform for condemning universal education: "There are thousands of enlightened persons who do not subscribe to the belief . . . that in popular education alone is to be found the panacea for all social political evils." Waddell added that education is even less useful when "applied to both races indiscriminately." But other whites, notably Charles B. Aycock, saw universal education as the South's salvation. As far as they were concerned, even African Americans could participate in the forthcoming redemption, though not in equal measure. Charles D. McIver, president of the North Carolina Normal and Industrial College for white women, tried to convince African Americans that disfranchisement would boost black education by encouraging parents to send their children to school, stating that "temporary disfranchisement . . . is a much less evil than permanent ignorance." Aycock, who had threatened to refuse the Democratic Party's gubernatorial nomination if the time limit on the grandfather clause was extended, later threatened to resign the governorship if the state legislature allowed whites to tax themselves separately for the benefit of their own children. His threat sprang partly from compassion—"Let us not be the first state . . . to make the weak man helpless"—but partly from his concern that such a move would encourage the U.S. Supreme Court to find the amendment unconstitutional.

The racial inequities of school funding have been well documented, but the efforts of black students and teachers to keep their schools from starving cannot be celebrated enough. Even in the best black schools, for example, the Charlotte graded school, there were few desks and "two and sometimes three small pupils sat crowded in a wide seat." The state gave so little—inadequate furniture, a meager library—but teachers made so little go so far. "There was much blackboard space in a room which was a good thing," Rose Leary Love recalled. "At the time, blackboards were not termed visual aids, but they really were the most important available ones." The teachers used them to explain lessons; the pupils used them in lieu of paper. In the state's eyes, African Americans were not training to be full citizens; they needed no civics classes, no maps, no copy of the Constitution, no charts on "How a Bill Becomes a Law." That left teachers on their own to define citizenship. Somehow they did. Teachers chose talented students to "draw the National Flag or the State Flag on the blackboard," Love remembered. "These flags were assigned a place of honor on the board and they became a permanent fixture in the room for the year. Pupils were careful not to erase the flags when they cleaned the blackboards." Despite whites' efforts to rob African Americans of their country, black teachers taught each day under the flag.

A centralized state bureaucracy grew to oversee the curriculum in African American schools. In 1905, Charles L. Coon, a white man who had recently been superintendent of Salisbury's schools and secretary of the General Education Board, accepted the newly created position of superintendent of the state colored normal schools. According to his boss, Coon's oversight would "send out into the counties each a larger number of negro teachers, equipped with the knowledge and the training, and filled with the right ideals necessary for the . . . most practical, sensible and useful education of the negro race." By putting African American normal schools under the control of a white man, the state hoped to produce teachers who embraced industrial education and to force the private African American normal schools out of business.

Ironically, state oversight created controversy rather than quelling it primarily because of Coon's independent personality. An amateur statistician who often challenged authority, Coon created a furor by proving that the state spent less on African American education than the taxes blacks paid in. In fact, Coon produced figures to prove that black tax dollars educated white children. Coon's boss, James Y. Joyner, distanced himself from Coon's argument and decried him to Josephus Daniels. But Aycock admitted that Coon spoke the truth, and one white lawyer observed, "Our attempts to oppress the negro's mind are enslaving us just as bad as slavery did."

By the time Coon addressed the predominately female Negro State Teachers Association in 1909, his trial by fire had turned him into a political agitator. He argued that the tide had turned against white supremacy. "I do not believe we need to spend much more time upon that species of the white race who would doom any other race to mental slavery," he commented, "anymore than we should spend time fighting over again the battles of whether a man has the right to hold in bodily servitude another man of another race." He suggested that the teachers unite to work for better instruction, longer school terms, and improved school facilities in the next decade. Furthermore, he recommended that blacks "interest the white people in your schools. . . . Then get your churches, lodges, and societies to help. . . . We must see to it that we interest the local communities, white and black." Coon's prescription for African American education fit perfectly into black women's organizational missions and pointed up the political nature of black women teachers' jobs.

Whites quarreled a great deal more over funding black education than they did over its content, which white educators overwhelmingly agreed should be based on the Hampton model. Very little industrial training could begin, however, without spending dollars on equipment and tools. Ironically, it proved more expensive to build a bookcase than to explain an algebra problem on a broken piece of slate. Outside help would be critical. As a few dollars began to trickle down, black women teachers learned to exploit whites' support of industrial education. The Negro State Teachers Association recognized in 1903 that "the industrial and manual idea . . . is a much felt need in our public and private schools, since the development of negro womanhood is one of its immediate results." At the same time that black women recognized the potential of industrial education to improve home life, they began to clamor for a greater voice in its administration. When officials from the Rockefeller-funded General Education Board and local white educators met with black teachers in 1913, Charlotte Hawkins Brown told the group flatly that since women made up the majority of rural teachers, industrial education would fail unless philanthropists and white educators listened more closely to black women's suggestions and rewarded them for their efforts. African American women's tilting of the industrial education ideology was slight but important. While paying lip service to the ideal of producing servants for white people, black women quietly turned the philosophy into a self-help endeavor and the public schools into institutions resembling social settlement houses. Cooking courses became not only vocational classes but also nutrition courses where students could eat hot meals. Sewing classes may have turned out some dressmakers and cobbling classes some cobblers, but they had the added advantage of clothing poor pupils so that they could attend school more regularly.

The Negro Rural School Fund, a philanthropy administered by the Rockefeller Foundation's General Education Board, gave the state's black women teachers the basic tools they needed to incorporate social work into the public school system. Begun in 1909 as the Anna T. Jeanes Fund, it paid more than half of the salary of one industrial supervising teacher on the county level. County boards of education paid the rest. The Jeanes supervisor traveled to all of the African American schools in a county, ostensibly to teach industrial education. In 1913, the General Education Board offered to pay the salary of a state supervisor of rural elementary schools in North Carolina to oversee the thirteen Jeanes teachers already in place and to expand the work to other counties. In naming the supervisor, the board had a hidden agenda: northern philanthropists did not trust southern state administrators to allocate and spend their grants wisely. They wanted a white man loyal to them in state government, a professional who could walk the tightwire of interracial relations, placating obstreperous legislators at the same time that he kept a keen eye on black industrial curricula. They found their man in Nathan C. Newbold, who had been superintendent of public schools in Washington, North Carolina.

In his first report, Newbold displayed his facility for straddling the color line. He condemned white injustice to African Americans at the same time that he explained it away as a reasonable vestige of the past, now, fortunately, antiquated. "The average negro rural schoolhouse is really a disgrace to an independent, civilized people," Newbold wrote as he surveyed his new field. "To one who does not know our history, these schoolhouses, though mute, would tell in unmistaken terms a story of injustice, inhumanity and neglect on the part of our white people," he observed. If someone unfamiliar with the South's history stumbled upon such buildings, the newcomer would surely think North Carolina's whites "unchristian." But the stranger would be wrong, he explained, since the black schools were no worse than white schools had been twenty-five years ago. Now that whites had remedied their own situation, he was sure they would eagerly set about improving black schools. Newbold always offered whites a face-saving excuse for past inaction at the same time that he spurred them to action.

Nonconfrontational and optimistic, as state agent for the Negro Rural School Fund Newbold became an extraordinary voice for African American education. He quickly persuaded more county boards of education to fund half of a Jeanes teacher's salary at the same time that he forged strong alliances with the incumbent Jeanes teachers. By the end of his first year, twenty-two counties employed Jeanes teachers, who found themselves in the often awkward position of having to report to both Newbold and the county superintendent. Newbold appointed a black woman, Annie Wealthy Holland, as his assistant. The Jeanes board's initial expenditure of $2,144 in the state in 1909 grew to $12,728 by 1921.

Most women who became Jeanes teachers came to social service work through their own organizations. For example, the Jeanes teacher in Rowan County was Rose Douglass Aggrey, a Shaw University graduate, poet, and classical scholar. Her husband, J. E. Kwegyir Aggrey, was born in the Gold Coast, Africa, was educated by British missionaries, and came to the United States to attend Livingstone College. He taught at Livingstone until the Phelps-Stokes Association sent him back to Africa as a missionary in 1920. Staying behind in Salisbury, Rose Aggrey was active in the Woman's Home and Foreign Missionary Society of the AME Zion Church, forging close friendships with Mary Lynch and Victoria Richardson. Aggrey later became president of the statewide federation of black women's clubs. Aggrey's daughter remembered that her mother often appeared before the school board and the county commissioners to plead for money for school improvements, to lobby for a longer school year, or to facilitate consolidation of one-room schools into graded structures. Aggrey was extremely well connected within the Jeanes structure; in 1919, her friend Marie Clinton's husband, George, served on the national board of the Negro Rural School Fund.

Faced with local white administrators' neglect, Jeanes teachers had an enormous amount of responsibility. Sarah Delany, the

Jeanes supervisor in Wake County, recalled, "I was just supposed to be in charge of domestic science, but they made me do the county superintendent's work. So, I ended up actually in charge of all the colored schools in Wake County, North Carolina, although they didn't pay me to do that or give me any credit." Delany, raised as a "child of privilege" on the Saint Augustine's College campus, stayed overnight with parents in rural areas, where she encountered not just a lack of indoor plumbing but a condition even more appalling to a citified house guest: no outhouse. Delany went to her pupils' homes to teach their parents how to "cook, clean, [and] eat properly," and when General Education Board officials visited North Carolina in 1913, she agreed to serve on the statewide committee to establish a cooking curriculum. She painted schoolrooms, taught children to bake cakes, raised money to improve buildings, and organized Parent Unions. Jeanes teachers also transformed their students into entrepreneurs. In 1915, their Home-Makers Clubs, Corn Clubs, and Pig Clubs involved over 4,000 boys and girls and 2,000 adults in 32 counties. The clubs were intended to teach farming, of course, but they also enabled poor rural African Americans to make money on their produce. The students raised more than $6,000 selling fruits and vegetables that year.

Jeanes teachers saw themselves as agents of progressivism, and they combined public health work with their visits to schools and homes. Unlike Rose Aggrey and Sarah Delany, Carrie Battle, the Jeanes supervisor in Edgecombe County, had grown up desperately poor. Her mother worked at two domestic jobs and Battle went hungry to save money for tuition at Elizabeth City State Normal School. After she began teaching, Battle visited the homes of pupils across the county to organize a Modern Health Crusade against tuberculosis in the schools. Moving from school to school with a set of scales, she would not weigh ill-groomed boys and girls, nor would she weigh anyone in a dirty schoolroom. She made the children promise to clean up the room, bathe, use individual drinking cups, and sleep with the windows open. One boy reported, "Pa said that was too foolish—I would catch cold and die if I slept with the windows up." Another outmaneuvered his father by waiting to raise the window until the man was snoring. Soon Battle had established Modern Health Clubs in every school and a total of 4,029 children enrolled as Crusaders. Her work attracted attention from the white community, and she began to cooperate with the white Red Cross nurse to produce public health programs. Many of Battle's students had never been farther than ten miles from their homes. She brought the world to them through regularly scheduled visits of the "Moving Picture Car," a truck equipped with projection equipment used to screen films on health education.

Jeanes teachers also built schools across the state—schools for which the state took credit and of which the counties took possession. Weary of asking for their fair share of tax dollars, black communities simply built their own schools and gave them to the county. For example, in the academic year 1915–16, thirty-two black schools were built and thirty improved at a total cost of $29,000. African Americans contributed over $21,000 of the total: $15,293 in cash and the equivalent of $5,856 in labor. The school at Chadbourn represents a typical case. Local African Americans deeded to the county "a large building nearly completed to contain four class rooms, and nine acres of land." Moreover, they pledged more than $850 the next year to pay additional teachers and make further improvements to the building. In Mecklenburg County, the white chairman of the school board told African Americans that the board was "willing to help those people who would help themselves" and that if African Americans "could pay half of the expense in as far as the board was able it would pay the other half." Amazingly, the black community was "encouraged" by this offer, built six schools, and forced the board to make good on its promise.

The next year, the Julius Rosenwald Committee, a Chicago-based philanthropy, appropriated $6,000 to stimulate public school building in rural areas of North Carolina. Although this amount was a great deal less than African Americans were already raising annually to build their own schools, Rosenwald grants often embarrassed state and county officials into contributing funds for building black schools. The Rosenwald grants would provide a third of the cost of schools, local African American communities would raise a third, and tax dollars would account for a third. The Jeanes teachers organized teachers, parents, and students to support school-building projects by raffling box lunches, setting aside part of a field to grow a crop for the school, or providing the building materials for the structure from their own lands. Their efforts made the Rosenwald seed money flower. For example, the first "Rosenwald" school built in North Carolina cost $1,473, of which the fund contributed $300. By 1917, Jeanes teachers saw to it that the state's twenty-one Rosenwald schools teemed with activity night and day. Parent Unions met there, and teachers returned in the evenings to conduct "moonlight schools" where adults could learn to read.

The unique role of the Jeanes teacher points up the distinctiveness of southern progressivism and provides clues to the reasons for historians' difficulties in finding and understanding it. The Jeanes teacher had no counterpart in the North. She did social work on the fly, leaving neither permanent settlement houses nor case files behind through which one might capture her experience. She understood the latest public health measures and passed them along even in the most remote areas. She fought to obtain Rosenwald school money to build schools that were airy and modern, then turned them into clubhouses in the evenings. By establishing Parent Unions, she provided a new organizational center for black communities. She lobbied school boards and county commissions for supplies and support. And she accomplished all of this while trying to remain invisible to the white community at large. To locate the progressive South, one must not just visit New South booster Henry Grady in Atlanta but find as well a schoolroom full of cleanly scrubbed Modern Health Crusaders, lined up for hot cereal cooked by the older girls in Rosenwald kitchens, each Crusader clutching the jelly jar that served as his or her very own glass.

At the same time that black women used progressivism to reshape black life and race relations, an organizational approach slowly began to replace racial "paternalism." The black community in Salisbury would not listen to influential whites who told them to clean up their communities. Nothing happened until whites recognized black women leaders, met with them publicly, and gave them authority. Then the city was "completely transformed." Despite whites' extensive efforts to undermine black education by imposing a nineteenth-century version of industrial education, black women's progressive ideas made industrial education modern and useful by linking it to the sanitary science movement. Contacts between

white and black women with progressive agendas set the ground-
work for inclusion of African Americans in formal social service
structures. Her desire to help solve civic problems gave Lula Kelsey
the right to appear before city officials during a period when black
men risked their lives if they registered to vote for those officials.

This is certainly not to argue that disfranchisement was a positive good or that African Americans were better off with limited social services than they would have been with full civil rights. It
means that black women were given straw and they made bricks.
Outward cooperation with an agenda designed to oppress them
masked a subversive twist. Black women capitalized upon the new
role of the state to capture a share of the meager resources and
proceeded to effect real social change with tools designed to maintain the status quo.

In *Gender and Jim Crow: Women and the Politics of White Supremacy in North Carolina,
1896–1920* (Chapel Hill, 1996), 147–65, 174–75.

CREDITS

Charles L. Black Jr.: "The Lawfulness of the Segregation Decisions" *Yale Law Journal*, vol. 69 no. 3 (Jan. 1960) is reprinted by permission of The Yale Law Journal Co., Inc.

Rev. James F. Burks: "Integration and Segregation" sermon delivered on May 30, 1954, published in *The Religious Herald*, May 3, 1956. Reprinted by permission of the publisher.

Countee Cullen: "Incident" from *Color* (1925). Copyrights held by Amistad Research Center, Tulane University. Administered by Thompson and Thompson, New York, NY.

W. E. B. Du Bois: W. W. Norton wishes to thank The Crisis Publishing Co., Inc., the publisher of the magazine of the National Association for the Advancement of Colored People, for the use of material first published in the May 1919 issue of *Crisis Magazine*. W. E. B. Du Bois "Georgia: Invisible Empire State," *The Nation*, vol. 120 (Jan. 21, 1925) is reprinted with permission of the publisher. For subscription information call 1-800-333-8536. Portions of each week's *Nation* magazine can be accessed at www.thenation.com. From *The Souls of Black Folk* by W. E. B. Du Bois (Penguin Classics, 1989). Copyright © the Estate of W. E. B. Du Bois 1903. Introduction copyright © Viking Penguin, a division of Penguin Books USA Inc., 1989. Reproduced by permission of Penguin Books Ltd. "The Niagara Movement: Address to the Country" from *The New York Times*, August 20, 1906 is used with the permission of the David Graham Du Bois Trust. From *Against Racism: Unpublished Essays, Papers, Addresses, 1887–1961*, ed. Herbert Aptheker (U of Mass. Press, 1985) is reprinted by permission of the publisher.

INDEX